Land Development

National Association of Home Builders
15th and M Streets, N.W.
Washington, D.C. 20005

Land Development
ISBN 0-86718-297-0
Library of Congress Catalog Card Number 87-60765

Copyright © 1987 by the
National Association of Home Builders
of the United States
15th and M Streets, N.W.
Washington, D.C. 20005

All rights reserved. No part of this book may be reproduced or utilized in any form or by any means, electronic or mechanical, including photocopying and recording, or by any information storage and retrieval system without permission in writing from the publisher.

When ordering this publication, please provide the following information:

TD
163
.L36
1987

Title
ISBN 0-86718-297-0
Price
Quantity
NAHB membership number (as it appears on the *Builder* or *Nation's Building News* label)
Mailing address (including street number and zip code)

Contents

    Acknowledgements................................. 11

    Introduction 15

1. **Market Research** 17
   - Who Should Conduct Market Research 17
   - Selecting a Market Researcher 17
   - How to Use Market Research 18
   - Useful Sources of Market Data 22
   - Other Elements of Market Research 24
     - Consumer Research 24
     - Competitive Audit 26
     - Absorption 26
   - Conclusion 27

2. **Site Selection and Analysis**....................... 29
   - Feasibility Study 30
     - Offsite Factors.................................... 32
       - Utilities 34
       - Zoning.. 35
     - Onsite Factors.................................... 36
   - Site Analysis 39
     - Natural Environmental Conditions 40
       - Climate 40
       - Geology 41
       - Topography 43
       - Hydrology 44
       - Soils 44
       - Vegetation..................................... 45
       - Wildlife 47
     - Manmade Environmental Conditions................ 47
       - External Odors, Noise, and Views 47
       - Solid and Hazardous Waste 48
       - Access 48
       - Regulations and Restrictions..................... 48
     - Composite Site Analysis 50

Case Study: Savage Farm, Cayuga Heights, New York 51
   Feasibility Checklist 51
      Access to the City of Ithaca 52
      Market Indicators 53
      Site Size and Geometry 53
      Offsite Factors 53
         Transportation 53
         Site Accessibility 53
         Municipal Utilities and Services 55
         Parks 55
         Fire and Police Protection 55
         Library 55
         Rights-of-Way 56
         Views 56
         Architectural Context 56
      Onsite Factors 56
         Vegetation and Streams 57
         Topography 57
         Soils 58
   Summary of Feasibility Study 58
   Detailed Site Analysis 59
      Natural Environmental Conditions 60
         Surficial Hydrology 60
         Surficial Geology 61
         Soils Suitability 61
      Manmade Environmental Conditions 61
      Development Suitability: Composite 61
      Summary 63
   Final Project Description 63
      Central Facilities 63
      Townhouses 65
      Single-Family Houses 65
      Apartments 65
      Phasing 65

3. Local Land Use Regulations and Plan Processing 69
   The Origins of Zoning 69
   The Conventional Zoning Ordinance 71
      Special Exceptions and Variances 73
   The Subdivision Ordinance 74
      Unified or Land Management Ordinance 75
   The Legacy of Traditional Land Use Controls 75

  Reevaluation of Standards Necessary............... 75
  Exclusionary Zoning............................... 76
 Innovative Zoning: Responses to Today's Issues........ 77
  Planned Unit Development Zoning 79
  Incentive Zoning 80
  Conditional Zoning................................ 81
  Impact Zoning 82
  Performance Zoning 83
  Transfer of Development Rights 84
 Multiple Tiers of Regulation.......................... 86
 Case Law Pertaining to Zoning and Subdivision
  Control... 87
 Processing a Zoning Application 89
  The Art of Positive Compromise.................... 91
   Establish a Constituency 91
   The Negotiation Process 92
 Processing a Subdivision Plan 94
  A Time-Tested Procedure 94

4. Financing Land Development: An Overview ... 99
 The Transformation of Real Estate Financial Markets .. 99
  Shifts in Inflation Expectations....................100
  Partial Deregulation of Financial Markets 100
  Loss of Real Estate's Preferred Investment Status....102
 Site Selection and Acquisition 102
  Site Selection.....................................103
  Financing Land Acquisition 103
   Purchase Money Mortgage 104
   Purchase Option 104
   Long-Term Lease Plus Option 105
   Joint Venture..................................105
 Land Development Financing 106
  Obtaining the Loan 106
  Minimizing Lender Risk 107
   Release Price Repayment........................107
   Phased Disbursement Financing..................108
   Other Considerations...........................108
 Construction Financing 108
  Characteristics of Construction Financing...........108
  Risks Involved in Construction Lending 110
  Steps in Negotiating the Construction Loan 110
   Property Analysis..............................110
   Loan Analysis 110
   Loan Commitment and Closing....................111

Loan Disbursements 112
  The Take-out Commitment......................... 112
    Commitment Duration 112
    Commitment Rate................................ 113
    Commitment Cost................................ 113
    Special Commitment Terms...................... 113
    Sources of Commitment Funds 114
  Permanent Financing................................ 114
  Equity Financing.................................... 115
    Joint Ventures................................... 115
      Role of Participants........................... 116
      The Partnership Agreement..................... 116
      Summary....................................... 117
    Syndications 117
      Syndication Agreement 117
      Syndication Documents 118
      Syndication Funds 118
      Summary....................................... 119
  Tax-Exempt Financing.............................. 119
    Special Districts................................. 119
      Uses of Metropolitan Service Districts............ 120
    Tax Increment Financing (TIF).................... 121
  Summary 122

5. The Selection of Housing Types 125
  Housing Types and Examples 125
    Single-Family Housing............................ 126
      Large Lot, Single-Family Detached 126
      Example: Tymber Creek, Florida 126
      Small Lot, Single-Family Detached 128
      Example: Wood Creek Courts, Chicago, Illinois 128
      Zero Lot Line..................................... 130
      Example: The Landing, Fort Worth, Texas 131
      Duplex... 132
      Example: Turtle Rock Glen, Newport Beach,
        California..................................... 134
      Triplex 134
      Example: Stoney Brook, Denver, Colorado.......... 136
      Quadruplex 136
      Example: Beacon Hill Vistas, Laguna Niguel,
        California..................................... 139
      Townhouses...................................... 139
      Example: Heather Glen, San Diego, California 139
    Multifamily Housing.............................. 143

Garden Apartments/Stacked Flats	143
Example: The Valley on Roswell Road, Atlanta, Georgia	144
Midrise	146
Highrise	146
Example: Key Colony, Key Biscayne, Florida	147
Considerations for Choosing a Housing Type	150
Planning as an Approach to Choosing Housing Types	150
Choosing Housing Types Based on Compatibility	153
Choosing Housing Types Based on Solar Access and Sun Control	154
Choosing Housing Types Based on Site Specifics	158
Housing Type Choices	159

6. Earthwork and Stormwater Management 161

Erosion and Sedimentation Control	161
Erosion Control Measures	162
Vegetative Soil Stabilization	163
Nonvegetative Soil Stabilization	163
Structural Measures	164
Sediment Control Measures	166
Trapping	167
Filtration	167
Planning an Erosion and Sediment Control Program	169
Environmental Effects	171
Damage During Construction	171
Level of Protection	172
Stormwater Management Considerations	172
Quantified Performance Estimates	173
Site Planning	173
Maintenance Requirements	175
Grading	175
Grading Analysis	176
Grading Requirements	177
Other Considerations	178
Stormwater Management	179
Basic Principles	179
Stormwater Management Criteria	180
Hydrology	181
Design Considerations	181
Estimating Runoff	183
Drainage Systems	185

  Flood Plains.. 190
   National Flood Insurance Program 190
   State and Local Regulations 191
   Flood Plain Management Objectives 191
   Flood Plains and Site Design 192
    Channel Modifications 194
    Flood Plains and Residential Construction......... 195
  Natural Open Drainage Systems 195
  Closed Drainage Systems 197
   Location of Closed Drainage Systems.............. 197
   Drainage Pipe Selection........................... 199
   Culverts.. 202
  Water Quality..................................... 202
  Runoff 204
   Infiltration and Velocity Reduction Techniques..... 206
   Retention/Detention Techniques................... 208
  Maintenance 214
  Conclusion 215

7. Water and Sewer 217
  Water Supply Systems............................. 217
  Public Distribution Systems 217
   Fire Demand 218
   Storage 219
   Pumps... 220
   Pipe Capacity 220
   Pipe Pressure 220
  Subdivision Water System......................... 221
   Materials and Cost 221
  Private Supply Systems 221
  Wastewater Collection, Treatment, and Disposal
   Systems... 222
  Public Facilities................................... 223
   Basic Design Parameters 223
   Sewerage.. 224
   Pressure and Vacuum Sewerage Systems.......... 227
   Treatment Levels 230
   Types of Treatment Processes.................... 231
   Treatment Plant Site Amenities 232
   Disposal 234
  Onsite Treatment Systems 237
   Site Selection................................... 237
   Treatment Processes 237
   Methods of Treatment 239

	Disposal Systems 241
	Alternative Onsite Treatment Systems 246

8. Residential Streets 249
Hierarchy of Streets 249
Street Width 251
Design Speed 254
Geometric Design 254
    Horizontal Alignment 255
    Vertical Alignment 256
Typical Street Section 257
Intersection Design 258
Curbs 260
Pedestrian Traffic 261
Community Roadway Plans and Standards 262

9. Energy Conservation 265
Housing Types 265
Heating and Cooling of Structures 266
    Solar Characteristics 267
    Topography 269
    Street Layout 270
    Solar Heating 270
    Tree Locations for Solar Efficiency 271
    Regional Site Design Guidelines 279
Regulatory Effects on Energy Conservation 281

10. Landscaping 283
Benefits of Landscaping to the Development 283
Existing Vegetation 283
    Preserving Valuable Vegetation 286
    Tree Protection 286
    Pruning and Repair of Damaged Vegetation 287
    General Guidelines 289
    Open Spaces 290
    Planting Design 290
Functional Uses of Plant Materials 293
    Climate Modification 293
    Erosion Control 294
    Safety 294
    Maintenance 294
    View and Noise Control 295
Plant Selection and Purchase 295
Tree and Shrub Planting Methods 296

   Tree and Shrub Spacing 300
   Lawns 300
      Topsoil Spreading 300
      Seeding...301
      Sodding...301
   Landscaping for Individual Units 302

Notes 303

Appendix 306

Additional References 329

Index 331

Acknowledgements

This edition of *Land Development* represents a team effort by industry professionals and NAHB staff. Contributors are as follows:

Chapter 1. Market Research
>Sanford R. Goodkin
>Mark Rodman Smith
>The Goodkin Group
>La Jolla, California

Chapter 2. Site Selection and Analysis
>David Crandall
>Peter White
>Environmental Design and Research
>Syracuse, New York
>
>Peter Trowbridge
>Trowbridge-Trowbridge
>Ithaca, New York

Chapter 3. Local Land Use Regulations and Plan Processing
>William G. Hengst
>John Rahenkamp Consultants, Inc.
>Philadelphia, Pennsylvania

Chapter 4. Financing Land Development: An Overview
>Kenneth D. Bleakly
>Laventhol & Horwath
>Denver, Colorado

Chapter 5. The Selection of Housing Types
>Stephen Mead
>Stephen Mead Associates
>Des Moines, Iowa
>
>Michael F. Shibley
>Director, Land Use and Development Services, NAHB
>
>Susan D. Bradford
>Director, Publications, NAHB

Chapter 6. Earthwork and Stormwater Management

> David Johnson
> General Development Corporation
> Miami, Florida
>
> Kenneth A. Ford
> Manager, Civil Engineering, NAHB

Chapter 7. Water and Sewer

> David Johnson
> General Development Corporation
> Miami, Florida
>
> Kenneth A. Ford
> Manager, Civil Engineering, NAHB

Chapter 8. Residential Streets

> David Johnson
> General Development Corporation
> Miami, Florida
>
> Joseph R. Molinaro
> Land Use Planner, NAHB

Chapter 9. Energy Conservation

> David Crandall
> Environmental Design and Research
> Syracuse, New York
>
> Joseph R. Molinaro
> Land Use Planner, NAHB

Chapter 10. Landscaping

> Environmental Design and Research
> Syracuse, New York
>
> Michael F. Shibley
> Director, Land Use and Development Services, NAHB

This edition of *Land Development* was prepared in cooperation with the 1987-88 NAHB Land Developers Committee, Mark Tipton, chairman; Jack Harter, vice chairman. It was produced under the general direction of Kent W. Colton, NAHB executive vice president, by the following staff members:

James E. Johnson, Jr., Staff Vice President, Information Services

Denise L. Darling, Staff Vice President, Publishing Services

Michael F. Shibley, Director, Land Use and Development Services

Joseph R. Molinaro, Land Use Planner, Land Use and Development Services

Kenneth A. Ford, Manager, Civil Engineering, Land Use and Development Services

Susan D. Bradford, Director, Publications

David Rhodes, Art Director

Introduction

Since the first edition of *Land Development* was published in 1950 (under the title *Home Builders Manual for Land Development*), the degree of business acumen and technical expertise required to successfully develop land has increased significantly. There was a time when the land developer could simply be a shrewd entrepreneur. Now it is necessary to be a mystic, an engineer, an architect, a soil scientist, a tax accountant, a land use attorney, and a politician. A wide range of technical skills must be acquired and effectively applied to be successful in today's market. This newly revised and expanded edition of *Land Development* provides a detailed look at the complexities of developing land.

The degree of risk involved in developing land has increased exponentially as well. The prudent developer now needs a much broader and more sophisticated data base upon which to make initial acquisition and development decisions. External factors beyond the developer's control have increased the risks. Rising land prices, increased citizen activism, stronger environmental regulations, hazardous waste disposal, growth management and control policies, water quality issues, and the provision of infrastructure have emerged as issues fundamental to the land development process. This edition of *Land Development* has been updated to address these issues and to provide the developer with a guide to the land development process from the market research phase throughout project development.

Chapter 1, Market Research, adapted from NAHB's *Higher Density Housing: Planning, Design, Marketing*, covers the first step in the land development process—determining market potential. The chapter outlines what kind of market research is needed and how to conduct it, sources of information, and how to make the most effective use of research findings.

Another essential part of the process is site analysis. Chapter 2, Site Selection and Analysis, provides an overview of the feasibility and site considerations that must be analyzed before purchasing land. It includes a case study of an actual feasibility study and site analysis.

Local land use and development ordinances are constantly evolving and changing. Developers should be familiar with zoning options and how to negotiate with local officials. Chapter 3, Local Land Use Regulations and Plan Processing, includes a discussion of the zoning concepts in use today, as well as guidelines for processing development approvals.

Just as local ordinances have increased in complexity and number, so have the options in the real estate financing market. Chapter 4, Financing Land Development, is a new section that gives an overview of the financing market and provides important information on options and methods for obtaining financing for land development and construction. Additional information on this topic may be found in NAHB's publication, *Financing Land Acquisition and Development*.

Selecting the most suitable housing types for a project site and market directly affects land planning, development costs, and marketability. Chapter 5, Selection of Housing Types, offers a discussion of various unit types, with actual examples of each housing type discussed.

Water-related issues are addressed in Chapter 6, Earthwork and Stormwater Management, and Chapter 7, Water and Sewer. These comprehensive chapters cover erosion and sedimentation control, grading, drainage, water supply systems, and wastewater collection, treatment, and disposal systems.

Chapter 8, Residential Streets, provides a discussion of street designs that are appropriate for neighborhoods and cost-effective for communities to maintain. It covers street widths, intersection design, curb and gutter, pedestrian traffic, and community roadway plans and standards.

Energy efficiency is a constant consideration in designing and siting housing. Chapter 9, Energy Conservation, covers energy-efficient housing types, heating and cooling of structures, and the effects of regulation on energy conservation.

Land Development concludes with Chapter 10, Landscaping. This chapter provides an overview of planting design, guidelines for existing vegetation, functional uses of plant materials, plant selection and purchase, tree and shrub planting methods, and landscaping for individual units.

It should be noted that each jurisdiction has different regulations, development standards, and markets. Developers are urged to perform the necessary homework to become as familiar as possible with the development process in their community. NAHB believes that the information provided in *Land Development* will give developers a sound framework for successful land development.

Chapter 1
Market Research

Market research and analysis provides a framework builder/developers can use to analyze their markets and reduce the risks that are inherent in real estate development. This chapter gives insights into the research process so that builder/developers can better utilize the services of a market research company.

Before launching any multi-million dollar project, it is wise to examine the market for which the product is intended. Opportunities to increase market capture can be maximized when a project is designed specifically for its given marketplace, and properly marketed and merchandised to respective market segments. By conducting market research before a development plan is formulated, a builder/developer can better design a project to respond to market opportunities.

Market research is the science—and art—of bringing together product and market.

Who Should Conduct Market Research

Depending on a company's size, market research can be handled in-house or by an outside consultant. A small company may not have the capital to hire market research professionals. Many builder/developers find, however, that comprehensive market research requires staff time and expertise beyond their in-house capabilities. The argument can be made that market research conducted by an outside consultant pays for itself in increased sales. It also provides an independent third-party analysis for use by lenders or joint venture partners, architects, and land planners.

Selecting a Market Researcher

The best way to find a market research consultant is by referral. The local home builders association or other professional associations may be able to provide names; fellow builders may also have suggestions. The *Yellow Pages* are a last resort. Once a market research firm has been identified:

- Ask for references—and check them.
- Meet with the person(s) who will be working on your project, and make sure that they understand your needs.
- Get all agreements in writing: specify due dates, prices, and type of research to be conducted.
- And finally, stay in frequent contact with the researcher(s) throughout the research and analysis phases to ensure that work is progressing according to the original agreement. Interaction between the builder/developer and the research organization enhances the service provided, yielding more valuable information.

How to Use Market Research

As the builder/developer works with the researcher to plan a market research strategy, certain basic elements must be considered.

Who will be the primary user of the information?

For example, a lender is looking for precedents in the marketplace and statistical evidence that his/her risks have been carefully measured. A builder, on the other hand, strives for market entry and rapid absorption, so bottom line projections are vital.

The builder/developer's project team—architects, engineers, landscape architects, interior designers, and other professionals—can benefit from market research. A creative "team" approach to product development, starting with the market research phase, is helpful and welcomed by many of these professionals.

What should the research accomplish? What specific questions should it answer? What is the condition of the marketplace in terms of:

- Products on the market (Figure 1-1)
    Single-family
    Multifamily
- The resale market
    How long homes are on the market before they are sold
    Characteristics of resale homes
    Asking and selling price
    Most active areas, product type, and price range
- The competition—perform an audit of all competition (Figure 1-2), to determine:
    Their merchandising and marketing formats
    Their locational advantages and disadvantages
    Pricing, absorption, product mix
    Financing plans they offer

Figure 1-1. Total New Residential Units

Year	Single-Family	Two-Family	Percent Single Family	Multi-Family	Percent Multi-Family	TOTAL UNITS
1976	14,966	716	54	13,504	46	29,186
1977	8,102	256	72	3,287	28	11,645
1978	8,536	214	93	675	7	9,420
1979	12,024	234	84	2,319	16	14,577
1980	20,052	306	86	3,207	14	23,565
1981	20,388	414	74	7,363	26	28,165
1982	16,488	450	76	5,265	24	22,203
1983	11,117	212	71	4,660	29	18,991
1984	11,573	156	77	3,552	23	15,281
1985	12,920	296	67	6,507	33	19,703
1986	23,664	532	75	8,211	25	32,237

Source: The Goodkin Group

    Where their buyers are moving from (location and length of time they lived there)
    Where their buyers work
    Their buyer lifestyle, including types of recreation preferred, extent and formality of home entertainment, amount of traveling
    Features buyers like and dislike about competitor communities
- Economic forces affecting market conditions (Figure 1-3)
    Employment conditions
    Job growth and employment centers
    Characteristics of growth
    Expansion of existing companies and arrival of new companies
    Prevalence of two-income families
- Demographics (characteristics of the local population)
    Total population
    Population growth
    Number of households
    Household growth

Figure 1-2. Sample Competitive Audit Form

Audit Date
4/10/86

Project #: 4192

Project Name
LOMAS SERENAS

Market Area
Escondido

Developer/Builder
LOMAS SANTA FE, INCORPORATED

Architect
NAEGLE ASSOCIATES, INCORPORATED

Map #
THOMAS BROTHERS 27 E/3

Product Type
Detached

Location
WEST I-15 ON VIA RANCHO PARKWAY

Sales Organization
LOMAS SANTA FE, INCORPORATED

Sales Office Phone #
(619) 587-1455

Data Opened
3/31/79

Lot Characteristics
20,000 SQUARE FOOT MINIMUM

Interior Designer
R. CARLISLE

Model Merchandising
6 FULLY FURNISHED

Engineer
N.A.

Construction Lender
N.A.

Plans	Bed/ Bath	Square Foot	Stories	Overall Units Avail.	Overall Unit Sold	Monthly Units Avail.	Monthly Unit Sold	Current Base Price	Prior Base Price	Date of Last Change	Premium to:	Current Price per Square Foot
6	3/2.50	2232	1	24	22	2	0	199,000	203,000	9/06/85	33,000	89.15
7	3/2.50	2502	1	13	13	0	0	Sold Out	217,000	12/05/85	8,000	
8	4/3.00	2708	2	18	16	5	3	239,000	225,000	3/12/86	10,000	88.25
9	4/2.50	2841	1	23	21	2	0	255,000	245,000	3/12/86	10,000	89.75
13	5/2.50	3195	1	25	23	2	0	285,000	275,000	12/05/85	10,000	89.20
22	4/3.00	2875	2	8	8	0	0	285,000	276,000	3/12/86		99.13
5	4/3.00	2299	2	8	6	3	1	222,000	225,000	1/09/86	17,000	96.56

FINANCING

Down	Interest	Loan Type
	MARKET	CONV.

FINANCING NOTES

NO SPECIAL FINANCING OFFERED.

	Current Month 4/10/86	Last Month 3/12/86	Total Project 3/31/79
Total Sales	4	3	220
Sales per Week	.96	.61	.60
Escrows Closed	2	1	201

INSITES™

SUBDIVISION FEATURES

Maintenance Fee: $25.00 / QUARTER *
Pool Sauna Spa
Rec. Room Tennis Putting Green
Security
*FEE COVERS ROOF INS.& STREET UPKEEP
Driveway ASPHALT
Parking 3 CAR GARAGE
Fencing Height NONE
Landscaping NONE
Balcony: NO Patio: NO
Roof Type:
Utility Room Location IN HOUSE
Washer/Dryer NONE
Walk-in Closet: MASTER OTHER
Flooring CRPTS/TILE ENT. & KIT.
Luminous Lighting: KITCHEN BATH
Heating: F/A Air Cond. INCLUDED
Tub Type and Surrounding PORC/CERAMIC TILE
Shower TILE
Pullman Tops CERAMIC TILE
Counter Tops CERAMIC TILE
Pantry CUPBOARD
Sinks DBL/PORCELAIN
Oven Brand of Type G.E./SGL/ELC/S.C.
Microwave: OPTIONAL
Dishwasher Brand or Cycle G.E./2 CYCLE
Fireplace WOODBURNING
Wet Bar: YES Drapes: NO
TRASH COMPACTOR. GARAGE DOOR OPENER.
SPA TUB IN MASTER BATH. G.E. COOK
TOP. CENTRAL VACUUM OPTIONAL.
SKYLIGHTED ENTRY PLANS 8 & 9.
PLAN 7&9 OPTIONAL DEN,
PLANS 7&9 FAM ROOM. G.E. COOKTOP.

SUBDIVISION ACTIVITY

Development Size 306
Acreage

Tract/Unit Filing Number	Number Built	Under Const.	Approved	Planned	Sales Started	Number Sold	Standing Inventory
9064/1-4	111				3/31/79	111	
9064/V	19				9/01/83	19	
9064/VI	22				12/01/83	22	
9064/VII	13				6/01/84	13	
9064/VIII	21				11/01/84	21	
MODELS	6				NOT RELEASED		6
9064/IX	25				5/15/85	19	6
9064/X		19			12/14/85	15	4
Total	217	19				220	16

BUYER PROFILE

Singles
Single w/c 10%
Young Couple w/c 70%
Young Couple wo/c
Couples w/teens 10%
Empty Nester 5%
Retirees
Investors 5%

Area Previously Lived In OUT OF TOWN/LOCAL
Area Working In LOCAL/SAN DIEGO/SAN MARCOS

ADVERTISING/TRAFFIC

Newspapers 30% TV
Magazine 10% Signs 45%
Radio Other 15%

ADVERTISING NOTES

HOMES FOR SALE AND THE SAN DIEGO UNION
OTHER=REFERRAL
LOCAL PAPERS SPOT BASIS

ADDITIONAL NOTES

CUMULATIVE MIX BEGINS WITH PHASE V.
REMAINING INVENTORY: PHASE IX - PLAN 5:2, PLAN 6:1, PLAN 8:3, PLAN 9:1, PLAN 13:1.
PHASE X - PLAN 6:1, PLAN 8:1, PLAN 9:1, PLAN 13:1.
MODELS: PLANS 5, 6, 7, 8, 9 & 13
SALES REP: "LIZ" (619) 587-1455

The Goodkin Group

Source: The Goodkin Group

Size of households
Household value
Average and median ages, and distribution of age by range
Average and median incomes, and distribution by range
Commute patterns
Length of residence
Distribution of housing types, including single-family, multi-family, and mobile homes

Combined, the above statistics can be used to analyze a market to determine who lives there now. These factors, combined with projected community trends, help determine who buyers will be in the marketplace.

Has the market been changing in any way? Are there new market segments?

Identify specific market segments within the community. "Home-

Figure 1-3. Employment Projections by Occupation and Industry

LABOR MARKET AREA: 1985 - 1990 Occupation	1985	Projected 1990	% Change 1985-1990
Managers & Officers	74,206	87,688	18.2
Professional Occupations	143,150	166,924	16.6
Technical Occupations	32,968	38,551	16.9
Service Occupations	127,431	149,466	17.3
Maintenance & Production Occupations	227,133	267,846	17.9
Clerical Occupations	174,456	205,936	18.0
Sales Occupations	59,208	70,150	18.5
TOTAL*	838,552	986,561	17.7
Industry			
Mining	27,100	35,200	29.9
Construction	46,900	55,200	17.7
Manufacturing	127,400	148,000	16.2
Transportation, Communication Public Utilities	53,600	63,800	19.0
Trade	210,500	249,800	18.7
Finance, Insurance & Real Estate	61,300	73,700	20.2
Services	272,600	313,500	15.0
Government	72,800	82,600	13.5
TOTAL	872,200	1,021,800	17.2

*Occupational listings not additive to total.

Source: The Goodkin Group

buying Segments" in Appendix A defines a number of distinct homebuying segments that can be used when conducting market research.

Are there market opportunities that the competition has not discovered? Can your company have a locational, price, or design advantage? Will your company be introducing a new product type or price range to the community?
- If so, take full advantage of the opportunity to bring something new into the community.
- If not, how successful has that product type or price range been so far?
- How well have those homes done in the resale market? Determine whether they sold because of attractive pricing and financing, or if there is lasting marketability for that product in the community.
- Have design and planning been a drawback to acceptance of that type of housing?

Useful Sources of Market Data

The market researcher can draw on numerous free or low-cost sources to answer the economic and demographic questions discussed above. These sources include:

- U.S. Census
- Local chamber of commerce
- State and local economic development agencies
- Local utilities
- Title companies
- Local universities (unpublished studies as well as published reports)
- Moving companies
- Furniture stores
- Board of education
- Telephone company
- State or U.S. Department of Labor or Employment Services
- Local news clippings and real estate sections
- Local legal newspapers and transcripts
- Local bank reports

The researcher then analyzes the data gathered from these sources, possibly with the aid of a computer. The computer digests the information, cross-references it, and produces reports that provide valuable trends and indications for the builder/developer (see Figures 1-4, 1-5, and 1-6).

Figure 1-4. Population and Household Demand

YEAR:	1970	1980	1984 (est.)	1989 (proj.)
Population	125,961	151,323	160,893	172,745
Growth 1984-1989	11,852 people			
Annual Growth 1984-1989	2,370 people			
Households	35,206	50,967	54,834	59,705
Growth 1984-1989	4,871 units			
Annual Growth 1984-1989	974 units			

Source: U.S. Census, Urban Decision Systems, Inc., The Goodkin Group

Figure 1-5. Projected Employment by Economic Sector

1970-2000 (Number in Thousands)

Employment Sector	1970	1980	1990	2000
Mining	4.90	18.12	27.90	33.60
Contract Construction	28.00	46.20	71.40	85.40
Manufacturing	85.90	104.30	181.30	234.40
Transporation and Public Utilites	76.40	65.40	71.80	92.40
Wholesale and Retail Trade	118.00	181.50	272.40	357.50
Finance, Insurance and Real Estate	29.80	53.90	80.20	104.00
Services	88.40	167.80	229.10	312.90
Government	90.50	137.50	172.20	223.20
Total Non-Ag Wage And Salary	481.50	794.78	1116.30	1412.40
Agriculture (3)	6.50	5.80	5.10	4.00
Military (3)	10.10	11.10	11.10	11.10
All Other (3) (4)	40.70	57.50	76.10	97.00
TOTAL EMPLOYED (NUMBER OF JOBS)	1060.70	1643.90	2314.90	2967.90

Source: The Goodkin Group

Figure 1-6. Projected Housing Unit Demand

COUNTY STATISTICS 1970-2000	1970	Actual 1980	1983	Projected 1990	2000
Total Population	8.40	25.20	31.50	104.70	196.50
LESS: Non-Household Population	0.06	0.10	0.10	0.11	0.13
Household Population	8.30	25.10	31.40	104.60	196.40
Average Household Size	3.30	3.19	3.07	3.00	3.00
Households (Occupied Units)	2527.30	7868.30	10228.00	34863.30	65456.70
Vacancy Factor	5.00	5.00	5.00	5.00	5.00
Total Housing Units	2653.60	8261.80	10739.40	36606.50	68729.50
Incremental Demand Per Period	–	5608.10	2477.70	25867.10	3213.00
ANNUAL DEMAND	–	560.80	825.90	3695.30	3212.30
ANNUAL SINGLE FAMILY DEMAND	–	454.30	669.00	2993.20	2602.00
ANNUAL MULTI-FAMILY DEMAND	–	106.60	156.90	702.10	610.30

Source: The Goodkin Group

Other Elements of Market Research

In addition to the market research strategies already discussed, the builder/developer should consider other elements to ensure a comprehensive market profile. These include consumer research, competitive audit, and absorption projections.

Consumer Research

Many builders don't even bother with consumer research. Yet no other manufacturer will engage in product output before knowing the profile of his/her prospective buyers. The best way to do this is, simply, to talk to the people who are interested in your product.

The builder/developer must establish an objective for developing consumer information, because the objective frequently determines the research techniques to be used. Two major approaches to research include shopper surveys and consumer surveys.

Shopper surveys can take place at your existing project, a competing project, or at other high traffic areas such as shopping malls. They ask about prospect preferences and reactions to your product. If certain patterns emerge, these can be accommodated in your community. Consumer surveys can be performed at competitive communities. Findings are then incorporated into the overall project scheme. See Appendix A for preference questionnaires.

Focus group interviews are an in-depth, qualitative research method conducted by well trained group leaders. Select 10-15 random names from your prospect list, and invite them to an informal evening session to learn more about your product. Show them attractive renderings of the homes as well as specific site plans and floor plans. A skilled group leader will be able to develop a profile of the target consumers' homebuying needs, preferences, and motivations based on several of these focus group interviews. The results will be intuitive rather than statistical—an invaluable addition to other market research findings.

Below are some of the techniques often used in consumer research:

- Traffic analysis of prospects circulating in the marketplace. What drew them to your product? How far were they willing to travel to see the product? What did they like and dislike about it?
- Traffic analysis should take place over a four-weekend period at points of sale, with followup once a month for the subsequent four months. Traffic analysis can also be used to test the effectiveness of advertising, merchandising, and salesmanship.
- Move-in analysis of buyers at competitive projects with similar characteristics to yours. Why did they choose the competition rather than your product? Where did they live before? How far are they willing to commute to their workplace? Within which market segments do they fall?
- Mail and telephone interviews using mailing lists developed with professional help. Mailing lists are available for almost any socioeconomic category of prospects.

For the consumer research phase of the market analysis, budget $5.00 to $30.00 per interview, including computer time. Interpretation must be the work of skilled analysts rather than "number crunching" statisticians. Consumer research should take between 3 and 7 weeks to do from beginning to end, with longer-term followup as necessary.

Competitive Audit

One effective way of staying in touch with the market is to know what the competition is doing. No one has a better "feel" for the competition than a good field auditor. For a complete picture, the auditor should speak not only with sales personnel, but with the developer of the competing project as well. Both telephone interviews and onsite visits may be used, though an onsite audit offers the added advantage of face-to-face contact (Figure 1-2).

Absorption

One of the key questions to be answered about the proposed development is how long the absorption period will be. The absorption period refers to the amount of time it will take to sell out or lease up a real estate project.

There are two levels of absorption analysis:

- Total market absorption, which involves a review and reconciliation of supply and demand factors in the market, and
- Site-specific absorption—what is often referred to as market capture.

Total market absorption is, in essence, total effective demand. To determine this, the market researcher first audits competitive supply within the market area. This includes a survey of all competitive projects currently selling, under construction, and proposed. Second, population growth and employment increases are forecast to identify demand. Absorption time is projected by reconciling supply and demand. It estimates how much demand—how many months or years of population and employment growth—is necessary to reach an equilibrium with (or "absorb") total supply.

For example, let us assume that the population within the primary market area is projected to increase by 2,250 persons per year over the next 5 years. If the average number of persons per household is stable at 2.25, then one could assume a demand for 1,000 housing units per year during that time period (excluding allowance for population living in group dwellings, and vacancy rates). The total number of unsold dwelling units that are existing, under construction, and proposed within the same market area is 2,500. Under this scenario, it should take the market approximately 2.5 years to absorb the current supply, assuming newly forming households are the same size as past households. Competitive analysis should provide this information.

This is a general analysis. A more specific delineation of supply and demand will be helpful. For example, what portion of total supply is comparable in price and function to your product? What portion of demand wants a home in this price range and function? In other words, can you clearly define the demand from your market?

Why is absorption so important? Because it affects the bottom line. Given the cost of construction financing, the absorption time becomes critical to success or failure. A development that is profitable if sold out in 18 months may be a loser if it takes 3 years to sell out.

The second level of absorption analysis, market capture, evaluates the subject site in terms of its capture of projected demand. It is at this level of analysis where the value of market research becomes most evident.

The site's percentage capture within a given area reflects how well the project is suited for, and marketed to that marketplace. The market research identifies market segments, consumer preferences, effective advertising and merchandising techniques, proper pricing, and other items. Projected market capture is an assessment of how the development plan at the subject site relates to these factors. Obviously, those projects that are better suited for the marketplace should realize stronger sales.

A good basis for determining market capture may begin with a "fair share" analysis of the market. Determine the number of competing projects that are likely to be marketing homes (try to be specific to your market— attached, detached, or rental), and divide into total demand for this type of housing. The result shows the fair share capture of each project competing in the market. As a cross reference, compare this number with the absorption rate of product now in the market. If the numbers correspond, the market may be stable and homogeneous. Variations may indicate changing supply/demand factors or a variety of product quality in the marketplace. Fair share calculations can be compared with the current and past market performance of competing products.

Conclusion

In summary, market research can reduce the risk inherent in real estate development. It takes time and discipline. However, absolute dollar investment may be only $5.00 to $25.00 per unit, depending on the scope of the research and project size. This is not a high price to pay to target your market. If managed properly, market research can be of assistance during the development process, from project conception to closing the last escrow.

Market research is being used more and more frequently. Lenders are increasingly motivated to require market and site feasibility research and analysis for projects that they fund with construction and take-out loans. Builders see a changing market with increased and more sophisticated competition, as well as changing economics and demographics.

Finally, opportunities for market research are increasing. The increasing availability of information from a variety of sources allows a more refined analysis of the housing consumer. This creates opportunity for better design and more effective, efficient communication with target markets. The result: lower costs and increased profits.

This chapter is adapted from NAHB's *Higher Density Housing: Planning, Design, Marketing.*

Chapter 2
Site Selection and Analysis

Although the importance of location in the site selection and analysis process cannot be overemphasized, there are many other factors that must be considered. The past two decades have seen an increased environmental awareness among the public which has resulted in scores of federal, state, and local environmental laws. Developers and land use planners must now be accountable for their actions, not only to appropriate governmental agencies as required by law, but also to the highly discriminating public.

Land planning for a development project begins its formative stages with the feasibility study. The feasibility study, together with the other elements discussed in this chapter, leads to a schematic plan to determine lot yield and potential profits. Points of access, schematic circulation plans, relationships to existing neighborhoods, utility placements, grading needs, and other site-sensitive features can be mapped at this stage. These will help form the basis of the final land plan if the project is determined to be feasible.

The value of a well-thought-out land plan cannot be overestimated. Aside from financing, it is potentially the most valuable of the pieces in the land development puzzle. Developers undertaking a land development project, whether they are experienced or in the business for the first time, should put together a land plan that is sympathetic to site conditions and the target market. Seeking the assistance of a qualified land planner is one of the developer's best investments. The collection and interpretation of data during site selection and analysis provides a strong foundation for the project.

Problems encountered during the land approval process can often be traced to a poorly conceived land plan. Lack of sensitivity to site constraints, site character, neighborhood characteristics, geology, and drainage, among others, will inevitably lead to conflicts with local regulatory and development agencies, citizen groups, and local approval boards. Armed with market research data, an understanding of the target market, and a complete site analysis, the astute developer should discuss with the design team how the elements of the project will fit together. Design, theme selection (perhaps based upon an outstanding site feature), site construction techniques, marketing, and product presentation are all interrelated. But it begins with the land plan. Discussions among all team members during the planning process can highlight areas that may need special attention.

Feasibility Study

As urbanization spreads, more and more sites being considered for development are on land once considered physically marginal. Although some land is marginal only in comparison to other available land, some sites are marginal either because of drainage, soils, or stability problems, or because of topography that requires extensive earth moving.

As a consequence, a preliminary feasibility study is more important than ever before. The feasibility study should include an engineering survey to identify the improvements necessary for development, and their cost. Such information can dramatically affect the site selection process by determining the improvement time and costs that must be added to the base selling price. Market, resource availability, and other offsite factors are also part of the predevelopment feasibility study and must be considered early in the site selection process.

Development conditions should be broken into two categories: threshold (essential for development) and nonthreshold (alterable through design or construction). In a single-family detached housing development on large lots without public utilities, satisfactory percolation rates for septic fields would be considered threshold conditions, as would the ability to drill wells for household needs. Nonthreshold conditions would be view or noise. The feasibility study deals primarily with threshold conditions, those that allow development. Qualitative aspects of a development are dealt with primarily in the site analysis phase.

The feasibility study often requires that information be collected firsthand in the field, or from reliable and expert sources. All information should be collected in an orderly and easy-to-read manner. All this information should be documented at one scale on a surveyed base map to make it comparable.

The market study is the first consideration of any proposed development (see Chapter 1). Before the site feasibility is begun, a clear need for the development program should exist. The market potential and profitability of such a program should be evaluated. Factors that must be considered directly include population centers, per capita and expendable incomes, major economic sources in a community, vitality of other development in the community, and average age and age distribution of residents. The type of development planned determines the value a developer or investor places on this information. Some of this information can be acquired through a visual survey, but most of it will be derived from the most recent U.S. Census for the community in question.

Site size and geometry or shape as they affect a particular development program should be considered early during the feasibility study. Rough area calculations of program requirements should be tested against the site size. Consideration of site geometry and shape is important, as well as the amount of developable land the site yields. The area and geometric configuration of a particular parcel can be determined from local tax maps, which can usually be obtained from the county tax assessor's office or from the bank or individual(s) holding title to the site (Figure 2-1).

Figure 2-1. Tax maps can be used to determine property descriptions, assessed value, and disposition of adjacent land parcels. Tax maps are drawn to scale, giving an approximate base plan on which to develop feasibility studies. The development program might be sketched over the tax map to determine if site size and configuration are appropriate.

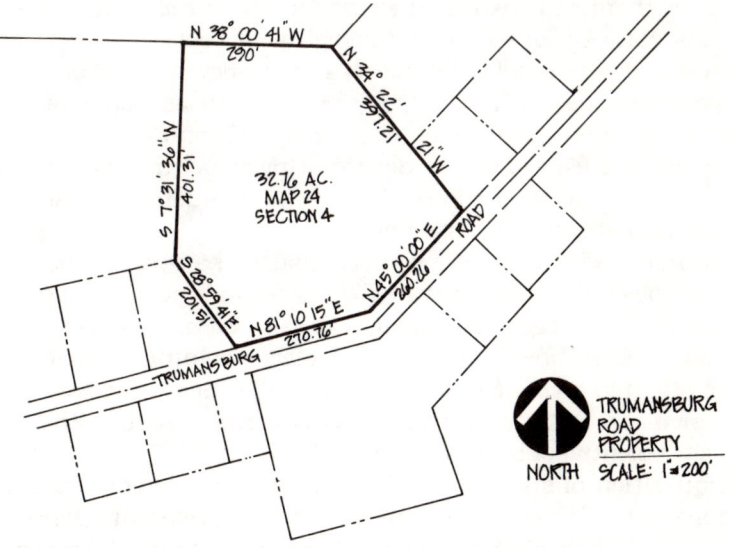

Source: Environmental Design and Research

Offsite Factors

The importance of offsite factors that affect development potential cannot be overstated. The existing and future development of adjoining properties contribute to the overall development climate of a given area, and must be considered. Many important considerations of nearby land uses can be detected easily from site inspection, but inspections at various times of day for an extended period may be necessary to detect some conditions accurately.

Existing land uses are major considerations, but proposed development should also be anticipated. Local planning boards, city or town engineers, and zoning board officials should be contacted for information about the future disposition of land close to the site being investigated.

Evaluating the relationship of the site to other types of development in the area is critical at this point. The type of development planned determines the relative importance of other types of development nearby and of proximity to them. For example, in residential developments, unit prices depend heavily upon location and factors determined by location, such as the cost of the land and the distance of the development from work, schools, and shopping. Typically, the distance from home to work should not be more than 30 to 40 minutes; to schools and neighborhood shopping centers, not more than 5 to 10 minutes; and to regional shopping centers, not more than 20 minutes.

The strength of new-town or large-scale projects is that the planning for them can insure adherence to an overall image and that various planned locations can complement each other. Site alternatives and design flexibility increase when development of adjacent property can be planned in conjunction with development of the site being investigated. Such coordinated planning can minimize the negative effects of nearby deteriorating structures, poorly maintained property, or incompatible land use such as noise, toxic fumes, and visual inconsistencies.

Acquiring surrounding property insures harmony of uses and helps protect the investment in the site under consideration. In areas that are largely developed, a broad development perspective should consider how to aggregate parcels adjoining or close to the main site into a single development concept. Such coordinated development prevents fragmented land use and enhances the development potential of both properties.

Acquisition of surrounding land requires up-to-date property and market information and discretion. The premature disclosure of an acquisition plan may either alarm surrounding landowners who do not favor development, or it may raise surrounding land prices high enough to prohibit purchase.

The acquisition effort begins by securing accurate ownership information from a title company or from the local property tax rolls. This information should include the owner's address, the property's size and zoning, and the current assessed value of land and improvements. Surrounding property should be checked to determine which parcels are most critical to development of the main site, their condition, and how they can be linked to create a commanding position in the market.

Several alternative approaches may be necessary to acquire surrounding land. Where land cannot be purchased outright, a joint venture may be feasible. Often government-owned property can be acquired through a land swap. Long-term lease agreements are also possibilities; however, terms should be reviewed carefully.

Offsite conditions should be documented on a map that includes a reasonable amount of land in proximity to the site being evaluated. This map will allow easy recognition of adjacent development, highways, industry, commerce, population centers, schools, parks and recreation areas, and mass transit facilities (Figure 2-2). Other

Figure 2-2. Site location map, putting the site into a regional context including land use and significant physical features.

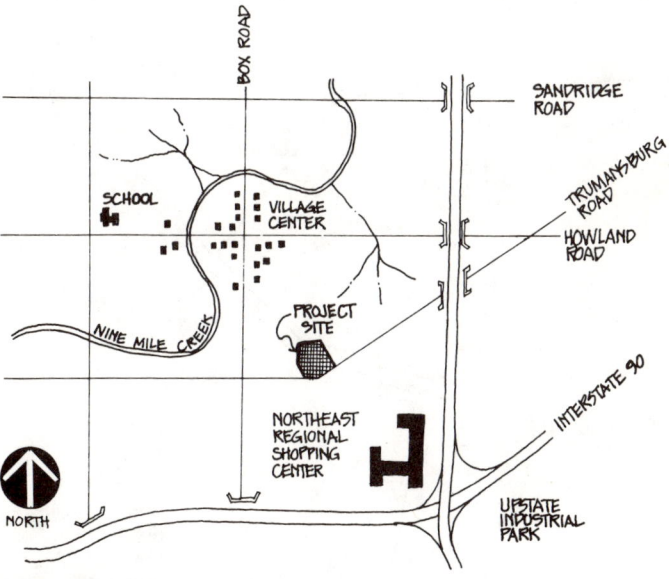

Source: Environmental Design and Research

less observable offsite factors such as existing utilities, zoning, and easements and rights-of-way should also be documented.

Utilities

Existing utilities are often critical threshold conditions for most development (Figure 2-3). The availability of public water and sanitary and storm sewers should be documented initially. Tie-ins to other utilities such as telephone, electric, gas, and oil tend to be less costly over longer distances.

Refer to local ordinances to determine whether all utilities must be placed underground. The cost of placing these utilities below grade is often borne by the developer and reflected in land development costs.

Water—Water supplies may be found onsite in the form of wells, but most developments of any size require water as a public utility. The local responsible agency or municipality should be contacted to determine the location of existing water lines. If direct connections to the site are not available, the developer should investigate the potential for water line extensions, the costs and sizes of water lines

Figure 2-3. Utilities plan documents all utilities. Overhead electric, cable, and telephone wires should be noted as well as easements and rights-of-way.

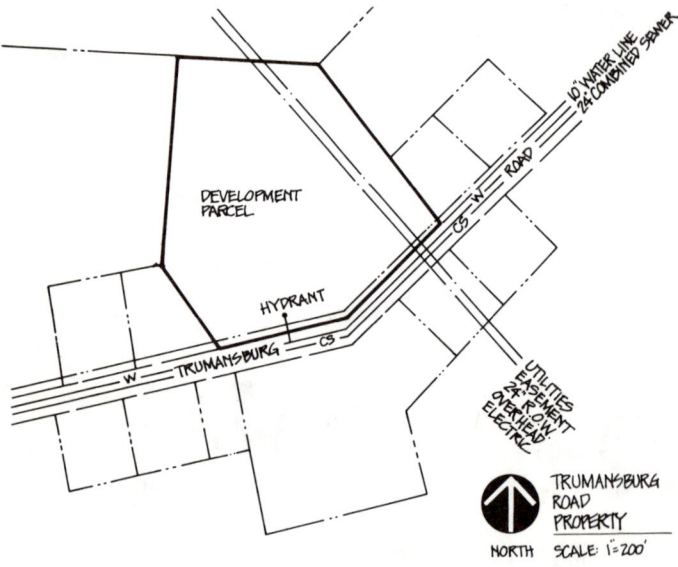

Source: Environmental Design and Research

required, pressure, tapping fees, and lateral lines. For large developments, outlying water mains may be insufficient. An estimate of site-related water needs must be made to determine if sufficient water service is available.

Sewers—Sanitary and storm sewers, if necessary for a development, should be placed according to municipal utility plans, generally available from the city or town engineer's office. Again, the development requirements should be estimated and compared to trunk line capacity. The site's location in relation to existing utilities is important, because sewers are generally gravity fed. If sewers are located at an elevation higher than the site, costly pumping stations may be necessary. Storm and sanitary sewers may exist separately or as a combined utility. This factor should be taken into account in the utility study. Not all developments require public sewer utilities. If they are not required, the site must be able to accept leaching fields and perhaps catchment and holding ponds for surface runoff.

Energy—The other utilities such as electric, gas, oil and telephone should also be documented on the utility plan. The connections to these utilities are often less complicated than connections to public water and sewer. Availability and capacity should be considered in terms of the development program.

Zoning

Existing zoning for the site being studied should be determined from the local zoning map, if zoning exists within the community (Figure 2-4). Zoning maps and interpretative guides are available from local planning offices, the city or town engineer's office, or the local zoning board of appeals. Be sure to determine whether zoning is in the process of being changed.

If zoning for the site in question is not compatible with the proposed development program, rezoning may be a possible alternative. Do not purchase or invest in a property unless a contingency clause requiring successful rezoning is written into the purchase agreement.

Look closely at both existing and proposed zoning limitations—setbacks, densities, height restrictions, minimum lot sizes, frontage requirements—to be sure the development planned is feasible.

Easements and Rights-of-Way—These existing site intrusions may not be evident from a site inspection. Compare utility plans to the site to see if utilities, abandoned railroad rights-of-way, or access to adjacent properties exist through the site. Previous title searches may be viewed at the bank or with the persons who are holding title.

Figure 2-4. Local zoning plan and interpretations should be documented. Information should be rescaled and drawn on the tax map base plan to be compared with other types of information.

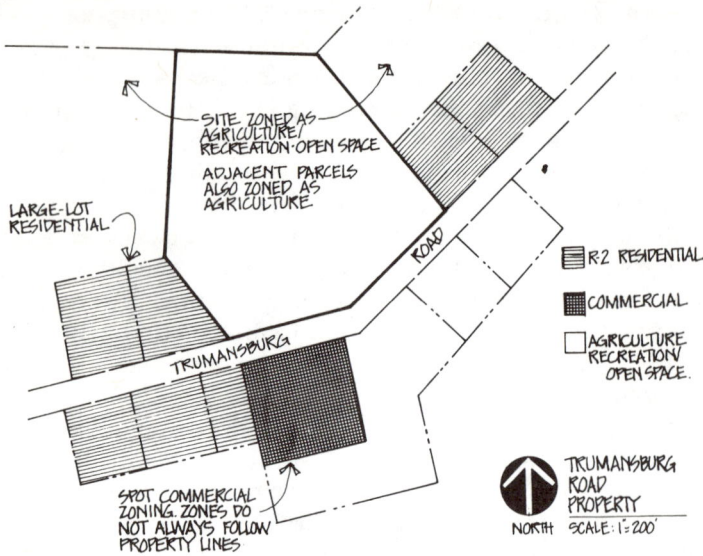

Source: Environmental Design and Research

Onsite Factors

After a site is found to be generally suitable based on size, geometry, and existing and proposed adjacent land uses, a comprehensive study should be made of onsite factors. Such a study may be conducted quickly before acquisition to determine if a site is suitable.

Many of the physical factors that determine the site's suitability for development are derived from geological and soils information. The local Soil Conservation Service (SCS) or the local U.S. Geological Survey (USGS) office should be contacted to determine specific conditions of the site. The SCS often has field representatives knowledgeable about the area who can tell whether the soils and geological structure are suitable for the planned development. An abundance of information can be garnered from soils data such as engineering properties, depth-to-water table (water saturated soils), depth to bedrock, and slope.

Conditions determined to be threshold or essential to development should be tested. For example, percolation tests can establish the potential for septic or leach fields. Soil bores can determine soil characteristics and average depths-to-bedrock more accurately than surface tests. Soil bores may not be necessary if soil types are known and reasonably consistent throughout the site. Glaciated regions of the country, or filled or manmade sites, should definitely be tested for soil characteristics, depth-to-bedrock, and water table. Many times irregularities exist on these sites, such as artificially perched water tables, fragipan (a semi-impervious soil layer), or erratics (large boulders randomly spread throughout the site) (Figure 2-5).

Topography, vegetation, trees, shrubs, and grasses should be noted and identified as either assets or liabilities to development (Figure 2-6). Be most careful to note wetlands and wetland vegetation. In many states, fresh water and tidal wetlands are protected by law from development. Often a buffer around the wetlands is also protected.

Contact the local conservation department to be sure that the site is not a habitat for a rare or endangered species. The conservation officer will know if the site is locally considered a critical habitat. If so, strong opposition would result if development were suggested.

Figure 2-5. Soils map information and interpretations can be rescaled and drawn on the tax map base plan.

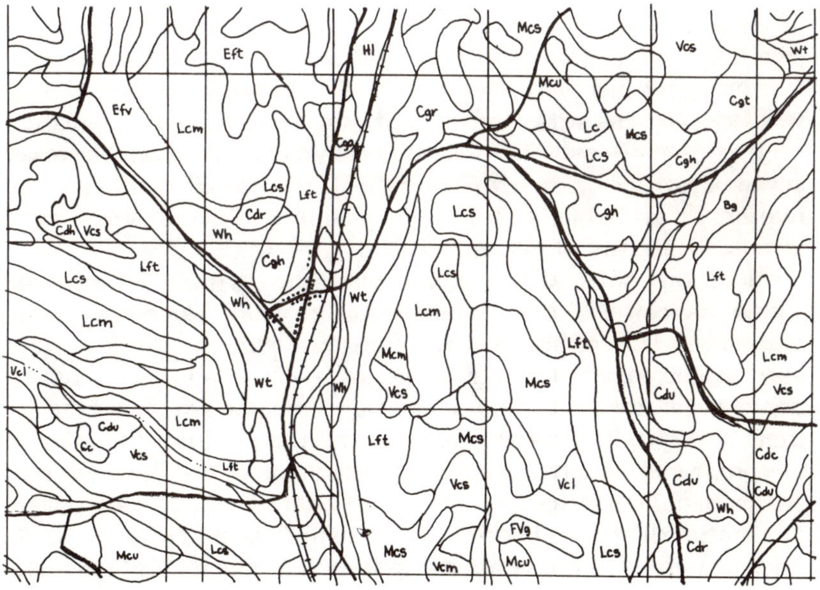

Source: Environmental Design and Research

Figure 2-6. The U.S. Geologic Survey map, topography, vegetation, and land use can also be rescaled and drawn on the tax map base.

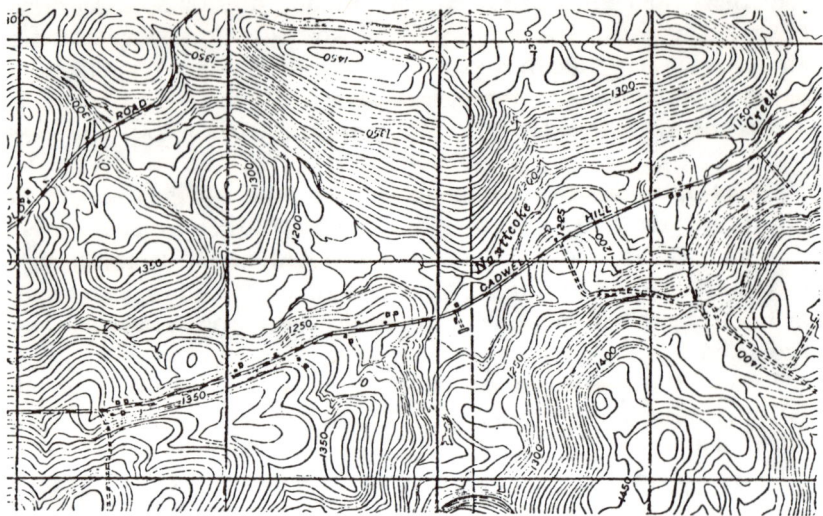

Source: Environmental Design and Research

Determine whether the site is situated in a flood plain or flood-prone zone. Conventional construction techniques, financing, and salability can be greatly affected by these physical site factors.

In an age of energy conservation, builders need to investigate local weather patterns and site exposure before development. Weather conditions can easily be determined by contacting local weather stations, airports, or farm bureaus. Documented weather information, if available, will make it possible to establish climatic trends, facilitating decisionmaking.

Conditions such as direction of prevailing winter and summer winds, aspect of slopes (the direction in which slopes face), and annual rainfall and snowfall give clues to site suitability. If a site is open and exposed to winter winds, the costs of additional insulation or vegetative buffers must be considered. Passive solar benefits from slopes that face southeast, south, and southwest also must be considered. Much of this information can be documented from onsite visual surveys.

Potential clients are becoming increasingly sophisticated in their understanding of the relationship between climate and site. The marketability of a particular development may well be dictated by factors of microclimate related to site.

The time and investment put into a site feasibility study reflect the nature and scale of the proposed development program.

Available resources—time, money, information, and expertise—will determine the nature of the prepurchase feasibility study. The feasibility study may be terminated quite early in the process if the site's disposition, size, or other offsite or onsite factors conflict with the development program. Often only outdated or incomplete site information is available, and a more thorough site analysis is necessary to determine site suitability.

The feasibility study should make clear whether the site is suitable for development. If essential or threshold conditions cannot be met, development becomes risky, if not impossible. If the site seems acceptable at this point, the mapped documentation—tax map, site location map, utilities map, zoning map, soils map, and U.S. Geologic Survey map—will become essential to the in-depth site analysis that follows the feasibility study.

Site Analysis

After the site has been found reasonably compatible with a development program, a detailed site analysis should be conducted. At this point the developer has a general idea of the site, its legal boundaries, surrounding land uses, observable physical features and characteristcs, and significant legal restrictions. A more detailed relationship must be developed that considers more carefully the qualitative conditions of a parcel.

Before any additional information is gathered, determine what information is necessary for the specific components of the program. For instance, a site analysis for single-family homes with basements in an area without public sewers, should include a determination of depth-to-bedrock, depth-to-water table, percolation rates, and slope and soil suitability, as well as vegetation, views, orientation, and climate.

The site analysis, unlike the feasibility study, is qualitative in nature, requiring sources of both essential (threshold) and secondary (nonthreshold) information. Careful site analysis results in a functionally, environmentally, and socially appropriate product. The site analysis is broken out into two major areas of concern: natural environmental conditions and manmade conditions. The natural environmental conditions include, but are not limited to, climate, geology, topography, hydrology, soils, vegetation, and wildlife. Manmade conditions include existing and historic land use; conditions external to the site such as odor, noise, view, site accessibility, and utility availability; and legal conditions such as zoning, restrictions, and covenants.

Natural Environmental Conditions

Climate

Every site has a general climate typical of the region within which it is located. This general climate is usually expressed in terms of possible sun days, annual precipitation, solar angle, length of day, relative humidity, and prevailing wind direction.

General information is most useful when it is applied to a particular site. Climate can influence the orientation of buildings, their exposure or buffering from the sun and the wind, the requirements for insulation, air-conditioning, heating, fenestration, material selection, and planting design. Climate becomes most important in housing, as the developer and designer attempt to define the optimum temperature and humidity, relationship to sunlight and shadow, and seasonal air movement.

The specific physical conditions of a site modify general climatic factors. The effects of a microclimate—climate that is specific to a site because of external physical factors such as slope aspects, vegetative cover, nearness to large water bodies, and relative elevation—require close consideration.

Wind—Wind direction is seasonal and can be enhanced or altered on a particular site. For instance, vegetative buffers have historically been used to modify the effects of winter winds. Building orientation can also be used to block undesirable seasonal winds or capture desired wind patterns.

Solar Energy Potential—Solar orientation has received considerable attention in building design during the last two decades. Passive solar heating during winter months has become an essential part of home design and building orientation. Sites that have topographical relief and face east, south, or west have the greatest potential to benefit from solar orientation (Figure 2-7). Solar potential can also be enhanced by building siting in favorable relationships to vegetation that allows seasonal filtering of light, or by building design and orientation.

Precipitation—is often a critical site factor. In some zones the developer will want to capture precipitation and contain it on a site; in other zones excessive precipitation is a development concern.

Rainfall is generally dealt with as site runoff. Some landscape features depend upon rainfall. For example, housing projects with lawns and ornamental plantings in arid parts of the country need

Figure 2-7. Climate mapping—generalized topography and vegetation developed from U.S. Geologic Survey map.

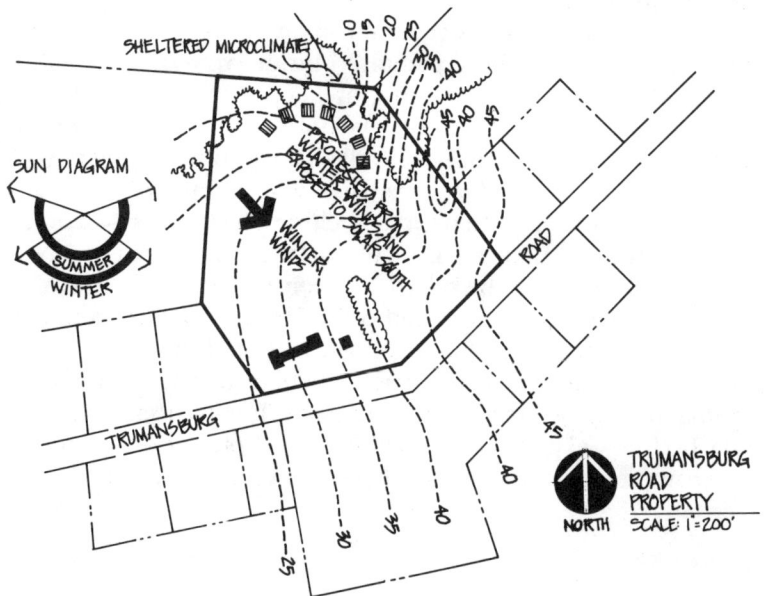

Source: Environmental Design and Research

to keep as much rainfall on the site as possible, whereas in more temperate climates water removal is a concern.

Snowfall must also be considered. Snow in combination with prevailing winter winds creates onsite drifting and accumulation that should be taken into account. Vegetative buffering or filtering might be considered.

Other microclimatic considerations might be noted such as frost pockets, areas that receive extremes of full or little or no sunlight, highly exposed or well-sheltered zones, or places that seem to encourage wind tunneling.

Geology

Within even a relatively small site, geology—structural landform and controlling rock conditions—can vary greatly. Regions of the country that have been glaciated tend to have the greatest geological variability.

In the context of development, specific geological conditions represent both assets and liabilities. For example, a developer documents bedrock conditions to determine not only the ways in which conventional construction might be altered, but also the characteristics of drainage and the ways in which a site can support plants and development (Figure 2-8).

Structural landforms are generally characteristic of a particular geological condition. Many glaciated landforms such as eskers, kames, and drumlins are rich in gravel deposits and fill materials. Such onsite sources of fill can be a valuable asset. Other landforms such as ledge, which is rock-controlled, may indicate the need for more expensive and restricting development practices.

Controlling rock conditions may include bedrock, boulders, and rock outcroppings. Bedrock is a subsurface rock formation. Depth from the soil surface to the bedrock becomes critical in excavation, such as basement excavation and utility trenching. Random boulders, called erratics in glaciated areas, can often be considered as significant as bedrock in construction when they are so large that heavy machinery or blasting is necessary. Rock outcroppings are usually bedrock-exposed at the soil surface. Conventional construction techniques may need to be altered on rock-controlled sites.

Figure 2-8. Geology map, derived from interpretive Soil Conservation Service information.

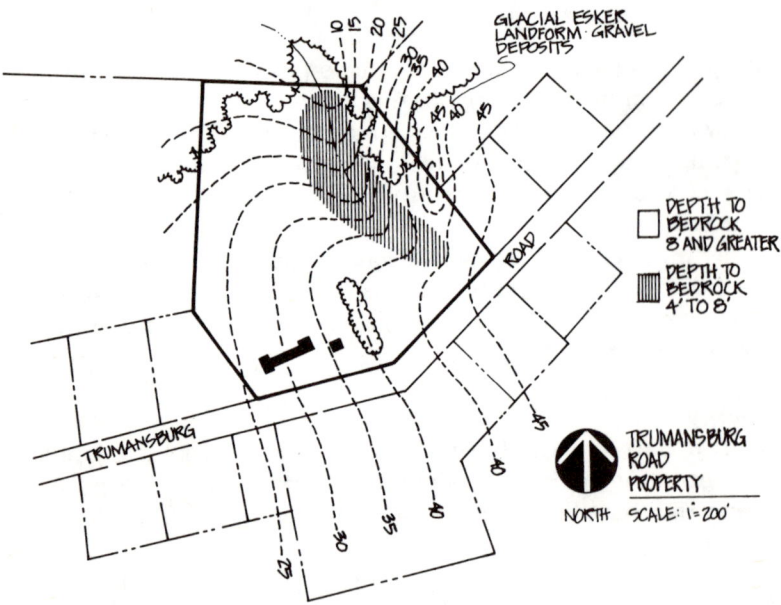

Source: Environmental Design and Research

Topography

Topography is the slope gradient of a site expressed as a relationship of vertical feet of elevation over horizontal feet of distance, as well as the visual lay of the land. Topography has specific implications for site development. It controls the location of roads and pathways, buildings, and utilities (such as sewers, which rely upon gravity feed) and generally affects the overall visual character of a site. The developer and the designer must be able to read the slope gradients and determine appropriate use.

In most climates and locales, zero to 8 percent is an optimum slope range for driving a vehicle or walking. Depending upon building design, a site can accommodate structures on grades of zero to 15 percent. Slopes of more than 15 percent are prohibitive for most uses. Optimum gradients for general development are 2 to 8 percent. Slopes of less than 2 percent require grading to enable drainage, whereas slopes more than 8 percent often require excessive grading as well as costly structural solutions. Although severe topographical conditions often create dramatic landscapes, the ability to develop steeply sloping sites in conventional ways is limited (Figure 2-9).

Figure 2-9. Topography map developed from generalized topographic information from the U.S. Geologic Survey.

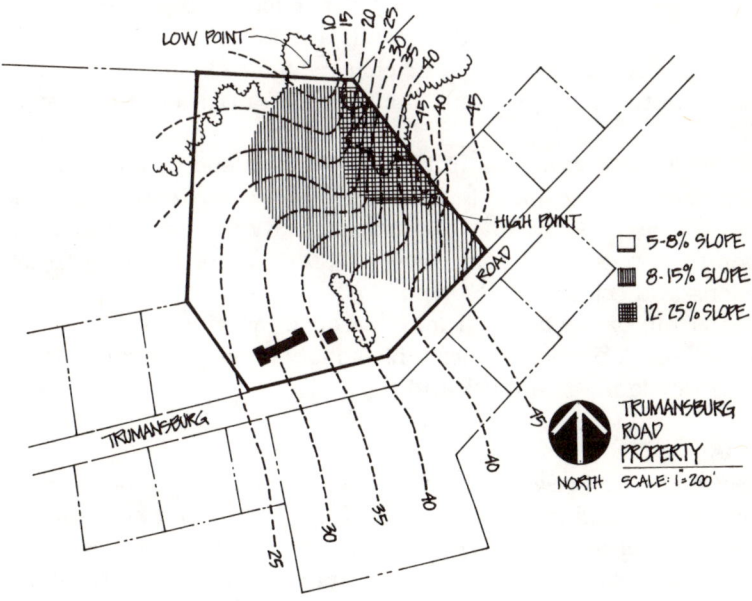

Source: Environmental Design and Research

Other topographical characteristics such as low spots or high spots in the landscape can offer clues for development. Low spots tend to be "sink" locations where site runoff accumulates, and are generally not good locations for most development. On the other hand, high spots are often exposed to the elements, create highly visible locations for development, and result in additional construction costs for buffering and insulation.

Hydrology

Hydrology refers in general to water above the ground, or surficial hydrology. Subsurface hydrology is generally referred to as water table. Surficial hydrology includes all visible water: lakes, ponds, streams, wetlands, and tidal areas. Although development in or on bodies of water is not common practice, high value is placed on developing in proximity to most bodies of water. Flooding must be considered, however. Certain bodies of water such as streams, rivers, and some lakes have a zone near their banks, the flood plain zone, which should be avoided for built development. Flood plains are classified in what is referred to as year-storms, or the probability of flooding once in a number of years. Development in a flood plain not only can affect salability but often can make mortgages and insurance difficult to obtain.

Wetlands require special attention, because they are generally an abused hydrological condition. For years wetlands were used as places to dump garbage and to fill over for development. In many states fresh water and tidal wetlands are protected by law. The characteristics of wetlands must be checked for each site. Wetlands can also be natural locations for site runoff and rich grounds for wildlife.

Water table is the level of water-saturated soil in relation to the surface of the ground (Figure 2-10). A depth-to-water table of less than 8 feet becomes a development liability because cellar excavations then require almost constant sump pumping to keep foundations and cellars dry.

Water tables can be artificially "perched" over bedrock or fragipan conditions. A perched water table should be noted because it often limits development significantly.

Soils

Soils and soil-related information is essential for most development. Not only should soil type be documented, but also soil characteristics: permeability, erodibility, agricultural value, and bearing strength. Most of this information may be extracted directly from the U.S. Soil Conservation Service's soil surveys for the county

Figure 2-10. Hydrology map—Surficial hydrology is mapped from the U.S. Geologic Survey. Subsurface hydrology, a function of soil, is derived from Soil Conservation Service information.

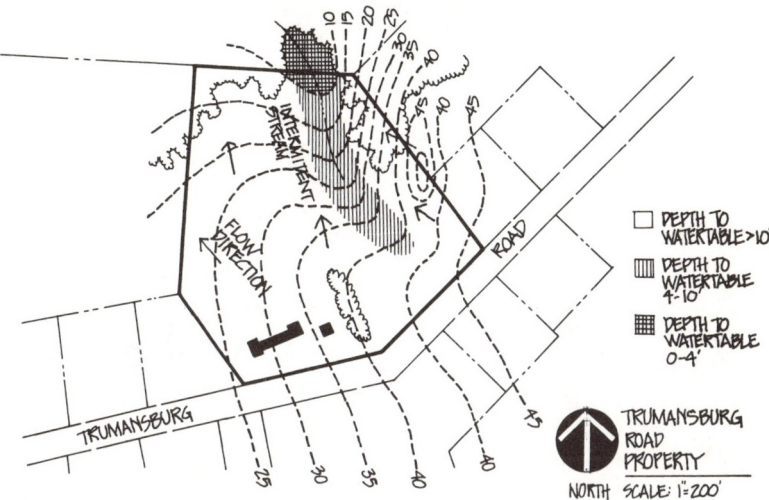

Source: Environmental Design and Research

within which the development site is located. These engineering properties are evaluated for each soil in terms of slight, moderate, and severe limitations for specific kinds of development. Areas of the site with severely limiting soil properties should be noted.

Although soil type is mapped, soil type in itself conveys little information. It is necessary to use the SCS interpretive guide to determine engineering requirements for each soil type. Soils are defined on the soils map legend (Figure 2-11).

Vegetation

Vegetation analysis includes locations and descriptions of trees, shrubs, field grasses, and wetlands vegetation (Figure 2-12). Vegetation can be both an asset and a liability to the developer. Mature trees in housing developments can create a 5 to 6 percent increase in market value for new developments. At the same time, vegetation conservation during construction entails certain costs.

Appropriately located vegetation not only has visual value, but it also screens or buffers the summer sun or prevailing winter winds. Vegetation also be valuable for offsite noise attenuation.

45

Figure 2-11. Soils map of the site derived from the Soil Conservation Service survey.

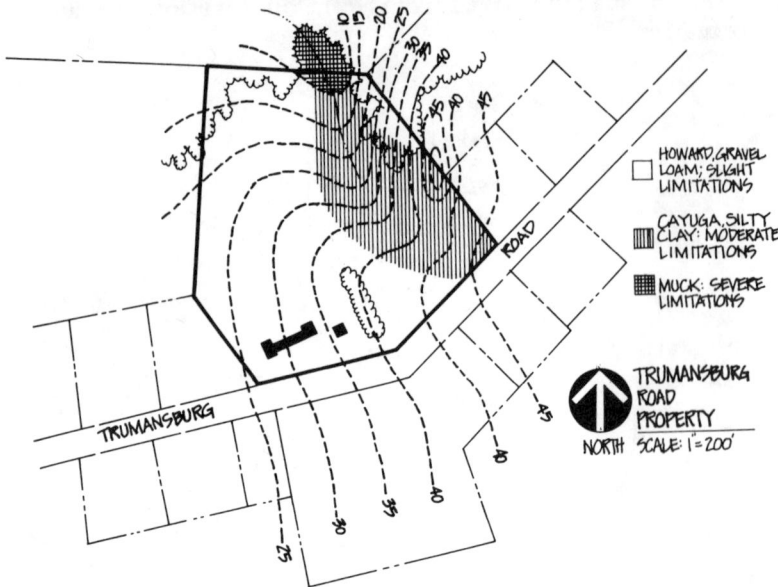

Source: Environmental Design and Research

Figure 2-12. Vegetation map, derived from the U.S. Geologic Survey map and field surveys.

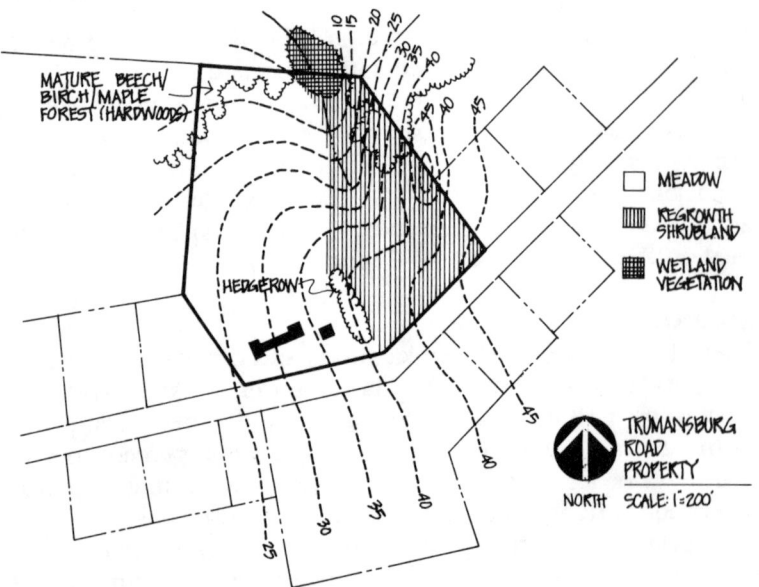

Source: Environmental Design and Research

Wildlife

Wildlife and wildlife habitat are necessarily considered simultaneously. Habitats for some species that live close to man are often enhanced by development. Rich and varied conditions such as wetlands and marshlands should be documented for their potential for compatible wildlife.

Manmade Environmental Conditions

Manmade conditions can often be determined by site inspection. Both onsite and offsite land use conditions should be documented. Land use information can be derived from tax maps and aerial photographs. Compatible and incompatible land uses must be considered as they relate to the planned development. Historical buildings or cultural sites with regional or national importance will greatly affect development alternatives (Figure 2-13).

External Odors, Noise, and Views

Both offensive and pleasant odors, noise, and views should be noted. Attractive views can greatly enhance a project by providing

Figure 2-13. Historic structures located from tax maps and verified through the local historic preservation league.

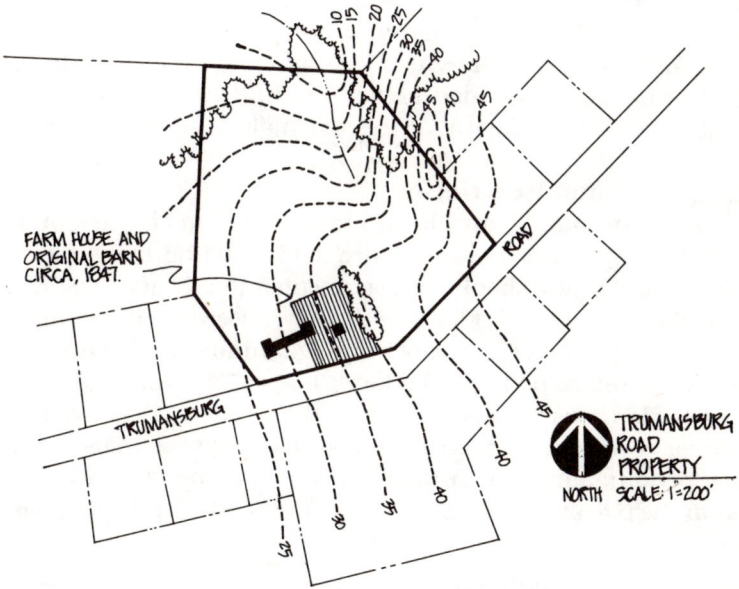

Source: Environmental Design and Research

beneficial orientation and qualitative conditions that must be noted. Views of the ocean or mountains, for instance, have not only a qualitative value, but a monetary value as well.

Solid and Hazardous Waste

The presence of any waste materials should be investigated. Buried solid waste, including construction waste or cleared vegetation, can cause added problems and expense.

Builders must also be aware of the potential liabilities of hazardous or chemical waste. There are many undocumented hazardous waste disposal sites that may be uncovered only when a site is analyzed or actually developed. Sources of soil and water contamination that may substantially affect developability as well as owner liability include leaks from underground fuel or chemical storage tanks, abandoned surface storage impoundments, and unlicensed dump sites. These possibilities are not always obvious. Frequently, evidence of past waste disposal is obscured when property becomes overgrown, is regraded, or existing structures are razed.*

Access

Site access must be determined early in the development process. The development program will determine to what degree both physical and visual access are necessary. All points of access should be noted.

Utility access must also be determined early in the feasibility study. The development program will dictate which utilities are needed for development in which locations. All existing utility and right-of-way locations documented during the feasibility study should be considered again for the site analysis (Figure 2-14).

Regulations and Restrictions

Zoning, covenants, and legal restrictions on the use of land should be mapped or noted (Figure 2-15). Zoning maps used for the feasibility study should be documented in site analysis. Existing deeds and titles should be carefully reviewed and a full title search begun to determine not only legal limits of the parcel, but also deeded restrictions on the land, if any. The responsible planning boards or review agencies should be contacted to determine any other covenants or restrictions on use of the site. Discussions of any pending changes in master plans or comprehensive rezonings can help to avoid delays at a later stage of the land development process.

*Builder Beware: The Risks of Hazardous Waste (Washington, D.C.: National Association of Home Builders, 1982)

Figure 2-14. External conditions mapped from site inspections and existing utility plans.

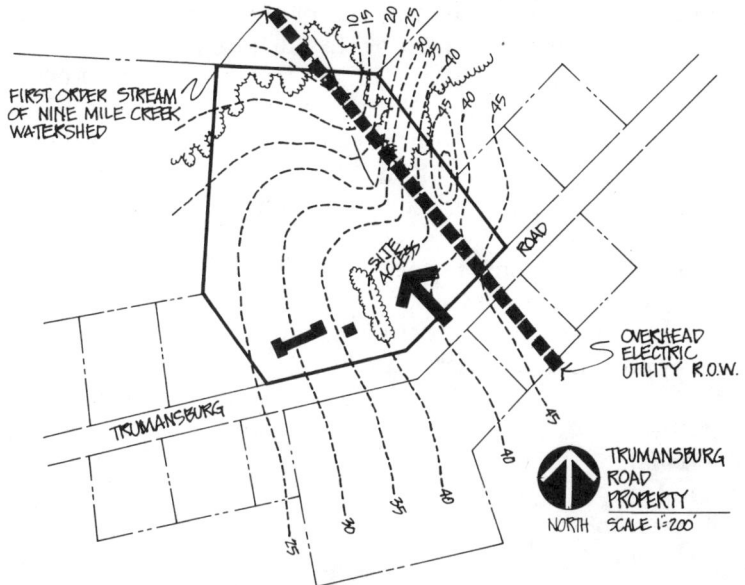

Source: Environmental Design and Research

Figure 2-15. Legal restrictions developed from the zoning map and title and deed restrictions.

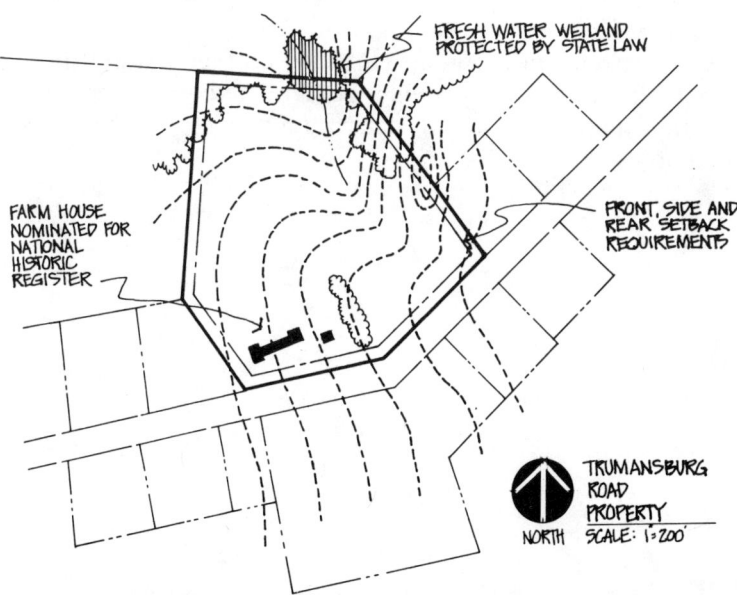

Source: Environmental Design and Research

Composite Site Analysis

After all relevant information regarding the site has been documented and mapped, the elements of the development program must be organized as dictated by the site analysis.

Some information is obviously more important than others. Development conditions should be identified as either threshold criteria, or important but nonthreshold criteria. Then the developer must consider the site analysis information as it limits development. Rank all mapped information in terms of limitations on the development program:

1. Severe limitations (negative threshold)
2. Moderate limitations (nonthreshold)
3. Slight limitations (positive threshold)

The appropriate numbers should be marked on transparent or semitransparent sheets over maps for each of the following categories:
- Climate
- Geology
- Topography
- Hydrology
- Soils
- Vegetation
- Wildlife
- Land use
- External conditions
- Legal restrictions

Design development drawings can then proceed using this composite site analysis document as a guide. Reference to the original information maps can help to determine specific site limitations and potentials.

Case Study: Savage Farm, Cayuga Heights, New York

The importance of analyzing every project cannot be overstated. Specific case studies may require feasibility study, environmental review, and site analysis procedures that vary considerably, depending upon the state and municipality within which the project resides. Each project has an individual set of constraints and requirements that are reflected in the analysis process. The conclusions drawn from an analysis of physical environmental conditions or manmade conditions may become critical to the success of a project. These analyses may then be more or less emphasized, depending upon the nature of the project. Resources spent on the feasibility study and site analysis should reflect the time, expertise, and risk involved in each particular project.

The following case study involves a site with both positive and negative physical environmental conditions that became apparent during the site analysis process.

Feasibility Checklist

The Savage Farm site is the last large contiguous land parcel remaining in the Village of Cayuga Heights, New York. The site has been maintained as agricultural land by Cornell University and consequently exists in contrast to the surrounding densely developed areas. These developed areas are older residential neighborhoods with an abundance of mature vegetation. Since the site is primarily open, it commands distant views of the Cayuga Lake basin, one of the largest of the Finger Lakes.

Savage Farm is strategically located with easy access to regional transportation routes, shopping, and the Cornell University campus. This unique setting immediately adjacent to the desirable Cayuga Heights community makes the site extremely attractive in the greater Ithaca real estate marketplace.

The simple geometry of the site will allow for efficient yet flexible site design.

Access to the City of Ithaca

Savage Farm is less than .25 miles from the intersection of Triphammer Road and Route 13 (Figure 2-16). Route 13 is a limited access four-lane highway which allows access to downtown Ithaca in less than 5 minutes. A resident of Savage Farm could walk to the regional shopping centers at the intersection of Route 13 and Triphammer Road, or drive to specialty shopping on the Ithaca Commons. Vehicular trips to Cornell University from the site would take less than 5 minutes. The site also allows for a brisk walk to the Cornell University campus.

Figure 2-16. Location plan for Savage Farm, showing transportation routes and proximity to regional points of interest.

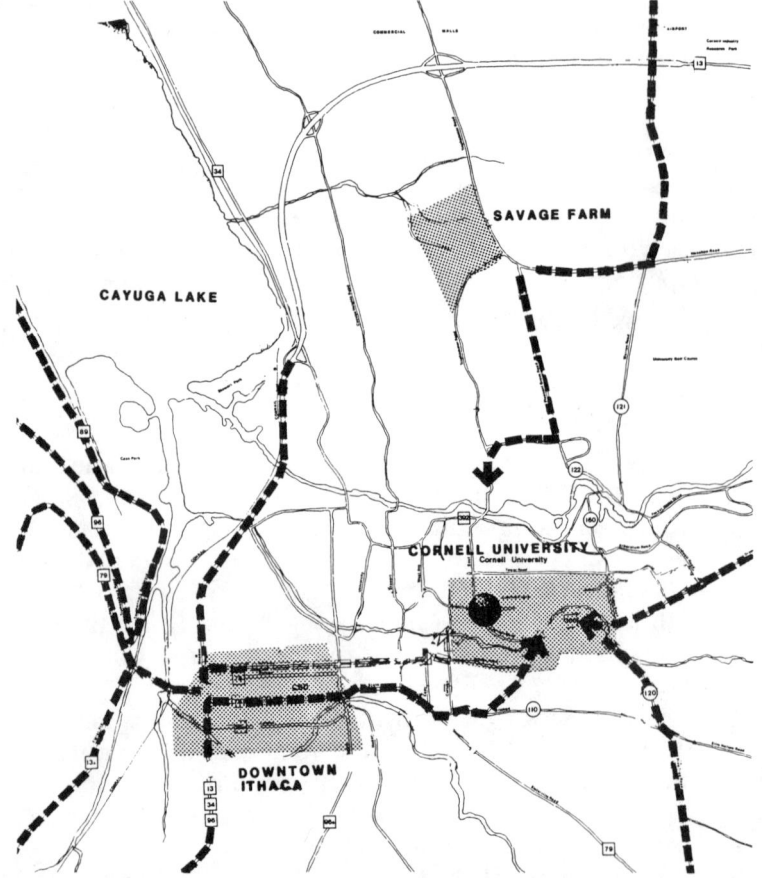

Source: Trowbridge-Trowbridge

Market Indicators

From all indications, a strong market clearly exists in Cayuga Heights for both condominium units and single-family detached houses. Developed resources in the community confirm a strong and vigorous economy. A more rigorous conventional marketing analysis has been completed prior to this phase of physical site feasibility. The market indicators survey is an offsite verification of potential marketability through the inventory of public facilities (schools, health centers, churches, recreational opportunities, and highways), and private investments (housing development, commerce, and industry). In addition, housing in the Cayuga Heights community is the most sought after in the Ithaca area. No other parcels of land of any substantial size exist in Cayuga Heights.

Site Size and Geometry

A rough estimation of acreage required to accommodate the proposed mixture of 84 condominiums, 71 single-family detached units, and 48 rental apartments verifies that the development program can be accommodated on the 105-acre site. A prototype building grouping and density has been developed and distributed across the site to test the adequacy of site size and geometry (Figure 2-17).

Offsite Factors

The most influential offsite factors for the development program are transportation, site accessibility, municipal utilities and services, utility rights-of-way, and views from the site.

Transportation

The transportation system connecting the site with downtown Ithaca and the Cornell campus is presently based on motor vehicles: automobiles, buses, or trucks.

The major regional highway is Route 13. Triphammer Road intersects Route 13, which is the site of regional shopping. Triphammer Road connects the site to the Cornell campus.

In short, the site is well served by the local network of streets, which permits access to Route 13, the most significant regional highway in the Ithaca/Cayuga Heights area.

Site Accessibility

The site has frontage on Triphammer and Hanshaw Roads plus access rights-of-way from Sevanna Park, a condominium project. The site entrance points are approximately .5 miles from Route 13.

Figure 2-17. Prototype building grouping and density distribution.

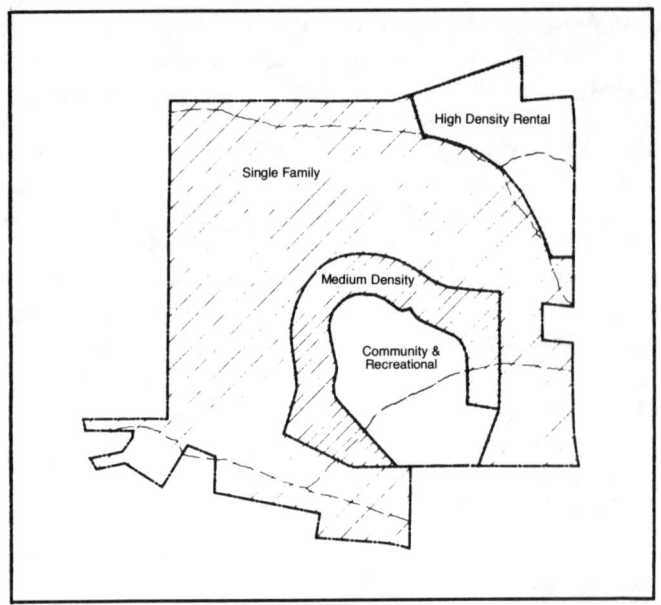

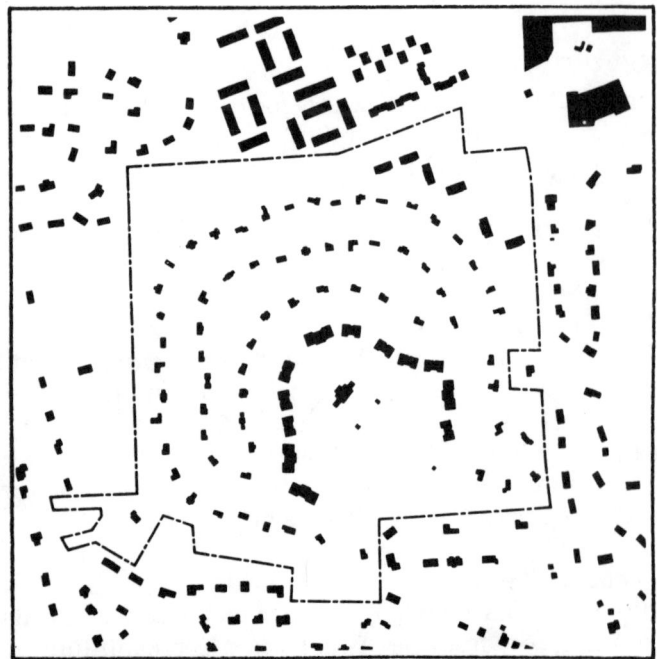

Source: Trowbridge-Trowbridge

The streets surrounding the site are residential in character, and are well maintained.

Municipal Utilities and Services

The Village of Cayuga Heights is well served by municipal utilities. All of the village is linked to the municipal sewage system. The site has ready access to all major service utilities. Connections to water and sewer can occur along Triphammer and Hanshaw Roads and along the north boundary of the site at Sevanna Park. Electric, telephone and television cables are easily accessed. Garbage pick-up must be arranged by a local service.

A large high-voltage powerline easement runs along the northern boundary of the site. This acts as an institutionalized separation between this project and development to the north. This powerline has little effect on development of the site.

Since two major drainage ways already traverse the site, surface and storm drainage can be diverted to these creeks. Sedimentation and control ponds could be developed along these ravines to control possible flooding, and add open water as a possible site amenity.

Parks

No parks border or are in walking distance of the site. However, numerous parks exist within a 5-10 minute drive. Stewart Park, a nineteenth century strolling park, sits at the foot of Cayuga Lake just off Route 13. Three state parks—Buttermilk, Treman, and Taughannock—are all within 10 minutes of the site, offering some of the most scenic areas, waterfalls, and gorges in the northeast United States. Another city park, Cass, has a full range of recreational facilities including a hockey rink and ice skating, a community pool, outdoor theater, a 400-boat marina, twelve baseball diamonds, and eight tennis courts.

Fire and Police Protection

The Village of Cayuga Heights provides good fire and police protection at Community Corners, a neighborhood commercial area within .25 miles of the site. The City of Ithaca provides a large back-up service to the Village of Cayuga Heights. The enormous tax base of the village allows for outstanding community services.

Library

The Village of Cayuga Heights does not have a public library, but the City of Ithaca has a large new facility. In addition, residents have access to Cornell University and its world-class libraries.

Rights-of-Way

Three rights-of-way affect the site. New York State Electric and Gas has a 60-foot R.O.W. at the north edge of the site which is occupied by a large high-tension powerline. The site has access along the north property line from a R.O.W. along the Sevanna Park access road, a residential boulevard. A pedestrian R.O.W. exists along the west of the site connecting to Highland Park, an exclusive single-family detached housing development.

Views

The Savage Farm site has excellent views toward Cayuga Lake and the surrounding countryside. The open, soft, rolling topography of the site allows for a variety of pastoral settings with distant views of 25-30 miles.

The topography is characterized by a broad plateau in the center of the site which slopes gently to the west and more steeply to the north and south. The two streams, which flow generally east to west, cut ravines through the site that reach depths of up to 30 feet. These ravines give restricted views to West Hill, a green agricultural vista.

Architectural Context

The site is bordered on the east, south, and west by uniform development of large single-family detached homes. This is predominantly post-war development. On the north, the site is bordered by Sevanna Park, an apartment-condominium conversion of largely undistinguished concrete and brick structures. This high-density development contrasts sharply with the context to the south, and acts as a transition to the commercial zones to the north—Pyramid, Cayuga, and Triphammer Malls (Figure 2-18).

Onsite Factors

The site has been found to be generally suitable based on size, geometry, and existing and proposed adjacent land uses. At this point a comprehensive study has been made of onsite factors. Such a study was conducted quickly before site acquisition to determine the site's suitability.

Many of the physical factors that determined the site's suitability for development were derived from vegetation, geological, and soils information. The local Soil Conservation Service (SCS) and U.S. Geological Survey (USGS) offices were contacted to determine specific conditions of the site. The SCS regional office is located in the Village of Cayuga Heights and has field representatives knowledgeable about the site who knew about the soils and geological struc-

Figure 2-18. Architectural context at Savage Farm site.

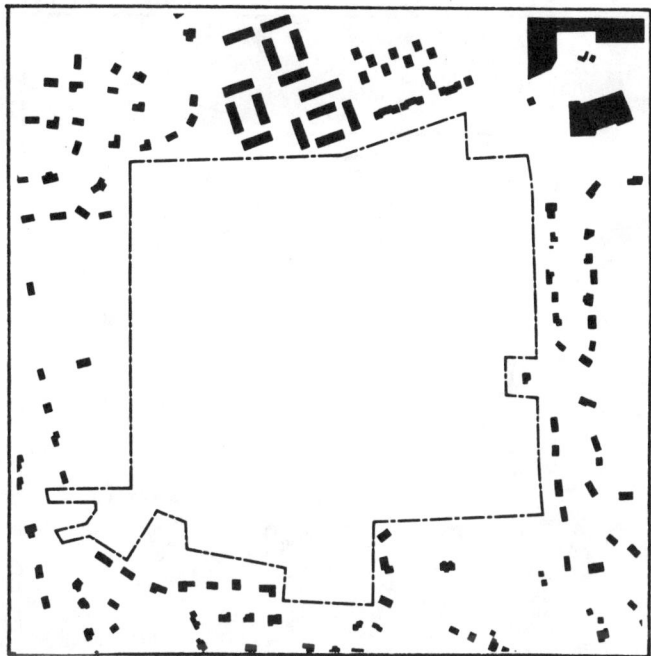

Source: Trowbridge-Trowbridge

ture relating to the planned development. An abundance of information was garnered from soils data such as engineering properties, depth-to-water table (water saturated soils), depth-to-bedrock, and slope/topography.

Vegetation and Streams

Since the site has been used primarily by Cornell University as agricultural plots, the landscape is largely open meadow. Two major drainage ways traverse the site. Mature wetlands vegetation follows these swales, giving a rich and diverse character to the site. Black willows, grey and redtwig dogwood, red maples, and an abundance of water-loving herbaceous plants line the creek beds and become natural buffers to the otherwise open site. Mature evergreens along Spruce Lane act as an existing foil to the southeast (Figure 2-19).

Topography

The topographic vantage of the site will allow for solar access to units as well as even sun from sunrise to sunset. This is unlike many sites in Ithaca which exist in valleys or on steep slopes adja-

Figure 2-19. Vegetation and streams at Savage Farm site.

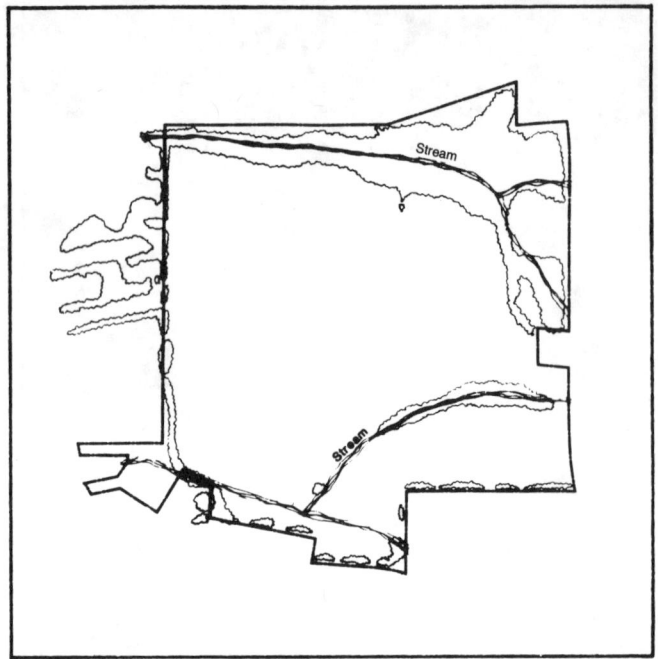

Source: Trowbridge-Trowbridge

cent to Cayuga Lake that are shaded part of the day. The natural topographic vantage also exposes the site to prevailing winds. While summer breezes are a site advantage, winter winds will require onsite buffering. Topography does not limit conventional building construction (Figure 2-20).

Soils

The soils are typical of the region. Glacial overburden, a moderately well-drained material consisting of clay soils and gravel, exists over the entire site. The soil is fertile and should allow for high-quality landscape development. It offers no limitations to residential development. It has good shear strength and compressibility.

The soil texture allows for good percolation, but it must be supplemented with subsurface drainage to eliminate the potential of wet areas in low points on the site.

Summary of Feasibility Study

The site appears to be a major undeveloped parcel in a rapidly developing region. Transportation access, public utilities, and ser-

Figure 2-20. Topography at Savage Farm site.

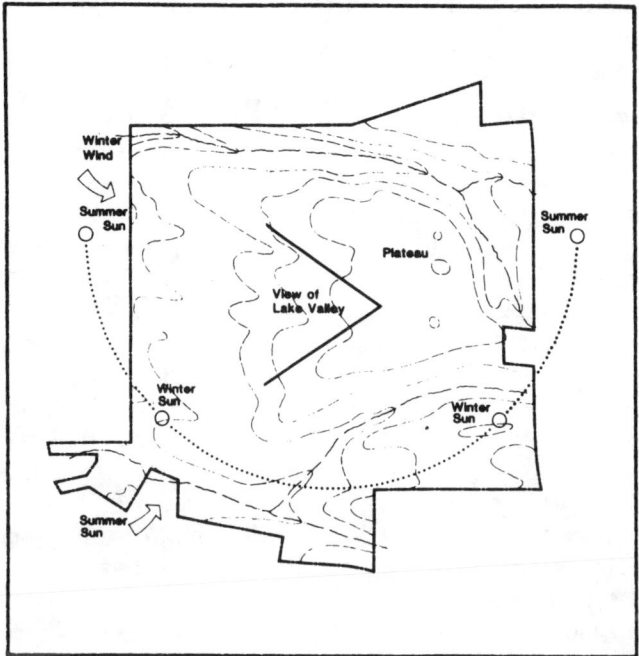

Source: Trowbridge-Trowbridge

vices to the site are exceptionally good. The visual characteristics of the site make it attractive for the proposed housing program. Zoning the parcel to include condominiums may become an issue in a village such as Cayuga Heights that protects the property values of an exclusive single-family housing community. Rezoning does not seem to be a restrictive factor, however.

The physical onsite factors such as drainage ravines and topography, which make the parcel so scenic, may limit development. These site factors are not considered sufficiently restrictive to preclude development, however, and sufficient information is available to warrant further study of this parcel.

Detailed Site Analysis

The Savage Farm parcel was sufficiently suitable for the developers to pursue a detailed site analysis to determine the most effective approach to residential development. Two major sections of the analysis were considered: natural environmental conditions and man-made conditions. These conditions have been documented systematically using an "information overlay" site analysis approach, which allows a cumulative understanding of all relevant onsite information.

Natural Environmental Conditions

The site shows the results of the glacial period that characterize much of Central New York State. The site is composed of three major physical forms: two ravines running east-west, which are the main drainage system, and a topographic plateau that defines highlands on either side of the ravines. The elevations run from 170 feet in the lowlands to 230 feet at the plateau level.

The topography includes a series of moderately steep slopes that occur all over the site in different locations. Of special interest are the slopes greater than 8 percent, which make road building very expensive, and those greater than 15 percent, which make building construction expensive. The mapping of these two slope thresholds shows that they are concentrated along the ravines.

The soil composition is predominantly Tompkins stony loam and is of glacial origin. Bedrock never occurs less than 6-8 feet from the surface.

The physical site characteristics greatly influence development programming and planning because of the difficulties that may be involved in excavation for different construction purposes, and because of general environmental constraints.

The vegetation is of three types: willows and dogwood in the ravines, swamp maples and various oaks in an intermediate zone, and open meadows in the dry plateaus.

A preliminary conclusion is that low wetland and ravine areas could be left in reservation for water conservation and open space, offering a unique opportunity for future recreational development of the site.

A detailed physical analysis of the site must include the soil structure, depth at which bedrock appears, surficial hydrology and depth-to-water table, and the relative costs associated with road, storm drainage, drainage, and sewer line construction.

A full physical analysis of the site was conducted, which included natural environmental conditions (surficial hydrology, surficial geology, soils suitability), manmade conditions, and development suitability as determined by the data presented above.

Surficial Hydrology

The surficial hydrology analysis revealed a wealth of characteristics within the site such as streams, edge conditions, and wooded wetlands. Such wetlands were concentrated in the lowlands of the site. These types of wetlands are not protected through the provisions of the New York State Freshwater Wetlands Act since they are too small and lack indicator vegetation species. They are, however, subject to regulation under Section 404 of the federal Clean Water Act. A Section 404 permit may have to be obtained prior to the placement of any fill in the wetlands.

Surficial Geology

The surficial geology analysis showed the glacial structure of the site such as bedrock overlaid by glacial till.

The water table is often perched and irregular because of the site's fragipan. This condition results in elevated wetlands and an interspersed drainage system.

Soils Suitability

The soils were analyzed to determine their constraints or suitability for construction operations. Soils unsuitable for development have the potential for low percolation rates and poor drainage, liabilities in shear strength, and compressibility and potential expansion. Proximity to bedrock and water table and the presence of fragipan are also considerations. Soils considered by the Soil Conservation Service to have moderate development limitations predominated the site.

Other soils on the site associated with wetlands were not considered suitable for development unless they were site-verified.

Manmade Environmental Conditions

These conditions were summarized from the regional feasibility study, documented at the same scale as the natural environmental conditions and incorporated into the composite development suitability map (Figure 2-21).

Development Suitability: Composite

The previous analysis makes possible a synthesis of the development suitability of the different sectors of the site. The property has been divided according to the following classifications:

Slight limitations—Depth to bedrock is at least 8 feet from the soils surface; depth-to-water table is not a construction limitation; the soil type is relatively suitable for development. (The corresponding SCS classification is moderate to severe.)

Moderate limitations—Depth to bedrock is 0 to 8 feet from the soil surface; drainage is poor because of fragipan near the surface; the soil type is not necessarily suitable for development. A site check is necessary to determine most suitable areas.

Figure 2-21. Manmade environmental conditions at Savage Farm site.

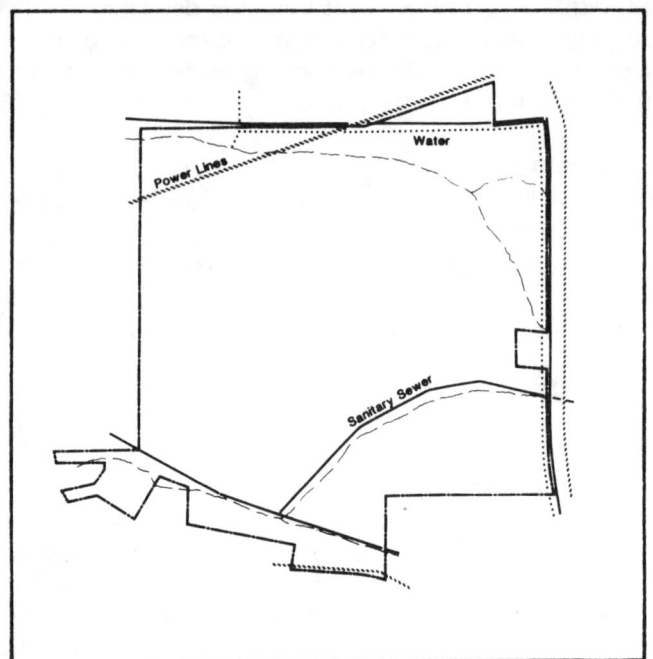

Source: Trowbridge-Trowbridge

Severe limitations—Depth to bedrock is 0 to 3 feet from the soil surface; the slope condition is often limiting in this soil type; depth-to-water table is 0 to 5 feet from the surface; soil type is not suitable for development.

Very severe limitations—None exist for this site.

Development suitability is determined with a ranking of site limitations established by the Soil Conservation Service, including the soil potential for frost action, soil percolation rates and sewage disposal, soil shear strength, and soil compressibility and potential expansion. In this region it also includes depth to fragipan, water table, and bedrock.

The typical geological section can be represented at the edge condition, where the plateau meets the ravine. The plateau is formed by glacial action. The glacial till covers the bedrock, and in turn is covered by organic soils forming the lowland. Often the water table appears at the surface of the lowland; the fragipan line is found within a few feet below the glacial overburden surface. This condition means that development potential is good. It is important to avoid the wetlands and ravines.

The plateau areas have no limitations for development. The edge condition has some limitations to development:

- The water table may be perched over the fragipan, although saturated soils usually are not encountered within 5 feet from the surface.
- The soil types may not always be suitable for development.
- The bedrock, or ledge, may be encountered within 8 feet from the surface.
- The slopes may be severe, and fill would be costly since no on-site source for fill exists, at least on such a large scale.

Summary

As a result of the site analysis, the following observations were made: more than 80 percent of the site, approximately 82 acres, can be considered for conventional development. The remainder of the site, approximately 20 percent or 13 acres, is considered to be feasible for development with some limitations. The land under the New York State Electric and Gas right-of-way was computed as not being conventionally developable.

This assessment is not final, however. Land must be contiguous or highly accessible to be considered developable. In the present case, some parcels may be disconnected from the rest and their development would involve additional costs to extend utilities and roads over ravines and wetlands.

Thus, easy accessibility is added to physical suitability as a criterion of development.

Final Project Description

The following is the proposed development scheme as configured in response to the site analysis (Figure 2-22).

Central Facilities

At the center of the site, situated on the plateau and facing southeast, would be the community center. It is envisioned as a clubhouse, with facilities for recreational activities, food preparation, library, meeting rooms, and hobby activity. If feasible, the center might also include a small medical facility and a limited number of guest rooms.

Parking for the center is located off a cul-de-sac north of the building. This area might also be used as a bus turnaround for

Figure 2-22. Proposed development scheme for Savage Farm based on site analysis.

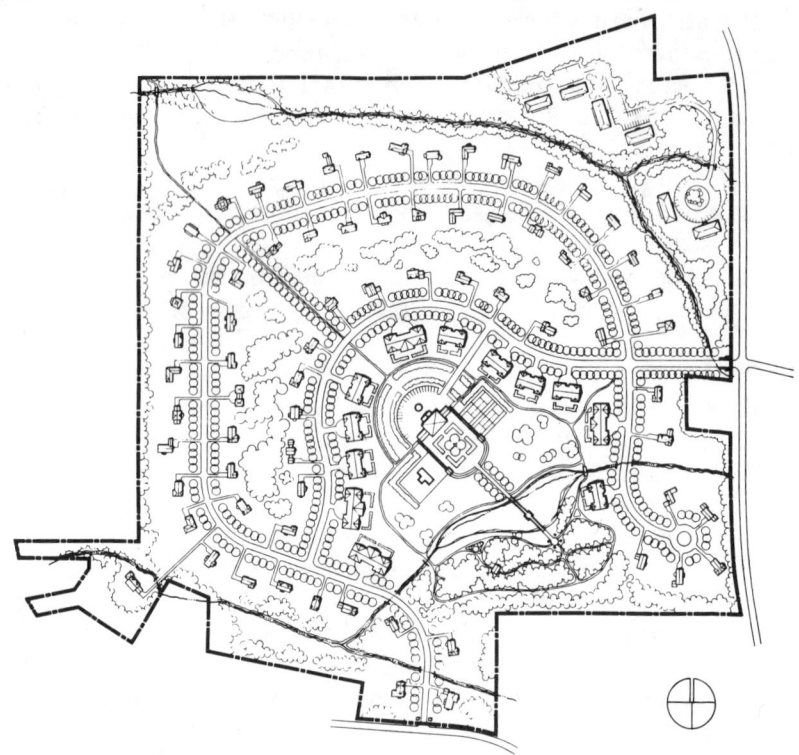

Source: Trowbridge-Trowbridge

public transit servicing the project. Its central location and convenience to the condominiums and clubhouse would make this an excellent collection point.

On the south side of the building is a large open terrace which serves as the community's central square. In addition to acting as an organizing element of the design, it would be the main outdoor activity space of the complex, hosting both organized and informal events in much the same way as the Ithaca Commons and the Cornell Arts Quad serve their communities.

Flanking the central space are two outdoor recreation areas. In the current configuration, one contains a swimming pool and the other, two tennis courts. These, however, are subject to change as a further assessment of needs is developed.

The entire central zone is surrounded by a green space which buffers the adjacent townhouses. The area slopes downward to the southeast, where a large pond is located. Serving both as drainage control and as a visual element, the pond would support a small population of ducks and would be an attraction to other wildlife. A low wooden bridge crosses the pond, connecting the community center to a wooded park to the southeast. Footpaths winding throughout would tie the common areas together.

Townhouses

Surrounding the community center is a ring of 84 deluxe condominiums. Organized in clusters, they include attached garages on the street side and private gardens on the community center side. Footpaths link the units to one another and to the common facilities.

The townhouses themselves are conceived as being one- and two-story units designed specifically for senior citizens and adaptable for use by physically handicapped persons. A typical unit would have two bedrooms, two baths and would encompass 1200 to 1400 square feet. Each would have continuous electronic monitoring for fire and smoke, as well as temperature variations, intrusion, and water entry. The monitoring system would also be available for residents' use in the case of medical emergency.

Single-Family Houses

Expanding upon the circular site design, the central facilities and townhouses are encircled by a zone of 71 single-family lots ranging in size from a half acre to more than one acre. The radial configuration is designed to optimize use of the site within its natural boundaries, integrate with the topography, and take advantage of views. It is contemplated at present that these lots would be sold individually. Control over design, size and placement of structures, and site development would be achieved through covenants and deed restrictions.

Apartments

Located in the northeast corner of the site, the 48 rental apartment units share a greater affinity with Sevanna Park, which they border, than with the low density housing. Vehicular access to the apartments is via Sevanna Park Road, while the stream and existing vegetation form a natural buffer for the single-family housing.

Phasing

It is proposed that development of the site be accomplished in four consecutive construction seasons, although a deceleration could be required based on the market absorption rate (Figure 2-23). The design lends itself to a phasing which takes advantage

Figure 2-23. Development phases at Savage Farm.

Phase 1

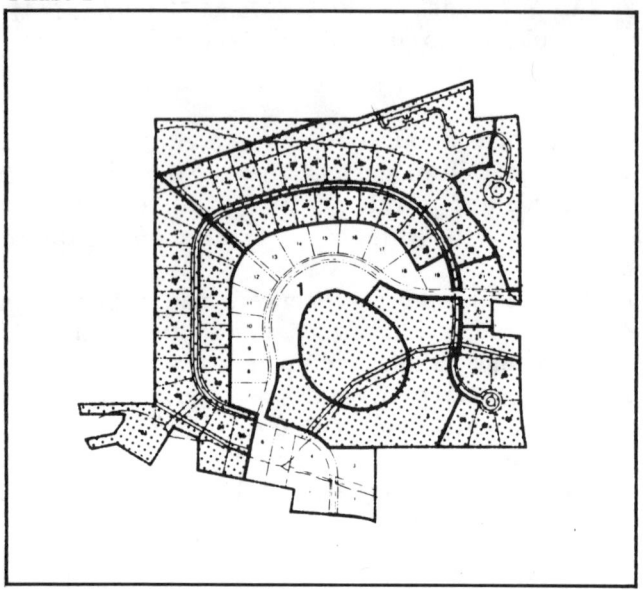

Phase 2

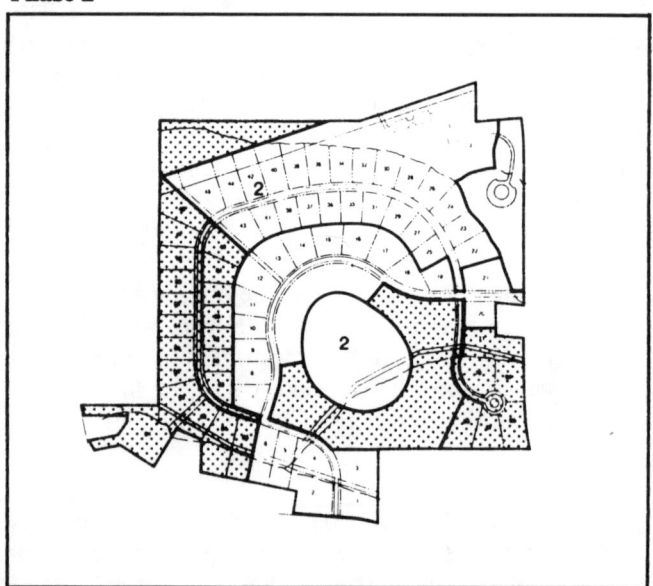

Source: Trowbridge-Trowbridge

Phase 3

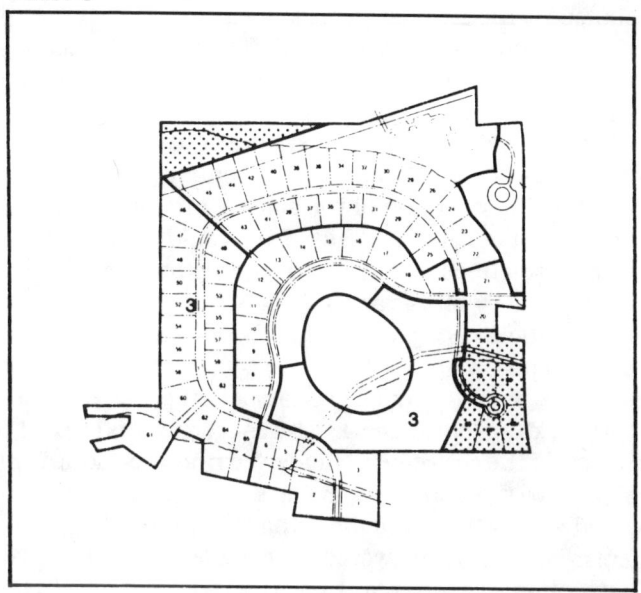

Phase 4

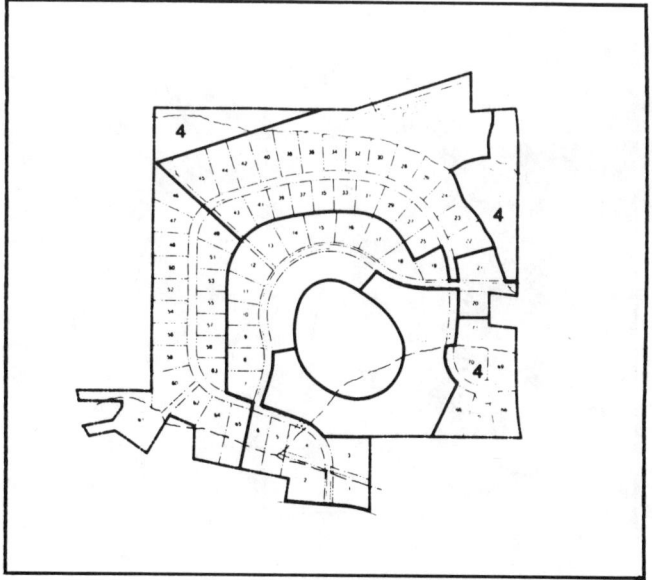

of existing vehicular access points and utilities, while respecting the impact of ongoing construction upon adjacent housing.

Phase One assumes construction of the inner loop road and utility extensions which would provide for the potential sale of 42 retirement condominiums and 21 building lots. Landscape development of the inner loop road would also be performed in Phase One.

Having established the inner nucleus of the project, Phase Two would continue development by expanding the outer ring with an additional 24 building lots and further enhance the retirement village core with construction of the community building and central recreation facilities. Also, Phase Two would include the first 32 units of apartments located at the northeast corner of the site. Accessed separately off Sevanna Park Road, construction would be isolated from the adjacent single-family building lots being concurrently developed.

Phase Three would complete construction of the outer loop road, adding 20 building lots at the southwest corner, and would complete construction of the retirement village townhouses, adding 42 units. Landscaping of the core area to the south of the central retention pond would also be completed during this phase.

The entire development would be completed in Phase Four with the construction of the remaining 16 apartments and related road extension, the southeast cul-de-sac and 6 remaining building lots, and site development of the northwest corner.

Chapter 3
Local Land Use Regulations and Plan Processing

All across the nation, local officials are facing decisions regarding the use of land in their communities. These are the decisionmakers who weigh the potential value of the local government's adoption of innovative zoning programs and who reconsider subdivision standards and approval processes. Their decisions have significant effects on developers as well as consumers of housing.

The Origins of Zoning

The American institution of zoning arose as a response to the evils of the 19th century industrial city. During the last half of the century, the mass exodus to urban areas began. In America, people came not only from the farms but directly off boats from other countries. The cities teemed with an ever-expanding population employed in the factories, and vast accounting bureaucracies created by the dawning industrial revolution. At the time, the use of land was strictly a private affair, with minimal regulations keyed mostly to the tracking of ownership. It was the age of the surveyor creating vast areas of gridded rectangular lots available for any and all uses over time.

Reformers came in many styles. Combating disease and implementing sanitary sewer systems brought a drive for scientific efficiency. The shift toward utilitarian structures on endless rectangular lots offended the aesthetic sense of the American elite, triggering in part the City Beautiful movements. Finally, the congestion and disparities of wealth inherent in cities created a fertile field for social critics.[1]

While desires for efficient, beautiful, and healthy cities came together as the basis for a city planning profession, the practice of zoning has stronger roots in the defensive protection of neighborhoods. The development pattern of Fifth Avenue in New York City led to the adoption of one of the nation's first zoning codes. Fifth Avenue was originally developed as a residential community for the well-to-do. These original residents were displaced over time by retail establishments. The expanding garment industry was, in sequence, encroaching when the local merchants organized in support of public regulations controlling the sweatshops. This was a case of protecting lower value and less intense uses from being continually displaced as the city grew.[2]

Conversely, the wealth, resettling on the fringe of the city, feared that other uses on the city's periphery would diminish the value of their newly built mansions. While this economic elite accepted freewheeling capitalism in the factory, the constantly shifting urban pattern of land uses was both unsettling and, in the long run, inefficient. It is because of this defensive orientation that zoning often is referred to as the politics of first arrival: Those people who arrived first in a given community influence zoning and land use constraints from which all future land use decisionmaking is derived.

As the problems of unregulated development became evident, a solution loomed literally over the horizon. On the Continent, European society retained within it institutions grounded in an aristocratic past. Municipal charters, greater public landholdings, and a social system which imposed patron-like behavior on emerging industrialists allowed for greater public control over the development process. In Germany, the Zone Plan was developed to separate the noxious uses from residences. With American higher education strongly focused on European thought, this idea traveled quickly.

Transportation technology both triggered the immediate crisis and offered a solution. Elevators broke the vertical barrier, casting permanent shadows on the street and permitting dramatic increases in the intensity of land use. Simultaneously, rail systems allowed workers to escape from the congestion downtown or the factory district, making large-scale zoning in American cities feasible.

The ideas, tools, leadership, and political support gelled by the 1920s. In May of 1924 the Commerce Department published the Standard State Zoning Enabling Act,[3] which was widely circulated and adopted by most states. During the Roaring Twenties, adopting a zoning ordinance became as fashionable as bathtub gin.

In 1926 the U.S. Supreme Court decided *Village of Euclid v. Ambler Realty Co.*, which upheld the constitutionality of zoning as a reasonable exercise of the police power needed to protect the

health, safety, and general welfare of the community.[4] Since *Euclid*, the three basic tests for the legality of a regulation affecting property have been:
- It must promote the health, safety, and welfare of the public.
- It cannot be arbitrary and capricious.
- It must be reasonable.

Over the years almost every court at the state or federal level has recited these tests in zoning cases. The basic doctrine has survived significant changes in planning goals, regulatory techniques, and social conditions as the criteria are sufficiently broad and general to accommodate the facts of each case and the changing trends of the law.

The Conventional Zoning Ordinance

Each zoning district generally has a set of detailed regulations covering not only the type of use or structure that is permitted within the district, but also yard requirements, height limitations, permitted unit density, and coverage limits. In theory, only a few districts should be established to keep the system workable (Figure 3-1). However, the trend nationally has been for the number of different zoning districts in municipal zoning ordinances to increase as a response to greater variations in land use types (Figure 3-2). A hodge-podge of zoning districts occurs that is no longer a logical response to the community's land use policies. Typically, as more districts are created, tailored to specific styles of land use, fewer uses are permitted by right in each district. The likelihood decreases that an available site will be properly zoned to correspond or accommodate a developer's needs; as a result, zoning appeals and amendments proliferate.

Figure 3-1. Typical Zoning Districts in a Basic Ordinance

District	Permitted Uses
A-1	Agricultural activities
R-1	Large lot residential
R-2	1/2-acre lot residential
R-3	5,000-square-foot lot residential
MF-1	Apartments and townhouses
C-1	Commercial
I-1	Industrial

Source: John Rahenkamp Consultants, Inc.

Figure 3-2. Zoning Districts in a Complex Ordinance

District	Permitted Uses
AA	Agricultural
R-R	Rural residential—3-acre lots
R-1	1-acre lot residential
R-2	1/2-acre lot residential
R-3	10,000-square-foot lot residential
R-4	5,000-square-foot lot residential
MF-1	Townhouses
MF-2	Duplexes, quadruplexes, rowhouses
MF-3	Apartments
MF-4	Midrise apartments
MF-5	Highrise apartments
B-1	Business district
H-C	Highway commercial
P-O	Professional offices
PP-O	Planned professional office parks
I-1	Light industry
I-2	Medium industry
I-3	Heavy industry
PI-1	Planned industrial park
FP	Flood plain
E-1	Institutional district

Source: John Rahenkamp Consultants, Inc.

Each ordinance has a definition section, usually found toward the front.

These terms should be reviewed carefully whenever the ordinance is used. Zoning terms are technical and their meaning can vary from community to community. A quick example would be the term "front yard." Most ordinances require that buildings be set back a certain distance into the lot. The definition section should be read to determine whether to measure the front yard setback from the street line (pavement) or the right-of-way line (usually extending beyond the pavement). This difference influences the decision to locate a building on a lot. Many of these "standards" are arbitrary and therefore subject to question and potentially vulnerable to legal challenge.

Most states have an enabling act that authorizes the use of zoning. The definitions provided by the state legislation should be checked against those in the local ordinances. Surprisingly often, local draftsmen prepare zoning ordinances that are inconsistent with state laws. In fact, some major cases have been won primarily on this point. Local officials must stay alert to amendments passed from time to time by the legislature and update their codes accordingly.

The administration and enforcement sections of a zoning ordinance determine procedural requirements. These sections should be carefully tailored to the state enabling legislation. Consideration of a zoning change or amendment often requires public hearings. Care should be taken to see that public agencies abide by the rules. Time limits and notice requirements are specified and all parties should adhere to them. Most communities have a zoning officer who is empowered to administer the regulations. Larger towns may have an entire zoning office or department.

Appeals from the decision of the zoning officer generally occur through a zoning hearing board or zoning board of adjustment. Members of the board are appointed by the executive or legislative branch of the community and are often referred to as performing a quasi-judicial function—that is, they hear appeals, take testimony, and render judgments involving interpretations of the zoning ordinance. They also issue special exceptions and variances when conditions merit such action. Actions by zoning boards become the focus of much attention, particularly when the matter involves small parcels and commercial sites.

Special Exceptions and Variances

A special exception, or conditional use, is approval granted to an applicant to use land for a purpose other than what is permitted by right in a zoning district. Standards are generally provided to guide the zoning hearing board or board of adjustments in making decisions on special exceptions.

Special exceptions can be called special only because the ordinance does not allow them by right but rather lists specific uses to be treated by this process along with standards for compliance. For example, in a typical residential zoning district, an ordinance might provide for neighborhood commercial, nursing home, and public uses by special exception. The standards necessary for approval should be checked carefully, both in the ordinance and in the enabling legislation. In most cases they will be straightforward findings regarding public health, safety, and welfare, but some local governments create more complex standards.

Another major function of the zoning board is to render judgments on whether or not to issue a variance. An applicant seeking a variance is trying to obtain permission for something that does not conform to a strict interpretation of the zoning ordinance, such as building too close to a property line. In most cases the applicant must bear the burden of showing that a hardship will be suffered if the strict application of the ordinance to the property is required. Usually, just the demonstration of a hardship is not enough, and the applicant must affirmatively show that the public interest will not be endangered by approving the variance.

Variance law is quite technical in many jurisdictions, but a few basic rules usually govern:

- A landowner cannot create personal hardship by his/her own actions and then expect relief.
- The variance sought will provide relief with the least modification to the ordinance.
- The variance will not change the basic character of the neighborhood.
- The variance is necessary to allow reasonable use of the property.

Remember that although economics plays a role in determining when a variance should be granted, it is not the controlling factor. If a landowner pays a high price for a piece of land and then determines that a variance is needed to permit its profitable use, relief will seldom be given for that reason alone.

It should be noted that the term "variance" is often misused. Usually a change in permitted use of a property requires a rezoning, not a variance. A rezoning is accomplished by an amendment to the zoning ordinance, passed by the legislative body, either changing the zoning district or allowing the proposed use as a permitted use or special exception. Advice from the planning board usually is required before adoption of the amendment by the legislative body.

The administration section of each ordinance usually contains provisions for creating new districts or changing one district to another. This process can lead to "spot zoning," which violates the law in many states and, therefore, must be approached carefully. The true purpose of zoning, after all, is to provide for the general welfare and not to guarantee every landowner the highest return on an investment.

The Subdivision Ordinance

Local governments have a long history of regulating the subdivision of land into lots. Many factors spurred the evolution of the subdivision ordinance as it exists today, among them the desire to facilitate the recording of plans and deeds in the appropriate courthouse, the desire to have some influence over the design and construction of streets to be dedicated to and maintained by the local government, and the desire to prevent repetition of the failures of yesterday. In the absence of subdivision regulations, developers, particularly of small parcels, left roads unfinished and streets of different widths. Some areas had curbs and sidewalks, and others did not. Stormwater was treated as the common enemy to be disposed of in any way possible.

Subdivision ordinances have evolved to include much more than plat recording and requirements for building streets. Many ordinances include strict design standards regulating building design and the arrangement of buildings on a street or courtyard. Tree ordinances, whose purpose is to prevent existing mature trees from being removed from a site, are becoming commonplace. Landscape ordinances, which can require street trees or screening of parking lots, for example, are also common. While the intention of these development regulations may be to prevent poor quality development, they often inhibit a builder or architect/planner from using an innovative design; the result of too much control over design is a blandness and sameness to all projects.

Unified or Land Management Ordinance

Zoning ordinances evolved to deal with the intensity or type of land use permitted in particular areas of a community, whereas subdivision ordinances evolved as sets of design standards. The result is often two sets of regulations and two groups of people to administer them, resulting in inevitable conflicts.

Given that the two sets of codes are interdependent, some jurisdictions have combined the regulations into a unified ordinance, often called a land management ordinance. The unified ordinance typically combines all subdivision and design standards with all use and intensity requirements. From an administrative standpoint, using the unified ordinance appears to make more sense, particularly when more flexible zoning techniques are adopted.

The Legacy of Traditional Land Use Controls

As in all attempts to regulate society, land use controls provided salutary effects that were, by and large, intended. The rampant evils of the 19th century city were tamed. But regulations also bring about changes that are unintended.

Reevaluation of Standards Necessary

Subdivision standards have a tendency to become excessive over time. Development technologies and techniques are developed much more rapidly than codes are updated. While some lag is inevitable, in some communities it is nearly permanent! For example, natural drainage systems based upon swales and detention basins have been proven effective for over 20 years and are now standard fare in design schools, yet many local governments still require curb and gutter in all circumstances. This problem is caused by several factors, including the domination of the approval process by laypersons due to vigorous conflict-of-interest laws that keep knowledgeable professionals from serving on the various boards. If a town does not have adequate staff resources to handle all the necessary revisions and keep the subdivision code current, the latter suffers. Also, lack of resources dedicated to the planning function leads to inappropriate copying of available standards. For example, it is not uncommon to find state highway or turnpike paving standards replicated inappropriately in local codes.

Finally, there is no incentive for a local government to remain current. Based on the old adage that no one lost a job by being too careful, towns slowly add to existing controls: road widths expand, setbacks grow, landscaping requirements proliferate, etc.

In addition, cost-generating or density-reducing design standards can be used to surreptitiously achieve local goals that cannot by law be directly sought. For example, it is increasingly common that densities seemingly granted by zoning ordinances cannot actually be obtained following the corresponding design controls. Cost-generative standards ensure that the housing that is ultimately built will be more expensive, bringing in more "desirable" homeowners.

At a time when more than half the population cannot afford to purchase a new house, everything must be done to deliver a solid product trimmed of unnecessary costs. This concept, often referred to as least-cost housing, must be embraced by public officials to meet both legal and economic obligations. The subdivision ordinance is a good place to begin this reexamination of where the cost of housing can be reduced through regulatory reform.[5]

Exclusionary Zoning

Exclusionary zoning is a zoning scheme that bans a use from an entire community. Of course, zoning is meant to exclude certain uses from certain areas, but the legal doctrine of exclusionary zoning has arisen to describe an illegal by-product. If a community bans a reasonable or legitimate use of land from a reasonable portion of its land area, its action is subject to challenge. Over the years, the list of excluded uses has expanded, encompassing solid waste storage or processing sites, power plants, and even residential uses. For years communities have banned mobile homes, apartments, townhouses, and homes on small lots for economic and social reasons, or, as was often publicly stated, to "protect the character of the community."

Oftentimes, municipalities have tried to use regulatory constraints to "improve" their character. Mount Laurel Township in New Jersey, a community dominated by 1/3- and 1/4-acre lots, not only excluded unwanted uses but also rezoned the rest of the vacant land area for 2-acre-minimum lots.

Underlying arguments about community aesthetics, the fiscal health of a town frequently induces exclusionary desires. First, local bodies often rezone vast areas for nonresidential uses, hoping to capture a larger local tax base. Because market forces are at least partially a function of supply, the zoning classification of each piece of land in a community will affect the value of the remainder.

With little land zoned for residential uses, its cost can rise dramatically. Second, new development is viewed as a potential source of revenue that is not regulated by local real estate tax caps. Excessive permit and processing fees, contributions for offsite improvements, requirements for new public facilities, and parks within larger developments all tend to exclude new homebuyers by driving up the cost of homes.

Exclusionary zoning is being eliminated slowly through court challenges, property tax equalization plans, and the growing importance of housing allocation plans at the state level. The myths that certain kinds of land uses or housing types will destroy the economic or social fabric of a community die hard.

Innovative Zoning: Responses to Today's Issues

Conventional zoning and design controls met the concerns posed by the industrial city; however, they have largely failed to meet the demands of current development trends. They have not provided the flexibility necessary for local leaders and intelligent developers to deal with the issues of today. Protection of the environment, reduction of the steep increases in property taxes, new technological methods to resolve old problems, and provision of housing opportunities for all citizens have become almost impossible without innovative land use management approaches.[6]

Conventional zoning imposes controls that can be exclusionary and cost-generating. For example, an R-1 district for detached residential dwellings to be built on a certain size lot often is established without any correlation to adequate health, safety, and welfare criteria. Clearly, several alternatives are possible without compromising the community's health, safety, and welfare.

Innovative zoning can further high-quality development by encouraging the developer to contribute to the community by building a project that fulfills its broader goals, and the community can identify and encourage the type and quality of development it wants and must legally accommodate.

In conventional zoning, flexibility can be achieved only through the cumbersome variance or rezoning approach. In innovative zoning, flexibility is designed into the system, thereby encouraging creativity on the part of the developer. Flexibility is the heart of the concept. A developer is given a set of options subject to certain performance standards. Certain items are purposely left to negotiation, such as permitting a higher density in exchange for more permanently preserved open space.

Conventional zoning regulations tend to be prescriptive, that is, requiring that something be done in a set, rigid fashion, without allowing for departures from that standard based on the specific character of the site. Performance standards are more permissive in nature. They state clearly the objective to be achieved and then recognize that there will be more than one good way to accomplish the objective, or that at one site it may be done one way and that at another site a different method is needed.

Prescriptive standards which utilize minimum numbers for things such as setbacks, height, etc., too easily allow all parties to forget the desired objectives of the standards.

The difference between prescriptive and performance standards can be seen in the following example, which deals with parking:

A prescriptive standard would state:
- Required setback from parking to property line—15 feet.
- Parking must be landscaped.

A performance standard would state:
- Parking shall not be visible from public roadways or adjacent properties (as viewed from ground level).
- Parking lots shall provide interior landscaping to assist in establishing the visual and functional subsections necessary to provide for the safe and efficient movement of vehicles and pedestrians.
- There shall be pedestrian paths providing safe access from parking spaces to the activity served.

In order to satisfy the performance standards, a parking lot may take one of several options. To be visually screened from view, the parking may be screened in several ways, including landscaping, fencing, berming, or placement behind a building. Each applicant can choose the method most appropriate to the site. Thus, at a relatively cleared site, one could use berming and minimal landscaping, while a heavily treed site could utilize existing vegetation and no berming. Further, the setback may vary based upon the character of the screening or buffer area. Vegetation of different types and size may screen parking with a planting strip 15 feet wide, while other material may require a 30-foot planting strip.[7]

Several innovative techniques—planned unit development (PUD) zoning, incentive zoning, impact zoning, and transfer of development rights—are being used in various communities to provide more performance-oriented methods for managing land.

Planned Unit Development Zoning

Planned unit development (PUD) zoning is one of the earliest approaches to innovative zoning; it is used widely today throughout the country, primarily in the developing suburban rings. Most state enabling statutes now provide for, and in some cases encourage, the use of PUDs.

The PUD concept encompasses a wide range of approaches to land use control.[8] In its simplest form the PUD ordinance provides for the use of cluster zoning where single-family homes are grouped on small lots to facilitate the retention of open space and the creation of a general environment better than can be achieved through conventional zoning. At the other end of the scale, the PUD concept can provide for the development of an entire new community such as Columbia, Maryland.

In practice, PUD ordinances can provide for a mixture of land uses, such as housing, shopping, and industry, on a single large tract of land. Density is often greater than conventionally permitted in order to induce the inclusion of open space, public facilities, or other public benefits in the overall plan. A separate review process for PUDs is often required to enable all parties to work together to create an asset to the community.[9]

Such assets include reduction in road area, increased potential for saving trees and natural features, mixture of housing types, increased use of nonvehicular transportation through bike and pedestrian paths, balanced services and taxes, location of shopping facilities close to the customer, and improved marketability for the developer.

Deciding where PUDs should be permitted is often a tough issue for local leaders. Some communities create separate districts, and others use floating PUD zoning. The floating zone concept is preferable because it permits maximum flexibility, authorizing PUD use wherever certain planning criteria can be met by the applicant.

One frequently touted advantage of a PUD is the amount of open space preserved. This advantage has been evident, but consideration should be given to who maintains the land and to ways to link two open-space areas of adjoining developments to create a community system, and not just isolated green spaces. Most areas rely on a homeowners association to manage the permanently preserved open space. This concept is not without risks, although it has worked well in most cases.

Higher densities and clustering of units are generally thought to reduce development costs and provide more affordable housing. Although PUDs provide these benefits, they are not easy or inexpensive to plan and get approved. The expense of the recreational amenities that some communities require of a developer also offsets the lower development costs and reduces the chances for lower housing prices. On the average, the PUD still results in a better designed and environmentally sensitive development than does the conventional subdivision, and it has the potential to keep housing costs down.

Another attractive feature of the PUD is that tax revenues will generally exceed public service costs.[10] The higher densities and variety of housing types usually found in the PUD generate very favorable revenues, and the cluster design with recreation facilities, reduced street length, and the possible dedication of public facility sites keeps service costs down. With militancy in public attitudes toward property taxes, emphasizing this positive fiscal impact is particularly important.

The PUD ordinance can also provide for a large development to receive an overall conceptual approval, followed by approval and build-out of smaller sections or stages of the project. The community and the developer are assured of a single comprehensive review process, and the developer can plan a large project over an extended time frame, thereby amortizing the costs of major improvements. A community definitely benefits from being able to work with a developer and achieve economies of scale.

In recent years, higher interest rates and land costs have made large-scale development more difficult. As a result, there has been a trend toward smaller PUDs. Development at higher densities has also become more widespread.[11]

Incentive Zoning

Incentive zoning can help achieve the goals set forth in the community's master plan, particularly in urban areas. Benefits or bonuses are granted to the developer who implements some specific objectives. In urban areas, an example would be an increase in building height in return for the provision of a plaza accessible to the public. The public concessions and the private contributions should be identified clearly in the zoning ordinance (Figure 3-3).

The cost and nature of the public benefits attained in exchange for certain concessions must not be unreasonable. Communities must consciously seek the negotiation of a fair exchange. This approach is more likely to attract development that achieves the goals of the community's master plan.

Figure 3-3. Typical Public Benefits and Incentives

Public Benefits	Incentives
Parks	Tax abatement
Playgrounds	Increased density
Library site	Publicly financed street or highway improvement
Beach or waterfront access	
Historic preservation	Extra building height
Provision of least-cost housing	Extra building coverage
Mass transit stop	

Source: John Rahenkamp Consultants, Inc.

Incentive zoning in urban and established older suburban neighborhoods can provide an impetus for redevelopment by the private sector, relieving local governments of many of the large initial capital expenditures needed to spur the revitalization of neighborhoods or business districts.

Conditional Zoning

Similar to incentive zoning, conditional zoning binds the landowner to agree upon conditions in exchange for certain zoning concessions. Unlike incentive zoning, however, in which the private contribution and bonuses granted are specified in the code, conditional zoning involves a negotiation process between the landowner/developer and the local government. In exchange for a rezoning to higher intensity use, the local government requires that certain public improvements be made by the developer, such as construction of offsite roads or provision of parklands. While conditional zoning can provide density bonuses for a developer and can enable the developer to know that no further commitments could be exacted after rezoning is granted, there are some dangers to this approach. The local government may demand increasing and arbitrary public improvements in exchange for rezonings, and often these are rezonings that should be approved anyway because of neighboring land uses or designation in the comprehensive plan.[12] Sometimes, the demands of local government can become so specific that they could constitute site plan zoning. This can result in the local government pinning down a developer on his final plan well before he even owns the land. While conditional zoning can provide zoning flexibility for developers, it can result in abuses by the local government. There is a danger for violation of due process, as the local government might require exactions to enforce policies and requirements that have never been publicly adopted.[13]

Impact Zoning

One of the more recent forms of innovative zoning, impact zoning, establishes a framework for negotiation through the use of specific performance standards and evaluation methods.[14] Specific guidelines for project approval are established, but the need to keep abreast of rapidly changing conditions is weighed in the decision. Approval is contingent on proof that the development will have a beneficial impact on the community.

The applicant bears the burden of showing compliance with a set of performance standards. Some of these standards might include:
- No increase in the peak discharge of stormwater runoff leaving the site.
- Retention of a certain percentage of the site in open space.
- No fill deposited in flood plains.
- No creation of traffic congestion (a term that should be defined specifically).

Many impact zoning ordinances require some form of an environmental impact statement to mitigate the ramifications of the development. The local government must exercise care, however, not to burden every developer with a costly technical exercise that should be applied only to major projects that have a significant potential for environmental harm. Impact statements can be very expensive and time-consuming. In the use of impact zoning techniques, the building industry will have to improve management skills and the public sector will have to use more sophisticated review methods in order to avoid unnecessary costs to both the builder and the public.

Advanced impact zoning schemes rely on analysis (occasionally computer-assisted) of fiscal and infrastructure capacities and demand. The term *infrastructure* refers to services such as roads, sewers, and water supply, and sometimes is expanded to include facilities such as schools. Available capacities are compared to potential demands to identify the expected effects (Figure 3-4). A key element of the impact zoning process is the authorization for the developer to make improvements or contributions that will counteract many of the potentially undesirable effects of development identified in the review process. This provision enables the community to insure that the long-term effects of development will be beneficial to the existing residents and those who will follow.

Figure 3-4. Capacity v. demand analysis process

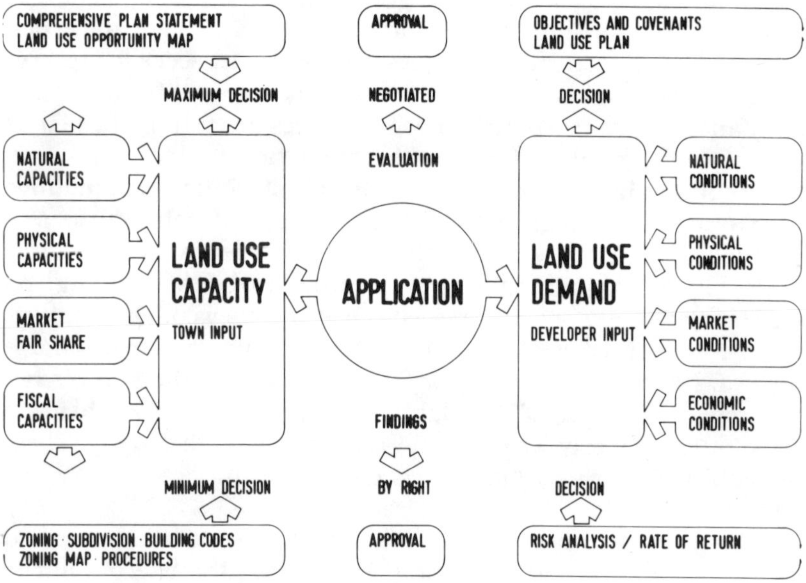

```
COMPREHENSIVE PLAN STATEMENT        APPROVAL            OBJECTIVES AND COVENANTS
LAND USE OPPORTUNITY MAP                                LAND USE PLAN

        MAXIMUM DECISION        NEGOTIATED                 DECISION

NATURAL                                                            NATURAL
CAPACITIES                      EVALUATION                         CONDITIONS

PHYSICAL                                                           PHYSICAL
CAPACITIES    LAND USE                        LAND USE             CONDITIONS
              CAPACITY      APPLICATION       DEMAND
MARKET                                                             MARKET
FAIR SHARE    TOWN INPUT                      DEVELOPER INPUT      CONDITIONS

FISCAL                                                             ECONOMIC
CAPACITIES                      FINDINGS                           CONDITIONS

        MINIMUM DECISION        BY RIGHT                  DECISION

ZONING · SUBDIVISION · BUILDING CODES   APPROVAL        RISK ANALYSIS / RATE OF RETURN
ZONING MAP · PROCEDURES
```

Source: John Rahenkamp Consultants, Inc.

Performance Zoning

Performance zoning permits a full range of housing types in all zoning districts rather than relying on rigid lot size, setback, and housing type requirements. Under this approach, development on a site is restricted by the site's natural features. No filling or encroachment is permitted on floodplains, natural retention areas, alluvial soils, streams, lakes, ponds, or wetlands. Often, large areas of a site must be set aside to meet these environmental protection standards. For this reason, clustering is an inherent part of performance zoning. Clustering permits attached or closely spaced dwellings, which can result in a broader range of housing prices and helps reduce costs for roads and utilities. Clustering also permits a developer to build the same number of units that would have been permitted had the entire parcel been built upon; therefore, the developer is not penalized for leaving environmentally sensitive land undeveloped.[15]

Transfer of Development Rights

Transfer of development rights, or TDR, is based on the idea that development rights can be separated from a piece of property and transferred or sold. This concept has been the practice with mineral or air rights for years. The right to the development potential of land is viewed as transferable and severable, a concept that combines legal and economic principles. New York City seeks to preserve historic structures with TDR; a few jurisdictions are trying to save farmland, and some suburban communities are trying to use it as part of their overall land management program.[16]

TDR might be used to preserve historic structures or buildings with architectural significance. The development rights of the parcel are determined by calculating what the permitted floor area under current zoning would be if the owner razed the building and constructed a new one in its place. These rights would be available for sale to another developer within the community, who could use them to increase the density or floor area of a building on his/her property. The owner of the rights could, of course, use them on some other property without selling them to another party. Theoretically, TDR provides a method of compensating for severe restrictions on land use.

TDR systems in suburban or rural areas are often implemented as part of a general downzoning. Restricting the use of land to extremely low levels of intensity is almost always politically difficult. TDR systems serve as a palliative as they work to ensure that landowners in the protected areas are compensated to some degree by landowners in developable areas.

One of the most successful TDR programs is that of Montgomery County, Maryland. The purpose of the program is to preserve farmland without resorting to purchasing land or downzoning. The county established a rural density transfer zone (sending area) and authorized development rights of one dwelling unit for each 5 acres.

Each of these development rights can be sold for use in a receiving area. Each development right purchased allows the buyer to build one additional residential unit per acre over the maximum permitted by zoning. Development in the preservation zone (sending area) is limited to one dwelling unit per 25 acres.

Real estate firms list and sell TDRs and collect commissions on sales, just as with any other real estate. Developers in Maryland have purchased over 2,000 one-unit development rights since the program's inception. To protect farmowners from a weak market for development rights, the county established a TDR bank to buy, hold, and sell development rights.[17]

True TDR systems are quite complex in management. For example, the ownership of "rights" needs to be tracked and local real estate tax implications arise. Further, future increases in levels of development permitted in the jurisdiction can pose intractable problems. For example, allowing a normal rezoning for more units on one parcel diminishes the value of the credits and causes the entire program to lose credibility. Alternatively, more "rights" could be issued, but they should be distributed as a stock split (to holders of original rights) or to landowners, some of whom already sold their last batch of rights. TDR systems are analogous to central banks, and local governments are rarely up to the task.

In order to keep the benefits of density transfers without creating currency-like rights, many jurisdictions simply broaden their PUD language to include noncontiguous parcels. In this system, all parcels must be brought forward as part of the same application, considerably simplifying the administrative procedures. The noncontiguous PUD system will not be an adequate substitute for a true credit system under certain circumstances, including:

1. When problems of title are endemic in an area. It may be possible to create a system in which development rights can be bought or sold without necessitating the proof of clear title.
2. When there is a need to hold development rights separate from the land over time. For example, if permitted densities are low and landholdings are small and diverse, it would be infeasible for a developer to simultaneously hold a controlling interest in enough ground to aggregate adequate development rights. A credit system would allow a more gradual accumulation.
3. When there is a need to move development rights across jurisdictional boundaries. This was the original justification for the Pinelands credit system in New Jersey. The Pinelands Commission could force municipalities with Regional Growth Areas to accept imported bonuses in their local codes.[18]

Multiple Tiers of Regulation

Land use regulation has never been the province of local government alone. The power to zone was delegated from the state government to the local government through enabling legislation. Since the early 1970s, the power and influence over land use decision-making has been increasingly assumed by higher levels of government, particularly regional, state, and federal agencies.

Regional agencies often have been used by the federal government to facilitate the disbursement of funds and the coordination of a variety of federal programs. When the Environmental Protection Agency (EPA) conducted its 208 Areawide Wastewater Management Plans, it used regional agencies almost exclusively.

The federal government is involved in land use regulation in many other ways. The Office of Coastal Zone Management has influence in coastal areas; EPA decisions affect sewer and water facilities; the Department of Defense controls base closings, which can affect neighboring communities severely; the Department of Transportation makes decisions every day on highway and transit funding that can play a major role in a community's future; the Corps of Engineers regulates wetlands; and the list goes on.

Regional commissions, set up by state legislatures, Congress, or local governments themselves, have proliferated. The Pinelands Commission was established to create a plan and program controlling the location of development in New Jersey's Pine Barrens, as well as preserving its most pristine areas. The Adirondack Park Commission regulates land use in northern New York through dedications from builders, rather than having to purchase the land for a conventional park. The San Francisco Bay Commission has considerable influence over land use decisions made in the area surrounding the bay.

The states have not been idle, either. The California Coastal Zone Conservation Act of 1972 regulated land within the coastal zone through a state commission. Maryland's Chesapeake Bay Critical Areas legislation, passed in 1985, will result in prescriptions for local government programs. Florida's Local Government Comprehensive Planning and Land Development Regulation Act of 1985 requires counties and municipalities to adopt comprehensive plans which must be approved by the state, and requires consistency between planning and development regulations. Maine, Vermont, Delaware, Oregon, Washington, and Hawaii have all adopted laws that give these states a major role in what for years were decisions handled at the local level.[19]

Planners, lawyers, and engineers who work for local governments are coming to realize the importance of this multiple tier of regulations. Frequently, the local decisionmakers, both public and private, must now keep abreast of and make recommendations to several agencies at these higher levels. Although many important decisions are still made at the local level, the process has become exceedingly complex. For better or worse, the days of conducting, planning, and filing zoning applications without relying on expert help and guidance are over.

Case Law Pertaining to Zoning and Subdivision Control

In processing a development plan through zoning and subdivision procedures, the most important element is to know the ordinances, state enabling legislation, and applicable case law that relate to the jurisdiction. Processing plans with any hope of approval relies on a working knowledge of, and not casual acquaintance with, the rules.

Today's realities tend to focus attention on the arbitrary aspects of many zoning ordinances and subdivision regulations in use across the nation. As more information becomes available, these regulations become harder to defend.

Methods of weighing the technical bases for conventional or traditional land management tools have become quite sophisticated in the past decade. Soils analysis has become more accurate, and the information is now more readily available. Aerial and satellite photography is now part of the information package available to planners and developers. Demographics and economics provide more definite data for land use decisions. Economists can now illustrate, for example, the added cost per new house that a town will force people to pay if it opts for 1-acre minimum lots versus clusters of 6,000-square-foot lots with open space. The per-unit cost of concrete curbs and gutters instead of grass swales can be calculated with precision.

Some of this new information is finding its way into the courtroom, and judges have been impressed. Minimum floor area requirements were found to exacerbate housing shortages and costs without advancing a single desirable social goal. Such zoning provisions were struck down as arbitrary, capricious, and unreasonable by the New Jersey Supreme Court in *Home Builders League of South Jersey, Inc. v. Township of Berlin*.[20] Requiring that every home be at least 1,100 square feet in size was held to be a form of "snob zoning."

Not every zoning or subdivision regulation that influences housing costs is unconstitutional, but local officials and planners should remember that such cost-inducing regulations must be clearly linked to health, safety, and general welfare.

The notion that land use regulations are a major factor in the alarming increase in housing costs should be no surprise. In *Oakwood at Madison v. Township of Madison*,[21] the Supreme Court of New Jersey identified this problem as the major obstacle to providing affordable housing. Later, the same court restated the affordability problem caused by local planning practices and forcefully imposed an affirmative duty on every municipality in the state to provide for its fair share of the region's low- and moderate-income housing needs (*Southern Burlington County NAACP v. Township of Mount Laurel*).[22] The *Mount Laurel* decisions resulted in hundreds of lawsuits and, finally, state legislation that created a mechanism for resolving housing and "fair share" disputes, resulting in the construction of thousands of affordable housing units.[23] The basic tenet of these New Jersey cases is that local government must bear the burden of proving the rational link between its land use regulations and public health, safety, and welfare.

The New Jersey judiciary is not alone in recognizing the local regulation and housing cost connection. Pennsylvania also adopted a "fair share" doctrine,[24] although it has since limited its original scope.[25] And lower level state courts in New York[26] and New Hampshire[27] have emphatically endorsed the *Mount Laurel* approach.

In *City of Boca Raton v. Boca Villas Corp.*[28] the District Court of Appeals in Florida struck down a growth cap ordinance because no rational relationship existed between the limit on the number of new dwelling units built each year and permissible government goals.

Growth management can serve a legitimate purpose when it ensures that new development does not surpass the growth capacity and natural resources of a community. When there are legitimate concerns over preserving public health and welfare, the housing needs of a community may necessitate builders to work with local government to determine how best to accommodate growth. Yet local governments increasingly are imposing growth controls for the purpose of stopping new development entirely, regardless of the larger public interest. The real charge of local government should be to manage, rather than to stop, growth.

Growth limitations have been imposed by municipalities across the country; Ramapo, New York; Petaluma, California; and Boulder, Colorado, are three well-known communities that have used growth controls. Most attempts by jurisdictions to limit public expenditures through growth moratoriums have backfired. No-growth communities have learned the hard way that growth more than pays for itself and is vital to a strong local economy and healthy housing market. Although they have yet to reject growth control in principle, Ramapo, Petaluma, and Boulder have repealed or revised their original growth management plans because of the unforeseen negative effect on the local economy.[29]

The case law pertaining to generic issues, such as housing opportunity or growth management, will indicate the soundness or vulnerability of a particular locality's zoning and subdivision regulations. An individual planning to file a zoning application for a development project must put together a team of experts who have experience with the approval process, the law, and the politics of the area.

Processing a Zoning Application

Since the late 1970s, there has been a decreasing reliance on conventional zoning standards to control land use and an increasing reliance on performance standards and impact assessment, in practice if not by statute. Increasingly, traditional by-right zoning seldom exists now without input from state and federal programs and detailed local negotiations. These processes generate findings from environmental impact assessments, such as water quality studies and standards that require technical analysis. Planned unit developments, clusters, and floating zones all demand a high level of design and management skill to produce a high-quality development. The concern over local tax rates expressed by many voters has resulted in the need for an applicant to do extensive economic homework on the fiscal effects of the proposed project.

Often planning boards and town councils must be educated about the changing population profile and the effect this has had on the housing market. Families with fewer children are deciding, often for economic reasons, to select a multifamily unit, attached home, or a small detached home. In 1985, according to the U.S. Census Bureau, 74 percent of the households in the U.S. had one to three members, as compared with 68 percent in 1975 and 61 percent in 1965. The tremendous jump in demand for townhouses, apartments, and condominiums is partially caused by this historic increase in the proportion of smaller households.

Figure 3-5 describes a typical zoning process. In addition to this formal process, there is a much more informal process of persuasion and negotiation which usually includes several players—the

Figure 3-5. The zoning process in Prince George's County, Maryland

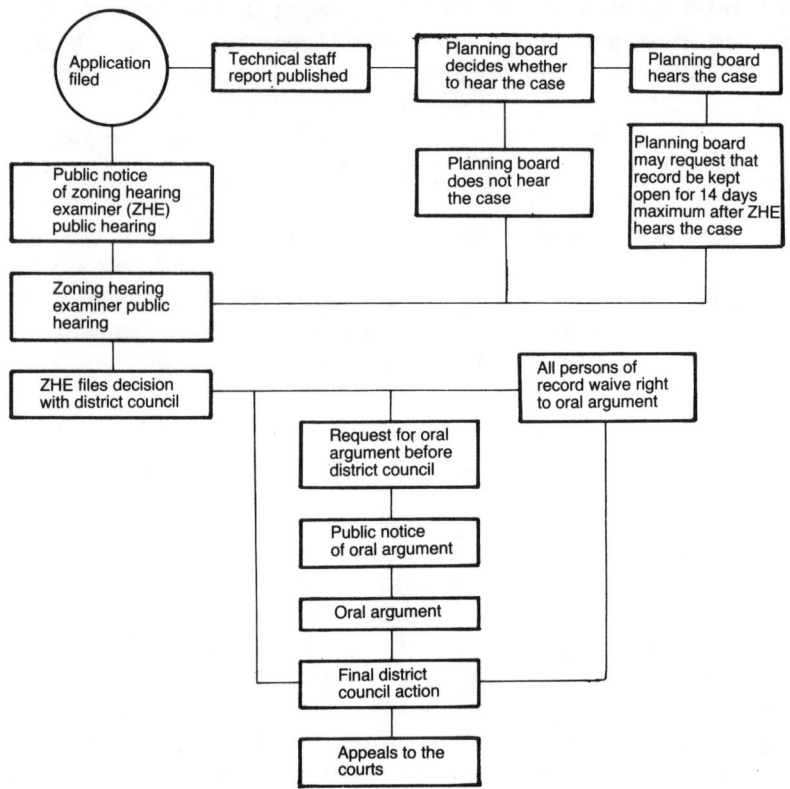

Source: Maryland—National Capital Park and Planning Commission (Prince George's County, Maryland)

builder/developer, the municipal elected official, the municipal staff planner, present and future town residents, environmentalists and preservationists, and state and federal officials.

Most of these players place the burden of proof on the builder/developer. They have to be convinced that the proposed project will be a positive contribution to their community or their interest. The builder/developers must therefore practice the art of positive compromise, entering into the negotiation process fully prepared to document all claims and answer all technical questions. By doing a thorough job on homework, developers can hope to build a constituency of support gradually.

The Art of Positive Compromise

The key strategy of anyone entering the zoning process must be to find the common ground among all the players. The real needs of all the parties must be addressed. The unresolved issues must be constantly narrowed until the officials are satisfied that approval can be granted.

Too many developers who have not done their homework adequately overcommit themselves and agree to "give away" items of a low priority without satisfying the real needs of the community. They try to impress municipal officials with experience that may not be applicable to the local situation. In the end, the result is often a loss of credibility and control over the outcome of the project.

Establish a Constituency

A major element in the art of positive compromise is establishing a constituency of support. This goal is accomplished through extensive personal interviews with key people and identified players in the decisionmaking process. Get their views and ask many questions such as, "Why does your office feel it's necessary to have concrete curbs in rural areas?" Differences of interpretation can provide tactical information that will be of use later. Successful applicants use controversies and negotiate them to their benefit.

The obvious place to begin building a constituency is with public officials or public employees. The objective is to find people who will support the builder/developer's goals. This process is also an excellent method for determining which departments do not agree on certain policy issues. At some point the builder/developer may need to play one agency against another in order to achieve united positions on issues that will benefit his/her project.

A young public agency employee can be an asset. If a developer's information is technically sound, such an employee will be more likely to endorse a position and defend it. This rule also applies to more established people, although they seem less willing to endorse developers' positions without airtight defense; therefore, the technical homework must be solid.

Politicians are not in the business of taking chances; they have to be convinced that both the public and private interests are parallel and not contradictory. Therefore, the developer must be prepared to take the risks. The developer should expect, when seeking support from politicians, that their positions may waver if the matter becomes politically sensitive.

As problems are identified, they must be resolved. Problems will not work themselves out or disappear; rather they always seem to come up at a public hearing when it is too late to do anything about them. During the interviewing of public officials, official positions must be questioned and challenged when necessary. "Curbs are necessary to control stormwater, so we require curbs," is the kind of response that cannot be allowed to pass unchallenged. The developer should not argue, but rather just present the facts to support his/her design or concept and look for alternatives to satisfy the goal at less cost. The developer must present a team that has proven land management skills, that can deliver on its pledges.

The art of positive compromise involves establishing trade-offs. Determine what the town wants, but always keep the goals of its master plan handy. In many cases, the developer can show that the proposal will help to implement the community's goals.

The developer should carefully review the plans and cash flow, and set aside several alternatives for use as potential trade-offs. The town often can be convinced to trade more quantity in exchange for higher quality. A strong selling point is usually that permission to build more units in clusters will save everyone money and open space.[30] Some potential trade-offs are—

- Providing additional open space
- Solving an existing drainage problem
- Preserving historic structures
- Preserving agricultural land using clustering techniques
- Providing community linkages with walkways, bikeways, open space, etc.

When weighing what to trade off as possible negotiable items, the developer should study the state enabling legislation, case law, the local master plan, zoning and subdivision ordinances, and cash flow. Identifying conflicts that can be helpful in the negotiation process is not unusual. Throughout this process the developer must constantly relate the facts to the legal standards. Does the ordinance rationally and reasonably support the public health, safety, and general welfare? If a lawsuit is ever forced, this process of identifying and narrowing of issues will be helpful in defending the developer's legal position.

The Negotiation Process

To achieve the desired results from the zoning process, the developer must keep several principles in mind:

- **Set the framework,** which means never attending uncontrolled public meetings. If the developer cannot sense support from at least one portion of those attending, the meeting will be a disaster. Support can often be gained from unlikely sources, such as the League of Women Voters, bankers, labor leaders, and other interest groups.

Here, too, problems must be identified before the public meeting and narrowed as much as possible.

- **Stay on the offensive.** Pressure must be maintained to keep the process moving. Of course, being on the offensive means being fully prepared. The developer should never have to request an extension of a time limit. The preferred position is to judiciously grant the municipality extensions of time.
- **Never eliminate the possibility of suing.** An applicant should not threaten litigation lightly, because it can add months and possibly years to the process. The municipality should be made aware, however, that the developer is not afraid to take court action, if necessary.
- **Stay well-informed.** An applicant who is well-informed and has performed all relevant background studies can often control the zoning process. Public officials, at all levels of government, often take positions supported by weak technical information. If they oppose the application, press them on their technical backup, and they will often seek a compromise in order to resolve the issue. A surprising percentage of decisions are assailable on the basis of faulty or insufficient support data. If public officials or employees are supportive of the proposal, the developer must provide them with sound technical information to buttress their position.
- **Never become overcommitted.** Municipalities are often made suspicious and defensive by developers who promise the moon from the start. The developer should never make a statement or promise something that cannot be delivered. Credibility and believability are essential features of a successful zoning negotiation. To keep promises, the developer must remain informed as to the cash flow and market situation.
- **Be responsive to community needs.** Throughout any presentation and conversations with community leaders, stress the ultimate aim of making a real contribution to the community, not just to building dwelling units. Knowledge of the area is crucial. The developer should study community needs so that the design features of the project that will address those needs can be stressed. For example, the developer might add trails to a development plan in an area trying to establish a network of pedestrian and biking routes. Or a town that has been searching for a piece of ground suitable for its recreational soccer teams might be favorably disposed toward a project that included a 3-acre parcel for public recreation.
- **Rely on logic and facts.** Never be dishonest or intentionally mislead anyone in a zoning matter. Such actions can rapidly tarnish the developer's professional reputation and hamper the chances of

success through litigation. The judge will not be impressed if the applicant enters the case with less than clean hands.

- **Remember that the process is a game,** and builders should not get personally involved in the arguments. The developer who keeps everything in perspective will not create friends and enemies based on how they react to a set of plans for a land development project.[31]

Processing a Subdivision Plan

Generally speaking, the subdivision review process takes less time and is less complex than the zoning process. Figure 3-6 describes a typical subdivision process. Typically, it does not require the usual string of public hearings before local planning boards, zoning examiners, and councils of various types (city, county, commissioners). Regular meetings of planning boards or councils are sufficient to handle the administrative matters of subdivision review. Public hearings usually are not necessary in the subdivision process.

The same rules of the game apply to subdivision processing, however, as to zoning. The builder/developer must be skilled in the art of compromise, establish a constituency, and benefit from the negotiation process. Research done ahead of time can resolve problems such as matching up proposed streets with those on adjacent properties, addressing public facilities needs, and establishing buffer areas. Public participation and potential opposition are generally less in the subdivision review process than in the zoning process because the property does not have to be posted and notices in the newspaper are not required. Both of these are standard requirements for a zoning application.

The builder/developer should be able to minimize the effect of any opposition by using the information gathered during the research phase to determine when problems might arise and to devise strategies for resolving them. At times, however, a strong-willed group of citizens can create havoc in the processing of subdivision plan proposals. A calm, organized, and informed approach to the problem will yield the best results.

A Time-Tested Procedure

The approval process for a zoning matter or a subdivision application can be approached in many ways. The following approach has worked with noticeable success over the years:
- Preprocessing (30 to 90 days)
- Heavy homework (additional 30 to 90 days)

Figure 3-6. The subdivision process in Prince George's County, Maryland

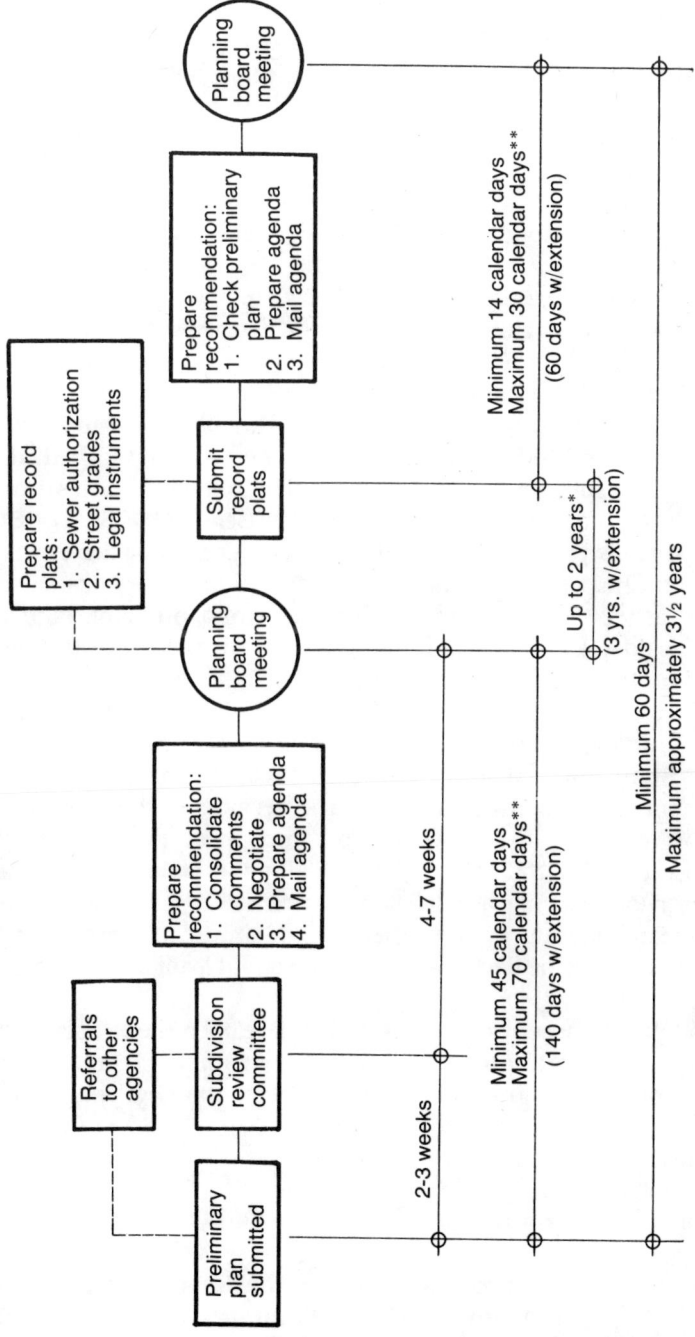

*Time consumed depends upon the time required to prepare and submit record plats.
**Automatic approval after this time period.

Source: Maryland—National Capital Park and Planning Commission (Prince George's County, Maryland)

- Preliminary approvals (time varies with local procedures)
- Final approvals (time varies with local procedures)

During the preprocessing—or investigative—stage, the developer needs to collect a wide variety of information and make as many contacts as possible. At this point holding an option on the land is preferable to owning it because of the uncertainty of development approval. The basic objective is to identify problem areas and note that they will need attention. This time should be devoted to initial interviews with public officials at local, state, and regional levels. These pre-application meetings should be used to establish the framework for a negotiated agreement.

An important part of preprocessing is a review of the applicable codes, ordinances, and performance standards. Language should be drafted to authorize the developer's desired use of the subject tract of land if the ordinances as written do not appear to allow it.

The buildable land on the site should be carefully identified by the use of the soil surveys, topographical maps, flood plain studies, and the staff of the U.S. Soil Conservation Service (SCS). The SCS is a technically proficient agency that consistently provides excellent service; its help on soils and stormwater management issues can be a real asset. The assessment of the amount of buildable land will permit the developer to do a rough layout of units to calculate what kind of zoning is desired or whether or not the project can comply with the ordinance as it is written. The buildable acreage figure is also essential for determining the economics of the project.

In addition to constraints identified through studying the soils and topography, the infrastructure and services of the community must be analyzed. Sewer, water, fire and police protection, solid waste, and school and road capacities all must be looked at closely. If infrastructure or service deficiencies are noted, have any arrangements been made to remedy them? Can any of the problems be alleviated to gain the developer support from at least some members of the community?

Throughout the entire process, the developer must assess the chance of gaining approval and weigh it against the potential return if approval is granted. Along the way, the developer will be faced with any of four options:
- Withdrawal from the project
- Compliance with the existing zoning
- Application for a zoning change or variance
- Litigation

At the end of the preprocessing period, the decision must be made to either drop out or proceed. If the findings reached during the investigative stage spell danger, dropping the matter, at least for the present, may be wise. If the decision is to press ahead, the developer may want to extend the option or enter into a joint venture.

The heavy-homework stage involves refining and expanding on much of what was begun during the first phase, resulting in the drawing up of the preliminary plan and supporting documentation necessary for government approval. More meetings with public officials, interest groups, and others will take place, detailing support for a plan the developer wants to produce and the community can support.

The preprocessing and heavy-homework stages apply equally to matters of zoning and subdivision, particularly for a property that has to be rezoned before it can be subdivided. The results of preliminary meetings and homework can be put to work when plans are reviewed for compliance with local subdivision regulations before preliminary plan approval and final plat approval. Usually, preliminary plan approval requires some changes to the original submittal, which is then revised and resubmitted for approval.

Final plat approval usually includes permits from all relevant agencies, not just the municipal government, such as sewer permits from the local utility, well-drilling permits from the local health department, or special permits issued by the county or state. More and more jurisdictions are now installing a one-stop building permit program that gives builders quick action on applications requiring more than one permit. Implementation and efficient use of this kind of program sometimes can save builders weeks that otherwise would be spent waiting for the normal permit process to grind out the approvals. Builders should make their local officials aware of the benefit of such a program if one does not already exist.

The steps necessary to obtain preliminary plan and final plat approval are often fully identified in the local codes. A lack of effort during the preprocessing and heavy-homework stages will make the final two stages difficult to negotiate.

In conclusion, to achieve success, the prospective applicant should observe the following basic rules when attempting to get land rezoned or subdivided to suit a development proposal:

- Do not assume that the zoning ordinance, subdivision regulations, and master plan are givens. Become familiar with the community and analyze the chances of gaining an amendment to the zoning, subdivision, or master plan.
- Do not buy land for development outright, except at a very low cost.
- For land priced at the prevailing market price, obtain an option. An option permits the latitude to secure the necessary zoning and other approvals. It would be foolish to purchase land out-

right at market prices without a modest degree of certainty that all fundamental approvals can be obtained.

- Do not attempt to calculate land value from raw land directly. It is a function of interrelated factors that cannot be assessed casually.
- Stress the fact that the developer represents the demands of the consumer and that a private developer is more efficient at meeting these demands at the least cost.
- Be a catalyst for affirmative decisions; that is the developer's role.
- Maintain a continuous dialog with local lawmakers and keep them abreast of problems and changes needed to reflect market conditions.
- Be aware that as the approval process becomes more complex and difficult, it becomes increasingly profitable for the builder/developer to be skilled at manipulating it.

Chapter 4
Financing Land Development: An Overview

Obtaining financing is one of the greatest challenges facing any developer. Without the necessary financial backing, developers are unable to transform their visions into actual bricks and mortar. Yet there is no special magic to securing financing for land development. Lenders and investors need good investment opportunities, just as developers need sources of financing. The secret is to put together a loan application that is attractive to lenders while it meets the project's financial needs.

This chapter offers an overview of the real estate financial market, and provides information on options and methods for obtaining land development, construction, permanent, and equity financing.

The Transformation of Real Estate Financial Markets

While project financing has never been easy to obtain, the transformation of the nation's real estate financial markets since the mid-1970s has added to the complexity. New sources of capital and the emergence of large regional and national development companies with the ability to directly enter financial markets are shaping today's development industry. The options available to a developer for financing a project have never been greater.

The principal transformations affecting land development financing include[1]:
- Shifts in lender expectations about inflation, and therefore, their expectations for a return
- The partial deregulation of financial markets
- The loss of real estate's preferred investment status

Shifts in Inflation Expectations

The high inflation of the 1970s and early 1980s forced lenders to alter their previous financial outlook, which had been characterized by low real interest rates and lending for long periods at relatively low fixed rates. In response to high inflation, lenders increased their real rate of interest to obtain higher returns and sought ways of lessening their exposure by offering adjustable-rate financing and shorter terms.

As a result of these shifts, the real cost of capital to developers has increased, with a corresponding increase in the uncertainty of financing. It has become more common for development financing to have higher rates of real interest; lenders adjust the interest rate as the market shifts. Likewise, future fund commitments are more important for insuring fund availability than for guaranteeing specific rates of interest.

Partial Deregulation of Financial Markets

A series of sweeping legislative reforms from 1979 to 1982 phased out the sheltered lending market that savings and loan institutions had traditionally enjoyed. These institutions began to compete more aggressively for funds, encouraging greater competition in the development financing field. As a result, developers have found a widening financial market for funding their projects. Savings and loans, commercial lenders, Wall Street investment houses, and financial subsidiaries of major manufacturing firms have entered the real estate finance arena in a major way. The savings and loans have also diversified their activities by setting up special subsidiary corporations to engage in joint venture arrangements with development entities and participate directly in the development of real estate.

Thus, deregulation has dramatically expanded the number and variety of financial vehicles available to the real estate developer. Many of the more innovative sources of funds, however, are available only to large, national development companies with direct access to capital markets.

As shown in Figure 4-1, savings and loans and commercial banks lead in making land loans to developers: 60.8 percent and 33.6 percent, respectively, of all land loan originations. The construction lending area has attracted significant involvement by mortgage banks and state credit agencies, but savings and loans and commercial banks still predominate.

As for long-term lending, traditional lenders are strong; however, pension funds, mortgage companies, and mortgage pools are providing an increasing share. The residential market is dominated by

Figure 4-1. Land Construction and Long-Term Mortgage Loans
By Major Lender Group 4/1/1986
(Millions of Dollars)

Loan Type	Commercial Bank $	%	Savings & Loans and Mutual Savings Banks $	%	Life Insurance $	%	Pension Funds $	%	Mortgage Companies $	%	Federal Credit Agency $	%	Mortgage Pools $	%	State Credit Agency $	%	Totals $	%
Land Loans	$11,350	33.6%	$20,555	60.8%	$ 693	2.1%	$ 6	0%	$ 1,154	3.5%	$ 0	0%	$ 0	0%	$ 28	0%	$ 33,786	100.0%
Construction Loans																		
Residential	21,108	36.4	25,846	44.5	108	.2	3	0	3,109	5.4	1,146	2.5	0	0	6,446	11.0	58,066	100.0
Nonresidential	46,723	61.9	22,062	29.3	777	1.0	13	0	5,904	7.8	0	0	0	0	0	0	75,479	100.0
Subtotal	67,831	50.8	47,908	35.9	885	.6	16	0	9,013	6.8	1,446	1.1	0	0	6,446	4.8	133,545	100.0
Long-Term Loans																		
Single Family Residential	181,855	13.9	534,089	41.0	12,223	.9	672	.1	13,592	1.0	112,135	8.6	400,305	30.7	49,262	3.8	1,304,133	100.0
Multifamily Residential	10,620	6.5	76,119	46.6	19,372	11.9	282	.2	477	.3	23,553	14.4	7,947	4.9	24,840	15.2	163,210	100.0
Nonresidential	96,696	29.4	91,860	28.0	126,147	38.4	1,207	.4	711	.2	6,355	1.9	82	0	5,420	1.7	328,478	100.0
Farm	10,284	13.8	592	.8	11,623	15.7	0	0	0	0	41,762	56.3	8,528	11.5	1,424	1.9	74,213	100.0
Subtotal	299,455	16.0	702,660	37.6	169,365	9.1	2,161	.1	14,780	.8	183,805	9.3	416,862	22.3	80,946	4.3	1,870,034	100.0
Total Mortgage Loan Credits	$378,636	18.6%	$771,123	37.9%	$170,943	8.4%	$2,183	.1%	$24,947	1.2%	$185,251	9.0%	$416,862	20.5%	$87,420	4.3%	$2,037,365	100.0%

Source: U.S. Department of Housing and Urban Development News Release HUD No. 86-80, "Survey of Mortgage Lending Activity First Quarter 1986"

the savings and loan industry, commercial banks, and mortgage pools, especially for single-family housing. The mortgage pools represent a comparatively new source of capital that wasn't available to the home building industry in a significant way before the 1970s.

Among commercial projects, most long-term financing comes from such traditional sources as life insurance companies, commercial banks, and savings and loans. The structure of these transactions has been changing, however, with greater lender equity participation, shorter terms, and more variable interest rates than in the past.

Loss of Real Estate's Preferred Investment Status

Since 1979, real estate has been gradually losing its preferred investment status due to sweeping changes in domestic priorities brought on by high inflation in the late 1970s and early 1980s, changes in monetary policy, and the recent overhaul of the tax system.

The Tax Reform Act of 1986[2] removed many of the special tax advantages associated with investing in real estate. The real estate industry effectively became just another form of investment, with comparable status to other popular investment vehicles. As a result, real estate investors are seeking high returns on their investment from the income of the project rather than looking for tax breaks to cover operational deficiencies.

The cumulative effect of these reforms requires developers to accelerate the economic performance of their projects. This in turn creates a positive cash flow for the investor/lender early in the development cycle, and should increase the demand for well-managed, well-located projects with strong appreciation potential. The successful developer will evaluate each of these transformations to determine the best source of funds for his/her project, to understand the changing role of the lender equity partner, and to structure the project to best fit the current investment market's preferences.

Site Selection and Acquisition

The developer faces two major tasks in the site selection and acquisition process: the analytic work necessary to select an appropriate site, and securing financing to develop the site.

Site Selection

The site selection process is described extensively in Chapter 2. From a financial perspective, however, site selection can involve a significant expenditure of funds. The developer typically assumes responsibility for coordinating all, and conducting many, of the site selection activities prior to actual acquisition. The resulting expenses may include:
- Legal fees
- Soil and water testing
- Title work
- Market analysis
- Appraisal
- Travel and expenses
- Preliminary planning/engineering studies

The capital to cover these services is either paid out of the development company's cash flow from other projects, or is provided on prospective basis by the various professionals involved who hope to continue working on the project.

Once the necessary studies have been completed to determine that the site is appropriate for the project, the developer is ready to acquire the site for development.

Financing Land Acquisition

The first challenge facing the developer in the land acquisition process is finding a source of financing. Relatively few major institutional lenders are involved in land acquisition financing because it is considered risky. Since the raw land will generate no cash flow, financial institutions must rely on the developer's creditworthiness for assurance that they will receive payment. Raw land may be difficult to resell should the project fail, which reduces its value as collateral.

The institutions that do finance raw land purchases typically provide no more than a 50 to 60 percent loan-to-value ratio, and the proportion of their real estate loan portfolio that can be used for this purpose is restricted.[3] Major financial institutions are more willing to finance land acquisition if it is part of the land development financing.

If conventional financing for land acquisition is not available, the residential developer is faced with four alternatives:
- Purchase money mortgage
- Purchase option
- Long-term lease plus option
- Joint venture

Each of these alternatives is discussed below.

Purchase Money Mortgage

The most common means of financing raw land acquisition is through the use of a purchase money mortgage that is taken back by the seller. The developer typically seeks a loan with no amortization or delayed amortization, and asks the seller to subordinate the first mortgage on the land to a subsequent construction financing lender (most construction lenders demand first liens).

Under the terms of a purchase money mortgage, the seller of the land accepts, in lieu of cash, the developer's note for the unpaid price of the land secured by a mortgage on the property being sold. This approach provides immediate financing for the developer and creates an investment for the seller secured by his/her own property. In return for this highly advantageous financing opportunity for the buyer, the seller receives a higher return than a financial institution would normally provide.

Purchase money mortgage agreements often require the developer to pay a significant downpayment. The mortgage term is generally short, although the purchaser may not want to pay the high monthly costs associated with a shorter term. Balloon payments are often used, where monthly payments are set on a 20- to 30-year schedule, but the loan matures in 10 years with the unpaid balance paid as a lump sum at the end. Prepayment of purchase money financing is common, and is generally favorable to both buyer and seller once development has progressed to the point that conventional financing is available.

The purchase money mortgage is an attractive approach for financing land acquisition, but it requires a landowner who can benefit from the transaction and is willing to take the risks involved.

Purchase Option

Options are among the most widely used techniques for securing control of land parcels for subsequent development. Under an option agreement, the developer purchases the right to control a given parcel while deciding whether to develop the land. The option allows the developer to assemble multiple parcels for a comparatively small cash outlay and, in the case of longer-term options, provides a vehicle for speculating on the future value of the land. Should the developer decide not to proceed with the project, it may be possible to resell the option to another developer at a profit.

Several different types of options are often used, including:[4]

Fixed option. Allows the developer to purchase the property a fixed price during the established option period.

Step-up option. Used for long-term options where the purchase price of the property increases in stages, often at the time of the option renewal.

Rolling option. Widely used by subdividers as a means of moving in sequence from one tract to another as the development progresses. The price of the land in later tracts often rises as property value increases.

Full credit option. Price of the option is fully credited against the purchase price of the land if the transaction moves forward.

Declining credit option. As an incentive to shorten the option period, the proportion of the option that can be credited to the purchase price declines over time.

The option process sustains the developer from the time when he/she needs to control the desired parcel of land until he/she is able to finance the actual purchase of the property. As such, it is often used as a first step in conjunction with other financing techniques.

Long-Term Lease Plus Option

Under a long-term lease plus option, the developer offers the landowner a lease, with an option to purchase during the lease term. This approach offers the developer two advantages: payments under the lease will be treated as rent and are therefore deductible; and nonpayment of the rent will not result in an automatic termination of the agreement, since the landowner would have to institute a legal action. Again, the feasibility of the approach depends on the seller's willingness to enter into this type of agreement.

Joint Venture

Joint ventures with landowners, or third parties, are an increasingly popular approach for securing control of the land and/or carrying out the development. Partners can be full participants making equity contributions and sharing in the proportional losses and gains of the project, or they may take a less active role. Joint ventures will be discussed more fully in the section on equity financing.

The principal advantage of joint ventures to the developer is that payments to the landowner may be delayed until the project begins to generate cash flow. In return for this deferral, the landowner may be able to negotiate a share in the venture larger than that dictated by the value of the land contribution. The proportion of the joint venture controlled by the landowner is often 35 to 55 percent, depending on the degree of risk assumed by each party.

Land Development Financing

Once the developer has acquired the land for a project, the next step is to obtain financing for land development. At this stage, the developer is seeking financing to increase the raw land value. Lending for land development is considered a high risk venture since value will not increase if the project fails. Land development financing is used to cover the following development activities:[5]

- Site preparation
- Installation of infrastructure (streets, sewers, etc.)
- Engineering and consultants
- Architect fees
- Zoning process
- Other soft costs

Obtaining the Loan

Most land development loans represent a first lien on the property. They are short-term, and involve interest rates 2 to 4 points above prime. Land development loans are made separately from construction loans when the raw land must be subdivided into smaller lots. They are considered riskier than construction loans because repayment of the development loan is contingent on the sale of building sites. Construction loans are generally backed by a commitment from the builder to assume the loan if the product does not sell.

Lenders making land development loans are primarily concerned with the creditworthiness of the developer and the project's feasibility and profitability. In making decisions on applications for land development loans, lenders evaluate a variety of factors related to the project. Some of the documents commonly required in the application are:[6]

- Current financial statements for the borrower
- Feasibility/market studies
- Appraisal reports
- Physical surveys of the land
- Site plans
- Area demographic studies
- Aerial photographs
- Environmental impact statement
- Estimates of hard and soft development costs

As was seen in Figure 4-1, among institutional lenders, commercial banks and savings and loans are most heavily involved in providing land development financing. These institutions benefit from a familiarity with the real estate development process. Moreover, they are frequently present in the market area where the project is being developed, and they enjoy ongoing relationships with certain developers that can involve them in the project from inception to completion.

To obtain land development financing, the developer, working with the lending officer, must prepare a loan offer for submission to the lender's loan committee. This offer typically includes:[7]

- Borrower's name and address
- Amount of the loan
- Term of the loan
- Interest rate on the loan
- Commitment fee charged to make the loan
- Primary purpose in making the loan
- Guarantors' names and a short summation of their net worth, a breakdown of the nature of their asset holdings, and a description of their background and projected annual net income
- Collateral for the loan
- Location of the property to be developed
- Description of the development plan
- Summary of estimated development costs
- Marketing approach to be used in selling the lots
- Breakdown of the projected sales to be made
- Release provisions for the sold lots
- Other conditions necessary to making the loans

Minimizing Lender Risk

Given the greater uncertainty of payment in land development loans, lenders impose several control procedures in an effort to increase their security in the transaction.

Release Price Repayment

Repayment to the lender is generally accomplished through a "release price" procedure. The release price per lot is calculated based on the lot's proportional share of the project's total financing cost, plus 10 to 20 percent.[8] Lenders require this 110 to 120 percent figure to minimize the risk associated with the development: it allows the lender to recapture the bulk of the loan before project close-out. The developer receives his/her profit from the sale of the lots at the end of the development period, which provides the lender with further assurance.

...ased Disbursement Financing

To minimize the risks involved in larger, more complex projects, lenders often require a phased disbursement approach for financing. The developer builds only immediately marketable products, and changes the product to address the needs of changing markets as the development progresses. This method limits the lender's liability for a particular project to the phase currently under development. To further assure repayment of land development loans, developers are frequently required to post a performance and payment bond with personal guarantees by the developer as a condition of obtaining financing.[9]

Other Considerations

Despite these performance requirements, the lending community considers land development financing to be risky (though less risky than straight land acquisition loans). Lenders generally also require some connection to the eventual end-financing for the project, so that they are assured of repayment. An eventual take-out commitment, a strong sales record, and strong developer equity are the key ingredients in a successful application.

Lenders are often willing to lend 70 to 80 percent of the appraised value of the finished lots, as long as that amount does not exceed the costs associated with land acquisition and construction.

Construction Financing

The next step in the development process is to secure construction financing. Unlike the land acquisition and development financing phases, many institutional lenders are interested in being involved in construction lending. The Urban Land Institute prepared an analysis of 518 construction loans from around the nation made during a portion of 1984. As Figure 4-2 shows, commercial banks made over half the construction loans during that period, and savings and loans made another 20.5 percent. A variety of sources accounted for the remainder of construction loans—life insurance companies, syndicators, mortgage bankers, and others. These lending patterns still hold true today.

Characteristics of Construction Financing

The principal characteristics of construction financing are:[10]

Short term. The term of the loan is usually set to cover the expected period of construction—usually from 6 months to 3 years. The lenders in the residential segment of the financial community expect payment in full at the end of the construction period. For

Figure 4-2. Sources of Construction Financing

	All Loans (in Millions)	Percent Total	New Construction (in Millions)	Percent Total
Total Loans	**$6,411**	**100.0%**	**$6,185**	**100.0%**
Banks	$3,324	51.8%	$3,243	52.6%
Savings and loans	1,316	20.5	1,264	20.4
Public financing*	157	2.5	129	2.1
Life insurance	586	9.1	579	9.4
Mortgage bankers	316	4.9	298	4.8
Savings banks	255	4.0	238	3.8
Credit companies	139	2.2	129	2.1
Syndications	64	1.0	58	0.9
Internal funding	49	0.8	46	0.7
REITs	58	0.9	54	0.9
Wall Street firms	101	1.6	101	1.6
Foreign lenders	46	0.7	46	0.7

Public financing refers to any tax-exempt loan or public loan

Source: Urban Land Institute, *Dollars and Percents of Development Finance*, April-December, 1984

commercial projects, construction financing can evolve into permanent financing. Construction loan funds are released as construction progresses, in a predetermined sequence. Thus the developer only pays interest on the funds disbursed. The lender's risk is reduced, since the outstanding loan is matched closely to the value of the construction.

Repayment at maturity. During the construction period there is no cash flow and no amortization on the loan. Repayment carries in full at maturity, usually from the proceeds of long-term financing or from sale of the residential units.

High loan-to-value ratio. Construction loans generally equal 100 percent of the total construction cost, if the developer can provide adequate security or a take-out commitment equal to the construction cost.

Take-out commitment required. The construction lender typically requires a first mortgage on the land and the construction in place, as well as an assurance of repayment through a take-out commitment for a permanent lender or an equity purchaser.

High interest rates. Because of the risk involved and the ongoing administrative burden, construction loans involve relatively high interest rates and substantial loan commitment fees.

Risks Involved in Construction Lending

Construction lending and land development lending share a unique set of risks associated with the real estate market.[11] First, loans must be based on estimates, projections, and judgments rather than facts. Lenders must assess the project's marketability, the accuracy of construction cost estimates, and the developer's competence—none of which is a known entity. In addition, construction projects are subject to many external factors that can dramatically affect their success, such as weather delays, material shortages, environmental and other regulatory barriers, and changes in market demand.

Lenders attempt to minimize risk by controlling these factors as much as possible. An understanding of the lender's viewpoint can help a developer in his/her negotiations with lenders.

Steps in Negotiating the Construction Loan

There are three major steps in the process of obtaining a construction loan:[12] property analysis by the lender, loan analysis by the lender, and loan commitment and closing.

Property Analysis

The lender considering an application for project financing will generally require the following information about the project:
- A map of the project
- Detailed unit plans and specifications
- A site plan
- A project cost statement
- Soil conditions
- Zoning approval
- Assurance of utility availability

Loan Analysis

If a developer has no previous experience with a lender, the lender will require documentary evidence of the developer's technical and financial ability to complete the proposed project. Information on banking relationships, creditworthiness, and references from those who have done business with the developer—architects, contractors, building materials suppliers—are often requested. The lender will require evidence that the developer has sufficient access to capital to assure project completion. The lender will also attempt to verify the construction cost estimates submitted by the developer by comparing them to industry standards.

Construction lenders generally require loan guarantees. Developers often must give personal guarantees—that is, pledge personal assets—to assure the successful completion of the project, particularly where the developer has established a "one-shot" or "shell" corporation for the development of a single project. First-time developers are usually required to obtain a performance bond and/or a labor and materials bond, which assure the lender that funds will be available to finish the project should the developer fail to perform.

Lenders frequently require a property appraisal at the time of project completion. The appraisal verifies that the project has been completed according to plan. The accuracy of appraisal reports has become a major issue in construction financing, because the reports are used to measure the project's success and effectively determine the viability of the loan commitment. Accordingly, lenders are increasingly requiring an appraisal that conforms with Federal Home Loan Bank Board Regulation 41c. This regulation requires consideration of discounted cash flows and the project's value at different points of completion to determine the value of a property.

Loan Commitment and Closing

The lender decides whether to fund the project based on the results of the project analysis and the loan analysis. If the decision is favorable, the terms of the loan will be spelled out in the commitment letter. If the terms are satisfactory to the developer and the developer is able to meet any additional requirements noted by the lender, loan closing can occur. Loan agreements document all of the obligations the lender and developer have agreed to assume.

In a building or construction loan closing, an agreement is drafted that contains all of the agreed-to obligations of the developer and lender. This document is critical in clarifying the relationship between developer and lender. The agreement commonly includes:

- A loan entitlement clause that requires the developer to pay interest on the amount of loan proceeds to which he/she would have been entitled on the basis of the construction schedule, whether or not the loan advance is actually made.
- A statement that requests for loan advances will constitute an affirmation that all of the representations made at the time of the agreement are still true.
- A requirement that loan advances will be made according to actual construction progress and the construction line budget,

rather than by a calendar schedule.
- A clause requiring assurance that utility services are in place or will be available.

Loan Disbursements

Once the loan is made, the lender and developer must follow a very strict loan disbursement process. Funds are made available as work progresses. Payouts are frequently authorized by the general contractor but go directly to the subcontractor to assure receipt of funds. The lenders conduct frequent inspections to make certain that the work is proceeding according to plan and that the funds are being disbursed properly.

The Take-out Commitment

Lenders of construction funding for residential properties often require a take-out commitment, which is an agreement by the builder to assume the permanent loan directly if the house is not sold within one year of the commitment date. The permanent loan to the builder would be at the same ratio as the construction loan, usually 80 percent of the sales value of the house. The builder still faces the problem of selling the house, but is responsible only for a monthly payment rather than immediate repayment of the full amount of the construction loan; and the construction lender receives full payment.

A wide variety of take-out commitments are available to residential developers. The major differences among them are duration, interest rates, and costs.[13]

Commitment Duration

While typical take-out commitments are a year in duration, the time frame can vary depending upon the characteristics of the project, the market, and the lender's motivation.

Builders need to balance conflicting objectives when negotiating take-out commitments. In inflationary markets, it is advantageous to lock in the interest rates as long as possible. The length of the commitment determines its cost, however, so builders also have a stake in minimizing cost by keeping the loan period short.

A rule of thumb is to seek a commitment for several months longer than one expects to need it. This provides a cushion in the event of unexpected project delays or other circumstances that would push the project beyond the commitment period—such as buyers who are unable to sell their existing residence. Developers often try to coordinate the start of their commitments with the beginning of actual construction.

Commitment Rate

There are a variety of approaches to setting the interest rate on a take-out commitment. Under a "fixed-rate commitment," all loans are at a specified rate. If interest rates are higher than the commitment rate—say, 12 percent versus the commitment at 10 percent—purchasers will use the commitment rate. If interest rates are lower, purchasers will go elsewhere for financing.

It is common practice for forward commitments to fix the rate on the upside only. For example, the commitment rate might be stated as 12 percent or the market rate, whichever is lower at the time of funding.

A "floating" or "over-the-counter" commitment typically does not specify the interest rate. It states that rates will be at the lender's market rate at time of closing, or uses some other index, such as Federal National Mortgage Association (Fannie Mae) auction rates. Thus, the floating commitment assures the developer of funds, but does not assure the interest rate. When only limited funds are available, this type of commitment is very valuable.

Commitment Cost

Lenders charge for the commitment based on their level of exposure. Commitments of shorter duration, and with more flexible rate terms, are generally less costly than lengthy or fixed-rate commitments. The lender takes a greater risk of exposure in the latter case, and prices the commitment accordingly.

For example, at a time of 10 percent interest rates, a one-year commitment for 10 percent financing will be more costly to the developer than one at 10.5 or 11 percent. In this instance, the lender cannot be certain that interest rates will remain at 10 percent for the coming year, yet will have to honor the commitment if rates go higher.

Special Commitment Terms

The commitment will often include special loan terms, such as:[14]
- Establishment of a maximum loan amount
- Maximum lending ratios (such as 90 percent on loans up to $100,000, 95 percent on loans up to $125,000)
- Criteria for qualifying buyers
- Policies regarding investor versus owner/occupant purchasers
- Buy-down policies on the loan
- Presale requirements stipulating that a certain percentage of units must be sold before closing on any loans (this is most common in condominium and PUD projects)

Sources of Commitment Funds

The principal sources of take-out funds are savings and loan institutions, commercial banks, and mortgage bankers. Given their traditional orientation towards real estate lending, savings and loans are aggressive lenders in the residential financing market. Those commercial banks which have a strong real estate orientation may provide take-out commitments as well. Mortgage bankers often specialize in take-out lending, and for this reason are often used by residential developers. Mortgage bankers tend to have more available funds than savings and loans during periods of deposit outflows, because mortgage bankers do not derive their funds from savings deposits.

Permanent Financing

Once the construction phase of the project has been completed, the next step in the financing sequence is to secure permanent financing for the project. In the case of residential projects, permanent financing is provided by end users on a unit-by-unit basis via mortgages on individual properties. In the case of multifamily rental, cooperative housing, and commercial development, the developer must seek permanent financing for the whole project.

As with other stages of financing, permanent loans have undergone a significant transition during the past decade. Historically, permanent financing was viewed as the most stable and lowest-risk way to participate in real estate lending. Since the project to be financed was already built, it allowed the lender valuable collateral for the loan which could be taken back if necessary and remarketed. The income to be generated by the project could readily be determined, further assuring payment on the loan and making it easier to establish value for lending purposes. Lenders typically would seek level payments based on fixed interest rates for an extended period of 25 years or more. Their return was based on the interest charged on the loan over the period.

These procedures have changed dramatically due to recent developments in the financial marketplace. Lenders now seek shorter loan terms, variable interest rates, and opportunities to participate in the cash flow from projects they fund. As a result, developers who in the past may have obtained one permanent loan now find themselves refinancing the property more often during its useful life.

The sources of permanent financing are highly varied. While insurance companies and commercial banks are playing a less dominant role than in the past, Wall Street firms, pension funds, and public financing agencies are becoming more active as deregulation of the financial markets continues. This diversity enables developers to match their financing both to the unique features of their project and to the investment criteria of lenders.

Equity Financing

The distinction between debt and equity financing has become increasingly blurred. One reason is the growing equity participation of investors who were previously involved only in debt lending.[15] These lenders have found that a combination of debt and equity participation is a more attractive investment position in a volatile economy.

Under debt financing, the lender's position is generally secured by the property, and the lender is reimbursed according to a payment schedule and interest rate set at the time the loan is made. The lender usually has no opportunity to participate in upside return on the project.

Under equity financing, the lender obtains an ownership interest in the property. He/she can participate in the property's cash flow as well as in its appreciation at the time of sale.

Another major distinction between equity and debt positions for a given project is the element of risk. While both positions involve risk, the equity investor assumes the primary risk based on his/her residual interest in the property. All project operating costs and the debt position must be satisfied before the equity investor realizes any return. Other investors will not suffer any losses until the equity position has been entirely drained.

The most obvious source of equity for a project is the developer. However, relatively few developers are willing and able to invest substantial amounts of their own funds. Today's real estate market features increasing requirements for developer equity as a means of providing greater lender comfort. As a result, developers are turning to outside sources of capital. Two primary means of securing equity capital are joint ventures and syndications. They are discussed briefly below.

Joint Ventures

In a joint venture, the developer and one or more outside parties join forces to provide capital and/or expertise for a project. A third party is often involved as a debt partner. The developer provides expertise and may also make a capital contribution. Pension funds, domestic and foreign investment groups, wealthy individuals, and savings and loan associations often provide capital. Increasingly, savings and loans use internal development subsidiaries such as service corporations to participate in residential joint venture projects. One advantage of a joint venture arrangement with a savings and loan is that it may lead to favorable terms for the permanent financing of the project.

Landowners selling to developers also frequently become equity participants in joint venture activities. As discussed earlier in the section on financing land acquisition, the landowner typically contributes land to the project in return for a proportionate ownership interest in the project.

Role of Participants

In any joint venture, the roles of the various parties must be negotiated and should be carefully spelled out in the partnership agreement. In some cases the equity investors may wish to exercise more control over the project and may even take the role of general partner. The degree of control is affected by such factors as level of confidence in the developer and his/her track record, the perceived risk involved in the project, the amount of equity contribution required, and the level of the developer's commitment to the project—including whether the developer has made a capital contribution to the project.

Several other significant issues should be discussed by prospective partners before entering into a joint venture agreement. For instance, it is important that the goals of the various partners be similar or complementary. A poorly structured agreement that did not acknowledge one partner's interest in the long-term appreciation of the project, and another's in the cash flow, might result in conflicts over project management. The prospective partners must also clearly understand the amount of risk each is willing to accept.

It is the developer's responsibility to provide prospective joint venture partners with complete information about the proposed project. This generally includes site plans, architectural drawings and building specifications, sources of funds used and required for the project, and financial statements and résumés of the principals.

The Partnership Agreement

The partnership agreement itself should contain a number of elements. Of obvious importance are the amount of capital to be contributed, who is to make the contributions, and the timing of the contributions. The agreement must also specify the return to each partner, including any preferred return, distribution of cash flow, tax benefits, and reversion. (Prior to entering into the agreement, a tax advisor should be employed to project the after-tax returns to each party involved.) The distribution of responsibility for any losses should be covered, as should a method for raising additional capital if needed, The agreement should also contain a dispute-settling method and provisions for withdrawal or death of a partner.

Once the project is under way, it is the ongoing responsibility of the developer to provide joint venture partners with timely progress reports, including regularly updated cash flow projections.

Summary

In summary, a joint venture agreement is a commonly used, practical way to secure the equity necessary for a project. However, it is also complex and variable, requiring detailed and careful consideration so that the interests of all parties are best served and protected. Competent legal and financial advice by experienced professionals is essential before entering a joint venture agreement.

Syndications

Syndications have become a common source of equity for real estate development during the past decade. While they are most commonly used in a wide variety of commercial projects, including multifamily housing, they are so prominent in the real estate industry that they will be discussed here briefly.

A syndication involves the sale of ownership shares in a project to raise cash for the developer. The syndication may involve a large number of investors, each making only a small equity contribution, or a small group of investors making more significant individual contributions.

Syndication Agreement

Developers may arrange syndications themselves, but they usually turn to professional syndicators when large amounts of capital are needed. When arranging a syndication, a developer draws on his/her own contacts and those of others involved in the project.

The developer must carefully spell out the amount of capital required, the risks involved, and the benefits (including tax benefits). Expert legal and accounting advice is required, especially with the passage of the 1986 Tax Reform Act. This tax law has specific definitions for classifying syndication income as "active" or "passive" based on the role the investor plays in the project.

An agreement with a syndicator can be structured in one of two ways. The syndicator may act as a middleman who simply markets the ownership shares to prospective investors. Under this option, the developer often remains the general partner in the project. Alternatively, the syndicator may actually purchase the ownership shares from the developer and resell them. In this case, the syndicator becomes the general partner and the developer provides expertise on a fee basis.

There are advantages and disadvantages to each arrangement. From the developer's perspective, the trade-off is between liability and control. If the developer remains the general partner, he/she retains the major decision-making position. However, as general partner, he/she has unlimited liability and limited opportunities to deduct losses from the project.

Syndication Documents

Syndication involves two major documents. The first is the offering memorandum, which is used to market the investment to prospective investors. The second document is the agreement between developer and syndicator. It is called the partnership agreement if the syndicator is playing a middleman role and merely marketing the ownership shares. If the syndicator is actually purchasing the shares from the developer, it is referred to as the purchase agreement. In either case the agreement should spell out all aspects of the ownership arrangement, capital contributions, roles of partners, and distribution of risks and benefits.

The syndicator's compensation is typically a percentage of the gross proceeds from the sale of ownership shares. The syndicator's fee depends on the amount of money to be raised, the time frame during which the money is to be raised, and the type of project.

Syndication Funds

The syndicator will determine the amount of equity to be raised. The developer must remember that the amount of equity that can be raised is not determined by the value of the project. Rather, it is based on the financial benefits projected to the equity investors. The developer must consider whether the amount of money that can be raised is enough to meet the capital requirements of the project, with enough excess funds remaining to provide a reasonable profit.

If the developer is to remain the general partner, the level of risk he/she is willing to take will directly affect the ease with which money can be raised, and the amount that can be raised. The more risk assumed by the developer—usually in the form of guarantees—the less risk to the equity investors, and the more attractive the investment. A certain minimum guarantee is nearly always required. This may include responsibility for operating deficits, construction cost overruns, and the like.

The distribution of risk is a negotiable issue. Syndications can be the sole source of financing, or they may be combined with debt financing. If debt financing is sought, the involvement of a reputable syndicator can increase the lender's participation, resulting in a more favorable loan package.

The capital contributions resulting from syndication may be made in a single payment or in installments over time. If payments are made in installments, their timing must be negotiated. The payment schedule can be established to coincide with the timing of various capital expenditures by the developer, such as the purchase of an option on the land, purchase of the land, and the beginning of actual construction.

Summary

In summary, syndications are used in a wide variety of projects and have been a major source of equity for many real estate projects during the past decade. It should be noted, however, that the 1986 tax reform law has had a major impact on syndications by limiting the deduction of losses allowed by limited partners. As this book goes to press, it is anticipated that this will greatly lessen the attraction of tax-motivated applications of syndication. Syndicators will instead seek transactions that can provide a positive cash flow and strong appreciation potential.

Tax-Exempt Financing

During the past decade, many developers have used the tax-exempt bond market to help defray costs associated with site preparation and infrastructure. The chief vehicle for developer access to the tax-exempt market has been the creation of special taxing and assessment districts, either jointly with local government entities, or independently through the issuance of tax-exempt bonds. As with many other areas of real estate, the tax-exempt market was significantly affected by the recent tax reform legislation. However, two forms of tax-exempt financing are still worth considering: special districts and tax increment financing.

Special Districts

"Special districts" is a general term for geographically based jurisdictions that are created to carry out a specific function or functions. Examples are special tax districts, public improvement ts, single-purpose districts, and metropolitan service districts, metropolitan service districts are most frequently used to finance infrastructure construction. They are established in an unincorporated area and are quasi-municipal corporations that operate independently of other jurisdictions. (The discussion below is based on Colorado statutes, but other states have similar procedures. A local attorney can provide information on your state's metropolitan service district statutes.)

Uses of Metropolitan Service Districts

Metropolitan service districts are used by developers to reduce the front-end costs of providing infrastructure for residential projects. A metropolitan service district can issue bonds, the proceeds of which are used to pay for the infrastructure. General obligation bonds are the most common type of bonds issued.

The tax-exempt status of bonds is a major attraction to investors. The costs associated with bond financing (beyond the actual cost of the infrastructure) are usually added to the purchase price of houses in the development. A combination of property taxes and fees is collected to pay the debt service on the bonds and the operating costs of the district.

Metropolitan service districts can be used to provide a number of services or facilities for a community, such as fire protection, hospitals, parks and recreation, and water and sanitation services and facilities. Water and sanitation are the services that most frequently motivate developers to establish a metropolitan service district.

In considering metropolitan service districts as a means to finance infrastructure, the developer should know that these districts are controlled by the qualified electors of the district through its board of directors. This means that as soon as the developer begins to sell land or homes, he/she is no longer in control of the district. The board may differ from the developer on such important items as timing of construction and tax levies and fees to be paid by homeowners. The developer must be prepared to work closely with the board.

As with most financing arrangements, liability must be considered. If the developer has given any guarantees, he/she shares in the district's liability. Bond purchasers will have a claim on all improvements within the district, including homes constructed. Therefore, it is wise to be conservative in projecting the revenues to be generated by the district. By building in a cushion when estimating costs, the developer can better cover debt service.

In summary, special districts—and metropolitan service districts in particular—are an important financing strategy for infrastructure related to development. This strategy can substantially reduce the developer's front-end costs. But, as with any financing method, the issues of risk, funding availability, and project control must be weighed carefully.

Tax Increment Financing (TIF)

Tax increment financing (TIF) has become a popular infrastructure financing device. It enables developers to work closely with local governments to help pay for the infrastructure improvements associated with their projects and create an economic stimulus for the local community. TIF is used to capture the increased tax revenue generated by a project. That revenue is then used to retire tax-exempt debt related to the project rather than putting those funds into the local government's general fund. Twenty-six states currently have enabling legislation to allow TIF.

Under the TIF approach, the municipal government establishes a tax increment district that must meet legislatively mandated criteria for being "blighted" or "an economic development area." Once the district has been so designated, the amount of tax collected from that area is calculated and "frozen" as the base year tax amount. As land is cleared and redevelopment occurs, additional tax collected from that project can be used to retire bonds or pay other obligations of the TIF district. Figure 4-3 illustrates the process.

The chief advantage of tax increment financing to the developer is that the tax he/she would have been paying to the locality anyway now provides a revenue source to the project. The debt issued for infrastructure-related costs is serviced, thereby lowering overall development costs for the project.

For local governments, TIF encourages the redevelopment of deteriorated areas of the community without using local revenues. It can provide a powerful subsidy to attract developers into areas where they would otherwise hesitate to do a project. The long-term benefit of TIF is to increase the local tax base and create a catalyst for new development.

In considering whether to use TIF, the developer must become thoroughly familiar with his/her state TIF law: what types of projects qualify, what types of tax revenues can be pledged, and the local government's objectives in establishing a TIF district. The developer should obtain advice from persons knowledgeable about state law and local priorities to determine what will be the most

Figure 4-3. Tax Increment Financing Process

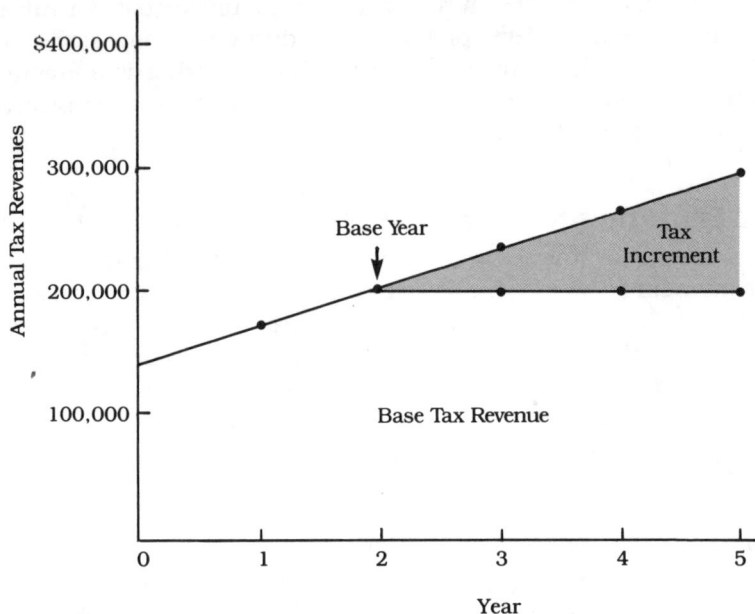

Source: Laventhol & Horwath

appropriate project for a TIF district in his/her area. (At this writing, the Tax Reform Act of 1986 was shown to have significant impact on the use of TIF through the limitation on "private purpose" bonds and the classification of qualifying activities. Before proceeding with a project, the developer must thoroughly research these issues within the local market.)

Summary

Real estate finance has undergone significant change due to federal government policy decisions during the late 1970s and early 1980s, culminating in the Tax Reform Act of 1986. As a result of these changes, developers face an almost bewildering range of financing alternatives as they move their project from initial concept through site acquisition, construction, and eventual operation.

These alternatives have proliferated as the number of financing sources has increased with the introduction of syndicators, Wall Street firms, and commercial credit corporations into the market.

Financing terms have also expanded with greater equity participation, variable rates, and an increase in the use of joint ventures and limited partnerships. Additionally, developers now have the option to use tax increment financing and special districts to draw on the tax-exempt financing market. This unprecedented range of options enables developers to target their financing to the particular needs of their project.

Chapter 5
The Selection of Housing Types

The single-family detached house has been the preferred choice of the homebuying and homebuilding public since the first stone shelters were built. In more modern times, the single-family detached house has held its own against a variety of newcomers to the housing market. For many years, local land use regulations did not permit much more than the typical detached unit, one per lot. Architectural styles varied, but the basic detached unit predominated.

More recently, however, local regulations have begun to permit more types of units as a result of changing market demands for housing. Not everyone can afford the American dream of a detached house with a big yard. To meet today's market needs, builders are searching for ways to provide a wider choice of affordable housing for more people. A variety of unit types and site development techniques has evolved that give the builder the flexibility to provide a range of choices to the consumer. Selecting the most suitable unit type for a project site and market greatly influences the land development costs and marketability of the project.

Housing Types and Examples

Although the generic name system of classifying housing types has drawbacks, it is used here to clarify some of the confusion that exists in housing nomenclature. Unit names and definitions will vary according to market and location, so be careful not to limit your design options through a strict interpretation of these definitions. They are intended only as a basic guide. Housing types are discussed in ascending order of land use intensity; specific projects are provided as examples of each type.

Single-Family Housing

Large Lot, Single-Family Detached

The single-family detached house on a large lot—10,000 square feet or more—has been the most common building type since the suburbs emerged after World War II. The structure occupies the entire interior space from ground to roof and is separated from other dwelling units by yard or other open space. It is, as the name implies, the living unit for one family (Figure 5-1).

Figure 5-1. Typical single-family detached house (Oak Cliff, Wichita, Kansas)

Source: The Bloodgood Group

Densities average four to an acre or less, and the units are built on fee simple lots. Generally, local development regulations require deep setbacks of 25 to 30 feet and side yards of 10 feet or more.

A subdivision of single-family detached units on large lots is usually the most expensive form of housing because of the requirements for land, roads, vehicular access, and provision of utilities. Floor plan configurations most commonly associated with detached housing are:
- The one-story (ranch) house
- The story-and-one-half house
- The two-story house
- The split-entry house
- The split-level house
- The multilevel house

Example: Tymber Creek, Florida

The developers of Tymber Creek in Florida chose to use single-family detached housing units in an effort to preserve the naturalness of a heavily wooded site. Using single-family detached units allowed each homesite to be planned individually to provide units with proper orientation for view and privacy. In addition, the choice of single-family detached units preserved the scale and texture of the natural amenities. The development is governed by a homeowners association that is responsible for maintenance and management of the common areas and amenities. It ensures that existing natural features are preserved and maintained.

Lots vary in size depending on location and relationship to natural features. Setbacks, rights-of-way, and buffer easements created a variety of open spaces that turned the development inward to minimize its impact on the surrounding area and provide interior interest (Figure 5-2).

Figure 5-2. Tymber Creek, Florida

Source: J.K. Shirah and Sons

Small Lot, Single-Family Detached

Small lot housing—housing on lots of 10,000 square feet or less—achieves medium density development. As in the large lot detached category, the single-family detached house on a small lot occupies the structural space from ground to roof and is physically detached from neighboring structures, except perhaps for the attachment of privacy walls or fencing. A typical small lot house requires less setback and smaller side yards than a large lot unit; however, the need to define exterior use areas becomes more important (Figure 5-3).

Figure 5-3. Small lot housing uses land more efficiently than large lot development

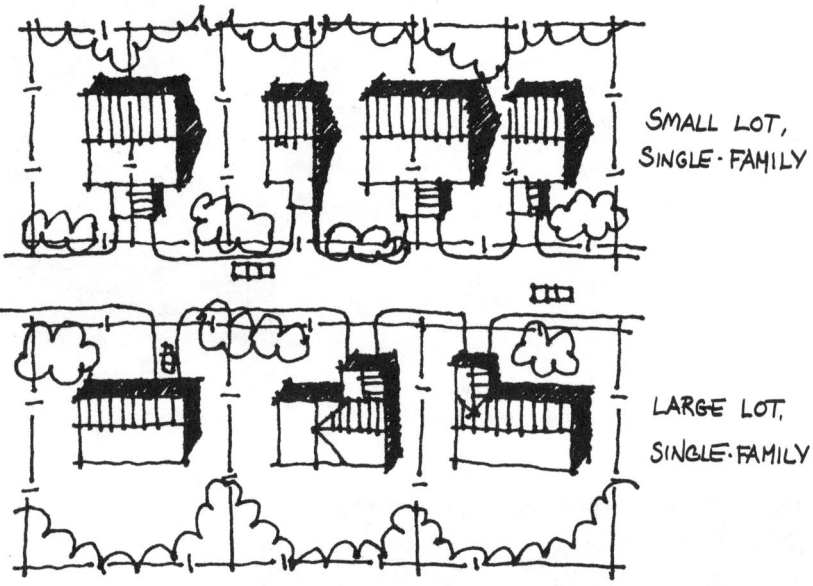

Source: The Martin Organization

Example: Wood Creek Courts, Chicago, Illinois

Environmental and market factors dictated the choice of housing type to be used in Wood Creek Courts, located in a suburban area of Chicago. Zoning in the area called for nominal one-half-acre lots yielding two dwelling units to the acre. The developer, concerned with preserving a natural environment and making the project cost-effective, proposed an increase in the total number of units to accomplish both goals (Figures 5-4a and b).

The choice of housing type was based on a land plan that first surveyed major growth and tree stands, and then suggested housing clusters intertwined with the natural amenities of the site. Individual sites were kept to a minimum of 5,000 square feet to

Figure 5-4. Wood Creek Courts, Chicago, Illinois

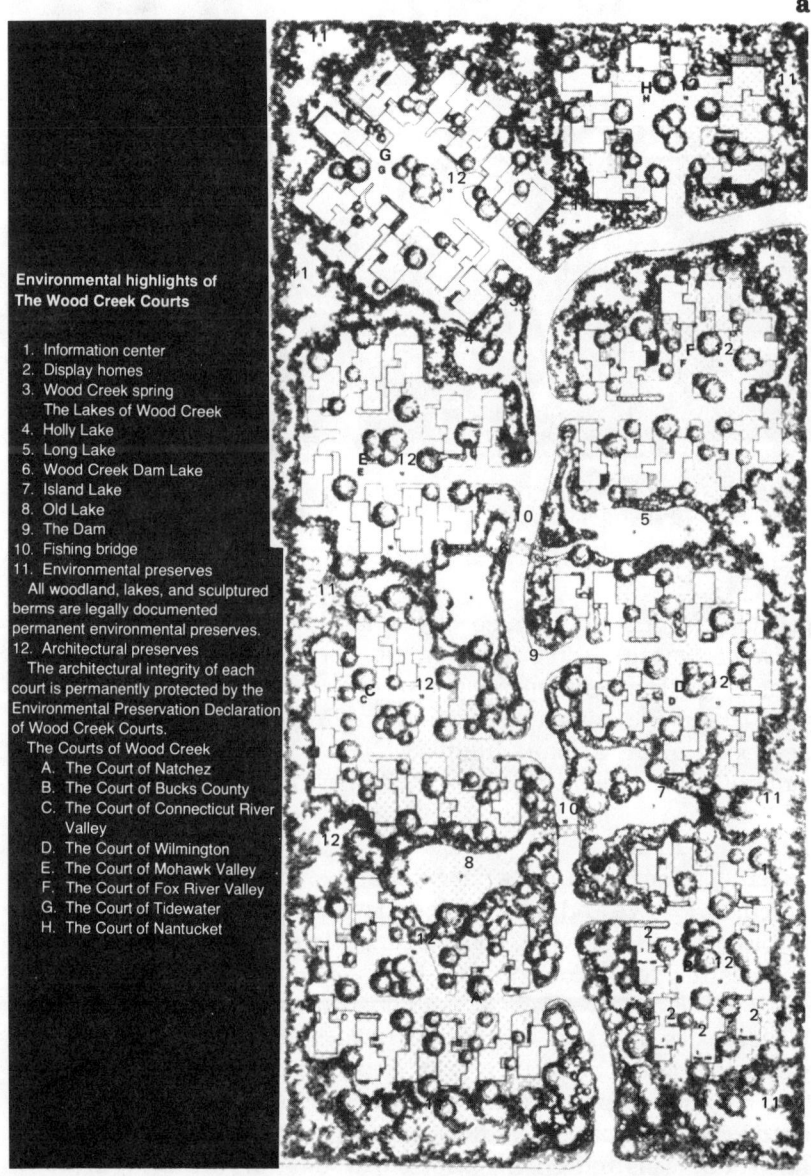

Environmental highlights of
The Wood Creek Courts

1. Information center
2. Display homes
3. Wood Creek spring
   The Lakes of Wood Creek
4. Holly Lake
5. Long Lake
6. Wood Creek Dam Lake
7. Island Lake
8. Old Lake
9. The Dam
10. Fishing bridge
11. Environmental preserves
   All woodland, lakes, and sculptured berms are legally documented permanent environmental preserves.
12. Architectural preserves
   The architectural integrity of each court is permanently protected by the Environmental Preservation Declaration of Wood Creek Courts.
   The Courts of Wood Creek
   A. The Court of Natchez
   B. The Court of Bucks County
   C. The Court of Connecticut River Valley
   D. The Court of Wilmington
   E. The Court of Mohawk Valley
   F. The Court of Fox River Valley
   G. The Court of Tidewater
   H. The Court of Nantucket

b

Source: Irvin A. Blietz
Photo: Hedrich-Blessing

provide just enough privately owned land for the house, a driveway, a two-car garage, and outdoor living. Forty percent of the land was kept in environmental preserves owned in common.

To lessen the impact of the surrounding area, large berms were developed along a main highway. Native trees and shrubs were stockpiled for replanting along the buffering berms.

Zero Lot Line

Zero lot line planning is often used in small lot detached housing to reduce lot size and thus reduce costs. Zero lot line planning often involves the use of patio, courtyard, and atrium houses that relate successfully to outdoor private spaces. A zero lot line house is sited so that one or more walls of the house sits directly on the lot line. With smaller lots, this technique provides more effective use of side yard space and maintains privacy and exterior space definition. The zero lot line or patio house also offers better use of the site for outdoor living space. Exterior spaces are defined by the structure itself or by walls and fencing attached to adjoining units (Figure 5-5).

Figure 5-5. Zero lot line

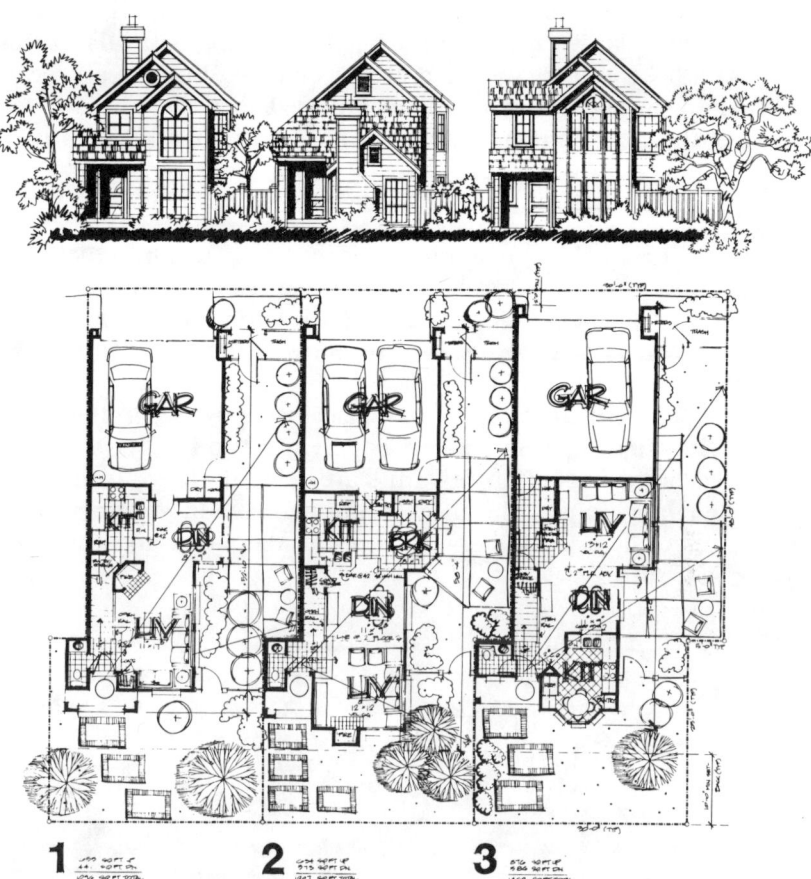

Source: EDI Architects/Planners

Zero lot line lots can be staggered or z-lot, angled to the street, in pinwheel clusters, square or semi-attached. All of these methods offer distinct advantages over conventional siting techniques. A mix of techniques may be used within a single project, although the appropriateness of each method depends upon site conditions and the preferences of the target market.

Higher density achieved by shrinking lot size reduces the land and infrastructure costs per lot while providing the amenities found in less dense, large lot developments.

Example: The Landing, Fort Worth, Texas

With a lake and topographical variations as dominant concerns, the developers of The Landing chose zero lot line housing to enable

131

residents to actually live on the lake rather than near it. The zero lot line unit type was selected to provide the market with a permanent and affordable single-family lifestyle. Existing natural features were studied carefully and used to provide views, buffers, and scale to housing groups. Each unit was placed to allow unrestricted views of the lake, and no unit was located more than a 1½-minute walk from it (Figure 5-6a, b, and c).

Duplex

The duplex is a single-family attached structure in which two units share a common wall or ceiling and floor. Duplexes can be designed as side-by-side or back-to-back units. The side-by-side configuration is the more widely recognized and frequently used type (Figure 5-7).

In the past, entrances have been placed side by side in the front, giving the building a clear identification as a two-family structure. More recently, however, duplex units are being designed to look like a single-family house. The effect can be achieved by separating the entrances or by orienting one entrance to the street and the other to the side yard.

Figure 5-6. The Landing, Fort Worth, Texas

Source: Columbia Communities, Inc. and Guaranty Service Corporation

Figure 5-7. Duplex

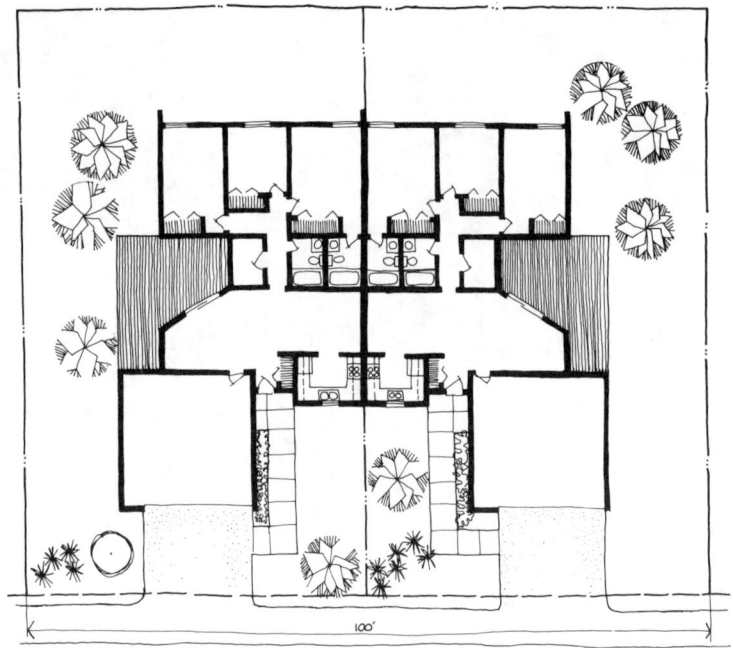

Source: Stephen Mead Associates

Example: Turtle Rock Glen, Newport Beach, California

The economics of site development shaped the choice of duplex units in Turtle Rock Glen to develop a sloping hillside with surrounding views. The project required the density of duplex units to be workable, but the surrounding single-family detached housing had to be considered. Expansive views were another development factor.

The duplex house solved these problems. It could easily be designed for uphill or downhill orientation, and the placement of each unit could take advantage of directional orientation when coupled with a curvilinear site plan.

The result is a development that uses the entire site wisely. The unit type chosen is worked into the topography and takes full advantage of the natural amenity of the site—the view (Figure 5-8).

Triplex

Three-unit single-family attached dwellings are commonly called triplexes. Although the triplex can be designed in several ways, the most common is the row configuration in which two single-family

Figure 5-8. Turtle Rock Glen, Newport Beach, California

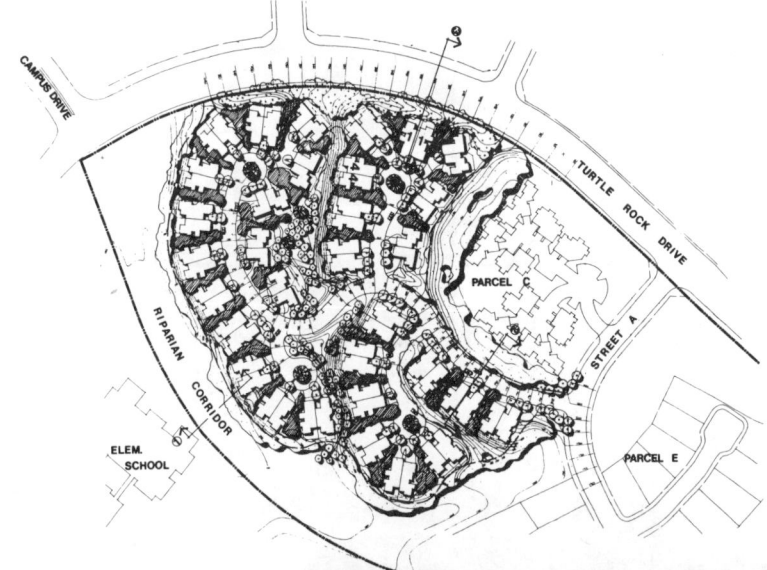

Source: Broadmoor Homes, Inc.

attached houses flank a third unit (Figure 5-9). Generally, each unit is sited on its own fee simple lot and contains all of the functions of a typical single-family detached house. The condominium form of ownership can also be applied to the triplex. In this case, the three units are sited on one common lot along with other units in the project.

Separate architectural identities can be used for each triplex unit, or the building can be designed to look like a large single-family house. Each unit of a triplex occupies the entire interior space from ground to roof. The units can be set back from each other or can follow a more typical linear townhouse configuration. Units do not have to be side-by-side in all cases; they can also be back-to-back.

135

Figure 5-9. Triplex

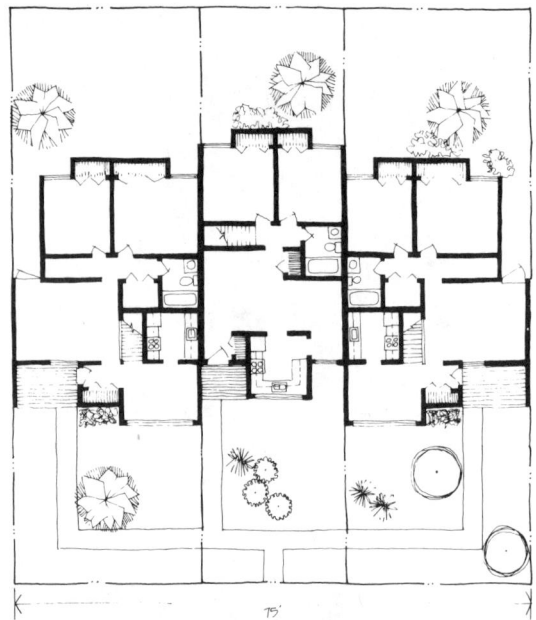

Source: Stephen Mead Associates

Example: Stoney Brook, Denver, Colorado

Stoney Brook was developed as a triplex community to take full advantage of a hillside site and create compact neighborhood clusters on a once-barren property.

The choice of housing type reflects the need to create a community with single-family character while maintaining the economic feasibility of developing a system of recirculating ponds, streams, and stormwater detention (Figure 5-10).

The unit design and individual unit siting allow total privacy. Units are staggered and positioned so that views are of mountains or of the ponds and streams meandering through the development.

The use of private streets, which require less right-of-way than public streets, allows more open area and economically feasible density as well.

Quadruplex

In essence, a quadruplex consists of four single-family attached living units. Like the triplex, fee simple lots accompany each quadruplex unit unless they are to be sold under the condominium form of ownership.

The quadruplex is most frequently used in higher density developments where the appearance of separate dwellings is desired. Structures are often designed to resemble an oversized single-family detached house. A typical quadruplex designed in this manner has a central two-story mass—actually two, two-story houses—flanked by a one-story house and a main-level car storage area with a living unit on the level above. Other configurations are also possible (Figure 5-11).

Figure 5-10. Stoney Brook, Denver, Colorado

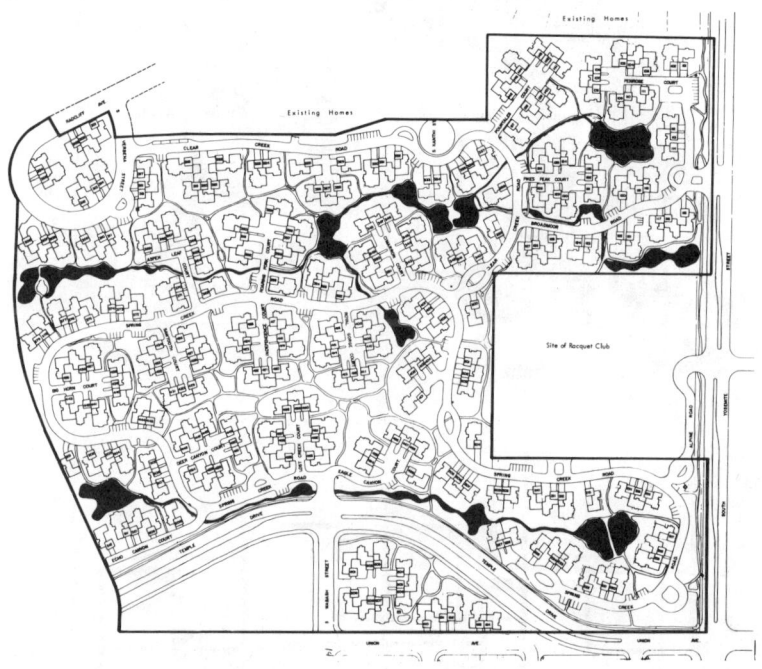

Source: Dusco, Inc.

137

Figure 5-11. Quadruplex

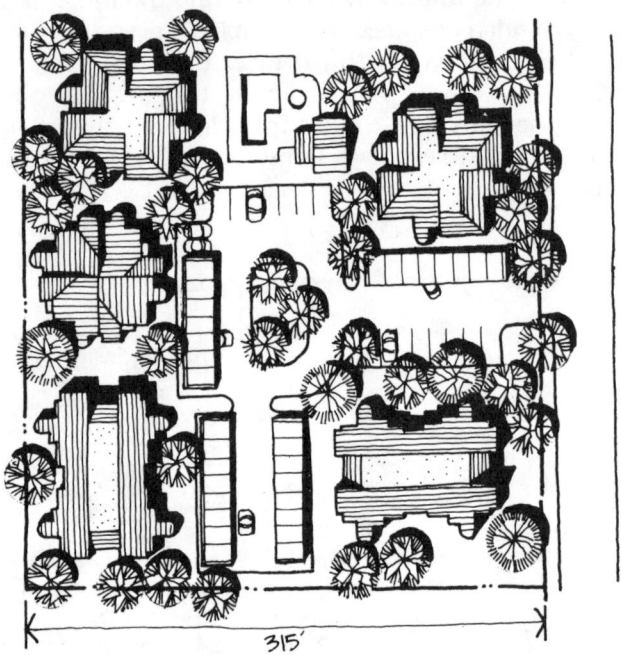

Source: Forbes Development Corporation

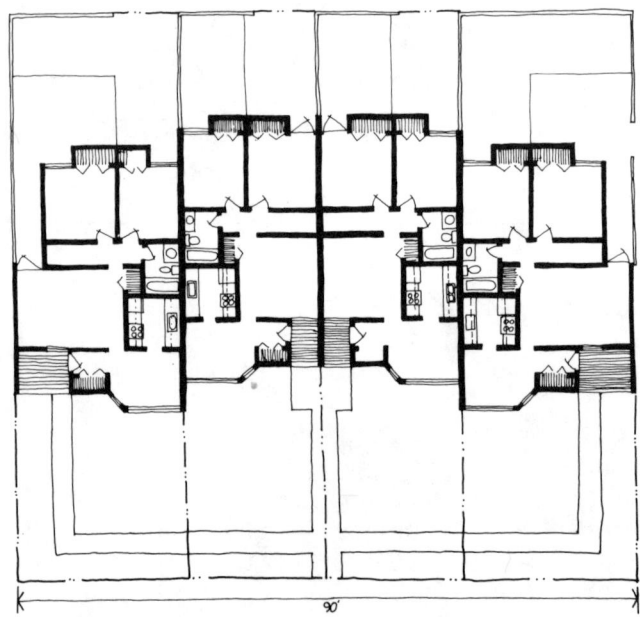

Source: Stephen Mead Associates

Example: Beacon Hill Vistas, Laguna Niguel, California

Beacon Hill Vistas is a sloping oceanside site developed to offer views of the Pacific to as many units as possible.

Quadruplexes in an over-under configuration are featured throughout the 13.2-acre site; overall project density is 11 units to the acre. The flexible over-under design maximizes ocean view potential while offering residents a choice of one- or two-story living (Figure 5-12a, b, and c).

The site was developed to include greenbelts, a trail system among buildings, and other recreational amenities that enhance the oceanside setting.

Townhouses

The townhouse is a single-family attached structure containing five or more units that share one or more wall or floor with an adjoining unit. While a quadruplex could be considered a townhouse, this book defines townhouses as more than four single-family units attached in one group. Within this definition there are multiple options for designing units and placing them on the site.

Options include the traditional side-by-side or linear arrangement, with common walls at the property lines; zigzag and staggered units and lots; a back-to-back configuration; and stacked unit arrangements. With the last two options, each unit has at least two walls or ceilings/floors in common with another unit, and interior units share common walls with three other units. In combination, these configurations have produced densities of up to 30 units per acre. It should be remembered that local regulations will often limit the flexibility the developer may have to utilize some of these options.

Example: Heather Glen, San Diego, California

The costs of existing land and the desire to provide homeownership potential in a central city area influenced the choice of townhouse units for Heather Glen, a small site in San Diego. The two-level units produce a density of 20 units per acre, yet maintain privacy, outdoor living, and view. Common spaces, enclosed parking, and landscaping help soften the project and allow it to blend in with less dense surrounding development (Figure 5-13a, b, and c).

The project, which replaced two existing small houses with 21 units, met its goal of retaining individual ownership within the confines of existing land costs.

Figure 5-12. Beacon Hill Vistas, Laguna Niguel, California

a

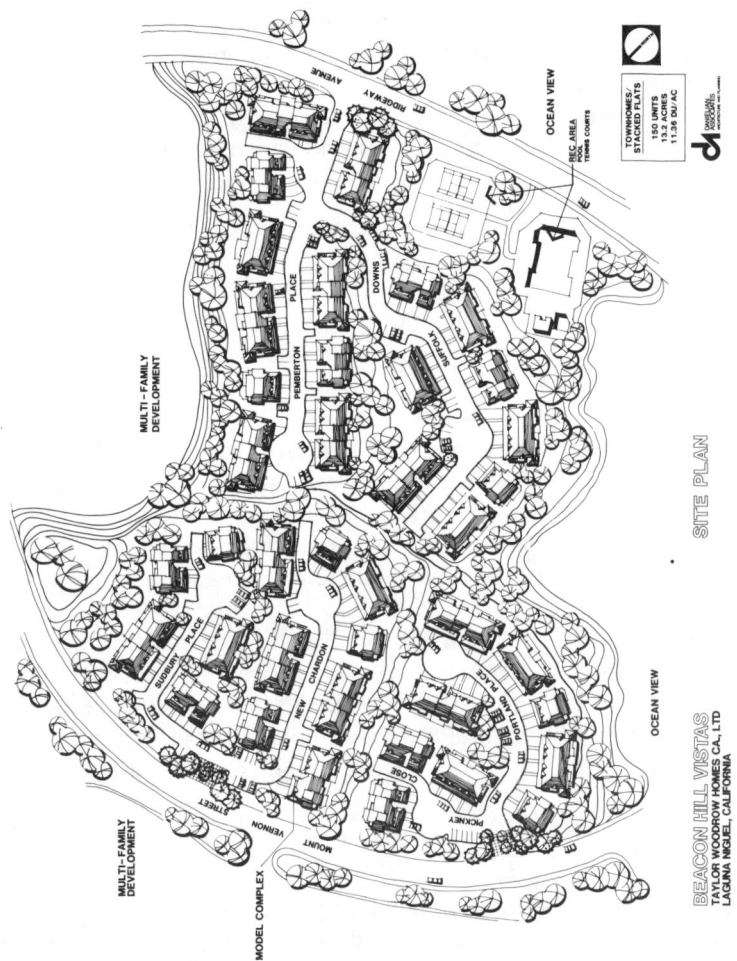

140

b

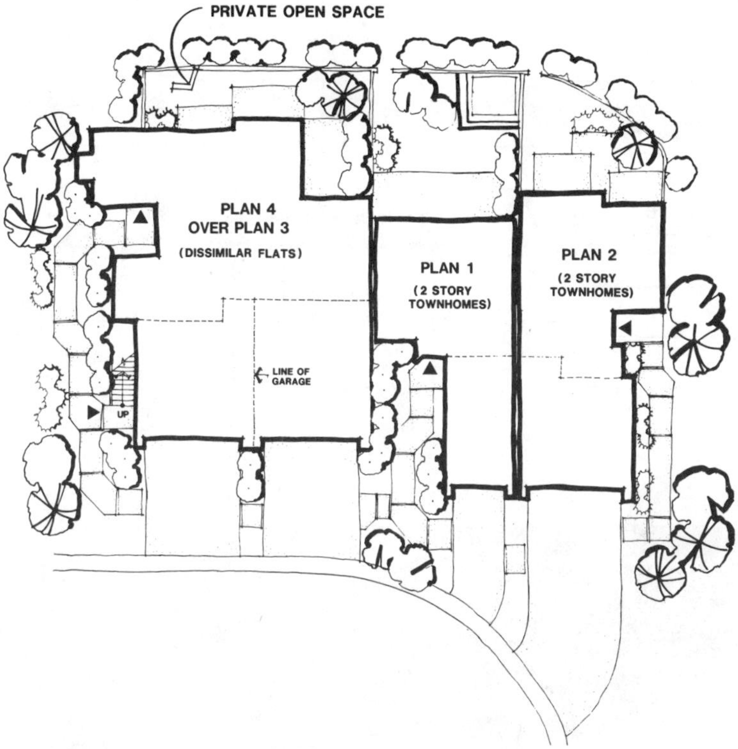

Source: Danielian Associates Architects/Planners
Photo: John R. Bare & Associates

Figure 5-13. Heather Glen, San Diego, California

a

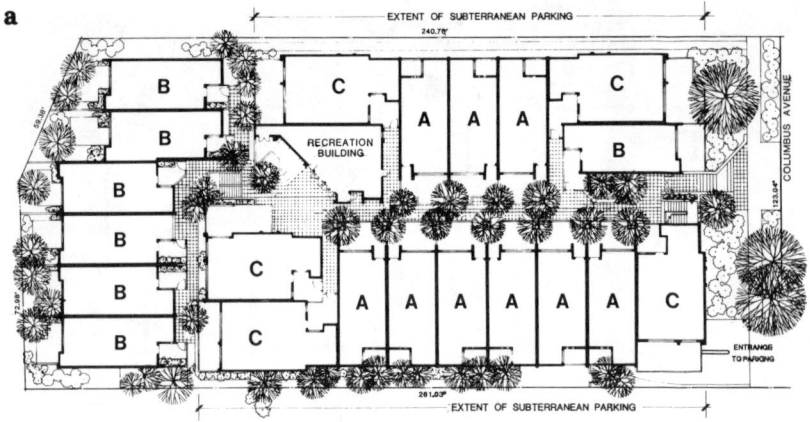

b

c

Source: Columbus Properties, Inc.
Photos: Sandra Williams Associates

Multifamily Housing

Garden Apartments/Stacked Flats

Garden apartments are two- or three-story walk-up buildings containing a group of living units on each level. Although they do not always open onto a garden or other private space, most garden apartment complexes have common recreational areas within the development. With the recent dramatic increase in condominium apartment ownership, the term "stacked flats" has brought a new respectability to the garden apartment.

Stacked flats feature a somewhat less rigid design approach than is typically found in conventional garden apartments, with respect to parking, common entry points, and the siting of units. The stacked flat provides a common entrance corridor, either open or enclosed, which allows the designer to slope or stack units in hill-town fashion on sites with no topographic variation. The density range for stacked flats can be 30 units per acre or higher.

Example: The Valley on Roswell Road, Atlanta, Georgia

The designers of this garden apartment complex, The Valley on Roswell Road, planned the buildings to step with the site by using interior as well as exterior retaining walls. Design features such as entrance bridges were made possible by siting the buildings to take advantage of the hilly terrain (Figure 5-14a, b, and c).

Figure 5-14. The Valley on Roswell Road, Atlanta, Georgia

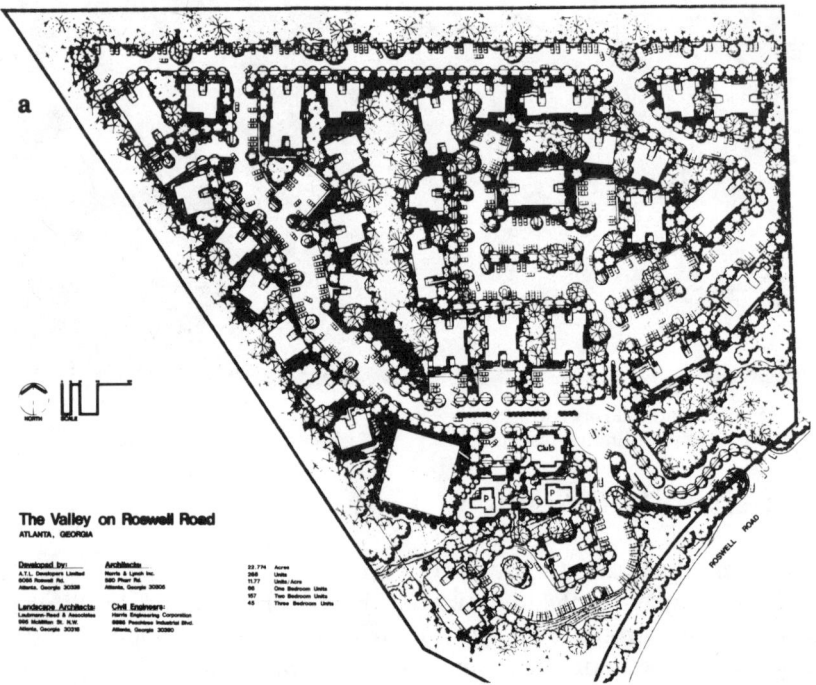

b

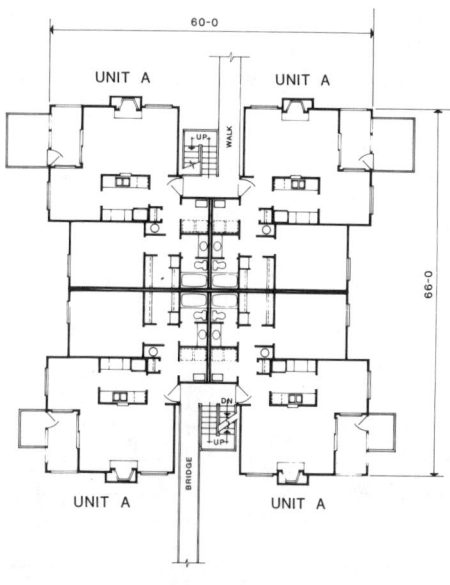

BUILDING TYPE ①
FLOOR PLAN

c

Source: Feifer and Associates

The entrance to the project features a dramatic, curved entrance drive sloping down through the trees to a textured open plaza.

The design allows for parking convenient to building entrances. Retaining walls and terraces allow circulation and parking to flow through the site. A pedestrian path system winds through the site and carries pedestrians to the recreation facilities.

Midrise

The midrise structure is usually four to no more than eight stories high. As with many buildings designed for rental, the structure has a central heating and cooling plant, and common laundry facilities and storage.

Often, a central hall provides access to each of the units on the same level. However, a central atrium or courtyard is sometimes used to provide circulation for vertical as well as horizontal movement (Figure 5-15).

Figure 5-15. Midrise

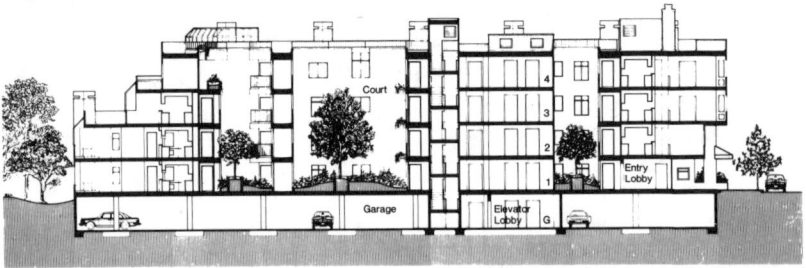

Source: Ocean Beach Associates

Highrise

The highrise structure usually consists of a building of more than eight floors, with one or more living units per floor. The building has an elevator for vertical movement within the structure.

Figure 5-16. Highrise

Source: deVitry, Gilbert and Bradley

Highrise structures can be freestanding or attached to other buildings in the development. Some buildings include residential as well as nonresidential tenants (Figure 5-16). Floor plans can vary between floors and on the same floor.

Example: Key Colony, Key Biscayne, Florida

Through its market acceptance, Key Colony illustrates the importance of combining the right location with the proper design. The project provides a variety of unit settings, from low- to mid- to highrise, without overwhelming the site.

Privacy was a design consideration for the terrace units on the stepped-down faces of the building, as was the ability to take advantage of the view. Stepping down the units from high- to low-rise permits better solar access than does the normal vertical plan with balconies (Figure 5-17a, b, and c).

Figure 5-17. Key Colony, Key Biscayne, Florida

a

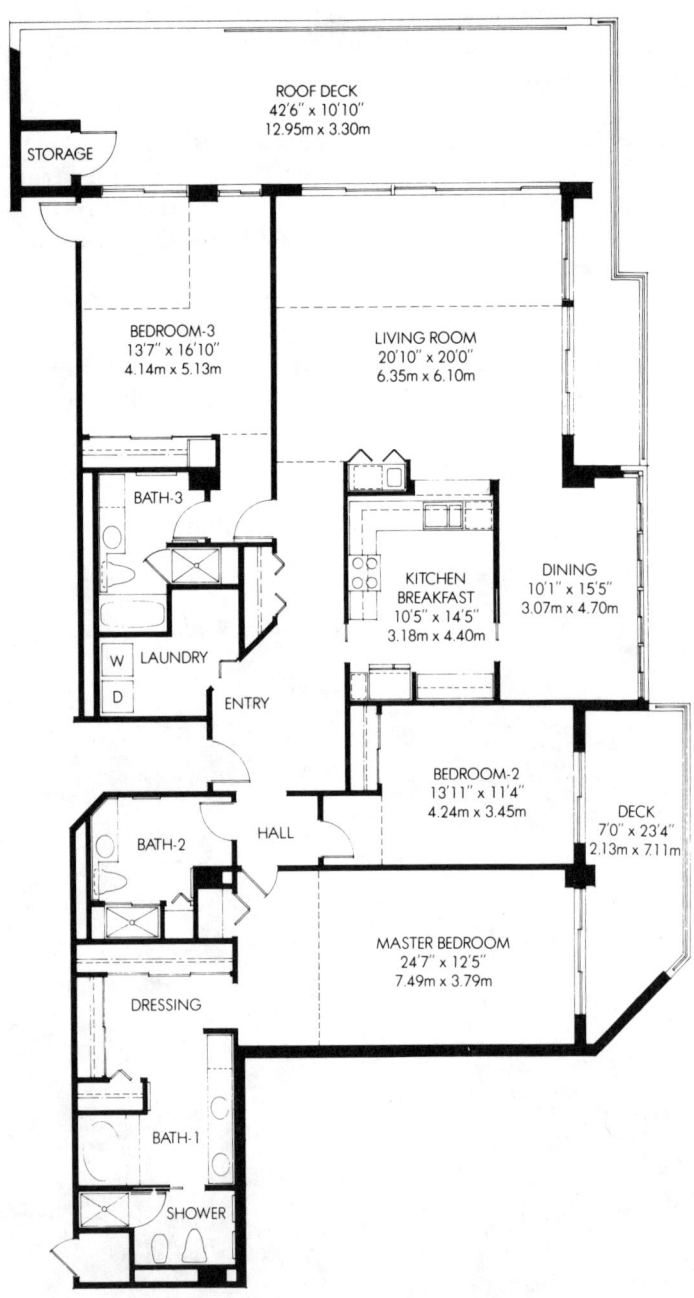

c

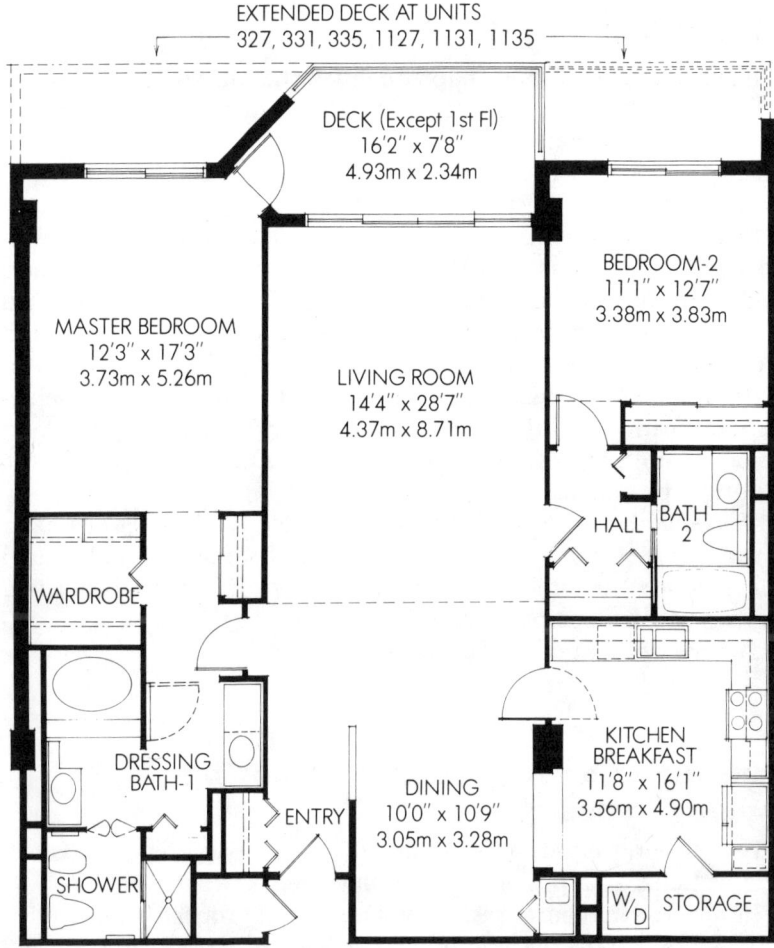

Source: Fininvest Limited

Considerations for Choosing a Housing Type

The first section of this chapter defined the range of typical housing types built in this country. These definitions do not address every single variation in design; rather, they illustrate the diversity of design that can be produced to create marketable and livable environments.

The choice of housing type must be based upon market research and a detailed site analysis (See Chapters 1 and 2). Market research should produce buyer profiles, analyses of existing and proposed housing stock, and unit preference information from residents and nonresidents. The site analysis should consider site location, orientation, topography, views, natural amenities, solar access, vehicular movement, and other characteristics, such as community land use or zoning plans that dictate land use and thus influence the building type choice.

Taken together, this information might tell the builder/developer that the project will be more cost-effective if it uses small lot, zero lot line cluster housing, rather than large lot single-family detached housing which does not take full advantage of the natural amenities, orientation, and scale of the site.

Planning as an Approach to Choosing Housing Types

The following exercise is designed to assist in the selection of suitable housing types for a particular site.

The site is a 166-acre, relatively flat piece of property surrounded by half-acre, quarter-acre, and estate-sized lots (Figure 5-18). Access is available from four sides, along which are existing utilities. The site is basically a moderately sloped meadow with several wet areas and two higher wooded areas. It is dominated by a prominent open hill featuring a mature orchard.

The land is zoned for a maximum density of three dwellings per acre on buildable land. Floodplain and steep slope land is classified as unbuildable. The maximum yield allows 472 dwelling units on approximately 157 acres.

The site analysis drawing highlights the physical characteristics of the site and shows the potential access points, open spaces, watershed areas, and amenities to be retained (Figure 5-19).

A cluster concept was proposed that would maintain all major wooded and orchard areas, achieve natural drainage channels

Figure 5-18. Existing site conditions

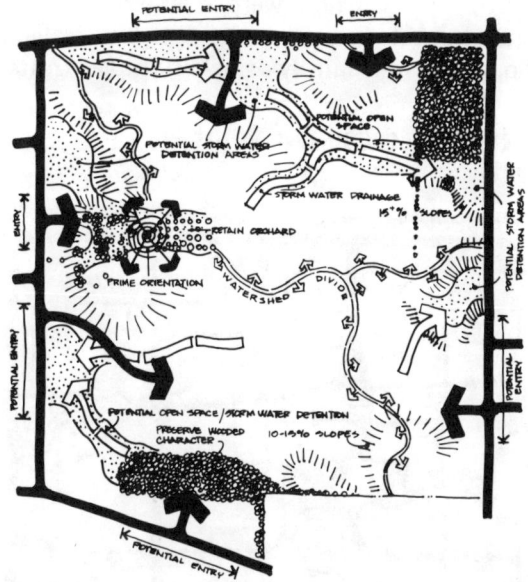

Source: NAHB

Figure 5-19. Site analysis based on existing conditions

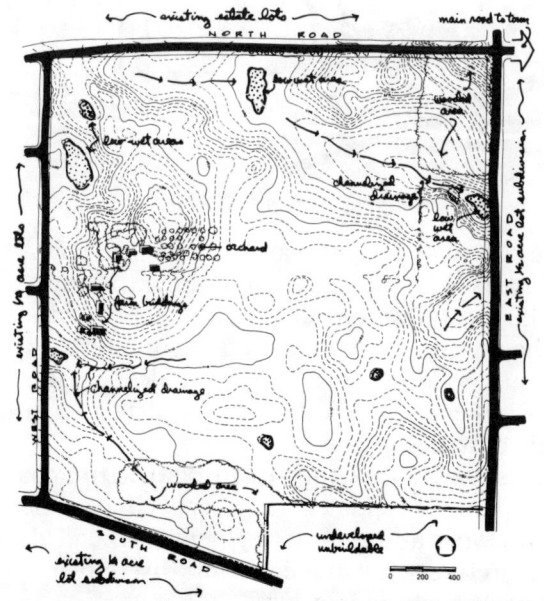

Source: NAHB

through open space, and retain the low areas as stormwater detention (Figure 5-20). The planners were able to offer a diverse range of housing consisting of conventional single-family detached, single-family patio, and single-family attached duplex units.

Figure 5-20. Cluster plan based on existing site conditions and site analysis

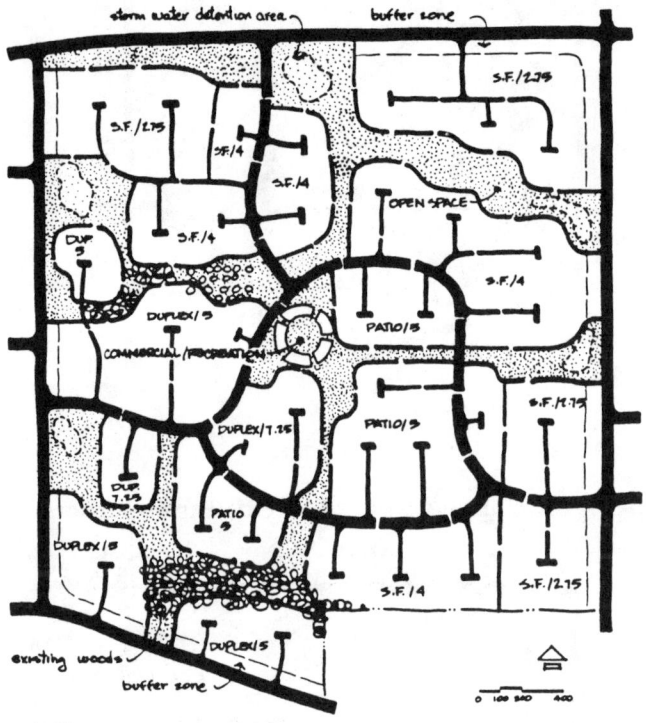

Source: NAHB

The choice of housing types was based on the characteristics of the site, as Figure 5-20 indicates. For example, the larger lot single-family detached units were placed on the perimeter of the project adjacent to the existing larger houses to maintain the character and scale of the surrounding area. The more dense patio units were positioned as buffers between the large lot detached units and the denser attached duplex units.

Figure 5-21 shows the savings in infrastructure costs achieved by the cluster plan. The cluster neighborhood also offers a greater mixture of unit types and contrasting neighborhood identities, and thus provides architectural and economic diversity in a more interesting and livable environment.

Figure 5-21. Summary of Site Development Costs

	Conventional		Cluster	
	Total Costs	Costs/DU	Total Costs	Costs/DU
Street pavement	$ 862,165	$ 1,827	$ 540,569	$1,145
Curbs and gutters	433,872	919	—	—
Street trees	412,496	874	374,640	794
Driveways	743,400	1,575	527,715	1,213
Storm drainage	696,464	1,476	278,295	590
Water distribution	746,044	1,581	492,792	1,044
Sanitary sewer	1,142,647	2,421	1,009,601	2,139
Grading	332,044	703	220,755	468
Clearing/grubbing	156,915	332	109,785	233
Sidewalks	209,250	443	197,775	419
Subtotal	$5,735,298	$12,151	$3,751,927	$8,045
Engineering fees (5.8%)	332,647	705	217,612	467
Total	**$6,067,945**	**$12,856**	**$3,969,539**	**$8,512**

Source: NAHB

Choosing Housing Types Based on Compatibility

Housing units that do not relate to onsite and offsite conditions are a result of poor planning. If units are arranged in an erratic fashion, if views are ignored, if solar access is not considered and natural amenities not taken advantage of, the end product will not be marketable, and the chance to create a livable environment will have been lost.

Compatibility is an essential ingredient in neighborhood planning, and it greatly influences the choices of housing type. Many compatibility factors are self-evident. In developing the cluster neighborhood just discussed, an attempt was made to preserve the character and fiber of the surrounding community. This goal was achieved by locating housing types similar to those existing in developed neighborhoods on the peripheral areas of the new tract, and changing character and density only within the development itself.

Locating higher density housing immediately adjoining a low- to mid-density area is not a wise decision from either an aesthetic or planning standpoint. If handled properly, however, an area of existing detached single-family houses could accept denser single-family or multifamily structures that preserve the scale and character of the neighborhood. These new units can act as a focal point for the surrounding area and create a balanced mix of resident types.

Compatibility is also essential in a planned unit development and has much to do with the selection of housing type. A mix of housing types of varying densities produces manageable, controlled, and sensible growth for communities. In this site plan (Figure 5-22), carefully planned use areas are evident. Residential building types were chosen to comply and blend in with surrounding uses.

The multifamily housing section is located in an area of commercial structures to blend better with existing building mass and volume. Single-family attached structures in the form of townhouses and other attached units are used as a buffer between small and large lot single-family detached housing. Office structures and highrise and midrise apartments share the same general location because their fabric, building mass, and orientation are similar.

The concept of planning and choosing housing types based on compatibility and integration with the existing community benefits both the builder/developer and the residents. A range of housing types means greater demographic diversity and more market flexibility.

Choosing Housing Types Based on Solar Access and Sun Control

Consumer awareness and common sense suggest that a housing site be evaluated for its energy potential. The selection and proper orientation of the housing types are critical (Figure 5-23).

The economics of site development and local development codes often dictate the directional and degree orientation of streets and the resulting lot patterns. The limited number of site design options, in turn, limits the range of housing type choices. These specific site conditions may result in variations from the ideal solar orientation. Exploring options in plan, site, and architectural detail can aid in solving this problem (Figure 5-24). In spite of limitations, the builder/developer should try to maximize the percentage of units in the project that can have ideal solar orientation, while seeking acceptable alternatives for the remaining units.

Figure 5-22. Planned unit development site plan

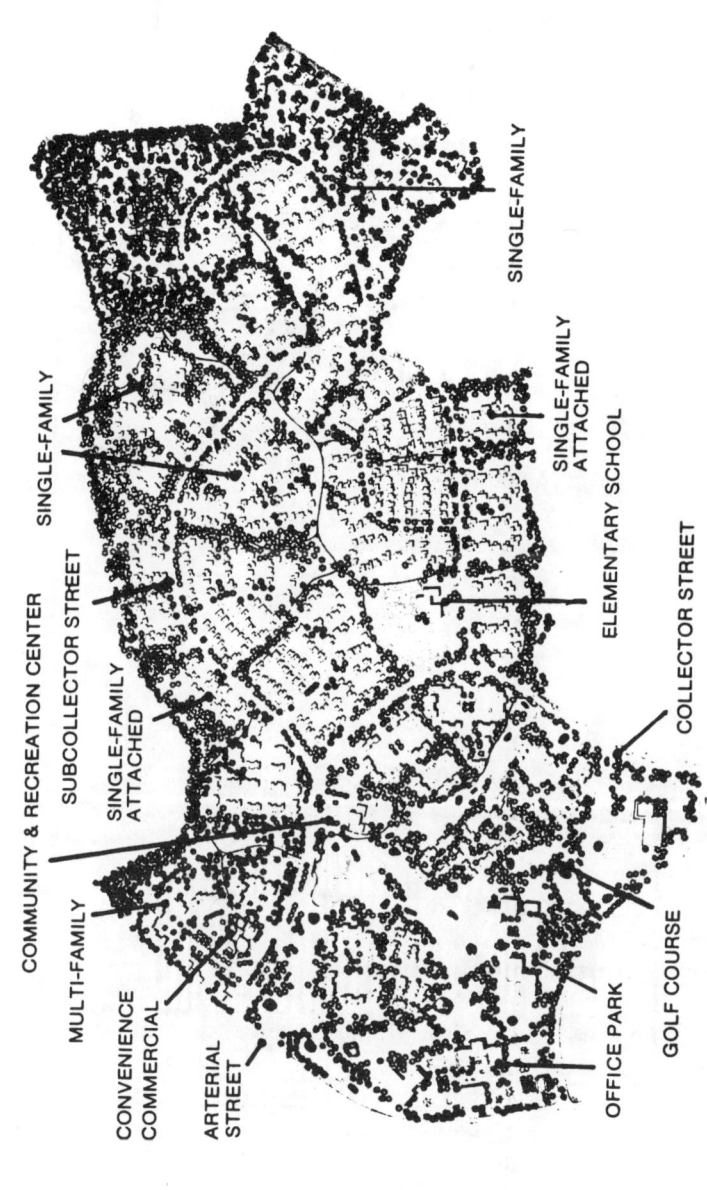

Source: NAHB

Figure 5-23. Sun angles and architectural design

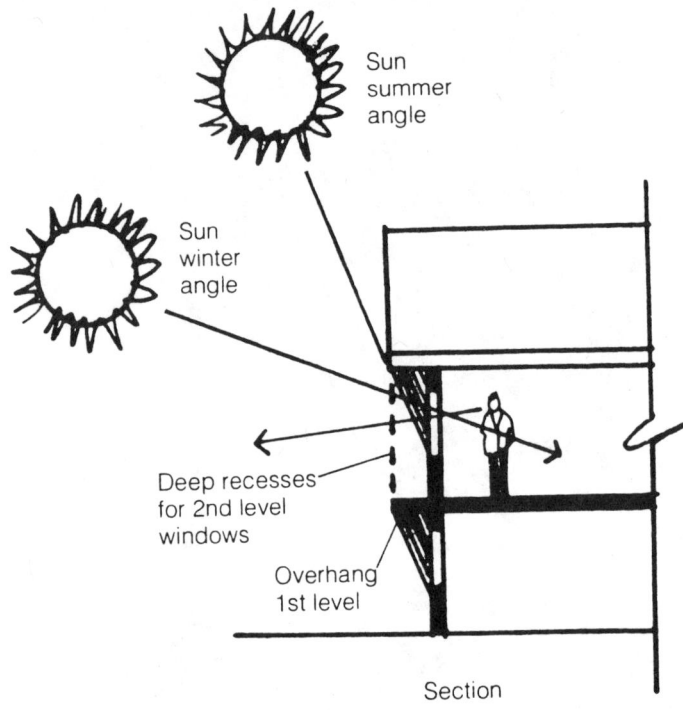

Section

Front elevation

Source: NAHB

Figure 5-24. Energy-efficient land planning (Burke Center, Virginia)

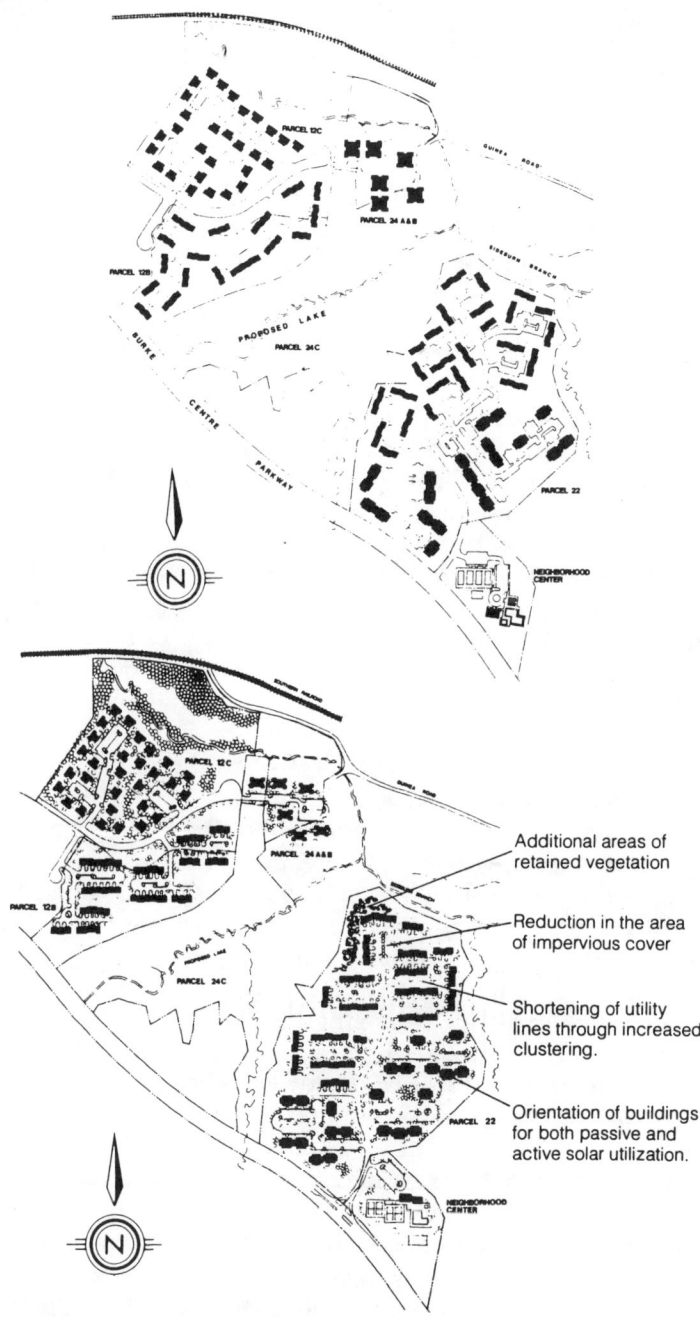

Source: U.S. Department of Energy

Choosing Housing Types Based on Site Specifics

The suitability of one housing type over another on a piece of property depends heavily upon the physical characteristics of the site itself. The most important considerations are listed below:
- Location.
- Availability of vehicular access.
- View. What are the views from the site to its surroundings? How will views from the buildings to be constructed relate to each other? The windows of units should not face each other at close enough range to destroy privacy.
- Interior space orientation to the view. Whether the view is natural or manmade, of mountains or an enclosed garden court, the time of day at which that view will be used is important if the housing units are to work properly on the site.

For example, if the prime view is best in early to mid-morning, the spaces within the structure that relate to the view should be usable at that time of day. A living space normally used in the afternoon or early evening should be located away from the prime morning view. Here, plan study and configuration begin to play a role in the selection of specific housing types.

While zoning requirements are overlooked in the following example, they may affect unit orientation. Given a site with a gentle slope toward a view to the east in late afternoon, how does selection of a particular housing type affect the site and its characteristics?

Single-family detached housing would be an obvious solution to take advantage of what the site has to offer, because the units are not confined by directional orientation.

A townhouse configuration might require careful planning for units located on the upper slope to have maximum view potential.

Multiplan configurations—such as a pinwheel quadruplex—are restrictive, because only two units could be oriented toward the view. Obviously, a quadruplex of this type would be a poor choice for the site.

A garden apartment with a single-loaded corridor away from the view, on the other hand, might be a solution because all of the units could be oriented to the view. If additional buildings are placed on the downslope, however, the land might require further sculpting to maximize the view.

Planning that determines housing type on the basis of site conditions is an absolute necessity. The full potential of each available building type must be understood and used to create a manmade environment that is visually interesting, that is sympathetic to any given site, and that provides neighborhood inhabitants with high-quality and well-thought-out housing.

Housing Type Choices

Advantages	Cautions

Single-Family Detached—Large Lot

- Orientation of interior spaces in any direction
- Privacy
- Adjacent outdoor living

- Land requirements
- Low density
- Infrastructure/lot improvement costs

Single-Family Detached—Small Lot

- Lower infrastructure and lot cost

- Reduced directional orientation options for each unit

Duplex

- Construction cost savings
- Reduced lot sizes
- Single-family detached character

- Indoor/outdoor relationships
- Privacy provisions
- Directional orientation

Triplex

- Access to grade from each unit
- Decreased lot sizes
- Design flexibility

- Privacy provisions
- Automobile access and storage
- Directional orientation
- Indoor/outdoor relationships

Quadruplex

- Construction cost savings
- Ability to buffer higher and lower density areas
- Design flexibility

- Indoor/outdoor relationships
- Directional orientation
- Automobile access and storage

Townhouse

- Floor plan and style flexibility
- Design flexibility
- Access to grade
- Single-family detached lifestyle

- Privacy provisions
- Adaptability to site
- Height limitations
- Automobile access and storage
- Indoor/outdoor relationships

Continued

Advantages	Cautions
Garden Apartment/Stacked Flat	
• Ease of construction • Land savings • Floor plan and style flexibility	• Directional orientation • Privacy provisions • Outdoor living availability • Automobile access and storage
Midrise	
• Mechanical equipment savings • Density trade-offs • Market flexibility	• Vertical movement • Automobile access and storage • Style flexibility
Highrise	
• View orientation • Density • Land costs	• Construction cost • Directional orientation for interior spaces • Effects of shadows on solar access of nearby buildings

Chapter 6
Earthwork and Stormwater Management

Residential construction before the end of World War II was mostly small scale. Since that time, the pattern of urbanization has changed from lot-by-lot development to the building of multi-unit subdivisions. With this change has come a growing awareness of the need to manage erosion, sedimentation, and stormwater. This has led to regulatory legislation at both local and state levels. Builders, developers, engineers, architects, and public officials must be aware of the erosion, sediment, and stormwater control laws that apply to individual project locations.

Erosion and Sedimentation Control

Erosion and sedimentation may have both beneficial and detrimental effects on the environment. Engineering and land planning should emphasize techniques that preserve, protect, and enhance natural features of onsite and offsite land. Each site has its own set of natural resources, environmental conditions, land use limitations, and occupancy requirements. These factors and their interrelationships must be considered by everyone from the initial planner to the eventual owner, in order to protect the site from the adverse effects of excessive erosion and sedimentation.

Study of the characteristics of each site is necessary to attain the following objectives:
- Give a perspective showing why erosion and sediment control have become important to the builder, planner, architect, and all others involved in the development of land
- Provide an understanding of erosion and sediment control philosophies, policies, and processes
- Encourage design resulting in effective facilities requiring minimum maintenance

- Develop better understanding of the long-term results of erosion and sediment control practices
- Encourage land use changes consistent with alternative design solutions, environmental quality, and sound judgment

In line with these objectives, a number of principles apply to residential development:

- Minimize changes in the rate of existing erosion and the amount of sediment movement during the life of a project
- Base control measures upon cost evaluation, subsequent benefits, and other needs
- Make long-term maintenance an integral part of erosion and sediment control design
- Consider protection, maintenance, or establishment of ground cover fundamental, except where permanent vegetative cover is not practical
- Create overall plans and objectives for catchment areas; they often help determine appropriate measures for specific sites
- Design specific plans for the prevention of erosion and sedimentation that recognize the risk, especially the projected frequency of events for which protective measures are designed and built
- Reduce or eliminate erosion and sedimentation problems before construction with good residential planning and development

Water and wind are the major causes of erosion, transport, and deposition of sediment. Water is by far the more important because amounts of soil locally removed by wind usually are small compared to those eroded and transported by water. Wind erosion tends to be related to drought and, although it can be problematic nearly anywhere, is primarily of concern in arid and semiarid regions.

Factors that affect water erosion include:

- Climate, particularly the amount, intensity, and frequency of rainfall, with special emphasis on its seasonal distribution
- Soil properties, such as particle size distribution, clay and organic content, porosity, capillarity, permeability, water content, soil structure, and specific gravity
- Slope gradient and length of downslope distance
- Vegetation establishment and maintenance

Erosion Control Measures

Temporary and permanent erosion measures and facilities have similar functions, but there are differences in design approaches, methods of construction and maintenance, and cost benefits.

Temporary measures and facilities are typically designed for the duration of the construction period. As field expedients, they may be in use only for several days, and, unlike permanent measures, they do not need to be designed or built to last for many years with minimal maintenance. Temporary control facilities, however, must be maintained regularly during their period of use to remain effective. Although initial costs for these measures may be low, frequent or intense storms during the construction period can lead to relatively high maintenance costs.

Permanent measures are intended to remain in place for at least 50 years with a minimum of maintenance; therefore they must be designed and built of durable materials.

Vegetative Soil Stabilization

Vegetative cover is the most natural method of soil stabilization. Fast-growing grasses and sod may be used on partially completed projects to protect them from erosion for short periods, but such temporary stabilization is costly and rarely can be salvaged or incorporated into final protective measures. In general, the need for temporary stabilization should be avoided.

Permanent vegetation should be long-lived and require a minimum amount of care or maintenance. Grasses and legumes are generally superior to shrubs and ground covers because of their more complex root systems which encourage formation of water-stable soil structure. Plants should be selected according to the specific site's growth expectancy, purpose, and projected level of maintenance. The general area should be examined to make sure that the plants chosen accomplish the intended purpose and to note the similarity between the other slopes, soil conditions, and maintenance expectancy in relation to the same factors for the specific site.

Nonvegetative Soil Stabilization

Nonvegetative soil stabilization measures may also be temporary or permanent.

Mulches, nettings, and chemical binders are typical temporary practices. Mulching protects soil from erosion even when no vegetation is used and provides a number of benefits when vegetation is being established. Common mulch materials include hay, small grain straw, wood chips, jute matting, glass fiber netting, plastic and asphalt emulsions, and various paper products.

Coarse crushed rock and gravel are commonly used materials for permanent stabilization of gradients no steeper than about five to one. Costs vary a great deal, depending on material availability and ease of application. For steeper slopes, areas of groundwater seepage, waterways subject to high flow velocities, or soils that do not absorb or retain moisture efficiently, structural treatment may be necessary.

Structural Measures

Structural measures are designed and built to fulfill specific functions. The most typical structures are built to intercept surface runoff and convey it to a safe disposal area to keep it away from erodible soil and to prevent gully erosion—advanced erosion resulting from concentrated stormwater flow.

Diversion structures are commonly soil or stone dikes, ditches or channels, and terraces or benches. Diversion and interceptor dikes are temporary ridges of compacted soil. Water collects behind the dikes in the ditches or on the benches, and flows along them at nonerosive velocities to an outfall where it can be released without causing excessive erosion. Temporary berms serve the same purpose, but are typically larger than diversion structures. These berms are mounds of earth that shorten vertical runoff distances on cut-and-fill slopes (Figure 6-1).

Figure 6-1. Diversion dike and filter berm

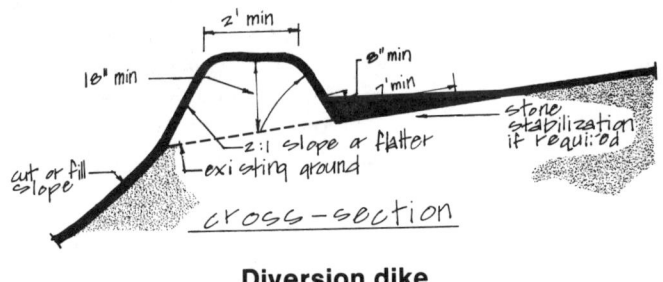

Diversion dike

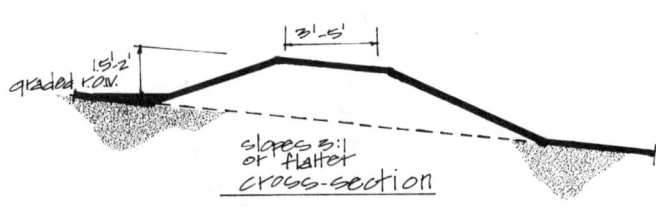

Filter berm

Source: National Association of Home Builders,
Residential Erosion and Sediment Control

Waterways are natural or manmade drainage channels that convey runoff to nonerodible outlets. They may be used to dispose of water from diversions, berms, benches, or other areas. Waterways are lined with vegetation, concrete, riprap, or asphalt. If lining is necessary, the type is determined by flow velocities. If the waterway discharges to a sedimentation basin, a lining may be superfluous. Swales (constructed channels) and other waterways are normally designed for a specific probable rate of runoff determined by their expected duration of use, and are located in accordance with normal storm drainage practices (Figure 6-2).

Figure 6-2. Swales

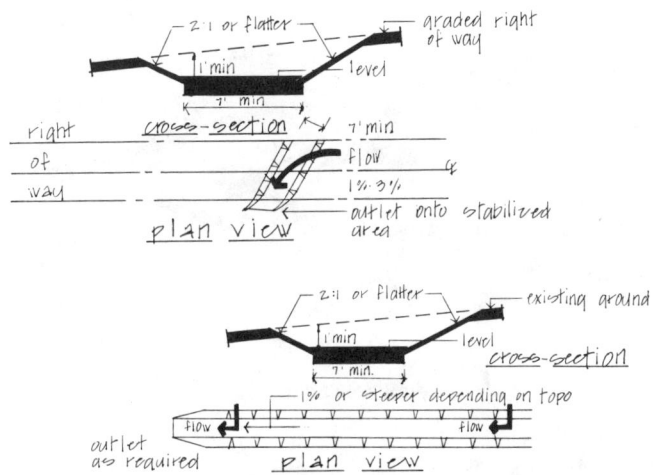

Source: National Association of Home Builders, *Residential Erosion and Sediment Control*

Disposal structures convey runoff collected by diversion structures to safe outlets. They are also used to convey runoff safely down slopes that otherwise would be subject to significant gully erosion. Flexible downdrains are conduits made of heavy-duty fabric, or other suitable material, and are usually installed for temporary use. Sectional downdrains are typically half-round pipes made of bituminized fiber, concrete, or metal, and are shingled and permanently staked into place. Flumes are channels made of metal, concrete, or asphalt. Level spreaders distribute concentrated runoff in such a way that it overflows at nonerosive velocities as sheet flow over lower undisturbed areas stabilized by existing vegetation (Figure 6-3).

Figure 6-3. Downdrain and level spreader

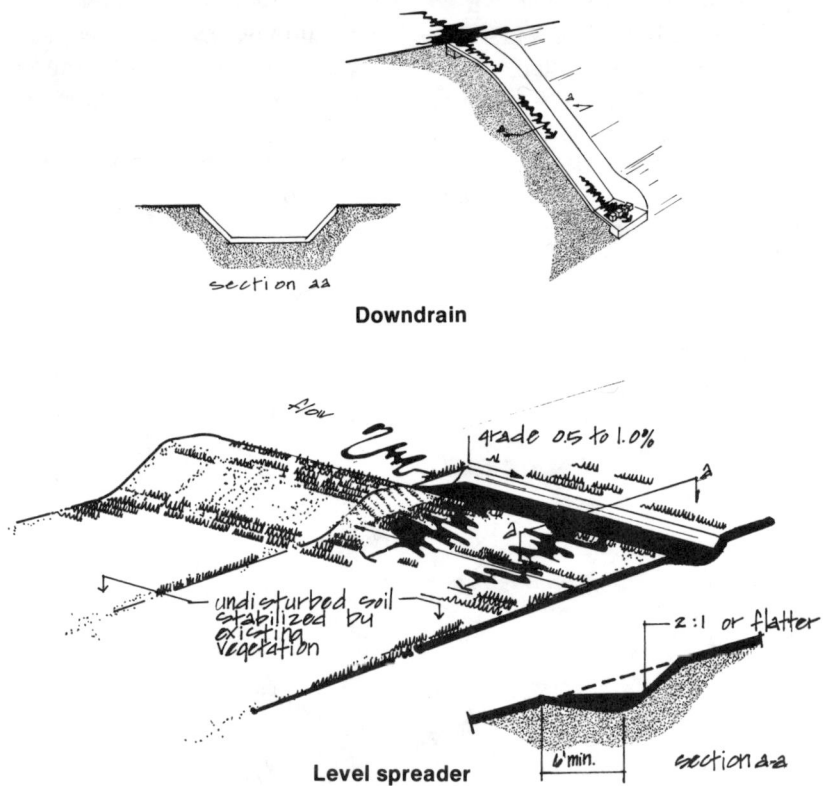

Source: National Association of Home Builders, *Residential Erosion and Sediment Control*

Sediment Control Objectives

The objective of sediment control is to ensure conditions that are conducive to deposition and that do not encourage suspension of particles in water at locations where deposition is desirable. Rate of particle removal is influenced by the size and specific gravity of the particles, the temperature of the water in which they are suspended, and the motion of the water. Heavier particles and warm and quiet waters lead to quicker settling out than do lighter particles, cold water, or turbulent flow. Very small particles, such as those found in some clays, will not settle out within a practical time period because other factors such as electrical charges keep them in suspension. The practical approach to this problem is to concentrate efforts to reduce the rate of erosion on sites with conditions that cause quick settling out rather than to make futile efforts to trap suspended sediments.

The reduction of runoff flow quantity and velocity is the basis for all sediment trapping measures. Trapping is the removal of suspended particles by reducing the flow velocity and turbulence of the suspending water and by preventing resuspension of these particles.

Trapping

Trapping measures are generally used where channel flows contain sediment in greater than acceptable amounts. Trapping is done with structures that retard runoff velocity, allowing sediment to accumulate and fall at a desired location, and permit the runoff to flow safely out of the structure without causing further erosion or other hazards. The most common of these structures are traps and basins, which function almost identically but are differentiated by their size, design, and construction.

Traps are comparatively small installations used for small drainage areas. Their construction can be inexpensive and their maintenance relatively simple. They are useful in areas that are unsuitable for larger sedimentation basins. Often, several traps can be substituted for a single basin if an area is divisible into smaller individual watersheds (Figure 6-4).

Basins are relatively large and frequently expensive to design, construct, and maintain. Although they are the most effective means of trapping sediment, their efficiency is often obtained at high cost. They consist of temporary or permanent impoundments, usually constructed by damming a waterway. Basins should be considered only when other approaches to site planning, erosion prevention, or trapping are inadequate to reduce offsite sedimentation to acceptable levels (Figure 6-5).

Filtration

Sediment removal also can be accomplished by filtration. Filtration removes sediment by straining it out of the water with grass, filter cloth, straw bales, or other materials that either trap or absorb the soil particles but permit clean water to pass (Figure 6-6). Filtration can be effective most often where contributory runoff areas are small. When used properly, filters and filter strips (natural vegetative buffers) offer high sediment removal efficiency with minimal maintenance.

Filtration is not universally useful, however, and should be used with caution. Excessive flows over a vegetative or other filter strip

Figure 6-4. Earth outlet sediment trap and embankment section through riser

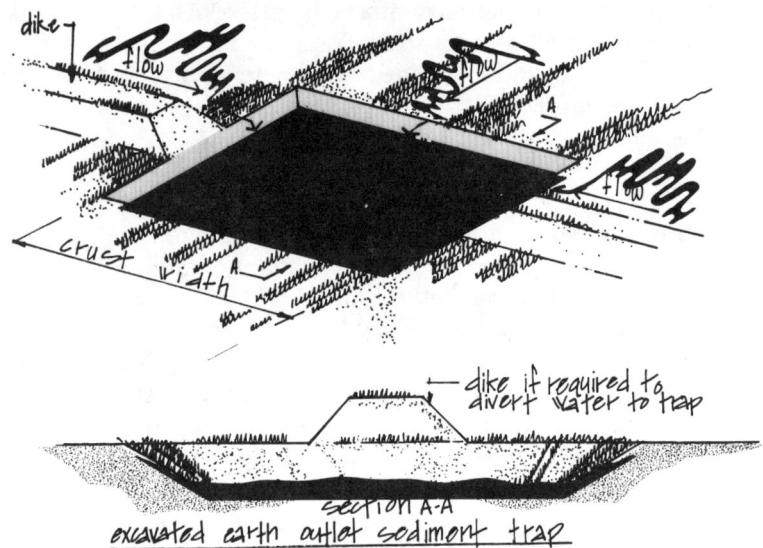

Earth outlet sediment trap

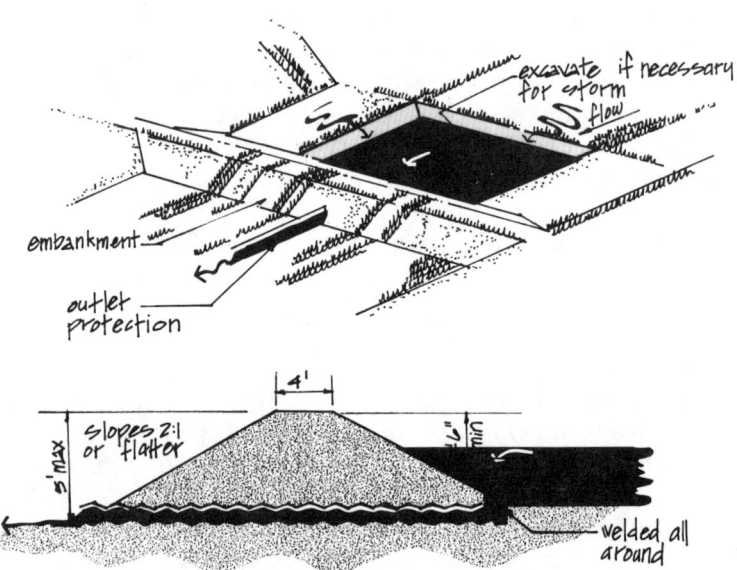

Embankment section through riser

Source: National Association of Home Builders, *Residential Erosion and Sediment Control*

Figure 6-5. Sediment basin

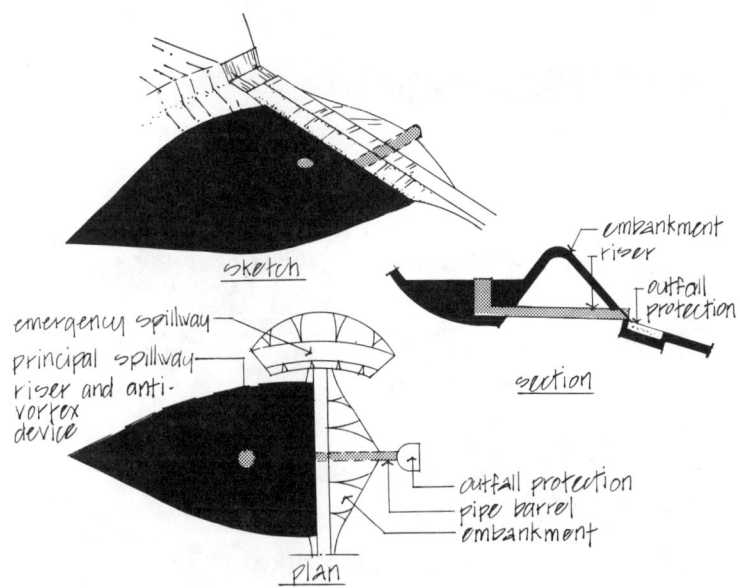

Source: National Association of Home Builders, *Residential Erosion and Sediment Control*

can smother or destroy the strip itself, or erode and carry away material previously deposited. The trapping efficiency of filter strips is difficult to quantify, and filters such as gravel barriers tend to clog and lose their effectiveness. Nevertheless, when dealing with problems in small areas or small parts of larger areas, filters can be practical.

Planning an Erosion and Sediment Control Program

Many variables are involved in planning an erosion and sediment control program for a residential development project. The developer must first determine what types of changes, if any, are likely to occur both on and off the site. After the nature of expected changes has been examined, the extent of these changes must be studied to determine what levels can be accepted without causing adverse environmental impacts.

If damage is unlikely, control measures are unnecessary. If damage is probable, its potential magnitude, character, and cause must be determined in order to select the most effective methods for

Figure 6-6. Straw bale dike and barrier with gravel outlet

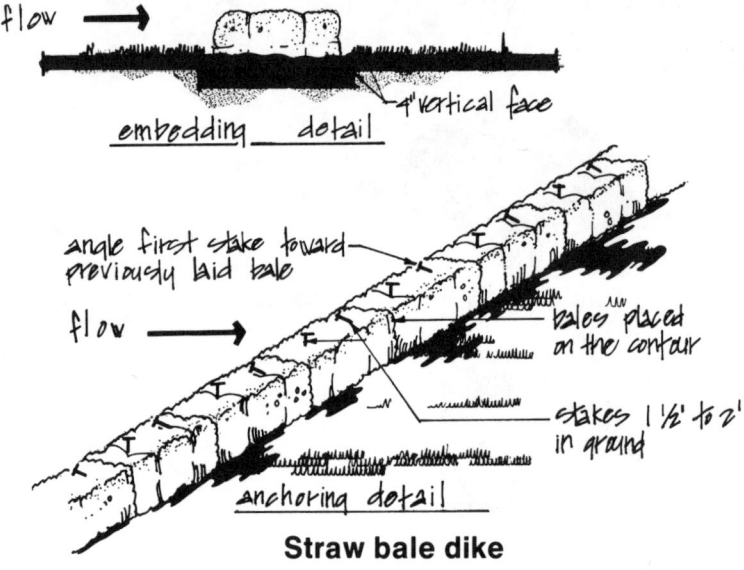

Straw bale dike

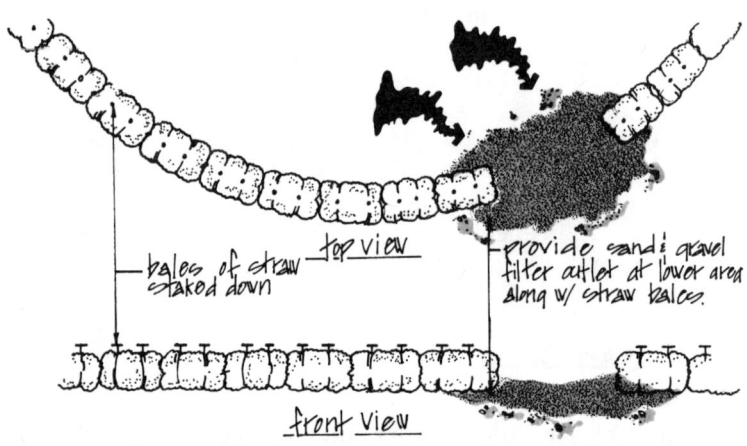

Barrier with gravel outlet

Source: National Association of Home Builders, *Residential Erosion and Sediment Control*

minimizing or avoiding the damage. The character of projected off-site environmental damage will determine the extent of public agency involvement.

Environmental Effects

Acceptable levels of environmental change differ widely, according to local laws, regulations, advice, liabilities, and attitudes of adjacent landowners. Factors other than public agency involvement that influence the level of acceptable adverse environmental effects include the site, climatic conditions, and the proposed uses of the affected land and its environs. The developer's self-interest will determine preventive or remedial measures to limit adverse onsite effects.

Erosion and sediment control can be overdone. Although deposited sediments can cause damage, they can also be beneficial. Some amount of stream channel nourishment by sediments is essential for channel stability. Channel bank and bottom erosion will be aggravated if sediment supply is cut off. Excessive reduction of erosion and sedimentation can cause disastrous effects upon stable biotic systems. Although effects of undercontrol of erosion, such as deposits of sediment, are often visible immediately, the effects of overcontrol may be long-term damage, such as loss of flood plain activity. The level of protection necessary need not be so high that it reduces the sediment, leaving the site to levels that are lower than under natural conditions.

The determination of acceptable levels of environmental change involves consideration of all the variables involved. Precise evaluation is impossible. Experienced scientific and professional judgment is required to set reasonable limits for allowable sediment movement of specific land areas.

Damage During Construction

Developers must take into account the probability that one or more damaging events such as a flood or storm may occur during construction. This risk must be determined before preparation of an erosion and sediment control plan in order to identify the kind, amount, and extent of measures necessary to reduce or eliminate foreseeable damage.

Erosion rates are related to the intensity, duration, and seasonality of rainfall and wind. In most cases the possibility that an event of a given magnitude may occur once during the period of construction can be determined and can be expressed as a probability or as a recurrence interval. The probability of a given event is represented by the numerical odds that it will occur within a given year. A recurrence interval indicates the average worst severity of a kind of event that may be expected during a given period of years—for instance, a 100-year flood plain.

The level of risk can be determined for rainstorms, wind velocities and directions, droughts, and other phenomena. When all possible types of offsite effects have been considered, the acceptable level of risk can be determined and specific measures for the protection of offsite areas can be designed and incorporated into the construction plans.

The level of risk can be determined by analyzing local and regional variations in climate, soils, topography, and vegetation, among other factors. These factors must be balanced against each other to arrive at realistic final decisions, Although the 5-, 10-, or 20-year storm or other "design" storm customarily provides a starting point, other factors such as environmentally sensitive areas or downstream life safety may also have to be considered.

Level of Protection

After an acceptable level of risk is determined, a preliminary erosion and sediment control plan can be prepared. The cost of implementing the plan should be estimated, and the cost of each suggested measure examined to compare the degree of protection required with the degree that probably will be realized. This comparison should include the consideration of losses that cannot immediately be measured monetarily. For instance, a proposed large sediment basin may trap a certain amount of sediment, but the total cost of the basin will include maintenance, loss of vegetation, scenic value, and other values at the basin site.

If the projected cost of adequate protection exceeds the anticipated damage, potential monetary loss, or potential environmental loss, a more cost-effective solution should be found. Proposed control measures should be reexamined, and possibly the required level of protection or the ability to repair damage after construction should be reevaluated.

Stormwater Management Considerations

Both erosion control and sediment control are intertwined with stormwater management, which prevents or reduces damage to property, rivers, streams, and lakes. As a measure intended to reduce loss of soil from a given site, erosion control is closely allied with stormwater management because channels and streams designed to receive managed runoff are less subject to damage than those that are not. Erosion continues after construction is completed, and a portion of the resulting sediment is deposited in stormwater management structures or downstream.

As an expedient intended to prevent or reduce deposition damage both onsite and offsite, sediment control is also connected with stormwater management. Sediment control measures that trap eroded soil particles in transport must be integrated with stormwater management measures, and they often become part of the permanent stormwater management facilities.

Quantified Performance Estimates

Erosion and sediment control methods should be evaluated numerically to estimate their probable effectiveness. Quantified performance estimates must be based largely on local experience and judgment. As is the case with determining risk and acceptable levels of environmental change, precise evaluation is not possible. For this reason, qualified engineering and scientific personnel must be engaged for professional estimates.

A typical erosion quantification model, the Universal Soil Loss Equation (USLE), gives an example of the complexities involved in such estimates. The USLE is useful only for certain types of erosion; gully and streambed erosion are excluded. It applies only to single, large, homogeneous areas where the setting involves long, regular, gentle slopes, and where changes during the season are relatively predictable. None of the model equations is reliable for estimating general erosion behavior on construction sites, but the USLE is perhaps the most generally accepted and illustrates the principles involved.

The basic form of the USLE is:

$$E = RK(LS)CP$$

E = Soil loss, in tons per acre per year
R = Rainfall factor
K = Soil erodibility
LS = Slope length gradient
C = Vegetative cover
P = Conservation practice

Factors likely to vary, such as mixed soil types and changing slopes (caused by grading), can result in a large number of calculations for a construction site.

Developed essentially for agricultural activities, the USLE is generally too conservative for estimating construction site behavior and may lead to overdesign. Still, the equation can be used for a rough evaluation of erosion control alternatives. It can provide insights into design alternatives at a given site, but such insights may not improve upon basic considerations of comparative soil erodibility.

Site Planning

Construction site grading and erosion control designs should be carefully integrated and reviewed. Attention should be directed to good site planning, construction scheduling, minimal grading, phased construction, and the cost-effectiveness of alternative measures for erosion prevention and sediment collection. Soil loss will be reduced if graded areas are kept as small as possible. Intervening undisturbed areas, which act as both filters and windbreaks, give added protection.

Careful site planning is the most effective method of controlling erosion and sedimentation. Consideration of the major factors affecting erosion can reduce or prevent many erosion and sediment control problems. One of the most obvious of these factors is the seasonality of rainfall. If possible, construction should be scheduled to avoid seasons when heavy rains are expected. Wind force and direction are also seasonal in many areas, but the adverse effects of wind erosion are comparatively negligible in contrast with potential water erosion problems.

Soil erosion potential, based on soil type and particle size, is another important factor affecting erosion. The least erodible soils should be exposed whenever possible, but the heaviest soil particles are the most easily trapped. For instance, the large particle size of sand allows it to be trapped readily. Minimal precautions such as installation of sediment traps and the diversion of runoff away from slopes can keep the amounts of sand leaving a construction site small. On the other hand, clay soils generally resist erosion better, but their extremely fine particles make them difficult to trap.

Both the length and steepness of a slope affect the rate at which soil is eroded. Grading can make slopes less steep, but the resulting exposure can be counterproductive. Terracing, also called benching, can reduce erosion caused by slope length. A terrace is an embankment or the combination of an embankment and channel suitably spaced across a slope to control erosion by diverting or storing surface runoff instead of permitting it to flow uninterrupted down the slope.

As noted earlier, vegetative and nonvegetative covers reduce both water and wind erosion. A mature forest can reduce water erosion to as little as one-thousandth of the rate on unprotected disturbed soil. In many circumstances, mature sod covers all, but eliminates soil losses caused by water erosion. When time needed to establish live cover proves impracticable, numerous types of mulches can be used for temporary cover. Mulches provide substantial protection from erosion, but they are not as effective as live covers. Every effort should be made not to disturb existing vegetation and to reestablish good cover as soon as possible after grading.

Other factors that influence design considerations include the condition of the exposed soil surface and the ratio of exposed area to undisturbed area.

To summarize, ideal planning balances all characteristics of a given site and incorporates the results into a final design that is functionally, environmentally, and economically sound. A site plan that is in accord with current erosion and sediment control practices will maximize retention of undisturbed areas and existing vegetation, and minimize the amount of clearing and grading to that which is absolutely necessary for the proper construction of homes, roads, and utilities. Erosion and sediment problems can usually be reduced to an acceptable level without placing undue burdens on the home builder, the homeowner, or the community.

Maintenance Requirements

Most erosion and sediment control measures require regular maintenance. Events such as droughts or storms may necessitate immediate repair or replacement. Regular preventive maintenance should be included in the construction program, and both the purchaser and the community should be made aware of control measures requiring future maintenance.

Vegetative cover normally requires watering and perhaps fertilizing until permanent maintenance responsibility is delegated. Structures formed by mounding may need to be rebuilt to restore them to their original heights. Channels may need to be recut if sedimentation or washover makes them ineffective. Maintenance of any measure placed across a traffic area will be made difficult by vehicle passage.

Maintenance equipment cannot be operated safely on slopes with gradients steeper than five to one. In fact, maintenance complications can arise on slopes no steeper than three to one. Accordingly, if excessively steep slopes are incorporated into the grading plan, the vegetation planted should be expected to flourish over the long term without maintenance.

During the construction period, maintenance is essentially a perpetuation of the control measures incorporated in the final design. Such measures may need to be restored partially or fully if their effectiveness becomes reduced significantly. Responsible planning will provide a written description of all maintenance needed to provide continuing protection to future owners.

Grading

The disappearance of easily developable land from areas near urban centers is necessitating the development of less desirable land. Conversion of such land into residential areas often requires more grading than usual. Grading design techniques should be

considered in the early stages of planning and should be selected to—
- Develop attractive, suitable, and economical building sites.
- Provide safe, convenient, and functional access to all areas of use and maintenance.
- Dispose of surface runoff from the site area without erosion or sedimentation, or collection of runoff as needed for basins, irrigation storage, or water features.
- Divert surface and subsurface flow away from buildings and pavements to prevent undue saturation of the subgrade that can damage structures and weaken pavements.
- Preserve the natural character of the site by minimum disturbance of existing ground forms and meet satisfactory ground levels at existing trees to be saved.
- Create an optimum onsite balance of cut and fill; stockpile suitable topsoil to be used to establish ground covers or planting.
- Avoid the creation of filled areas that will increase the depth or instability of building foundations and pavement subgrades.
- Prevent wavy profiles in streets and walks and avoid steps in walks.
- Avoid earth banks requiring costly erosion control measures, except where they are needed in place of costly retaining walls.
- Keep finished grades as high as practicable where rock is close to the surface, to reduce utility and other excavation costs and improve growing conditions for vegetation.
- Prevent the passage of runoff water over roadways. Ice forms during freezing weather and creates hazardous driving situations.

Modern technology has brought a new perspective to grading and other engineering practices. For example, in earlier days fill was not compacted; it was subject to settlement over a period of time until it reached a questionable degree of stability. Regulations of the times prohibited building on a fill unless the building foundations were deep enough to reach natural ground.

Modern compaction methods, equipment, and techniques have made grading more commonplace. A competent soils engineer can determine the amount of compaction necessary to prevent undue settlement for fills of almost unlimited depths. The amount of grading necessary is normally determined by the number of lots to be obtained and the amount of earth to be moved. These two factors are balanced to arrive at the most economical development method.

Grading Analysis

Decisions regarding the amount of grading are based on simple economics. With minimum earth movements, a given parcel of land will yield a certain number of lots conforming to the minimum lot size required by zoning. In areas where land costs and density requirements are low, grading will probably be minimal; where land costs and density demands are higher, grading is likely to be more extensive.

A topographical map showing the existing contours of the area is necessary for making a grading analysis of a site. From this map a number of trial calculations should be made to determine the most economical balance between cuts and fills. The first trial may indicate that an excessive amount of grading at an excessive cost is required to lessen the cost of improvements and increase the number of lots. Subsequent trials may reduce the amount of grading without significantly increasing other costs and lead to more economical and effective development. Conversely, subsequent trials may lead to the conclusion that conventional development is not feasible. In such a case the builder might consider a form of open space development, which leaves the rougher land to provide an open natural setting. Although this approach diminishes the number of lots available, it avoids grading and enhances the aesthetic setting.

Grading Requirements

The Federal Housing Administration specifies a number of grading requirements that must be followed. Unpaved areas adjacent to buildings must be sloped to direct surface water and roof drainage (including melting) away from buildings at a minimum slope of 6 inches in the first 10 feet of horizontal distance, not extending across sidewalks. Surfaces paved with portland cement concrete must have a slope of not less than 0.5 percent, and bituminous pavements must have a slope of not less than 1.5 percent to insure adequate drainage without ponding.

Those portions of the site not covered by buildings or pavement must have adequate continuous slopes to drain toward watercourses, drainage swales, roadways, and the minimum necessary storm drainage inlets. Drainage swales or channels must be sized and sloped to accommodate design runoff. Runoff should be carried under walkways in pipes with diameters of not less than 8 inches. Swales should be used to intercept water at the top and bottom of banks where large areas are drained.

For positive drainage, a slope of not less than 2 percent for turfed areas is usually desirable, but more permeable soils may have adequate drainage with a lesser slope. Turf banks, where required, should be graded to permit the use of gang mowers, providing a maximum slope of 1 vertical to 3 horizontal (if feasible, 1 vertical to

4 horizontal). Tops and bottoms of all slopes should be rounded gently in transition curves for optimum appearance and ease of maintenance.

Site areas must be roughly graded to comply with the foregoing criteria. Subgrade should be established parallel to the proposed finish grade, at elevations to allow for the thickness of topsoil or other surface. In fill areas, all topsoil, debris, and other noncompatible materials should be removed, and all tree stumps removed or cut out 18 inches below grade.

On sloping areas to be filled, if the original soil is clay it should be scarified to provide bond for fill material. Fill material should be free from debris and have a moisture content near the maximum when it is placed. Fill must be compacted to a density that would avoid damaging settlement to drainage structures, walks, or other planned improvements.

Other Considerations

Most projects with more than minimal grading are located on rolling to rough terrain, and geological problems may be present. Engineers can design grading plans that avoid most of the geological hazards; soils engineers can design corrective measures for unavoidable hazards.

With the exception of rock, clay is the most troublesome of common materials found on building sites. Expansive soils, which commonly have a high clay content, have caused major problems to home builders. Special foundations can eliminate house damage caused by soil expansion. In subdivisions designed for higher density, correcting the soil itself may be more economical. Techniques used for soil correction include controlled saturation, stabilization using lime, and reconstitution using closely controlled water content and compaction.

If the amount of cutting and filling to be done at a site is substantial, the builder must determine whether or not the in-place material is suitable for backfill. If not, and if hauling in large amounts of fill material is not economically feasible, other possibilities should be explored. For example, an area highway contractor may be searching for a suitable location to dump excess material.

Provision of proper drainage is another important consideration during cut and fill operations. Excessively flat grades, low spots, and entrapment can cause saturation of the fill, requiring expensive excavation, aeration, replacement, and recompaction of previously filled areas.

Labor, equipment, and costs involved in grading operations can vary widely, depending on the size of the development, the amount of earthwork necessary, and the nature of the problems encountered. The engineer should help select the types of equipment to be used, especially in the case of major operations such as large-scale compaction.

Wherever possible, street alignments should follow the natural terrain. Utility lines should be located within areas that will be graded or distributed for other purposes.

The benefit of aesthetic grading should be considered as an integral part of development. Scenic views, attractive uses of open space, and preservation of natural beauty can be balanced intelligently with minimal grading, cost, and marketing factors. These considerations, coordinated with a good site plan, will enhance the developer's reputation and provide a pleasant environment for human habitation.

Stormwater Management

A relatively new concept, stormwater management has developed into an important design factor for all residential, commercial, and industrial developments. The increased emphasis on the control of stormwater and pollution transported by stormwater has led communities to establish techniques designed to use the natural features of a site while accommodating new growth. As an integral part of a community storm drainage system, stormwater management serves two basic functions: to increase infiltration and to delay runoff. Stormwater management is a part of the storm drainage system and an important part of Section 208 of the Clean Water Act of 1977. Stormwater management techniques and other best management practices are control measures that are intended to reduce and prevent "nonpoint" source pollution.

Numerous documents address storm drainage issues on a technical basis or as an overview. NAHB's *Residential Stormwater Management* is an excellent bridge between the overall concepts of stormwater management and the technical issues surrounding the various approaches to stormwater management.

Basic Principles

In establishing a comprehensive stormwater management approach, several basic principles should be considered:
- A basinwide or watershedwide stormwater management plan designed to meet the objectives of stormwater control should be a primary goal of the public sector.
- The quantity of runoff from any given site should not differ

significantly from that generated before development and after development.

- Capital costs, operation and maintenance costs, liability, public convenience, risk of significant water-related damage, and environmental protection and enhancement should all be taken into account in the development of a stormwater management program.
- Natural features of a site should be preserved to enhance water pollution control, to maximize economic and environmental benefits, and to improve the effectiveness of natural systems.
- Site-specific characteristics vary considerably because of the natural environment and the regulations governing the development process. Stormwater management design parameters should be flexible to meet site characteristic variations.
- A balance between private and public ownership, operation, and maintenance responsibilities is necessary in developing a stormwater management program for any area.
- Use of a "blue-green" area for stormwater management facilities should be considered for aesthetic purposes in the subdivision design.
- Use of stormwater management facilities should be evaluated on the basis of their ability to reduce storm drainage facility costs, reduce erosion and sediment production, reduce maintenance costs of downstream natural channels, and reduce downstream flood losses and possibly the size of the flood plain.
- Groundwater recharge potential should also be considered.

Stormwater Management Criteria

Many localities are arbitrarily establishing stormwater management criteria regardless of the benefit attained upstream or downstream. The basic guideline is the design storm for which the facility is designed, and the design storm selected for the release of water. The most stringent requirement is designing the storage facility based on the difference of a 100-year storm before and after development. This approach would be appropriate for certain situations and generally only on a watershed basis. For development purposes, onsite stormwater management facilities should be designed to complement the storm drainage systems serving the subdivision.

Some areas of the country use stormwater management practices only on a watershed basis. However, if facilities must be incorporated in the subdivision design, the developer should only be required to provide management facilities for the stormwater originating on that subdivision or site. The facility design should not have to provide storage capacity for upstream runoff, but it should accommodate the passage of the flow through the facility.

Stormwater management criteria should promote flexibility in design because natural drainage courses usually do not follow property lines. In many cases subdivisions have several distinct drainage courses that require a multitude of control facilities. However, if the ultimate point of discharge is within the same watershed, possibly ample storage capacity can be provided at one location and reduce or eliminate a facility for another drainage course.

Stormwater management techniques vary from region to region, as do the requirements governing the approaches taken, but the requirements could be attained by:

- Providing a comprehensive watershed plan that is constructed and financed by local governments.
- Entering into a government-developer cooperative effort to provide various approaches.
- Entering into a cooperative effort with other developers.

Hydrology

Hydrology is a science concerned with the behavior of water under the ground, on the surface of the ground, and in the atmosphere (Figure 6-7). Stormwater systems for residential developments are designed primarily to accommodate water flowing over the surface during and after a storm.

Design Considerations

The analysis of any stormwater system requires data on the rate of flow, watershed characteristics, hydrology, and design methodologies. The most accurate method of determining peak rate of flows is keeping stream gauge records over a long period of time. Most localities have not undertaken a stream gauging policy until recently because of the Federal Emergency Management Administration's National Flood Insurance Program. However, stream gauging can be misleading in watersheds undergoing development. In addition, these data do not incorporate the total volume or time distribution of flow in the characteristics of a watershed. Rainfall, duration, and frequency data can be established by using the U.S. Weather Bureau's Technical Paper No. 40, published in 1961.

Developing the values for each of the hydrology relationships provides the design community with the necessary basis for designing stormwater runoff systems. Variations in seasonal precipitation, storm patterns, and runoff preceding the storm must be taken into account also in establishing the hydrology base for a community.

In summary, hydrologic design is the analysis of the peak rate of

Figure 6-7. Hydrologic cycle

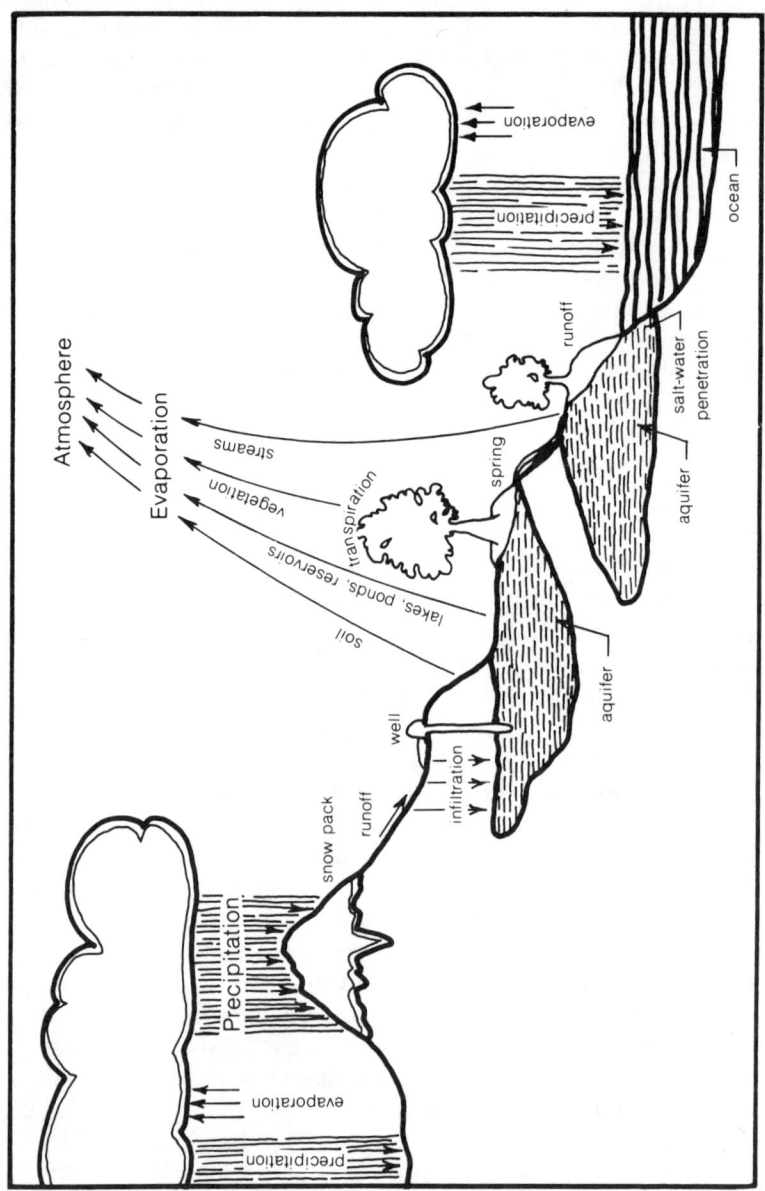

Source: National Association of Home Builders, *Residential Stormwater Management*

flow or runoff, volume of runoff, and time distribution of flow. The storm return period is a primary factor in the hydrologic design of storm drainage systems. The storm return period is the frequency with which a given storm is equalled or exceeded in a period of years. For any hydrologic approach, designers or developers should be aware of the watershed characteristics because a change can increase or decrease the drainage system costs for a particular site. Present and future land uses should also be considered, including the type of cover and percentage of impervious areas. In addition, soil type, vegetative cover, watershed slope and size, and existing and future drainage systems will all affect the watershed runoff to some degree. The hydraulic design of a storm drainage system is an empirical approach, and the accuracy of the calculations determines the effectiveness of the drainage system.

Estimating Runoff

Design of storm drainage, retention, and detention facilities can be approached in a number of ways. The most common method for estimating the design storm runoff is the rational method, which is based on the relationship of runoff to rainfall. This method was first introduced in 1889 and is generally used for drainage basins of up to 200 acres in size. For drainage basins that exceed 200 acres, a hydrograph method is generally used for the design of the drainage facilities. A hydrograph method is based on the residue of rainfall.

The rational method has limitations, but the formula can be used to estimate the peak rate of runoff at any location within a watershed. The rational formula is expressed as:

$$Q = CIA$$

Q = Maximum rate of runoff, in cubic feet per second.

C = Runoff coefficient representing a ratio of runoff to rainfall (Figure 6-8). This value varies according to the characteristics of the drainage area. The rational formula has limitations because the runoff coefficient does not vary with the storm frequency, the storm duration, or the size of the drainage area.

I = Average intensity of rainfall for a storm duration equal to the time of concentration, in inches per hour. The time of concentration to the point under consideration is the sum of the overland flow time and the travel time of the runoff, in an open or closed channel, improved or natural drainage system.

A = Drainage area tributary to the point under consideration, in acres.

Figure 6-8. Runoff coefficients

Description of area	Runoff coefficients
Business	
Downtown	0.70 to 0.95
Neighborhood	0.50 to 0.70
Residential	
Single family	0.30 to 0.50
Multi-units, detached	0.40 to 0.60
Multi-units, attached	0.60 to 0.75
Residential (suburban)	0.25 to 0.40
Apartment	0.50 to 0.70
Industrial	
Light	0.50 to 0.80
Heavy	0.60 to 0.90
Parks, cemeteries	0.10 to 0.25
Railroad yard	0.20 to 0.35
Unimproved	0.10 to 0.30

Character of surface	Runoff coefficients
Pavement	
Asphalt or concrete	0.70 to 0.95
Brick	0.70 to 0.85
Roofs	0.70 to 0.95
Lawns, sandy soil	
Flat, 2 percent	0.05 to 0.10
Average, 2 to 7 percent	0.10 to 0.15
Steep, 7 percent or more	0.15 to 0.20
Lawns, heavy soil	
Flat, 2 percent	0.13 to 0.17
Average, 2 to 7 percent	0.18 to 0.22
Steep, 7 percent or more	0.25 to 0.35

Source: American Society of Civil Engineers, *Design and Construction of Sanitary and Storm Sewers*

Before designing a drainage system, it is necessary to plan the most appropriate systems for the development. Advance planning of drainage systems can benefit the overall development design and help limit the development costs associated with drainage facility construction. The following factors should all be considered in determining the drainage needs of a subdivision:

- Right-of-way requirements
- Costs
- Availability of material

- Hydraulic capacity requirements
- Storage requirements
- Soil erosion and sedimentation criteria
- Topography
- Aesthetic and community character
- Street and traffic pattern
- Pedestrian traffic
- Recreational needs
- Maintenance

In accordance with accepted engineering practices, all hydrograph methods include the following basic steps:

- Computing the runoff for the design storm by increments of time.
- Determining a unit hydrograph for the drainage area.
- Applying the runoff for each increment of time to the unit hydrograph and using the resulting intermediate hydrographs to obtain the hydrograph of the design storm. A unit hydrograph is defined as a hydrograph of direct runoff resulting from an inch of effective rainfall uniformly distributed over the drainage area at a uniform rate during a certain time span (Figure 6-9). The unit hydrograph theory described comprehensively in professional publications has been used for determining runoff values for drainage areas varying from several acres to several hundred square miles.

Drainage Systems

The two basic components of a total stormwater runoff system are closed and open drainage systems. Each of these systems can be broken down even further into minor and major drainage systems. Delineating the different design parameters for major and minor systems is a matter open for discussion. However, the logical delineation would be for a major system to be designed to accommodate a 100-year storm, and a minor system to be designed to accommodate a 10-year storm. This section addresses only minor drainage systems.

Minor drainage systems include the components of site drainage facilities, swales, open channels, street drainage facilities, and closed-conduit systems. The primary objective of a minor drainage system is to collect surface runoff before it becomes an inconvenience to the public. The minor system conveys the surface runoff to an acceptable outlet within the major drainage system. Minor drainage systems are generally located in tributary areas, the upper reaches of a watershed, and within subdivisions (Figure 6-10).

Minor drainage facilities can be laid out in accordance with the development plans, topography, and existing conditions. In either closed or open systems, the total drainage approach should use natural drainage systems such as ditches, swales, or small streams instead of a closed-conduit system. Also, the alteration of the nat-

Figure 6-9. Hydrographs

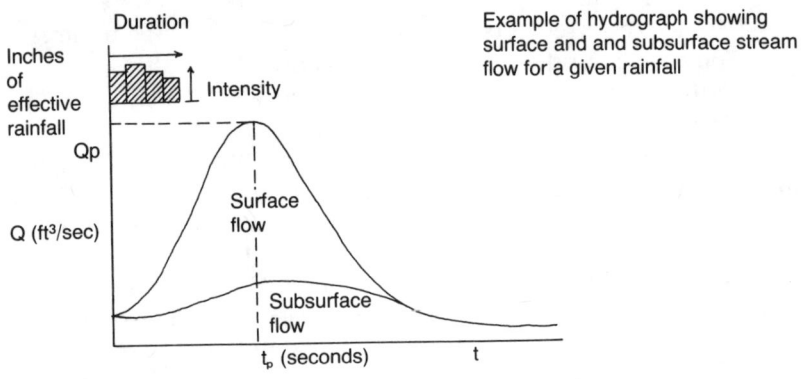

Example of hydrograph showing surface and and subsurface stream flow for a given rainfall

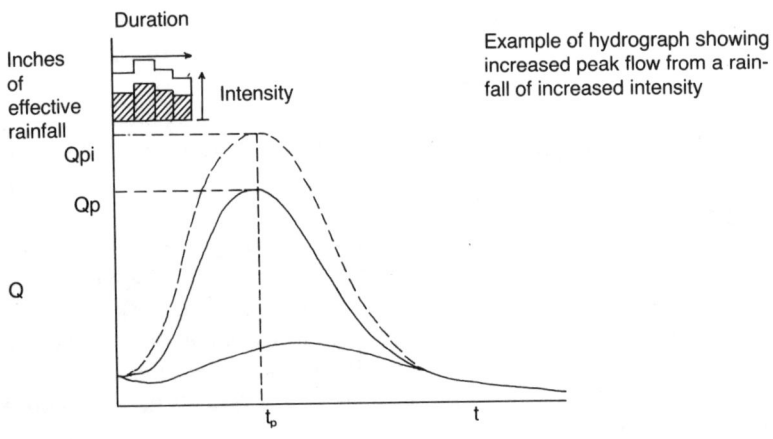

Example of hydrograph showing increased peak flow from a rainfall of increased intensity

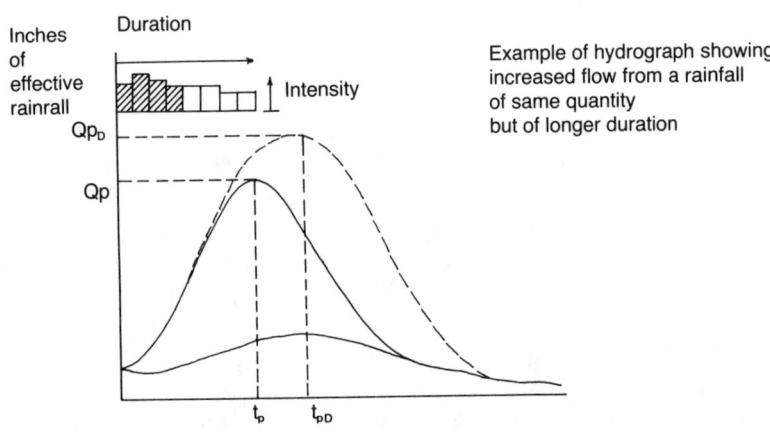

Example of hydrograph showing increased flow from a rainfall of same quantity but of longer duration

Source: U.S. Environmental Protection Agency

Figure 6-10. Example of watershed

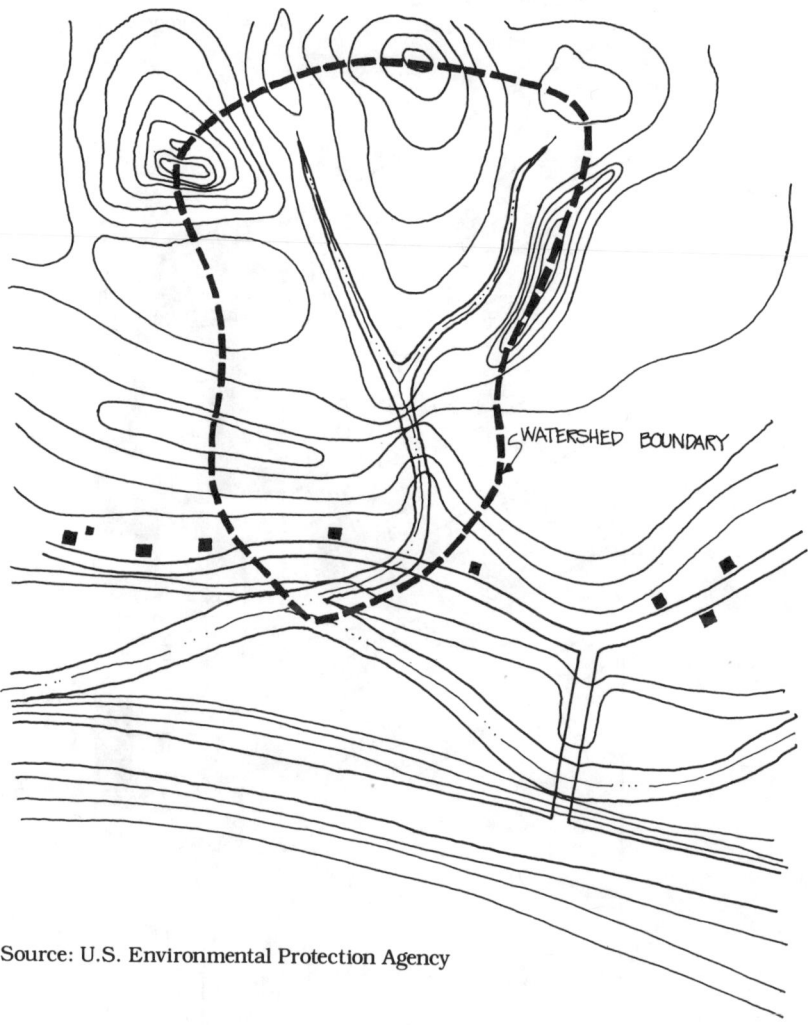

Source: U.S. Environmental Protection Agency

ural drainage ways, the location of collection or entry points into the system, the location of the discharge points, and the necessary rights-of-way should all be evaluated (Figure 6-11).

NAHB recommends a design change from wide, straight streets with curb and gutter to functional streets with roadside swales. However, from vehicular, pedestrian, and drainage perspectives, certain urban areas may need to design roadways with a totally closed drainage system that includes curbs and gutters, inlets, manholes, and closed conduits to convey the runoff to an acceptable

Figure 6-11. Summary of considerations relevant to design of channels and conduits

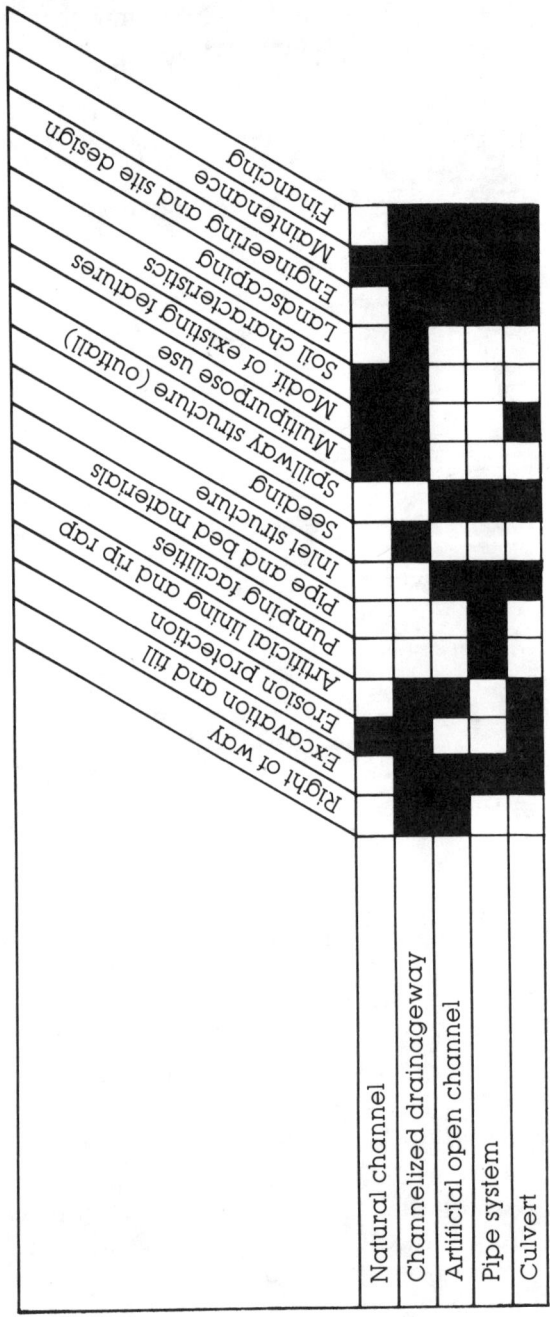

Source: Maryland Department of Natural Resources

outlet. In these instances, street patterns should be developed to reduce pipe lengths and to convey the runoff adequately from adjacent property and from the street. Stormwater runoff accelerates pavement deterioration and increases street maintenance costs incurred by the community. Stormwater runoff also affects the traffic-carrying capacity of the street. To ensure that the main function of a street as a traffic carrier is maintained, the following stormwater runoff conditions must be considered:

- Sheet flow across the pavement from water falling on the pavement surface
  - Gutter flow of runoff flowing adjacent to the curb
  - Stormwater runoff ponding at low points
  - Spread of the runoff flowing adjacent to the curb
  - Splashing of pedestrians caused by street drainage flow and vehicular traffic
  - Cross-street flow resulting from the water flowing across the pavement

The street flow can be estimated by the rational formula. Specific criteria—established to ensure that drainage capacities are maximized and that traffic movement during the design storm is maintained—dictate the street drainage design. The criteria for the spread of water across a street are contingent upon the cross slope of the street, the curb design, and the maintenance of through-traffic lanes. Cross slopes vary considerably from jurisdiction to jurisdiction, from street classification to street classification, and from normal crown streets to super-elevated streets; however, a steep cross slope can be established at 5 percent. Curbs should not be overtopped for any classification street, and two clear 10-foot lanes should be maintained for a collector street. One lane should be maintained as a subcollector, and a spread equal to one-half of the pavement width should be maintained for a lane or place.

Flow across intersections should be limited to ensure an adequate stopping zone area for the intersecting street and to lessen the pedestrian conflict in high-volume pedestrian areas. Probably the most effective method of reducing the flow across an intersection is the proper placement of inlets with adequate capacity to remove the runoff. This procedure is consistent with the approach for designing the sump inlets, or more commonly, the inlet at the low point in the grade. Sump inlets should be designed to decrease the chances of clogging; therefore, most designers prefer a curb-opening inlet or a combination grate and curb-opening inlet.

The capacity of either type of inlet is reduced by a certain percentage to account for clogging. Street inlets such as curb opening or grate inlets have a specific capacity based upon the cross slope and grade of the street. A grate inlet is a metal grid encased in a frame that is generally placed parallel to the gutter flow. The increased emphasis on bicycle traffic has made this configuration, although hydraulically efficient, a potential hazard.

Researchers have developed alternative approaches that may reduce the bicycle conflict but, in doing so, also reduce the hydraulic capabilities and therefore increase drainage costs. Several ideas involve the use of only curb-opening inlets and the provision of deflectors to increase the inlet capacity. The grade configuration can be altered to permit bicycle traffic and maintain the highest possible capacity. Obviously, the more inlets that are necessary to remove the stormwater runoff adequately, the higher the cost.

Proper development design eliminates the conflicts described. Federal Highway Administration circulars present the most authoritative data available on the capacity of curb-opening inlets. Research efforts by Colorado State University and Johns Hopkins University, among others, have helped designers, developers, and government officials place inlets so that they will intercept the maximum flow possible.

Flow velocity in the gutters is another important factor in providing adequate drainage facilities. *Residential Stormwater Management* recommends that the velocity in the deepest part of the gutter be limited to 10 feet per second. It goes on to say that the Manning equation can be used to compute the velocity in the gutter. This equation can be found in many hydraulic books. For this equation, the depth of the gutter flow at a point 6 inches from the face of the curb is used for determining the hydraulic radius for working out the equation.

Flood Plains

Flooding is an integral part of the hydrologic cycle. Natural drainage courses cannot, at times, transport the quantity of water within their banks. When this happens, the possibility of a threat to human life and property investment arises. Many communities, such as Johnstown, Pennsylvania, are "flood prone," and receive national attention when flooding occurs.

National Flood Insurance Program

Because the flood protection systems of some communities will never be adequate to withstand the forces of nature, Congress enacted the National Flood Insurance Program in 1963. The Federal Emergency Management Administration (FEMA) in the Department of Housing and Urban Development was charged with the administration of this program. FEMA identifies the flood hazard areas within jurisdictional boundaries. Of the 17,500 communities evaluated by FEMA, more than 2,200 have been identified as flood hazard areas.

The primary goal of the National Flood Insurance Program is to reduce the amount of property exposed to damage from flooding. The program was established to make flood insurance available at low rates to property owners in flood prone areas and to require flood plain management in flood prone communities. In essence, it is a federally subsidized insurance program, and communities can elect to participate in it. A community choosing to participate gains the insurance coverage, but only if the community regulates new construction and development in the flood hazard areas.

State and Local Regulations

The flood hazard area is delineated flood level that has a one percent chance of occurring in any given year. This frequency is defined as a 100-year flood by FEMA and by many states that have adopted legislation similar in intent to the FEMA program. Some communities do not use the 100-year flood as their base flood because the costs attributed to complying with its requirements can be burdensome to both the public and private sectors. They have opted for a more practical limitation of a 50-year storm. The difference in the water surface elevation from a 100-year storm to a 50-year storm is approximately one foot. That difference can be a dramatic and costly requirement to any community, and the removal of land caused by this flood area will be substantial under any topographical conditions.

Many local communities have developed comprehensive and often very stringent flood plain regulations and use zoning regulations and building codes to enforce them. Building codes for flood plains provide that the lowest floor elevation of a building adjacent to a flood plain shall be so many feet above the 100-year flood plain elevation. In some jurisdictions, 2 feet above the 100-year flood plain elevation is used. In some respects, the determination of the flood level already has safety factors built into the calculations. A local jurisdiction that imposes an additional elevation restriction seems to be overly conservative.

Flood Plain Management Objectives

The difference between stormwater management and flood plain management is that stormwater management is intended to control stormwater runoff, and flood plain management is intended to control the land use of flood hazard areas. The objectives of flood plain management for any community should:

- Protect adjacent, downstream, and upstream land, public and private, from flood drainage.
- Minimize unjustified costs to the private and public sectors caused by unjustified development within flood hazard areas.
- Reduce risks to the homeowner from threats to health, safety, and economic loss.

Where does the flood plain level of protection start? Does a flood plain exist along every stream, drainage course, swale, or channel? Technically, a flood plain area exists along each of these facilities, but to delineate a flood plain along each drainage course is not always practical.

Flood Plains and Site Design

Determining the limits of a flood plain is critical to any subdivision design. Several methods can be used to incorporate the flood plain area within the subdivision design. The primary methods of considering flood plains include separating the flood plain from the lots and deeding the area to the parks and recreation department as open space. As an alternative, the flood plain can be included as part of the lot with the flood area considered either a part of, or an addition to, the lot size.

Selecting the method of incorporating the flood plain area within any subdivision entails many considerations. The overriding consideration, however, is the selection of a method that allows lot planning flexibility to meet the intention of the overall subdivision design. Flood plain limits can be determined in several ways, one of which is a sophisticated computer program analysis. For a detailed hydraulic analysis, professional assistance should be used to determine the flood plain area.

Several components of a flood plain must be evaluated during flood plain analysis (Figure 6-12). The water surface elevation is contingent upon several hydraulic factors such as channel roughness or coverage, channel slope, channel cross section, and the total discharge to that point (see the drainage section of this chapter to determine the discharge value of flow). In residential neighborhoods the velocity of any flood waters can be a danger to life, and the damaging effect of the water increases as the velocity increases; therefore, the velocity should be held to a minimum.

Hydraulic analysis is a complicated process with many variables and critical parameters. One of the most important control points is the stream cross section. If the section changes, the characteristics of the flood plain also change. A common flood plain restriction is the amount of fill permitted within the flood plain limits. Generally, filling of the flood plain is permitted until the water sur-

Figure 6-12. Floodplain components

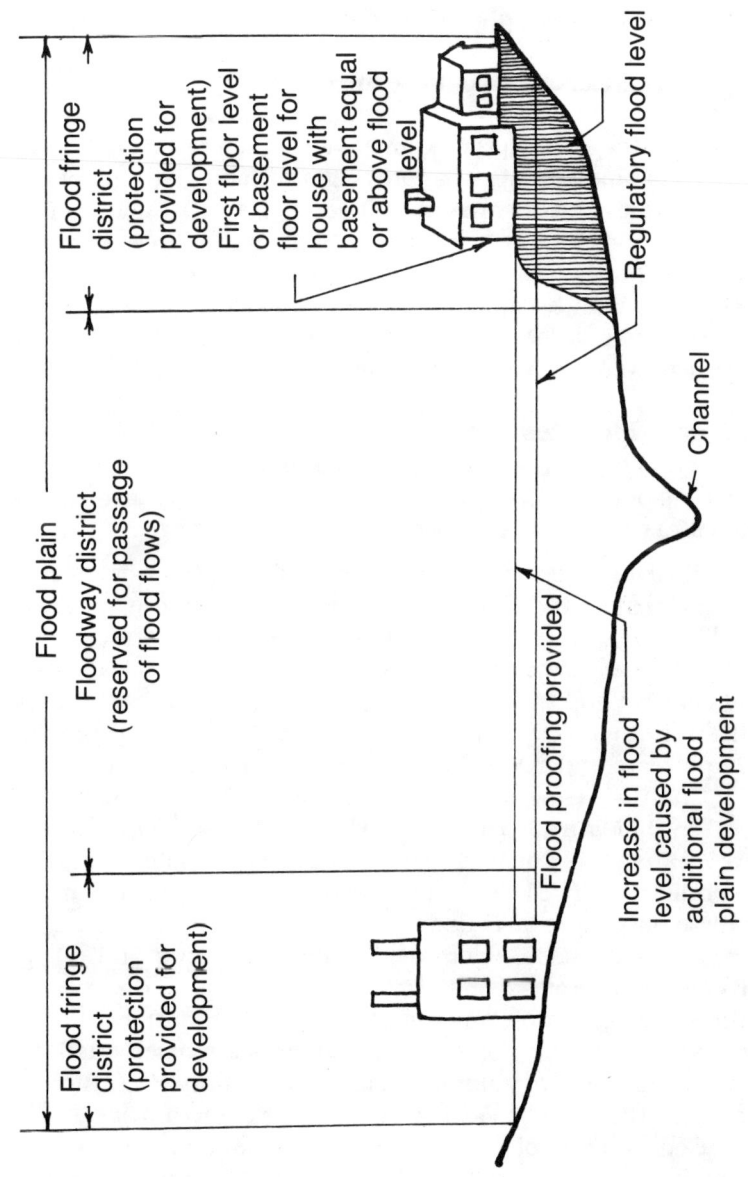

Source: American Society of Planning Officials, Planning Advisory Service Report 277, *Regulations for Flood Plains*

face elevation increases no more than one foot. If the flow is unchangeable and maximizing the land area of a subdivision is important, channel relocation or improvements might be economically feasible. Included with any channel improvement is the change in the cross sectional characteristics and the probable change in velocity.

In some areas of the country, the jurisdictional or agency responsibility for approving such changes to a flood plain varies according to the drainage area. For example, local jurisdictions in Maryland have the responsibility of approving any flood plain improvements up to a contributing area of 400 acres. For more than 400 acres, the Maryland State Department of Natural Resources has jurisdictional authority. This point should be considered when evaluating a parcel of land because delays can be associated with the review process and regulations of several governmental agencies. Hearings to review such proposals can take as long as a year in some areas.

Channel Modifications

Several channel improvement or modification methods can manage the flood plain better than by filling, and may also reduce the potential of in-channel erosion. These methods are:

• Clearing of debris and modifying blockages at bridges or culverts to restore the former hydraulic capacity of the channel. The total carrying capacity of the channel therefore improves.

• Channel excavations to reshape, enlarge, or relocate an existing channel and increase the capacity of the channel. This procedure requires adequate streambank protection, and the changes in upstream and downstream flow must be considered.

• Channel realignment to eliminate meanders that have developed in the natural streambed. This method is an extremely effective means with which to regulate a flood plain and stream within a subdivision. The lot layout would be more conventional and would achieve maximum land use.

• Construction of floodways to allow overflows and relieve the streambed of excessive stormwater discharge. This practice requires a considerable amount of financial commitment, land, and responsibility. A developer rarely finds this approach feasible.

• Use of temporary storage facilities to contain excess stormwater flow. Facilities can be located instream or offstream.

• Construction of retention structures, such as dams and controlling culverts, to reduce the downstream flow. The upstream land area requirements and hydraulic capabilities of the facility are vitally important to the success of this method.

Flood Plains and Residential Construction

The FEMA *Manual for the Construction of Residential Basements in Non-Coastal Flood Environs* clearly states that the technique of floodproofing residential basements should not be used to justify construction in a flood hazard area. Instead, those techniques should be used for construction that must be located in a flood plain.

The manual discusses two systems for waterproofing residential basements. The first system uses the conventional wall and slab surface treatments and a total drain, sump, and pump arrangement to keep water away from the basement walls. The other system uses a more watertight wall and slab surface treatment without a sump or pump. This manual is beneficial in evaluating whether a residential structure could be or should be built within or adjacent to a flood hazard area.

Flood plain regulations locally developed and implemented should be studied from a legal standpoint. As an example, the flood plain regulatory approach should be established as a guide for land use within a flood plain, not as a prohibition of all structures. No court decisions have been made on the reasonableness of flood frequency criteria, whether 25, 50, 100 or 500 years; flood plain restrictions developed for an area where flooding occurs every 50 years may not be appropriate where flooding occurs only once every 200 years.

Another legal question is the accuracy of the data used to define the limitations of a flood hazard area. Obviously, the flood plain limits must be based on supportive data rather than on arbitrary policy. The accuracy of the data is contingent upon the restrictiveness of the regulation and the stage at which information is used in the land development process. For example, a detailed flood plain analysis should not be required at the preliminary or sketch plan stage. A more detailed and comprehensive study is necessary at the final design stage to determine lot sizes and layout. Without question, a more detailed flood plain study provides the information necessary to evaluate the effect of a flood plain on a developable parcel of land.

Natural Open Drainage Systems

The use of open and natural drainage techniques will result in a comprehensive drainage system approach for any development. Natural drainage systems have four major advantages:
- They allow stormwater to filter into the groundwater
- They control the velocity of the runoff

- They extend the time of concentration by controlling the velocity
- They enhance aesthetic values of a site

A combination of these factors contributes to the control of stormwater at or near the runoff values before development. Natural drainage techniques reduce the rate and volume of runoff, provide an alternative method of routing runoff away from structures, and thus avoid inconvenience to the uses of the site. Management of open or natural drainage systems can benefit the community and the homeowners by increasing protection and decreasing costs. Open systems must be maintained to ensure that the system has adequate hydraulic capacity. Many open systems can be classified as natural drainage even if the capacity, alignment, and material differ from the site's predevelopment characteristics.

Overland flow can have the greatest impact on any drainage system design. Long overland flow distances, natural cover, existing topography, flat slopes, and preservation of natural woods all affect the peak rate of runoff. Overland flow time can be determined by various methods, some more rigorous than others. The approach to analyzing overland flow should be consistent because the information is essential to the design of the best storm drainage system possible.

Swales and open channels should be used to accumulate the overland flow and transport the runoff to an acceptable outlet. Wide, flat graded swales and open channels reduce the peak flow, but a flat grade should only be established after the capacity of the channel and soil characteristics have been evaluated.

The velocity of the flow depends upon the quantity of flow, channel configuration, grade, and surface cover, and can be calculated using the Manning equation. For all natural drainage facilities within developments, velocity is a critical factor. Excessive velocity can promote erosion, alter the hydraulic capacity, and cause maintenance of the system to be a problem until a sufficient ground cover is established. This problem can be managed by establishing maximum flow velocities for the different ground covers available for use in an area. Flow velocities can vary from 2.5 to 6 feet per second for easily eroded soils, to 3.5 to 8 feet per second for erosion-resistant soils with the same type of ground cover. Storage and the use of natural open drainage systems can limit minor storm discharge and predetermine flow rates.

David Lakatos, P.E., Water Resources Engineer at Walter B. Satterthwaite Associates, writes in NAHB's handbook *Practical Stormwater Management: Planning and Design Perspectives:*

In many cases, the impression of "problems" associated with a stormwater management system, e.g.—
- over-design or under-design
- excessive design and construction costs
- insufficient relief from downstream impacts
- regulatory concerns; approval delays or rejection
- loss of valuable development area to a stormwater management facility—

will likely be caused by a design that "force fits" the stormwater management system components into the site—as opposed to allowing the components to *blend well* into the natural site characteristics and the proposed development plan. A very important planning step for a system design is to fully identify the natural drainage patterns for a site. After doing so, try as much as possible to maintain the natural patterns and use the physical features of a site to the *advantage* of the stormwater management system.

This process also does not stop at the boundaries of the particular site, but should include the entire drainage area for the drainage paths that cross the site. An example of using nature features productively for a stormwater management system is illustrated in Figure 6-13.

Closed Drainage Systems

A closed drainage system consists of street inlets, manholes, and pipes. Inlets are located to intercept flow on streets, in swales, or in open channels. Closed drainage systems are becoming less popular than open natural systems, primarily as a result of the 1977 Federal Clean Water Act and the increased cost of providing materials for a closed system. Construction and maintenance costs for closed drainage systems are also increasing; these costs are associated with government services. Appropriate hydrologic and hydraulic design methods should be used along with other stormwater management techniques to reduce design discharge and the size requirements of the closed-conduit system to keep costs down.

Location of Closed Drainage Systems

Development designs generally require a closed storm drain system to be placed in an easement on a building lot or located in open space. In some areas of the country a homeowner is responsible for maintenance and replacement of a closed drainage system located on a building lot. An open space location can be the responsibility of a homeowner or condominium association. Both situations can result in an expensive proposition for the owners, and the system may not receive the required maintenance; therefore, a reasonable

Figure 6-13. Using natural features for a stormwater management plan

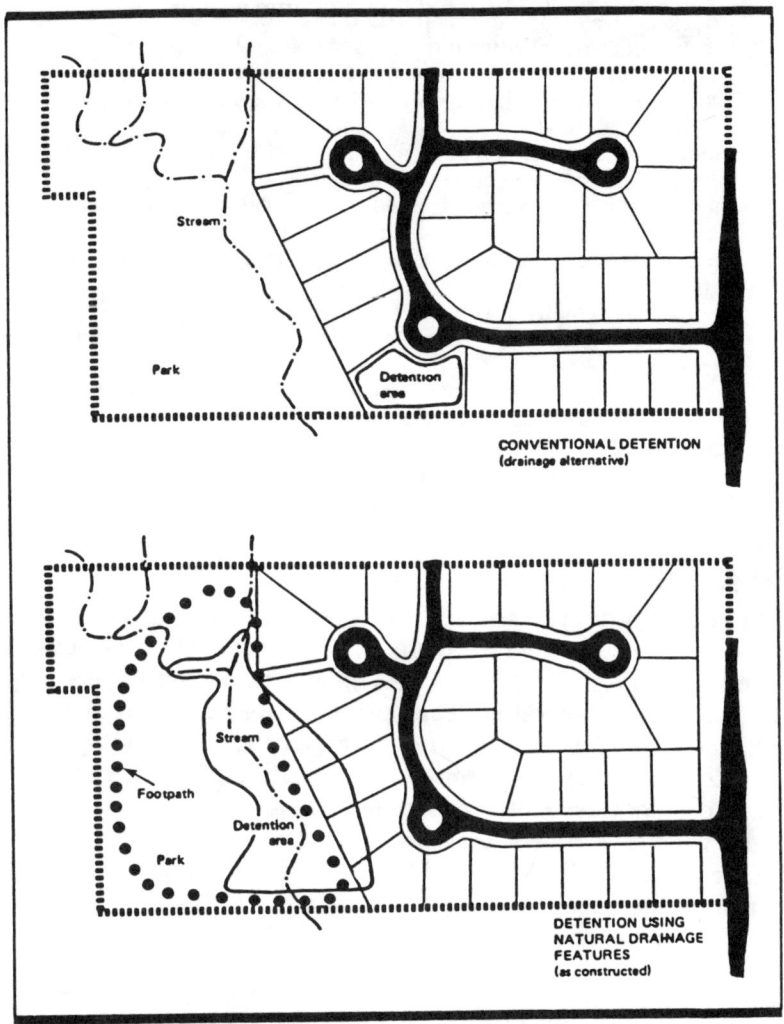

Source: National Association of Home Builders, *Practical Stormwater Management: Planning and Design Perspectives*

solution is for localities to accept drainage systems as a utility and maintain them in the same fashion as water or sewer lines are maintained.

Closed drainage systems that are located within a street right-of-way have a pipe network connecting storm drain inlets and manholes. Access points can include inlets, manholes, headwalls, and junction chambers. The hydraulic parameters of these access points alter the flow and should be taken into account in the design of the drainage system. Many local public works departments establish a maximum access point spacing. For use as a guideline, pipe sizes up to 33 inches should have a maximum spacing between access points of not more than 500 feet, and pipe sizes of 36 to 66 inches, a spacing of approximately 700 feet. Spacing of access points is not a controlling factor for pipes of more than 66 inches.

Horizontal and vertical alignments of a closed drainage pipe system are important considerations in the design, and a certain amount of flexibility is available. Storm drains can be situated on a straight alignment between access points or on a horizontal alignment that conforms to the curvature of the street. A curvilinear alignment provides design flexibility necessary for economical designs without reducing the quality of the system. Bell and spigot or groove and socket pipe can be opened up to a maximum of ½ inch at the joint to achieve a horizontal curve alignment. This approach can also be used for aligning a pipe on a parabolic or circular vertical curve. The common vertical pipe alignment is a constant slope between access points. This type of alignment simplifies the construction process. Storm drain pipe alignments should be coordinated with the location of the utilities: CATV, gas, telephone, water, sewer, and electrical. Joint trenching of several of the utilities helps minimize the alignment conflicts.

Drainage Pipe Selection

Other design considerations that are important in providing an economical and efficient system include material, pipe size, pipe shape, pipe cover, and hydraulic criteria. For any closed drainage system, selection of pipe material should be based on the following factors:

- Strength
- Durability
- Type of joint
- Flow characteristics
- Availability of pipe
- Availability of special shapes
- Installation and handling requirements
- Material and installation costs

In certain situations, pipe material of brick, cast iron, monolithic concrete, polyvinyl chloride (pvc), and vitrified clay can be used, but generally their use for drainage systems is limited by the high cost of material and labor.

The three most commonly used drainage pipe materials are:

	Advantages	Disadvantages
Aluminum pipe	Ease of installation, good structural strength	High friction coefficient, susceptibility to corrosion in acidic soils (can be coated with a bituminous material to improve the hydraulic capabilities and increase corrosion resistance at extra expense)
Concrete pipe (plain or reinforced precast)	Good hydraulic characteristics; good structural strength; wide range of sizes, shapes, and lengths	Weight for installation
Galvanized steel pipe (corrugated metal pipe)	Light weight, long laying lengths, strength, flexibility	Poor hydraulic efficiency, susceptibility to corrosion (can be coated with bituminous material or concrete to increase hydraulic capacity and corrosion resistance at extra expense)

Many local governments establish a minimum pipe size, regardless of the quantity or velocity of the flow. Such restrictive requirements increase development costs without benefitting the drainage system. If a government agency is not willing to consider an alternative, the excess pipe capacity could be used for a stormwater management facility. Pipes should be designed to maximize the cross sectional area, slope, and roughness characteristics of the pipe to accommodate the design flow. A rational formula is used to design the systems, and the travel time of the flow within the system must be taken into account (Figure 6-14). At an access point with several pipe branches, the time of concentration for each pipe branch is used for design, but for the main downstream trunkline, the longest time for concentration is used. A designer should analyze the hydraulic grade line and energy grade line of a system, starting from the downstream end. Pipe velocities should be used as guidelines in designing a system. A minimum velocity of 3 feet per second is necessary for self-scouring; while a 20 feet-per-second velocity is an acceptable maximum. With these parameters, the size of the pipe can be decreased in the direction of the flow. Strict

Figure 6-14. Rational formula showing relation of overland time of travel to overland travel distance, average overland slope, and coefficient C

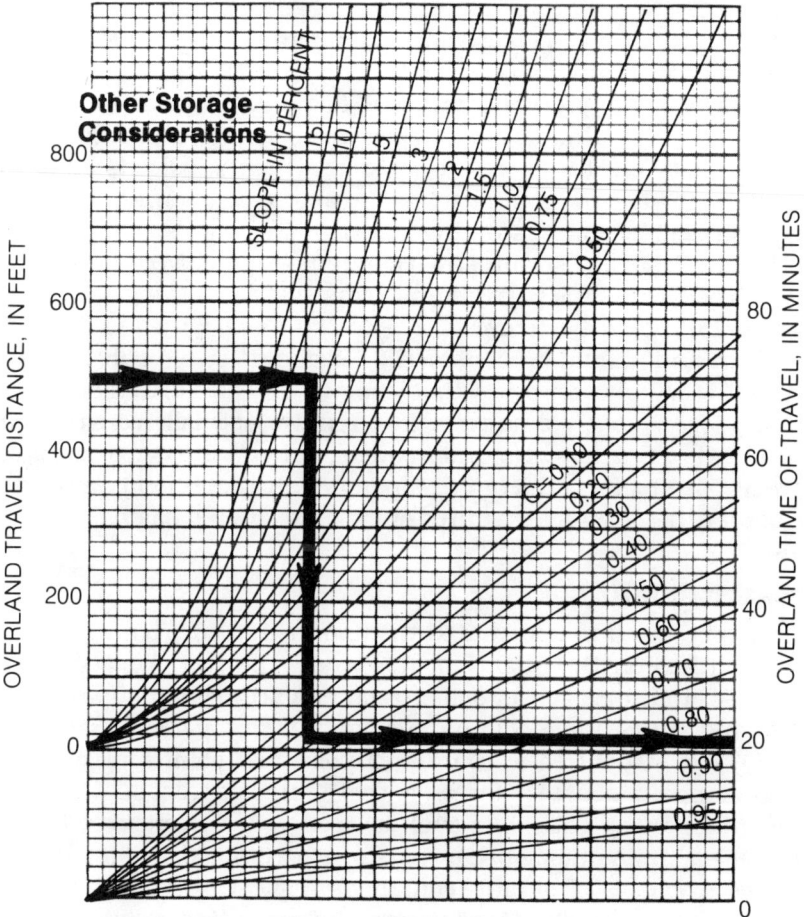

Source: Federal Aviation Administration, *Airport Drainage*

caution should be given to site specific circumstances in this approach, but the design guidelines remain valid.

Normally, closed drainage pipes are circular in shape. If, however, cover or lateral width becomes a problem in the design location, elliptical, longer axis—either vertical or horizontal—arch, and sectional metal pipes can be used instead of the circular pipes. As with any utility, the soil over every pipe should be compacted and covered adequately. Most pipe manufacturers provide a strength table that includes the gauge or class of pipe, cover requirements, and bedding criteria.

Culverts

Roadside swales, open channels, and natural waterways may require a culvert for street crossings. Culverts may also be needed at each driveway to provide continuous flow in a roadside swale; depending upon the swale cross slopes and quantity of flow, however, vehicles may be able to cross the swale without a culvert. Culverts tend to increase the water level in the upstream channel. The flow is controlled by culvert's inlet or outlet.

Federal Highway Administration circulars on culvert design adequately address the particulars of this storm drain segment (Figure 6-15). For major culverts a potential storage area exists upstream and should be considered. Roadside swale culverts are generally metal arch pipes that use prefabricated flared-end sections; larger concrete culverts may require specially constructed headwalls. As with storm drain outlets, culvert outlets may require energy dissipators. Energy dissipators can range from riprap to elaborate baffleblock structures or concrete stilling basins.

Water Quality

Builders need to understand the impact that environmental legislation has on the quality of the water. The two primary water quality guidelines are for soil erosion and sedimentation and surface and subsurface pollution. Section 208 of the Clean Water Act of 1977 is structured to control nonpoint and point source pollution. Nonpoint source pollution is that generated from surface runoff transporting pollutants such as road salt, insecticides, herbicides, lead from automobile exhausts, oil drippings, sediment, etc.

The emphasis of federal regulations implementing Section 208 ranges from controlling land use and implementing various zoning ordinances to revising subdivision regulations and implementing stormwater management requirements. Stormwater management facilities used to intercept the flow of water from a site also control soil erosion and sedimentation, and function as a collection point for the pollutants transported by surface runoff. In addition, many measures can be used after development has been completed to reduce nonpoint source pollution. Consideration should be given to street cleaning operations and alternatives for de-icing salts and monitoring the handling and application of chemicals. If these measures reduce the pollutants generated from a site, the need for stormwater management facilities may be reduced substantially.

Figure 6-15. Example: Culvert design tabulation form

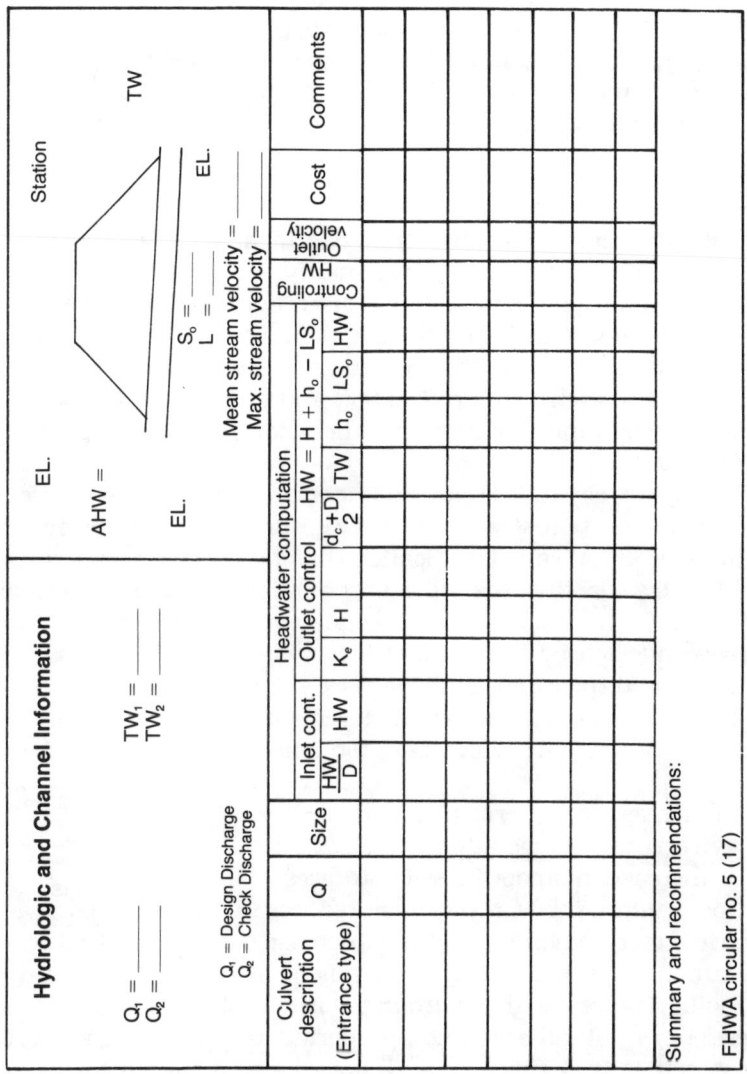

Source: Federal Highway Administration

Another means to reduce nonpoint source pollution and thus reduce the requirements for control measures is the adoption of zoning ordinances that include cluster and planned unit development alternatives. These design alternatives allow the same or greater overall project density while preserving open space to be used for the necessary stormwater management facilities. An approach such as clustering is compatible with the intent of the 208 program. In addition, cluster zoning permits a development design that requires less pavement, minimizes the need for curbs and gutters, reduces the need for closed drainage systems, and stabilizes the cost increases caused by development requirements.

Runoff

A comprehensive stormwater management approach includes the control of the volume, rate, and quality of stormwater runoff. The amount and rate of runoff at any given point is determined by the duration and intensity of the rainfall and by the characteristics of the ground surface across which the runoff must flow. These factors determine the velocity of rate of flow and thus the quantity of rainfall that filters into the ground rather than becoming a part of the runoff flow.

Infiltrative capabilities are an important ingredient to an effective program. The porosity of the surface, the length of time the water stands, and the soil classification directly affect infiltration capabilities by affecting the time in which runoff passes through a watershed, and thus affecting the quantity and rate of flow. Velocity can be affected by the slope of the surface, the roughness of the surface, and the extent of the surface (Figure 6-16).

In evaluating stormwater management techniques for any subdivision design, the following factors affecting runoff must be considered:
- Increase in impermeable surface
- Decrease in vegetation
- Increase in smoothness of surfaces

For example, roadway pavement reduces infiltration capacity; vegetative cover and impermeability increase the quantity and velocity of runoff. Technically, any development increases the quantity of runoff. However, with environmental site planning, reduction of development standards, and appropriate use of land, the increase of runoff is insignificant, and stormwater management facilities might not be necessary. Requiring stormwater management facilities to accommodate the increase in runoff caused by excessive development standards at the local level is certainly a questionable practice. Concepts relating to land development must be coordinated within the intent of environmental regulations. A diversified and fragmented development approach only leads to an increase in housing costs and a reduction in the quality of living environments.

Figure 6-16. Summary of considerations relevant to infiltration design

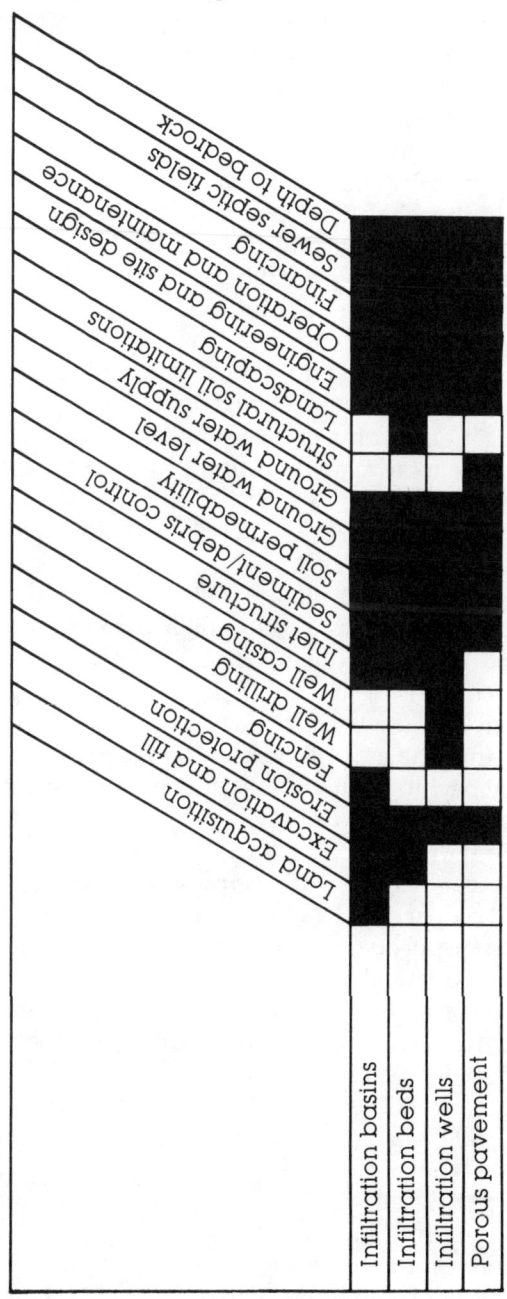

Source: Maryland Department of Natural Resources

Infiltration and Velocity Reduction Techniques

Increasing the infiltration capabilities of a site should be considered during the design phase. Techniques designed to increase infiltration can be used successfully to maintain:

- Runoff volumes and peaks at or near natural conditions
- Sufficient infiltration to shallow ground water
- Recharge of major aquifers

Local governments should be evaluating the use of the various infiltration approaches developed and studied over the years. Many of the approaches can be incorporated in the development design, and other options can be added later at relatively reasonable costs.

Dutch drains are gravel-filled ditches that intercept sheet runoff before becoming a concentrated flow. These ditches can have a drainage pipe in the base to maintain an adequately functioning system. If used properly and located appropriately within the drainage system, Dutch drains can accomplish the following:

- Reduce the total volume of runoff by increasing infiltration
- Reduce peaking effects of local floods
- Recharge groundwater by increasing infiltration
- Improve quality of vegetation
- Reduce the size of drainage facilities downstream

Porous pavement allows water to filter through the pavement and into the ground, thus reducing the runoff generated normally from parking lot or roadway areas. It functions by storing runoff within the pavement and the base, and then releasing the stored water at a slow rate into the ground. Porous pavement can be produced in conventional paving plants, and is stable, durable, and able to withstand freezing and thawing cycles.

Because a reduced storm drainage system reduces costs, porous pavement is competitive with conventional paving. Porous paving can be used on parking lots as well as on driveways and residential streets. When porous pavement is used, the local government should permit a reduction in the size of the storm drainage system. The cost of conventional pavement construction for a residential street with drainage is approximately $1 to $4 more than the cost of porous pavement construction.

Precast lattice blocks and bricks are commonly used for paving in Europe and Canada. The blocks are laid on crushed stone and soil that allows adequate drainage to increase site infiltration. This method of paving allows grass to cover the site and maintains a reasonable amount of stability. The option can be used for architectural landscaping, parking areas, common drives, or streets serving clusters. In addition, this method can be used for lining grass swales or channels to provide protection from soil erosion and sedimentation.

Seepage basins or recharge basins are normally used in areas such as Long Island, New York, to allow runoff to infiltrate the ground and recharge a valuable or sole-source aquifer. These types of facilities are not generally aesthetically acceptable to a residential development because the basins must be deep enough to increase the recharging capabilities and thus require constant maintenance and safety measures. The sizes of the basins vary, but the purpose is to recharge as much water as possible within the shortest period of time. Based upon these parameters, the land area requirements are sometimes less than those required for seepage areas.

Seepage pits or dry wells, unlike Dutch drains, collect and store runoff at one location until it percolates into the ground. The use of seepage pits or dry wells in the storm drainage design increases infiltration and thus reduces the flow from a site. This type of facility can be used effectively in areas where the soil has adequate permeability and where the seasonal high water table does not affect the facility. Seepage pits can reduce local flooding if they are large enough, or several of them are incorporated in the design. Storm drain sizes can be reduced and groundwater can be recharged by using seepage pits. Seepage pits, like dry wells, are more susceptible to clogging than are Dutch drains. Dry wells can be incorporated into the base of storm drain inlets to increase infiltration and allow for some storage of runoff.

Seepage beds are an alternative infiltration facility for areas where the percolation rate of the soil does not allow the use of seepage pits. Seepage bed construction is similar to the construction of a conventional absorption system designed for onsite waste disposal. The system can be constructed on any site except those with high water table or with poorly drained soils. Drains set in gravel ditches reduce the volume and velocity of runoff. The system covers a larger area, which reduces the chances for clogging. In some cases, it can be located under paved areas if the pavement's structure is not affected.

The selection of infiltration systems depends on the soil classification at the site. Infiltration systems require periodic maintenance to diminish the clogging problem. Some problems are associated with any stormwater management facility. The legal basis for requiring these facilities should be examined seriously. Water pollution control ordinances, building codes, flood control ordinances, zoning ordinances, subdivision regulations, and storm drainage ordinances have all been used to require stormwater management.

The legal responsibility for maintenance, damage downstream of a facility releasing excessive flows, and unsafe facilities should also be considered. Requirements for stormwater management facilities should be practical and effective for solving stormwater-related problems; they should not be established on a political basis.

The two remaining and possibly most important aspects of stormwater management require immediate attention from the regulatory sector. First, the financial burden imposed on land developers for constructing stormwater management facilities can be, and usually is, excessive. Local governments should seek design requirements that are practical, effective, and flexible to allow developers to use the method appropriate for the subdivision design and reduce the costs associated with stormwater management construction. Second, the lack of cooperation between governmental entities in establishing consistent design parameters fuels confusion among the building and engineering industries, especially when work is undertaken in several jurisdictions. Local jurisdictions usually allocate substantial funds to develop their own stormwater management criteria without consulting with adjacent jurisdictions. Unfortunately, until the state-of-the-art of stormwater management progresses, this fragmented approach by local governments will continue.

Retention/Detention Techniques

Most stormwater management plans use temporary storage, commonly referred to as a detention facility, to delay onsite runoff. Onsite detention systems are designed to store a quantity of runoff and release it at an appropriate rate of discharge. Detention facilities may provide some aesthetic benefits to a development design; however, the maintenance requirements must be met to ensure an aesthetic facility (Figure 6-17).

Generally, detention facilities can be incorporated without difficulties in any site design. Methods that delay the runoff are more cost-effective than are other types of facilities (Figure 6-18). Detention storage may reduce the size of the storm drainage system for the site. For each site design, storage can be located onsite or offsite.

Cluster developments, which concentrate the density while maintaining blue-green areas, allow for storage onsite via a detention pond, for an example. A high-density area in which the allocation of open space is not readily concentrated may require that a detention or retention facility be located on a stream offsite.

In *Storm Water Retention and Detention*, a report by Robert L.

Figure 6-17. Summary of considerations relevant to detention/retention design

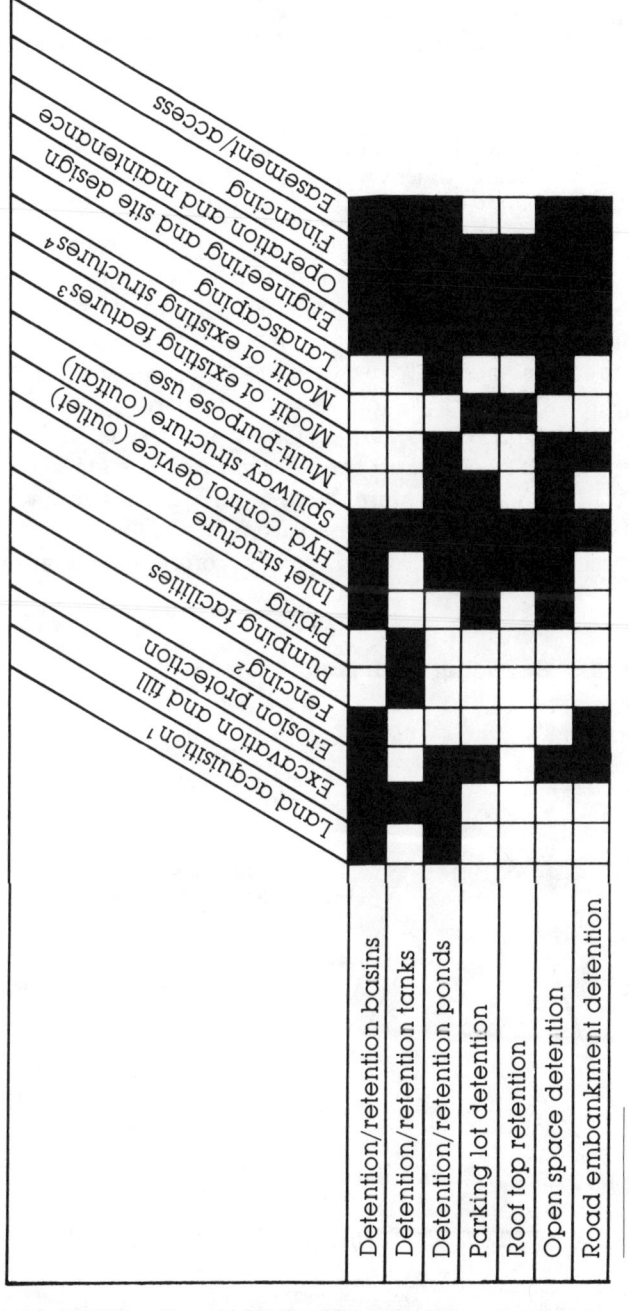

1. Acquisition of land exclusively for construction of control structures.
2. Fencing serving security and/or safety purposes.
3. Regarding, new roads, new bridges, etc.
4. Changes in design (roof tops, parking lots, etc.) serving a control function.

Source: Maryland Department of Natural Resources

Johnson and Robert A. Putt of Lehigh University, retention and detention are defined as follows:

> Retention refers to procedures and schemes whereby stormwater is held for considerable periods of time and causing water to return to the hydrologic cycle via infiltration, percolation or plant evapotranspiration and not via direct discharge to water course. Detention refers to holding runoff for a short time to reduce peak flow rates and then later releasing the runoff into natural or artificial water courses to continue in the hydrologic cycle. The volume of surface runoff occurring is relatively unchanged.

Temporary storage can be accommodated by many methods. As the state-of-the-art progresses, ingenious methods will be developed to meet the characteristics and economies of any development. Among the more commonly used methods for onsite detention are dry ponds, swales, parking lots, and rooftop and subsurface storage. The two design considerations for any of these facilities are the volume of storage needed and the release rate. The storage is basically the volume needed to store the difference in total inflow volume and total outflow volume measured from the beginning of the inflow. The release rate requirements vary from jurisdiction to juris-

Figure 6-18. Reducing peak runoff rates with detention

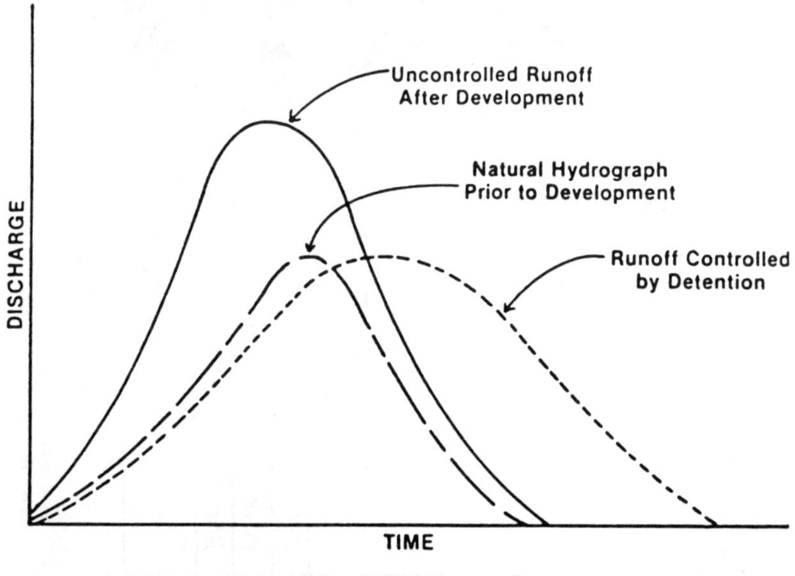

Source: National Association of Home Builders,
Practical Stormwater Management: Planning and Design Perspectives

diction. For practical purposes, a detention facility should be designed for a 10-year storm after development design frequency, and for a 10-year storm predevelopment release rate frequency. Storm duration must be considered in establishing practical parameters; it should be established in accordance with local conditions and watershed characteristics.

Detention ponds or basins can be used effectively to control onsite runoff where infiltration is infeasible (Figure 6-19). Detention ponds are commonly referred to as dry ponds because the facility only stores the runoff on a temporary basis. Detention ponds can be used effectively in cluster developments if ample open space exists. The primary disadvantage in using detention ponds is the constant maintenance required to ensure an aesthetic and properly functioning system. The cost and land area requirements can vary substantially, depending on runoff and site parameters. However, in well-defined topography, a detention pond can be constructed easily, and if it is located on a defined drainage swale, the pond can reduce the costs attributed to the collection system.

Swale storage is an inexpensive, effective, and relatively maintenance-free facility that can be incorporated into any development design. A restricted outlet in the swale will control the flow and, if it is large enough, the swale can be classified as a detention pond.

Parking lot storage is an effective way to use the facilities necessary to serve commercial, multifamily, and industrial developments.

Figure 6-19. Typical detention basin features

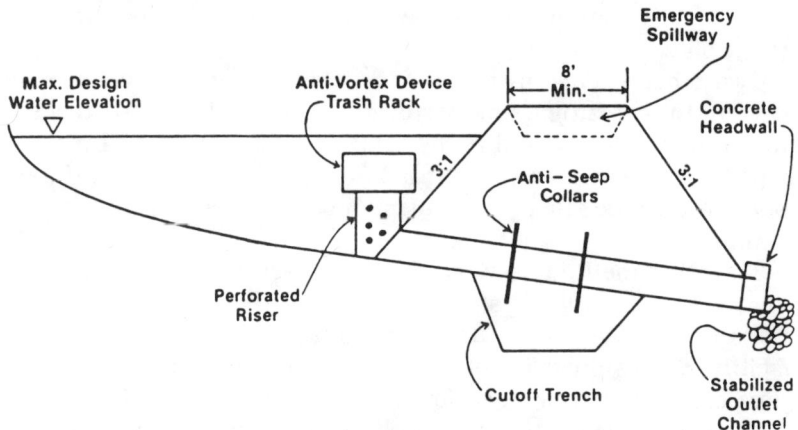

Source: National Association of Home Builders,
Practical Stormwater Management: Planning and Design Alternatives

Parking areas can be designed to store large quantities of runoff, and the development design should consider location of the parking area in relation to drainage requirements. Restriction devices controlling the outflow can vary considerably. However, periodic maintenance is needed to prevent clogging. The primary disadvantage to parking lot storage is the inconvenience to the users of the parking facility. Depending upon the design parameters, the inconvenience resulting from the depth of storage can be minimal. A 6-inch maximum storage depth for parking areas, specifically for automobiles, is a practical guideline. Parking areas for trucks can have a maximum depth of up to 18 inches.

Rooftop storage can be accommodated on commercial and industrial buildings without structural changes that would require a substantial increase in cost. Controlled outlets on flat or nearly flat roofs is an effective means of storing water and releasing it at a predetermined rate. Proper design can minimize the maintenance, potential leakage, and structural problems. The cost can be minimal for this method of stormwater management. Providing parking lot or rooftop storage allows for some trade-offs in locating the facilities to control an entire site. For example, a facility based on the entire site can be designed to accommodate the runoff from a portion of the site, and the remaining portion of the site can allow uncontrolled runoff.

Underground storage may be the last resort if the site cannot accommodate another type of facility or if the density does not allow a more flexible or less costly method. In expensive commercial areas, underground storage may be feasible in tanks, oversized storm drains, or other facilities. As with any stormwater management facility, maintenance remains an important consideration in the design.

Two other storage methods can be evaluated for a development design. Undersizing roadway culverts is an effective method of storing water upstream and releasing it at a slower rate. At times, the topography permits a substantial amount of storage that, if incorporated into the site's plan, can reduce construction costs significantly.

The other method uses the excess storage capacity, if any, in the storm drainage pipe system designed for the site. Local jurisdictions frequently will require minimum pipe sizes that result in a facility overdesigned for the contributing drainage area. The excess pipe capacity can be used for the storage of runoff. This is especially advantageous when the collection system has outlets into a stormwater management pond or lake.

A retention facility is generally located onstream and is designed to impound the runoff by maintaining a permanent pool elevation. Retention facilities can function as a multipurpose facility by being a part of the open space requirements, by functioning as a recreation facility, and by operating as a stormwater management facility. Design parameters for retention facilities differ somewhat from those for detention structures. An impoundment has a certain storage capacity, and if that capacity is exceeded, emergency spillway provisions must be included in the design.

Retention structures can provide an aesthetic advantage to any development, and the costs associated with the construction of such a facility can be offset by the increase in adjacent lot or land values. Again, maintenance requirements are a necessity. The primary maintenance problems come from trash and sedimentation, which can reduce the storage capacity of the facility and decrease its operational efficiency.

The land area requirements can vary considerably. For example, a certain type of soil may require 4 acres of watershed for each acre/foot of permanent pool. Guidelines similar to this should be developed for specific watershed areas. Dams or ponds (retention structures) must be designed in accordance with the minimum safety standards established by the State Water Resources Administration or the appropriate agency within each state. Onsteam retention facilities may have to be designed for a 100-year storm frequency. Similar parameters may counterbalance the cost-effectiveness and benefits of a retention stormwater management facility.

In some states, design parameters are established to clarify the review responsibilities of the various governmental agencies. The primary guidelines include the delineation of contributing drainage area, the normal depth of water at permanent pool state, and the normal surface area of the permanent pool or flood pool. In summary, a retention facility is a major component in any stormwater management plan and is an asset for any development design.

The construction costs for retention/detention facilities vary considerably from area to area. Approximate costs (on a percentage basis) for constructing a detention basin are as follows:

Construction Activity	Approximate Percentage of Total Construction Cost
Excavation	45
Pipe Work	40
Stabilization	15
	100 percent

Maintenance

The responsibility and maintenance requirements for each stormwater management facility should be determined and agreed upon before construction begins (Figure 6-20). Ownership and maintenance responsibilities can be accepted by a homeowners association, the public sector, a government agency, or a developer/owner. Homeowner and condominium associations are appropriate organizations to manage and maintain stormwater management facilities properly. The finances required for maintenance can be incorporated into the association's monthly operation fees.

Developer/owner responsibility may include stormwater management facilities on commercial, industrial, or multifamily sites. However, these facilities and the drainage systems ought to be considered public utilities similar to water and sewer facilities. Stormwater control and maintenance requirements are being de-

Figure 6-20. Operation and maintenance considerations

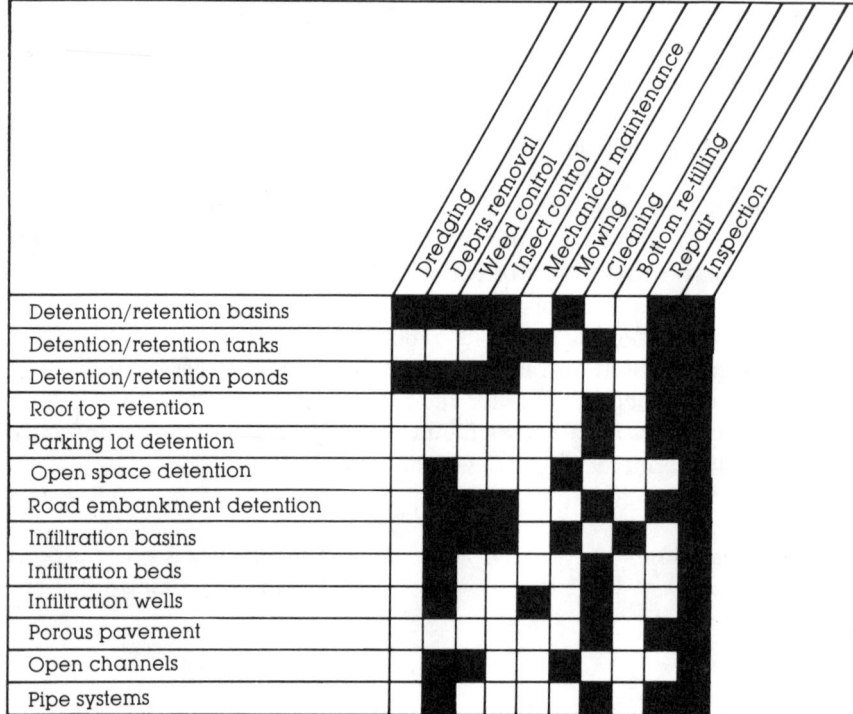

Source: Maryland Department of Natural Resources

veloped to manage runoff in urban areas and should be considered an integral part of the services provided by local governments. Local governments would, of course, have to allocate sufficient funding to hire staff to manage the drainage system properly. The ultimate goal is to provide a high level of service that will protect the basic health, safety, and welfare of the citizenry. Establishing the drainage utility concept is relatively straightforward. The following procedures can be used to formulate the concept of drainage as a utility:

- Define the drainage systems to be included, such as streams, improved channels, storm drainage systems, stormwater management facilities, etc.
- Define the problems and solutions regarding a utility system.
- Define budget needs and develop alternative funding approaches.
- Develop appropriate ordinances of regulations to establish the utility system.
- Organize the utility system, including staff operating procedures, etc.

This utility approach can be used to accommodate the entire urban drainage system or only specific components such as natural systems, improved systems, closed or open systems, and stormwater management systems.

Conclusion

Stormwater management will continue to be refined and modified to meet EPA's Section 208 requirements for urban area stormwater runoff. Prevention or reduction of nonpoint source pollution can be classified into two basic categories: management at the source and management of the collection system. Section 208 is concerned with the collection system management. Stormwater management practices satisfy the intent of Section 208 by reducing the amount and rate of runoff. The parameters established for stormwater management techniques determine whether the approach taken is cost-effective or not. Under the 208 program, stormwater runoff could be collected in stormwater management facilities and treated before it is released at a regulated rate. The costs and associated benefits of this practice will be points of discussion for years to come.

Chapter 7
Water and Sewer

The provision of potable water and the treatment of sewage are municipal functions in most communities. However, it is the developer's responsibility to provide the facilities for transporting water and sewage to the municipalities' sewerage.

This chapter provides developers with a basic understanding of water and sewer systems and their importance to the land development process.

Water Supply Systems

Public Distribution Systems

Public distribution systems are those that are owned and operated by a public body, usually a department of public works or a water works association. The water main does not have to be built or financed by the public agency, and for most new developments it is not. The system is typically built and paid for by the developer and then given over to the public body after an inspection of the system's worthiness or adequacy. Three parameters for the design of a water distribution system of a residential development follow:

Water use figure assigned to the individual—When this design figure was first formulated, it was used to cover all of the water use of a community whether it was business, industry, or fire use. As a result, the figure was placed unrealistically high, and in most areas this higher figure still applies as a per capita design figure. A study of residential use by Johns Hopkins University in 1963-65 shows a large variation in gallons used per capita per day (GPCD). The larger use figures were in the warmer, drier, and more affluent areas, and the smaller use figures were in the cooler, wetter, and less affluent areas. These figures range from 50 to 200 GPCD. Other factors that reduce water use are a high cost of usage and multifamily dwelling units. Conversely, lower usage cost and single-family dwellings increase usage.

Number of persons assigned to the average dwelling unit—This figure, too, has values assigned over a wide range from 2.5 to 5

217

persons per dwelling unit (PPDU). Some values were assigned based on the number of bedrooms per dwelling unit. A listing of the average PPDU is shown in Figure 7-1. Another method of computation using the type of dwelling unit is shown in Figure 7-2. In the recent past, a tendency for families to be smaller and for more people to live alone has caused a drop in the number of people per dwelling unit from 4.9 in 1924, to 3.3 in 1960, 3.1 in 1970, and 2.7 in 1985.

Figure 7-1. Average persons per dwelling unit
(based on bedrooms per dwelling unit)

Number of Bedrooms/Dwelling Unit	Design Value Persons/Dwelling Unit
1	1.8
2	2.8
3	3.8
4	5.0
5	5.5

Source: NAHB

Number of dwelling units per acre allowed under the zoning— This figure varies widely depending on the zoning. Where the zoning allows higher numbers of dwelling units per acre, the PPDU for these types of dwelling units is less because the development consists of apartments or townhouses.

The goal in setting a figure for each of the categories listed above is to arrive at a number of gallons a particular area can be expected to require for residential use, and then to use this figure and additional factors to design a pipe network to serve the area.

Fire Demand

The major volume allotted to the water distribution pipe is not for residential use but is set aside for use in case of fire. Most municipalities require that 500 gallons per minute be delivered to the site of a fire in a residential area of one- and two-story houses.

Higher fire flow figures are used for larger or higher buildings. The Insurances Services Office (ISO) has developed fire flow figures that take into consideration the type of construction, area of the building, number of stories, and the adjacent fire hazards. These figures have been published in the *Guide for Determination of Required Fire Flow*. The figures derived from this booklet are even higher than the 500 gallons indicated above. The use of this source requires a knowledge of fire protection and its principles and formulas because many factors affect the amount of water needed to control a fire. In addition, municipalities themselves are rated as to their fire fighting resources: equipment, location of fire stations, and the expertise and number of their fire fighting force. This procedure is described in ISO's *Grading Schedule for Municipal Fire Protection*.

The average design value of persons per dwelling unit also varies with the dwelling unit type as set forth in Figure 7-2.

Figure 7-2. Average persons per dwelling unit (based on unit type)

Type of Dwelling Unit	Design Value Persons/Dwelling Unit
Single-family	3.8
Townhouse	3.1
Low-rise apartment	2.9
Medium or high-rise apartment	2.7

Source: NAHB

Storage

Water storage facilities serve three purposes. First and most important, they store enough water for fire protection. The amount of water required during a fire is normally much more than can be furnished by the wells or other system sources; therefore, some water must be stored in a tank until needed.

Second, water storage facilities balance the peaks and valleys of user demand. The ability of storage facilities to store water and dispense it when demand is high allows the use of smaller supply sources and pumping facilities and therefore effects an economy of service.

Third, water storage facilities equalize pressures throughout a pressure zone. When water is maintained in the tank, pressure is maintained throughout the system.

Pumps

Pumps are used in a water system to move water from one area to another, usually the area of use. This process sometimes requires that water be pumped through successive booster pump stations until it reaches its destination. Pumps also maintain a minimum water pressure in the pressure zone, normally in conjunction with an elevated storage facility.

Pipe Capacity

Pipe capacity is directly affected by the diameter and the smoothness of the pipe. Smoothness is affected by the type of material and the age of the pipe. Because no formulas in general use age as a parameter, the engineer's judgment generally determines what smoothness coefficient is appropriate. Traditional formulas such as the Hazen-Williams, the Manning, and the Kutter formulas are used by most engineers to determine pipe capacity. These formulas are easy to use and widely accepted, although their accuracy in all cases is suspect. Newer formulas have been developed by the National Bureau of Standards, which are listed in the *Manual of Water Distribution Systems and Development Standards*, published by the NAHB Research Foundation, Inc. These formulas are more accurate.

Pipe Pressure

Pipe pressure is supplied to the pipe by pumps or elevated storage facilities. It is diminished by friction as the water moves along the pipe. The amount of pressure used up depends on the amount of water and the size of the pipe. A small pipe with a large flow uses up more pressure than a larger pipe with the same flow. Economic judgment is necessary when sizing the large distribution mains because a small main may cost less to build but require a larger pump to move the same amount of water and maintain the same pressure.

Pressures within the well-designed system usually vary between 20 and 50 pounds per square inch for one- and two-story structures. The minimum pressure should be higher where three- and four-story buildings are built. The higher pressure requirements are necessary to maintain proper pressure on the upper floors of the dwellings and to furnish water in case of fire. The lower figure and the more arbitrary of the two limits is chosen to minimize water use. Where higher pressures occur, the per capita use of water is higher and maintenance costs are also higher, especially in older systems.

Subdivision Water System

A water system in a subdivision is usually serviced from the outside by a small number of mains determined by the subdivision size. The mains are usually laid out as a network of mesh within the subdivision. Each portion of the subdivision should be serviced by a main that can be supplied from either direction. This practice is called "looping" and is evident in all well-designed systems. It equalizes pressure and in some cases allows the use of smaller pipe.

Fire hydrant spacing is normally based on the maximum distance that a piece of fire fighting equipment can be positioned from a fire hydrant and function as intended. This distance is based on hose lengths of 250 to 300 feet. The fire hydrant spacing is double this figure, or 500 to 600 feet. Another method used to determine fire hydrant spacing is to calculate the spacing required to furnish the necessary amount of water to the site. This calculation is described in ISO's *Grading Schedule for Municipal Protection*.

Within the street right-of-way, the water pipe is usually located on the high side for maintenance accessibility and out of deference to the sewer pipe, which is more economically located on the low side of the street. The water pipe is located on the high side of the street or on the side where the houses are higher.

Valves are installed at pipe intersections so that when a shutdown occurs, a maximum of only one block loses service. The valves should be placed close to the pipe intersections, but they should not be in a heavily traveled roadway.

Materials and Cost

The following types of pipe are allowed by most agencies: asbestos, cement, brass, cast iron, copper, polyvinyl chloride (PVC), reinforced concrete, steel, and ductile (wrought) iron. Asbestos cement pipe has been questioned increasingly by individuals and community groups concerned with the health aspects of this pipe. Whether proven or unproven, these concerns are causing the use of this pipe to be reduced, regardless of its construction cost advantages. The shift from cast iron to ductile iron pipe is caused by a shift by the manufacturers. In fact, ductile iron pipe accounts for the highest percentage of all new construction. PVC pipe is the most economical of all types to construct provided it is allowed under the local building code.

Private Supply Systems

The private water system is one that is not owned, operated, or maintained by a public body. A single well servicing a single house is a private system, but so is an area the size of Alexandria, Virginia, which is serviced by a privately owned water system.

Most of our larger cities' water systems started as businesses and were taken over by the public later. For purposes of this text, a private system is a system of more than one house, a system that would be owned and operated by someone other than the consumer unless it is owned by all the consumers through some organization, such as a homeowners association. Such a method of ownership can effect a savings in areas in which the drilling of individual wells would be costly, such as an area underlain by rock or a deep water table. In such areas, drilling of a few large wells may be the most economical way to service the entire area. Transfer of the system to another owner may be desirable.

Most developers should address this consideration as part of the decisionmaking process on whether a private system should be built or not. The requirements of a private system are generally those of the local Public Works Agency. Where requirements do not yet exist, such as in rural or developing counties, the state health department or public service commission is the determining agency or agencies. In any case, the engineering standards in general use should be used. This procedure would facilitate the transfer of the system to any public agency.

Wastewater Collection, Treatment, and Disposal Systems

The collection, treatment, and disposal of wastewater is of primary importance to this nation's goal of providing better housing for all its citizens. The collection phase of this effort is of major concern to the developer because it is an area of major expense. Collection systems began to be built for major cities in the latter part of the 19th century, although the treatment of wastewater did not begin until the 1930s, when the threat to public health and the pollution of recreational areas became obvious.

In the early days of collection, wastewater was deliberately dumped into the most convenient stream. It did not matter that stormwater, roof drainage, areaway drainage, and other storm-produced water was dumped into the wastewater sewers to flush the pipes. Construction methods of that era allowed groundwater to infiltrate the pipe because it had no effect on the system's operation.

Since the advent of wastewater treatment, the goal has been to keep at a minimum the amount of water that enters the system in order to keep treatment costs low. The efforts to accomplish this goal have been successful and are continuing. Design criteria from the era of combined storm and wastewater sewers are slow to keep pace, and many systems are overdesigned. The developer should be cognizant of which per capita wastewater flow figures are realistic and which may reflect the excessive infiltration of stormwater allowed in an earlier time.

Methods of handling sewage from a single home or a subdivision can be grouped into two general categories—

- Public facilities: Control collection lines placed together with either a treatment plant or a transmission line connecting to an existing municipal treatment system.
- Onsite disposal: Waste treatment at an individual site.

Public Facilities

Basic Design Parameters

The basic sewage design parameters for residential areas revolve around the per capita sewage contribution. Much of the per capita contribution is based on such factors as the amount and pressure of water available and type of housing in which the person lives. Seasonal and regional variations in the per capita use figure also occur; therefore, many standard per capita figures exist, and they can all be correct. The attempt here is to describe a norm or an average figure for use.

"Peaking" is another concept used in sewer main design. This describes the amount of increase in sewage flow over the average flow during the morning or evening, when the highest rates of sewage are being discharged.

Values used for a per capita flow figure vary between 75 and 300 gallons per capita per day (GPCD). The actual sewage caused by an individual is on the order of 60 to 80 GPCD. These figures are from EPA's *Optional Method of Wastewater Flow Estimating*. Another factor that increases this figure is the infiltration and inflow of ground water and rain into the pipe from the house to the treatment plant. Modern construction methods such as more efficient joint and manhole construction have greatly decreased this figure.

Figuring the peaking of sewage flow also varies widely between the regulating agencies. Peaking factors, which must be multiplied by the per capita sewage figure to produce the pipe flow design figure, range from 1 to 4. The recommended peaking factor is 2.5 times the average flow with an allowance of 500 gallons per inch of pipe diameter per mile of pipe for the ground water inflow and infiltration.

Other factors that affect the amount of sewage produced are the number of persons per dwelling unit and the number of dwelling units per acre. The first value has been dropping since the 1920s and is now in the range of 2.7 persons per dwelling unit. This figure, too, varies according to the size of dwelling unit or, more basically, the number of bedrooms in the dwelling unit.

The number of dwelling units per acre is entirely governed by the local authorities and is the means by which the amount of sewage from a particular area can be controlled. For instance, where half-acre lots, or 20,000 square feet per lot, are allowed, the number of dwelling units per acre of total land has been computed to be 1.5. This figure takes into account the land used up by roads and other nonresidential uses.

All these factors are brought together in the design problem shown in Figure 7-3.

Sewerage

The pipes that transport the wastewater from the house to the treatment facility are categorized by their purpose and by their sizes. The sewer house connection that carries the wastewater from the house to the public main in the street is the smallest of all the pipes, but it is not part of the public system and is generally installed when the house is built. The first public main into which the wastewater flows is called the collector. It is generally 6 to 8 inches in diameter. It collects the wastewater from a developed area and delivers it to the point where it will be carried offsite.

An outfall sewer delivers the sewage from the collector to the interceptor. Outfall sewers are slightly larger than collectors, generally 8 to 10 inches, and they are generally located beside a minor stream or swale that drains the developed area.

The final category of pipe is the interceptor sewer, which ranges in size from 8 inches and up. An interceptor flows directly to the treatment facility and is located along major streams.

The difference between an outfall and an interceptor is one of degree. If an outfall sewer serves several developed areas, it could be considered an interceptor. The most obvious differences are between the collector and the outfall-interceptor pipes. In many cases the collector does not follow the natural drainage, but goes where it is needed to service the designated lots. On the outfall-interceptor, usually no individual connections are allowed except at manholes. The primary purpose of these pipes is to transport sewage, not to collect it.

In order to do this, sewers should be designed to carry, when running full, the per capita flow of sewage and normal infiltration

Figure 7-3. Sewage volume calculation

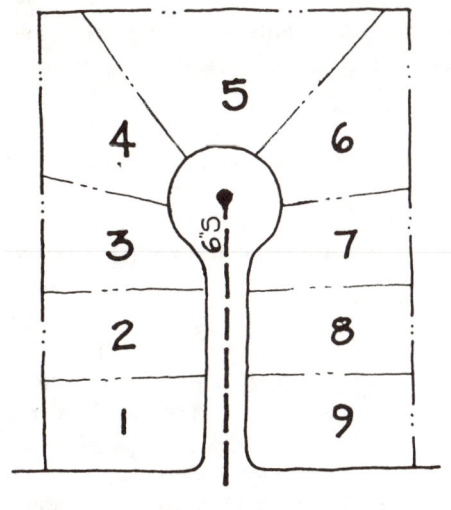

6 Acres
R-20 Zoning
(20,000 square foot lot)
Average house = 3.5 people/unit

6 Ac. × 1.5 D.U./Ac × 3.5 = 32 persons

85 gpcd × 32 = 2720 gallons per day

Inflow-infiltration from the site

600 feet of 6" sewer

$\frac{600}{5280} \times (6 \times 500) = 341$ gallons per day

2720 × 2.5 (peaking factor) + 341 = 7141 gpd

Note: If the actual number of lots can be determined, that number should be used rather than the 1.5 units per acre figure, which is an approximation to be used on undeveloped land to determine the approximate sewage that would be produced by the area.

Source: NAHB

at a flow rate of not less than 2 feet/second. The average per capita flow should not be less than 120 gallons/day. Sewers should be deep enough to receive sewage from basements (if utilized) and to prevent freezing.

Curvilinear sewers—The practice of installing sewer lines along a curved alignment, as opposed to the conventional straight alignment which requires a manhole at every change in direction, results in a sewer line with fewer manholes. Curved sewers can be constructed using both rigid and flexible pipe. Rigid pipe (ductile iron, asbestos cement, vitrified clay, concrete, ABS) is installed by deflecting the pipe joint from a straight position, while flexible pipe is deflected by bending the pipe itself.

A curved sewer has the advantages of requiring fewer manholes, being cheaper to construct, conflicting with fewer other utilities, and having a better hydraulic efficiency. The usual reason for public agency reluctance to permit their use is the possibility that the curve might affect the velocity in the sewer and thereby cause solids to deposit and block the pipe. A second objection is the possibility that maintenance equipment might not be usable on curved pipe. Many jurisdictions allow the use of curved sewers with complete success, however.

Pipe sizes, material, and costs—Pipe material is selected for its strength, durability, installation cost, and hydraulic characteristics. The available pipe materials are asbestos, cement, cast iron, ductile iron, clay tile, concrete, fiberglass reinforced plastic, and plastics. Each of these materials should be satisfactory if installed correctly. Some of these materials are only available in smaller sizes, usually up to 12 inches in diameter. Larger pipes are generally of concrete or asbestos cement.

The minimum pipe size allowed by most agencies is 8 inches for collector; however, the use of pipe smaller than 8 inches has been allowed by a few jurisdictions, and they have experienced no unusual maintenance problems. Hydraulically, the use of smaller pipes for areas of low flow may be an advantage because smaller pipes increase velocity and depth of flow. Again, the use of larger pipe minimums by some agencies may be a holdover from the days when a large infiltration could be expected.

Manholes—A manhole serves four major purposes. It allows horizontal alignment change, vertical alignment change, access for maintenance, and intersection of sewers. It also allows the venting of sewer gases. This gas venting should only be required on larger interceptors. The maximum spacing a public agency requires is based on the length of pipe that can be maintained from a manhole. In earlier times this distance was much less than is now possible. With television and remote pipe repair machinery, the length of pipe that can be repaired from a manhole is greatly increased. In the past, the most prevalent maximum distance in use around the country was 400 feet. This distance has been increased with use of modern pipe maintenance equipment to 600 to 800 feet. Within subdivisions, the most common use for a manhole is for alignment changes and pipe intersections rather than for conformance to the maximum manhole distance requirement.

Pressure and Vacuum Sewerage Systems

The use of pressure and vacuum sewerage systems is extremely site specific, and the costs should be considered carefully by both the developer and the approving agency. This type of design can, however, allow the development of some areas that would otherwise be undevelopable because of undesirable site conditions, or because no interceptor is available within the drainage area. Once built, these systems cannot easily be converted into gravity systems.

The main purpose of both systems is to elevate the sewage over a geographical obstruction that would be prohibitively costly to bypass by means of a gravity sewer. These systems can permit cost-effective development of land that was previously undevelopable because of the lack of sewerage.

The pressure system uses an onsite sewage pump to force the sewage from the site into pressurized lines and to the destination.

The system usually works in the following manner. The sewage flows from the house's interior system into a small holding or septic tank (Figure 7-4). When the tank fills to a certain point, the pump is activated and pumps the sewage from the tank into the pressurized lines in the street. From the point at which the sewage is pumped from the holding tank, the mains carrying it can be smaller than the usual gravity lines, and where grinder pumps are used to break down the solids, the sewage lines can be even smaller (Figure 7-5). If houses are lower than a gravity main in the street, this system can also be used simply to pump the sewage to the gravity main. The gravity main in the street could be constructed

Figure 7-4. Typical septic tank effluent pumping

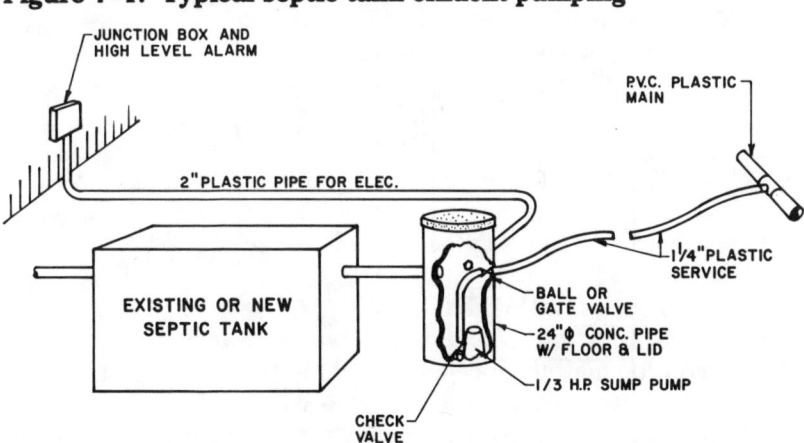

Source: National Association of Home Builders, *Alternatives to Public Sewer*

Figure 7-5. Typical grinder pump installation

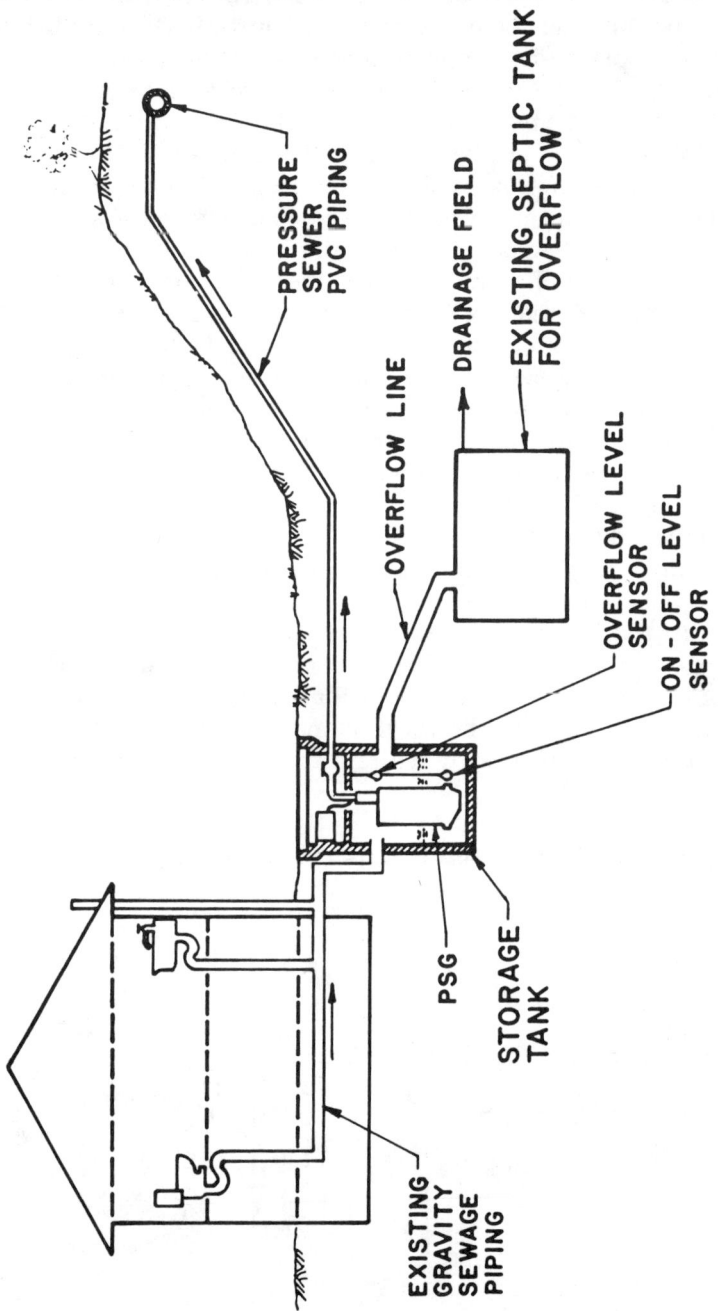

Source: National Association of Home Builders, *Alternatives to Public Sewer*

at a much shallower depth, thereby lowering construction costs. Because of power outages and other emergencies, a standby holding tank is usually necessary to catch and hold effluent from the house for a required length of time, usually 12 hours.

The vacuum system uses a central collection point where a tank equipped with both an air pump and a sewage pump is used (Figure 7-6). The air pump creates the vacuum in the tank and along the collection mains. After the sewage has been collected, it is pumped along to the outfall main or treatment facility. The onsite equipment includes a collection tank to collect the household wastewater, which is then periodically sucked from the collection tank along the mains to the central collection point. The system allows the use of smaller mains and curvilinear mains that can follow the contours of the land.

The basic advantages of these systems are that they eliminate the need for manholes and allow the use of smaller lines that can be laid just below frostline. In a subdivision layout, only a minimum amount of main is necessary. Where gravity sewer mains must follow a swale or steambed, which in many cases requires a right-of-way, a pressure or vacuum sewer can avoid this problem by staying in the road right-of-way.

The disadvantages are higher maintenance costs for cleanouts, system failures, and electric power, and the costs that result from damages to home and property during an overflow. The costs for a pressure system are shown in Figure 7-7. The costs for a vacuum system depend on the size of the area served because the size of the vacuum pump depends on the size of the area served.

Figure 7-6. Elements of a vacuum sewage system

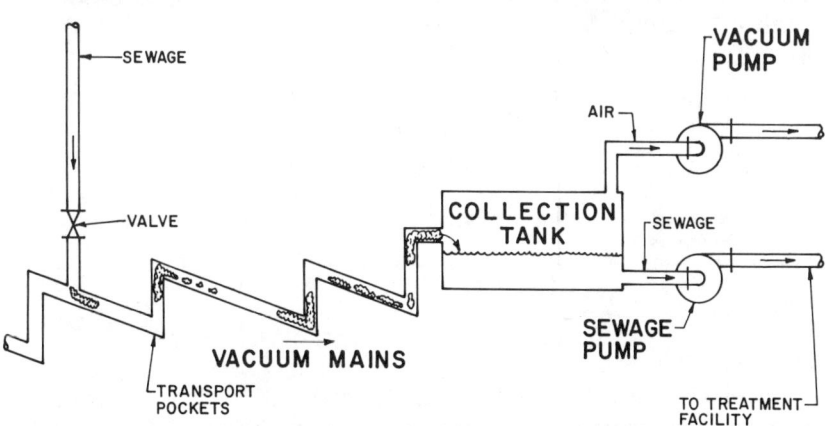

Source: National Association of Home Builders, *Alternatives to Public Sewer*

Figure 7-7. Pressure system construction cost

Home Service	Unit	Grinder Pump	Septic Tank Effluent Pump
Single pumping unit and vault, installed	Each	$1,500-2,500	$500-1,200
Double pumping unit and vault, installed	Each	2,500-3,500	800-1,800
Accessories (alarms, valves, sensors, etc.)	Per Conn.	300-800	300-800
Septic tank	Each		500-1,500
Service piping, 1"-2" in place	Linear Foot	2-6	2-6

Community Service	Unit		Pressure Main
Main piping, 3"-6" in place	Linear Foot		$9-15
Cleanouts, installed	Each		150-400
Air release valve and vault, installed	Each		120-350
Gate valve and vault, 3"-6", installed	Each		250-600
Check valve and vault, 3"-6", installed	Each		150-450

Source: National Association of Home Builders, *Residential Wastewater Systems*

Treatment Levels

Modern wastewater treatment involves three levels of treatment: primary, secondary, and tertiary treatment. Primary treatment is the removal of solids from the wastewater by physical means. Such methods include removing large solids with screens or racks, shredding other solids into smaller particles for easier treatment, allowing sand and grit to settle, skimming off oil and grease. Secondary treatment involves using bacteria to consume a large amount of the remaining organic parts of the wastewater for food because they give off waste products that are easier to handle or collect. These processes are approached differently with different methods, each having advantages and disadvantages. Generally, the bacteria method requires the presence of oxygen (aerobic); others do not (anaerobic).

Tertiary treatment, or advanced wastewater treatment, is the essential completion of the removal of suspended solids and organic matter. Chemical nutrients can also be removed during this process. This level of wastewater purification is done to satisfy the requirements imposed on the discharge of the effluent into a particular body of water. If the body of water has already been degraded to some degree by other pollutants, the regulations might require a higher level of treatment than if the effluent were to be discharged into a purer body of water. The requirements imposed on the effluent dictate the level of advanced wastewater treatment needed. This treatment includes removal of suspended solids by chemical coagulation and their settlement or flotation—removal of organic matter by treatment with activated charcoal. Removal of nutrients is generally by chemical means. The chemicals added combine with the nutrients and then settle or form a gas that is drawn off. Bacteria are also used to act on the nutrients and change them to a form more easily removed from the effluent. Nutrients such as phosphorus and nitrogen cause undesirable biological growths such as algae.

Types of Treatment Processes

Activated sludge—After primary treatment, bacteria and oxygen are added in the aeration basin, where the organics are acted upon by the bacteria. The wastewater is then sent to a settling basin, where the bacteria and the sediment settle out. They are returned to the aeration basin where the bacteria again act upon the wastewater just entering the aeration basin. Activated sludge refers to the sludge being activated with bacteria. Part of the sludge is drawn off to be disposed of, and the effluent is then disinfected and discharged.

Extended aeration—This method is the same as the activated sludge except that the wastewater remains in contact with the bacteria and oxygen for a longer period of time to reduce the amount of sludge to be disposed of. This method is advantageous to a package treatment plant, where sludge disposal would be a problem (Figure 7-8).

Contact stabilization—This method also uses the activated sludge method except that the wastewater is not held long in the aeration tank. The organic materials in the wastewater attach themselves to a settleable mass that once they are settled out the effluent is aerated in another tank. This method allows the wastewater processing tanks to be smaller and hence less costly; however, this system is more complicated and more difficult to operate.

Rotating biological contactor—Instead of diffusing air or oxygen through the wastewater mass, this method allows slowly turning plates to be exposed to the air part of the time and then submerged. The bacteria attach themselves to the disks when submerged and get the required oxygen when not submerged. This system is easy to operate and less costly to maintain; however, more sludge is produced, and low air temperature adversely affects operations. The latter problem requires the disks to be covered and heated in winter in some areas, which increases the construction and maintenance costs.

Biological tower—In this system the wastewater is aerated by letting it trickle over pallet-like wooden or plastic racks through which air can circulate. After aeration, the wastewater is collected and settled as with the other systems. Unpleasant odors and adverse effluent quality are major problems arising with this method of treatment.

Treatment Plant Site Amenities

Access—Access to the site is required for construction and maintenance, but is also needed for electric powerlines, waterlines, the wastewater source, and the effluent stream. However, too easy an access, especially by the public, leads to other problems.

Land area—The land area required for a treatment plant site varies depending on the type of treatment, whether the sludge is to be deposited onsite or offsite, and the width of buffer around the site required by local regulations (Figure 7-9). In addition to the plant itself and the sludge drying beds, an emergency storage pond is usually required to store effluents in the event of a system malfunction or power outage.

Utilities—Utilities servicing the plants are electricity and water for clearing and washing. A backup electricity source is a wise policy and is generally required. It can be an onsite generator or another electric line to the plant from a different electric grid source.

Sludge handling and disposal—Sludge handling and treatment constitute the major operations cost of a package system. Sludge

Figure 7-8. Extended aeration flow scheme

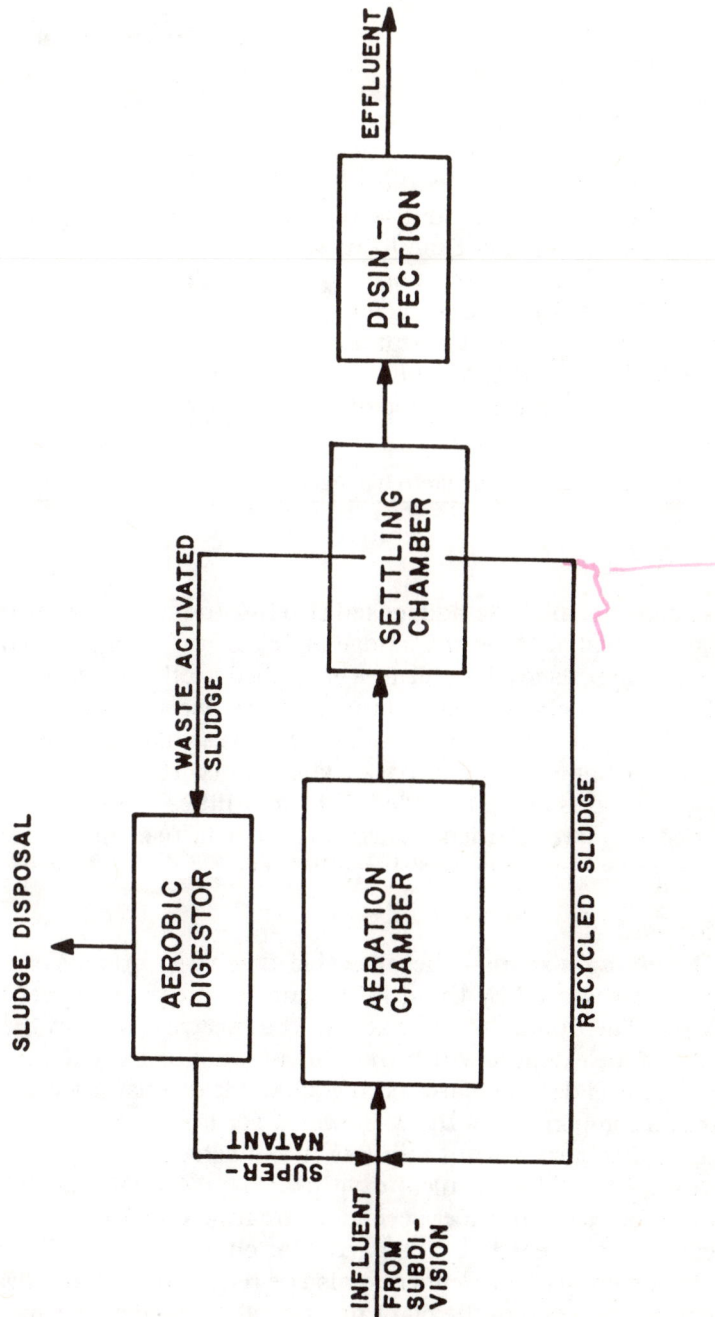

Source: National Association of Home Builders, *Alternatives to Public Sewer*

Figure 7-9. Area requirements for treatment plants

Plant Treatment Type	Area Required, in Acres	
	Without Sludge Beds	With Sludge Beds
.25 MGD Contract Stabilization	1.60	2.25
.25 SMGD Extended Aeration	1.60	2.25
.25 SMGD Biological Contractor	1.75	2.25
.5 MGD Contractor Stabilization	2.2	3
.5 MGD Extended Aeration	2.2	3
.5 MGD Biological Contractor	2.5	4
1.0 MGD Contract Sterilization	3.0	4
1.0 MGD Extended Aeration	3.0	4
1.0 MGD Biological Contractor	3.2	5

Source: U.S. Environmental Protection Agency

disposal normally is addressed during the permit acquisition phase of design. After the sludge is dried, it can be removed from the drying beds to a landfill area or applied to other sites specifically selected for such use. Many municipalities use sludge as a fertilizer for areas that have been grass-seeded, areas along new road construction rights-of-way, or parks where a new recreation area such as a ballfield is being installed. Private utilities sometimes use the sludge in flower gardens. Farmers also will use the sludge as a fertilizer as allowed by health regulations.

Disposal

Receiving stream—The allowable discharge quality of the effluent is dictated by the quality and quantity of the receiving waters. The quality of the water in the receiving stream therefore dictates the extent to which the effluent must be treated. Advanced treatment is designed around the allowable discharge levels for the various components of the wastewater. For instance, if a treatment plant's discharge permit requires it to discharge no higher than a certain level of biochemical oxygen demand (BOD) and that level cannot be reached under secondary treatment methods, advanced treatment is needed for this particular characteristic of the wastewater. Removal of nutrients may also be required, and the advanced treatment portion of the plant must be able to remove them also.

Land application—With EPA's affirmation of the good of zero pollutants, the use of land application has been reexamined as an alternative treatment of wastewater for small operations where large, sophisticated, and expensive systems would not be practical or even affordable.

There are three basic types of land disposal: overland flow, rapid infiltration-percolation, and irrigation. These methods are normally used after pretreatment.

The overland flow method requires a gentle slope of slightly impervious ground with dense vegetation. The wastewater is acted upon by bacteria living on the soil surface or on the plants. Nutrients are removed by the plants, and some are deposited in the soil. The wastewater then, in a purer state, recharges the ground water aquifer. For overland flow to work successfully, the ground water table must be low, and have no geologic formations through which untreated wastewater can seep.

The crop irrigation method is the most widely used land disposal method. The wastewater is normally sprayed onto furrowed cropland, where it is soaked up by the soil. The same physical, biological, and chemical action takes place as with the rapid infiltration-percolation method. Wastewater is disposed of by evaporation, transpiration through the plant leaves, and ultimately through percolation into the subsoil.

Figure 7-10 lists some characteristics of the land application approach.

The oxidation ditch system has been used in Europe for smaller systems for several years. It is larger than comparable package treatment plants, but it is easier to operate and may prove effective in nitrogen removal. This nitrogen removal ability may cause the widespread use of the oxidation ditch in those areas where nitrogen removal is required. The system is a circular or elliptical channel about 3 feet deep where the waste is circulated by means of aeration bubbles or brushes. The effluent is settled in another basin, then heated and disharged.

Aeration lagoons may be up to 10 feet deep. The wastewater is aerated by use of mechanical or diffuser aeration. The effluent is settled, treated, and discharged. Low temperature conditions affect the efficiency of the lagoons, and for that reason the regulations usually require a larger holding area. This size requirement limits the economic feasibility of this treatment method.

Stabilization ponds are shallower and larger than aeration lagoons. They are usually around 3 feet deep. The operation is the same, except that the wastewater is aerated by the algae that form on the surface and that produce oxygen by biological-chemical action with the sun. Low temperatures adversely affect the operation

Figure 7-10. Comparative characteristics of irrigation, infiltration-percolation, and overland flow systems

Factor	Irrigation		Infiltration-percolation	Overland flow
	Low-rate	High-rate		
Liquid loading rate, in./wk.	0.5 to 1.5	1.5 to 4.0	4 to 120	2 to 5.5
Annual application, ft./yr.	2 to 4	4 to 18	18 to 500	8 to 24
Land required for 1-mgd flowrate, acres*	280 to 560	62 to 560	2 to 62	46 to 140
Application techniques	Spray or surface		Usually surface	Usually spray
Crop production	Excellent	Fair	Poor	Fair
Soils	Moderately permeable soils with good productivity when irrigated		Rapidly permeable soils, such as sands, loamy sands, and sandy loams	Slowly permeable soils, such as clay loams and clays
Climatic constraints	Growing season only	Storage often needed	Reduce loadings in freezing weather	Storage often needed
Wastewater lost to:	Evaporation and percolation		Percolation	Surface runoff and evaporatioin with some percolation
Expected treatment performance				
BOD and SS removal	98+%		85 to 99%	92+%
Nitrogen removal	85+%		0 to 50%	70 tc 90%
Phosphorus removal	80 to 99%		60 to 95%	40 tc 80%

*Depends on crop uptake.
Metric conversion: in. × 2.54 = cm
ft. × 0.305 = m
acre × 0.405 = ha
Source: U.S. Environmental Protection Agency

of ponds even more than lagoons, because the ponds are shallower and more exposed to weather.

Onsite Treatment Systems

It is desirable for a builder to build at or near public sewer installations. However, the availability of public sewers has not kept pace with residential development in many areas. The latest census information indicates that nearly 20 million housing units, serving approximately 30 percent of the nation's population, dispose of their domestic wastes through onsite disposal units, and they are increasing at a rate of approximately 500,000 per year.

Figure 7-11 shows the diversity of onsite systems in use.

Onsite sewage treatment and disposal systems, in particular the septic tank system, are expected to be the primary methods of sewage disposal in the foreseeable future except in areas served by public sewers. The septic system is cheap and simple to operate, and, where adequate land area and soil conditions exist, this system should be used.

In the future, more and more land with inadequate soil conditions may have to be used, and more compact development may be required. The increasing cost of sewage collection and treatment may also bring about the reevaluation of the septic tank method.

Which methods would replace or augment these current sewage treatment and disposal methods is not settled; however, several methods now being used will be discussed in this section.

Site Selection

The objective of any onsite sewage system is to provide a means of disposing of household wastewater within the confines of the property in a manner that will protect public health and preserve the environmental quality. With most onsite systems, the environment provides the final treatment before the liquid from the effluent becomes part of the hydrologic cycle. The environment must be able to assimilate the pollutants without overloading its ability to naturally treat the effluent.

Criteria such as soil type, bedrock type and depth, slope, groundwater level, lot size, etc. will determine the usability and type of onsite systems.

Treatment Processes

The biochemical processes which take place in septic and aerobic methods of treatment are totally different. Both are affected by micro-organisms which are present in the sewage itself, and which use the organic material in the sewage as food to produce energy.

Figure 7-11. Onsite wastewater treatment and disposal systems

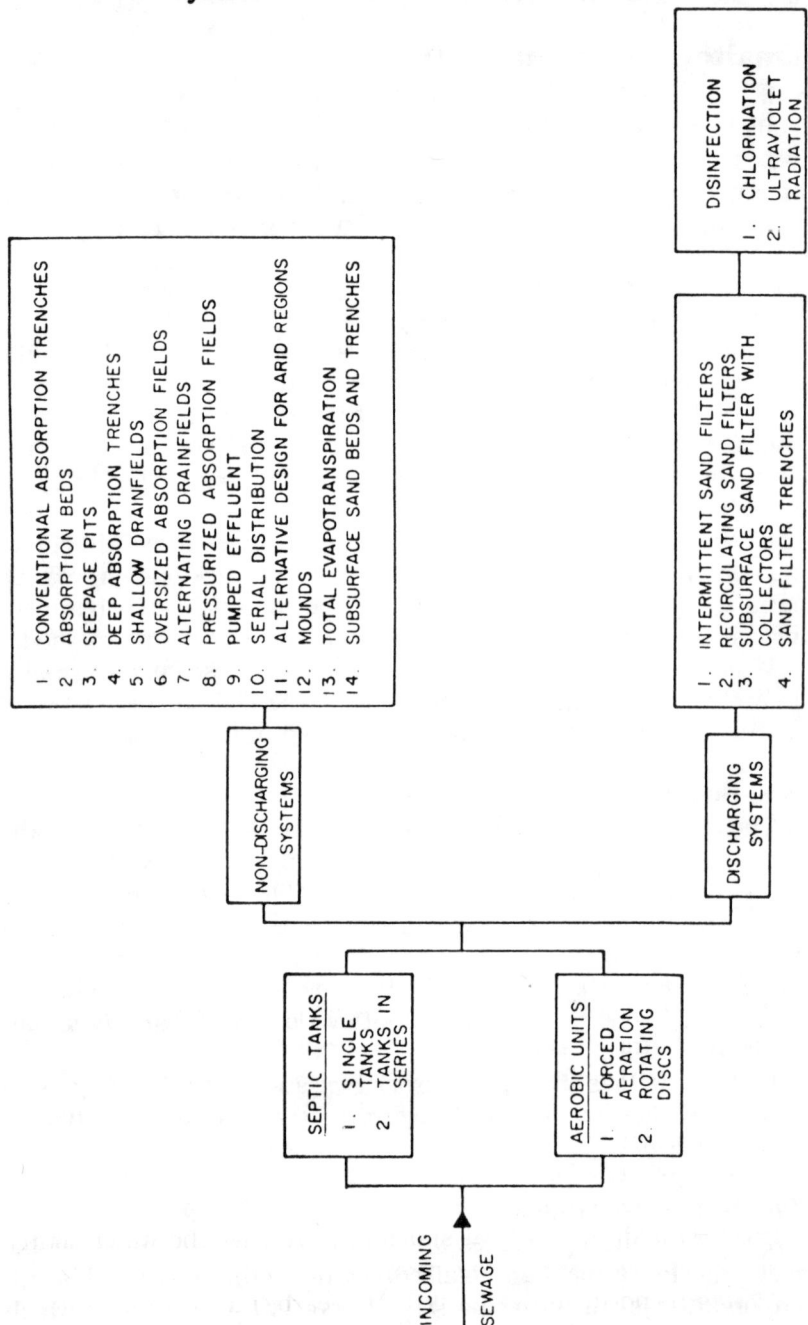

Source: National Association of Home Builders, *Residential Wastewater Systems*

Aerobic micro-organisms are dependent on oxygen to multiply and grow, or will die in an atmosphere lacking oxygen. Anaerobic (septic) bacteria and micro-organisms, on the other hand, live in an atmosphere devoid of oxygen and die in its presence.

In either process, aerobic or anaerobic, the organic matter in human waste contains material that is degraded biochemically. These chemicals are in combined form and include carbon, hydrogen, nitrogen, sulphur, and phosphorous derivatives.

Methods of Treatment

Septic tanks—Septic tanks are the most widely used of the individual sewage disposal systems. Since the 1930s the number of septic systems in use has exceeded 50 million and is increasing annually.

The septic tank system is simply the septic tank, usually made of concrete and open on the inside with the inlet and outlet both near the top of the tank, and the absorption field into which the drainage or leaching lines discharge (Figure 7-12).

The wastewater is discharged directly into the tank, where it is settled out with the uppermost fluid being discharged into the absorption discharge system. This fluid is evenly discharged into the absorption field where bacterial and vegetal action complete the treatment. Septage, that which remains in the bottom of the tank, must be removed every 3 to 5 years in order to prevent excessive buildup, which decreases the effective size of the septic tank. Failure to remove septage will cause more and more solids to be discharged into the leaching lines with the result that the lines and absorption field become overloaded, and sewage ponding and odor problems result.

The normal septic tank should give 15 to 20 years of service before modification, which normally means relocation of the absorption system. Naturally the type of soil, the depth of soil, and the elevation of the water table affect the operation of the septic tank by affecting the absorption field. Areas with impervious deep soils with a low water table are ideal for septic tank systems. Impervious soils or soils underlain with rock or damp soils are not good. The soil's absorption areas are generally tested for their absorption capacity by the percolation test, which measures the time required for a certain amount of water to drain into the soil from a standard-sized hole. The time required dictates the size of absorption field required. In addition, several states require that the water source and the septic system be separated by a minimum distance.

Septage is normally discharged into nearby public sewer systems, or more often disposed of through land application.

Figure 7-12. Septic tank

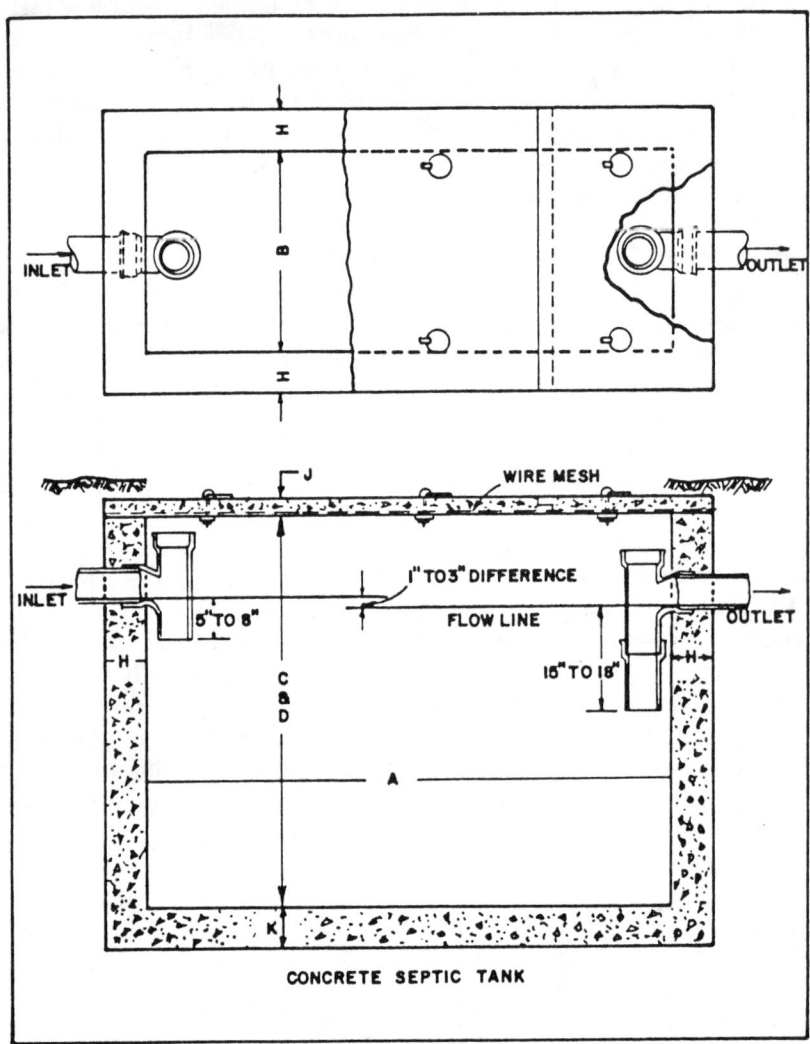

Source: National Association of Home Builders, *Alternatives to Public Sewer;* Virginia State Department of Health

Various other methods have been devised to handle and discharge the wastewater from the septic tank in order to rejuvenate old systems or improve new systems. These methods include pumping wastewater to another more suitable area nearby, constructing seepage beds or pits instead of discharging wastewater into the ground, and various methods of filtering before discharge.

Aerobic tanks—The home aerobic system is a small activated sludge system without refinements. The system's tanks usually consist of a presettling chamber, aeration chamber, and secondary settling chamber. In some units the presettling chamber is omitted. Activated sludge is formed in the aeration tank by the addition of diffused air and bacterial action on the wastewater. The effluent from these types of systems is of higher quality than that from the septic system. This fact allows the absorption areas to be smaller although state regulations in most cases are slow to recognize this.

Maintenance costs include the electricity to pump air and the normal sludge pumping, which must be done periodically. Drawbacks to this system are bulking sludge that does not settle and is carried into the drainfield, and poisons that harm the bacterial mass thereby retarding the bacterial decomposition.

This type of treatment facility was developed to allow direct discharge into streams. This procedure would normally involve a discharge permit and chlorine treatment, which would add additional costs both to construction and maintenance. The developer should weigh the cost of this system against the cost of the septic system.

Disposal Systems

Choosing the best onsite system for a particular installation requires a basic knowledge of the types of systems available and how they have been designed to blend with the various site conditions. Figure 7-13 has been prepared to assist in this decision.

Absorption fields—Subsurface absorption is usually the best method of wastewater disposal provided the site conditions are compatible (Figure 7-14). The system is simple to design and construct, is not costly to operate and maintain, and is stable. Subsurface absorption systems include trenches, beds, fills, seepage pits, and artificially drained systems. The selection of the most appropriate soil absorption system depends on the site characteristics.

The two methods used most frequently to size absorption fields are the percolation test and soil evaluation. The percolation test is easy to conduct, and it measures the liquid absorption rate of the soil. Most jurisdictions have established design data based on a range of percolation rates applicable for the locality. Soil evaluation is a somewhat more sophisticated approach to determine the ability of the land to support a soil absorption system. When properly interpreted, the results of a soil evaluation can be very accurate.

Other aspects of a site should be considered in evaluating its potential for a soil absorption system, such as:

Figure 7-13. Onsite disposal methods

	Site Limitations									
Onsite Disposal Methods	**Slowly Perme-able Soil**	**High Water Table**	**Soil Readily Clogs**	**Soil, Creviced Bedrock**	**No Soil Depth**	**Limited Space**	**Imper-meable Soil**	**Steep Slope (20-25 Percent)**	**Limiting Strata at Surface**	**Limiting Strata at 5 Feet**
Absorption Trenches	X									
Absorption Beds	X					X				
Seepage Pits						X			X	
Deep Trenches									X	
Shallow Drainfield										X
Oversized Absorption Field	X									
Alternating Drainfields	X		X							
Pumped Effluent							X	X		
Serial Distribution								X		
Mounds	X	X		X						X
Evapotranspiration		X		X	X		X			
Sand Filters		X		X	X		X			

Source: National Association of Home Builders, *Residential Wastewater Systems*

Figure 7-14. Septic tank and absorption field (trench)

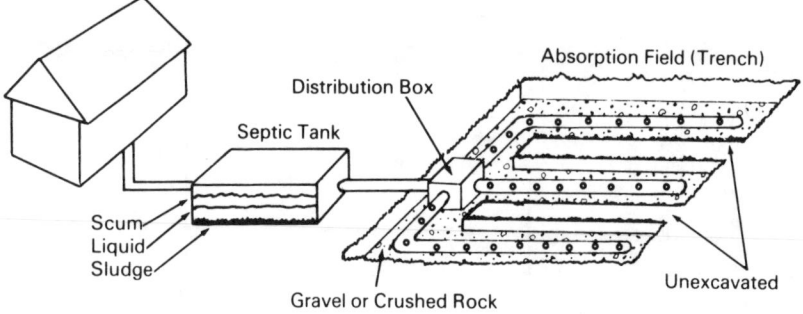

Source: U.S. Environmental Protection Agency, *Small Wastewater Systems*

- Soil depth beneath soil absorption system
- Ground water level
- Slope of the site
- Stoniness of the site
- Separation distances from structures and boundaries
- Flood plains
- Surface drainage

The construction phase of an absorption system is extremely important to a properly functioning system. The absorption lines can be of perforated plastic pipe, clay tile, concrete tile, or bituminous fiber drainage pipe. Aggregate used in the trenches should be crushed stone sized between ½ and 2½ inches. The stone should be covered with untreated building paper, straw, or similar material to prevent it from becoming clogged with the earth backfill.

Mound system—An alternative to the conventional substance soil absorption system is the mound system (Figure 7-15). It is essentially an absorption field above the natural soil. The mound is constructed of a suitable fill material, such as sand. The effluent from a septic tank or aerobic unit is pumped to the gravel seepage trench layout or seepage bed for percolation into the sand and down to more permeable topsoil.

The mound system has been researched and studied quite extensively in Pennsylvania and Wisconsin. It is an alternative and should not be considered if a subsurface system can be constructed, because it may cost as much as $2,000 more than a subsurface septic tank system. Mounds are appropriate options on sites with slowly permeable soils, shallow permeable soils covering perma rock formations, and permeable soils with seasonally high groundwater. Before a mound system is selected, other variables must be consid-

Figure 7-15. Plan view and cross-section of a mound system for problem soils

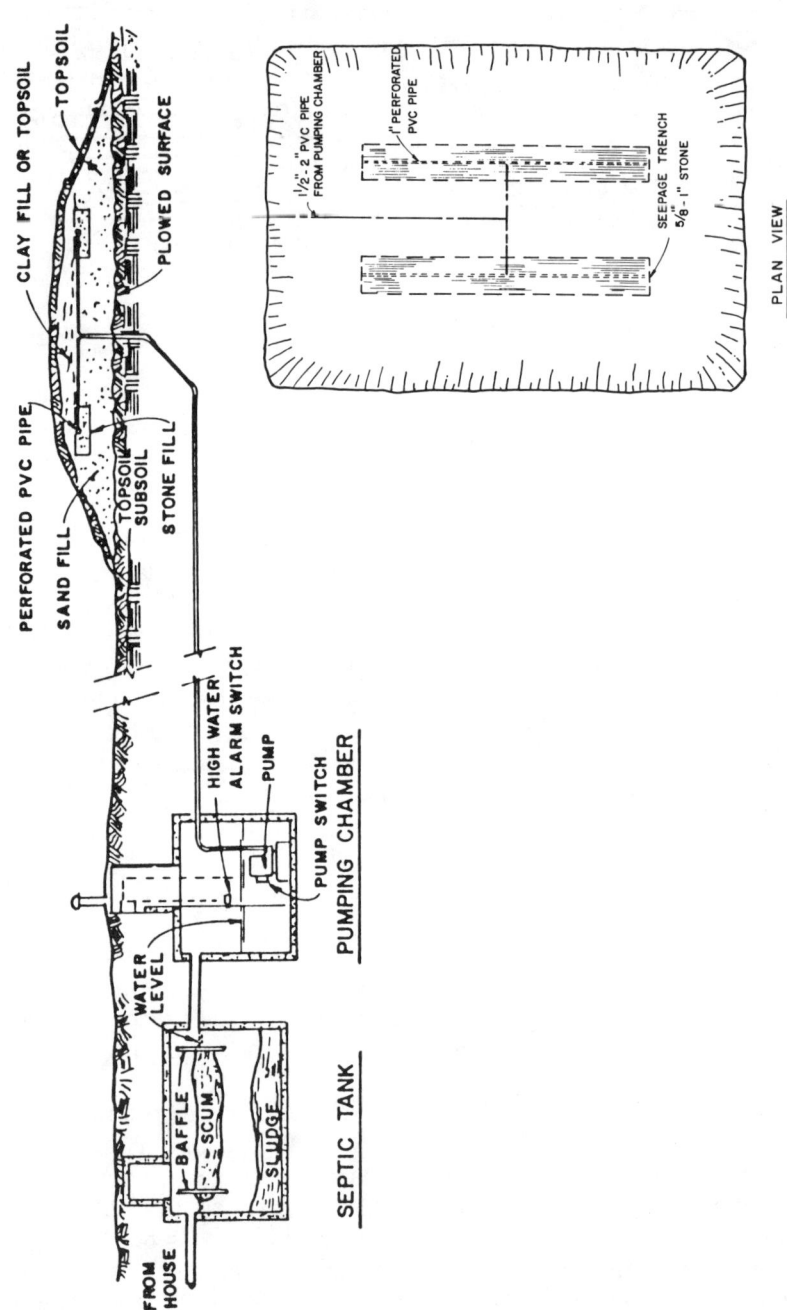

Source: National Association of Home Builders, *Alternatives to Public Sewer*

ered, and they include slope of the ground, flood plains, surface water, landscaping, and weather conditions.

Evapotranspiration bed—The name is a combination of evaporation and transpiration, which describes the method of effluent disposal. Effluent from septic or aerobic systems is discharged to beds of gravel and sand that are isolated from the soil by an impervious plastic lining (Figure 7-16). The system, therefore, is neither affected by, nor affects, the surrounding soil. Capillary action raises the effluent to the surface, where it is either evaporated directly or absorbed by surface plants and transpired to the air via the roots to the leaves, with the plant using whatever nutrients are available from the effluent.

Areas with heavy rainfall require a larger bed area than those with a drier climate. This system must be carefully researched and designed for each site, and its advantages and disadvantages compared to those of other systems. Areas of light rainfall and low humidity are ideal for evapotranspiration beds. This type of effluent disposal should not be used if the beds are subject to freezing. Salt building up within the bed could clog the flow and retard plant growth.

Figure 7-16. Evapotranspiration bed

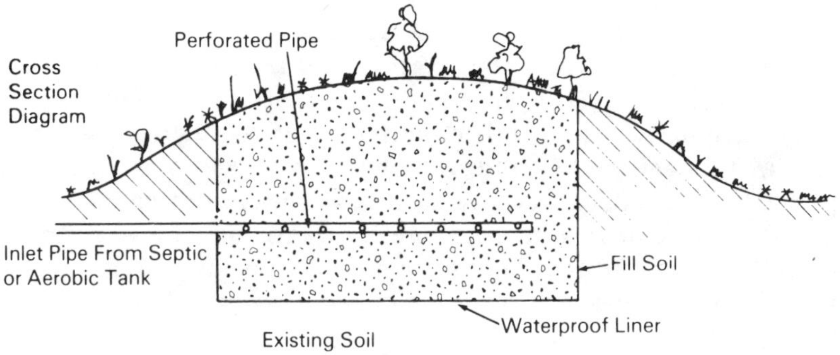

Source: U.S. Environmental Protection Agency, *Small Wastewater Systems*

Alternating absorption field—The failure of a drainfield is generally caused by a buildup of organic material in the voids of the soil of the absorption field. One method of restoring the bed to its previous efficiency is to take it out of service for enough time to allow the natural bacteria and organisms to break down the clogging agents. This goal can be accomplished by using two drainfields and alternating use of them every few months. This procedure allows the drainfields to clear themselves naturally.

Pressure dosing—In this system the effluent is pumped through small-size pipes to the drainfield. When the back pressure on the pump increases, the pump shuts off, so that the field accepts only what it can handle in any one pump cycle. The system reduces clogging caused by a slow-moving effluent, and the reduced clogging attracts larger organisms that increase porosity by their movements through the soil.

Leaching field chambers—These large rectangular concrete blocks or modules, approximately 13 feet × 4 feet, are buried with the open end down. The effluent flows into these chambers and is absorbed into the subsurface soil. This process allows the absorption to occur farther below the surface than usual and to involve a larger area. It is used where more permeable soils are overlaid with soils of lesser permeability.

Pump and haul system—As the name indicates, in this system the effluent is collected in a tank and periodically pumped out and hauled away. This method is most expensive and is normally used only when the health of citizens is endangered. It is never used as a permanent operation or initiated for a new development unless a sewer line extension is forthcoming and the operation would be temporary.

Alternative Onsite Treatment Systems

Blackwater-greywater preparation and treatment—Blackwater is wastewater derived from organic waste, primarily toilet waste. Greywater derives from other household areas such as showers, sinks, and washing machines. Greywater produces more of a liquid in the combined wastewater, and generally is not considered a threat to human health; therefore its treatment is less extensive than that of blackwater. This system would require an entirely separate inhouse collection system and two separate treatment facilities.

One method suggested for treating blackwater is to have a separate septic tank for each kind of wastewater. The blackwater treatment system would be smaller and have a smaller drainfield, and the treatment within the tank could be intensified toward the organic wastes.

Blackwater treatment also includes using toilets that treat and store sewage within the toilet itself, such as:
- Incinerator toilets, which burn the sewage to ash and which are periodically cleaned.
- Chemical toilets, which deposit waste directly or with a mini-

mum amount of flushing water, into a chemical holding tank, which is periodically changed. This type is used in vacation homes.

- Recycling toilets, which recycle the fluid for flushing back for reuse, and treat and dispose of the waste usually by biological means.

Most of these types of toilets are rarely used on a permanent basis. They are more likely to be used in a vacation house.

Most methods for the treatment of greywater are the same as for regular wastewater. The difference is that greywater systems require a much smaller drainfield, usually only about half the regular size, and they are seldom out of order because of clogging.

Two septic tanks in series—This system allows some remaining solids to settle in the second tank, leaving the effluent with fewer solids. The fewer the solids, the longer-lived the drainfield. This system was used initially for soil with low permeability because it clogs much faster than normal soil.

Waterless/low-water systems—All of the systems described below treat blackwater. Separate greywater treatment and disposal is required (Source: U.S. Environmental Protection Agency, *Small Wastewater Systems*).

Composting: No water
   Anaerobic decomposition creates an inoffensive black humus-like substance that can be used directly as fertilizer. Time frame, one year or more. No valve; venting required.

Incinerating: No water
   Electricity, gas, or oil burns solids and evaporates liquid. Small amount of ash is removed weekly. Roof vent. Proper care essential.

Recycling Oil Flush: No water
   Similar to water-flush toilet but uses oil for flush. Oil and wastes go to large storage tank where wastes settle at bottom and oil rises to top. Filtered oil recycles for flush. Storage tank is pumped and oil replaced periodically. Uses electricity. Proper care essential.

Recycling Chemical: Low water
   Water-chemical flush mixture is pumped into toilet bowl. Mixture and wastes go to storage tank. Filtered liquid recirculates for flush. Permanent or portable types. Permanent needs water hookup. Storage tank is pumped and chemicals added periodically. Uses electricity. Proper care essential.

Recycling Water: Low water
   Various systems. Some reduce wastes to water, gas, and vapor. Treated wastewater recycles to flush toilet. System vents to outside. Multiflush commercial units available. Most systems use electricity. Professional maintenance essential.

Chemical addition system—For use in slow percolating soils, this system resembles the normal septic system, except that it employs a second tank into which the effluent flows after being settled in the first. This effluent would normally be discharged into the absorption areas, but is now collected in a second chamber where coagulants are added. These coagulants bring together the fine solid particles in suspension, and they then settle out in the second chamber.

The effluent from this chamber is discharged into porous concrete blocks sealed together to form a long rectangular pipe or a series of pipes, if necessary. It is then passed through the blocks, which act as a filter for any remaining solids. This system is not accepted in all states, so a check with the health department should be made before it is used.

Chapter 8
Residential Streets

The early development of residential street standards by local governments was a response to immediate problems of unpaved streets. Post-World War II America experienced a great increase in automobile ownership and traffic, and public dissatisfaction with alternatively dusty and muddy unpaved streets spurred towns and cities to quickly adopt measures to stimulate street paving.[1]

Unfortunately, little research went into this standard-setting process for residential streets. The zenith of highway engineering, however, occurred in the 1950s. Studies of highway design geometry, capacity analysis, and level of service resulted in the development of highway standards which focused on the safe movement of large volumes of traffic at high speeds. Curiously, these same concepts and standards were used for low-density streets. But most residential streets do not need to move high volumes of traffic at high speed. In traffic terms, their only function is to provide access to properties.

By the 1960s, many builders and planners recognized that residential streets were being overdesigned and overbuilt. Neighborhood interaction, pedestrian safety, and environmental quality were finally seen as more important concepts than design speed.

Designing residential streets to highway or city street standards had only encouraged driving at excessive speeds. Residents in many neighborhoods began requesting installation of speed bumps and barricades—an unmistakable sign that streets had been overdesigned and were encouraging through-traffic and speeding.

Aside from these considerations, building streets to excessive standards has significant effects on the cost of housing and maintenance costs to municipalities. Excessively wide streets use up more land, cost more to build and maintain, and also result in increased stormwater runoff.

Hierarchy of Streets

A street system should keep routes which carry through-traffic separate from routes which provide access to residential properties.

All streets can be described in terms of their relative service for through-traffic movement. Interstate highways, for example, are designed for high-speed through-traffic but do not provide direct access to properties. Residential cul-de-sacs, on the other hand, are designed only for access—they should be considered part of the residential neighborhood more than part of a traffic system.[2] (Figure 8-1.)

Another way of describing a street hierarchy is by traffic volume. Through-routes that serve large areas can be expected to have larger volumes (measured by Average Daily Traffic, or ADT), while streets which are dead-end and exist only to provide access have very low volumes.

Knowing the development plans or the zoning of the adjacent land can be of assistance in planning a street network to expand or

Figure 8-1. Hierarchy of street types

- COLLECTORS: CONDUCT TRAFFIC BETWEEN MAJOR ARTERIALS AND/OR ACTIVITY CENTERS...28'-36'
- SUBCOLLECTOR: TYPICAL RESIDENTIAL STREET ....24'-26'
- PLACE OR LANE: CUL-DE-SACS UP TO 300' IN LENGTH ....20'-22'

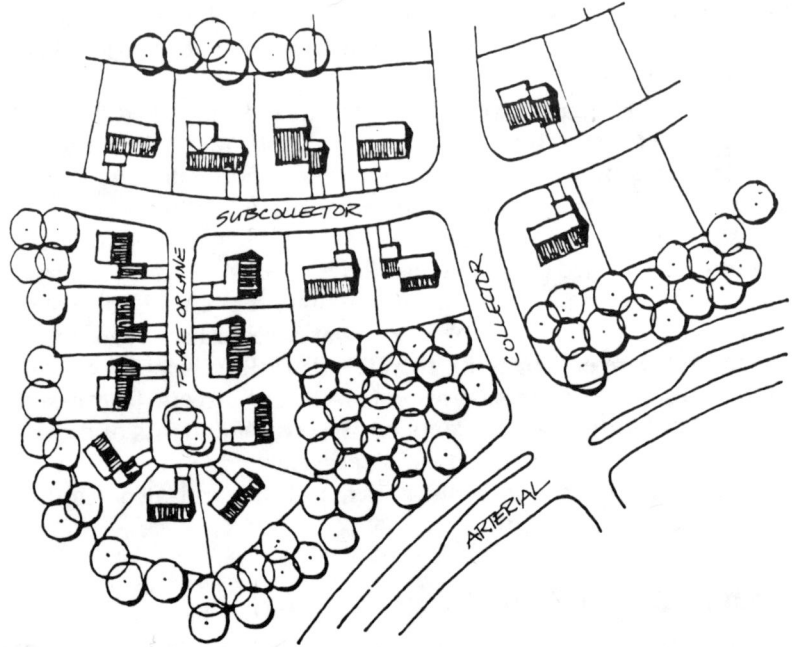

Source: HOH Associates, Inc.

isolate a development. Most jurisdictions have planned capital improvements projects that should be investigated because they may affect a proposed subdivision. Improvement projects can be used to the developer's advantage; however, they also can be used to the developer's disadvantage if the jurisdiction requires the developer to improve any portion of the publicly owned roadway. A road that serves traffic other than that generated from a development is normally considered to be the responsibility of the local or state government.

The road classification chart (Figure 8-2) is a summary of the most important design parameters for each roadway classification. To arrive at these limitations, the philosophy of residential streets must be analyzed. The road's level of service is the basis of these parameters and is a function of speed, volume, and composition of traffic. The ultimate goal of a street is to allow adequate movement, a goal achieved through use of a design that allows this free flow of traffic. Land use and land development will determine the anticipated volume of traffic. To determine the volume, the trips generated are calculated by estimating the traffic load from the various land used. This process is extremely difficult because many of the factors that influence the traffic volume, such as employment dispersal, gasoline prices, and carpooling, are overlooked. The ADT values shown on the road classification chart can be used as a guide in determining the density of a development that the various road classifications can serve.

This evaluation is only the initial step in determining whether the road classification selected will accommodate the development design. Street width, design speed, and roadway alignment will be the determining factors in providing a roadway that can accommodate the traffic and be economical, safe, and an aesthetic part of the development. This analysis may change under other circumstances, site conditions, and development characteristics, but providing residential roadways that exceed those parameters would be impractical. Using the notion of street hierarchy, a street system can be designed so that the width, geometry, and pavement characteristics are appropriate to the function of each street.

Street Width

The width of a street should take into account the role that street plays in the street hierarchy. A street whose major function is to provide access to residential properties need not be as wide as a street which is meant to move large volumes of through-traffic. Based on this principle, for a street classified as a place or lane, a

Figure 8-2. Road classification chart

Classification	Usual ADT Range	Right-of-Way Width	Pavement Width	Maximum & Minimum Grades	Minimum Radius
Place	0-100	pavement + 2 ft.	20 ft.	maximum 10-14% minimum 0.5%	100 ft.
Lane	75-350	pavement + 2 ft.	20 ft.	maximum 10-14% minimum 0.5%	100 ft.
Subcollector	200-1,000	varies	26 ft.	maximum 8-12% minimum 0.5%	200 ft.
Collector	800-3,000	varies	28 ft.	maximum 6-8% minimum 0.5%	as designed by state or local highway dept.
Arterial	more than 3,000	varies	as designed by state or local highway dept.	as designed by state or local highway dept.	as designed by state or local highway dept.

Source: National Association of Home Builders

width of 20-22 feet is sufficient, while a subcollector should be 24-26 feet wide and a collector 28-36 feet, depending upon traffic volume. Appendix C contains examples of ordinances that are based on the street hierarchy concept.

Residential street turning requirements at the end of a cul-de-sac should accommodate the vehicles intended for that particular roadway. Designing a cul-de-sac with a turning radius that will accommodate a moving van is unreasonable. A cul-de-sac turnaround should have a turning radius that will accommodate cars (Figure 8-3). It does not need a radius that can accommodate an occasional moving van or emergency vehicle, for those vehicles can easily maneuver within a lesser area if absolutely necessary. Circular turnaround areas of 30-feet radius are sufficient, according to the American Association of State Highway and Transportation Officials.[3] This size allows automobiles to make an easy U-turn

Figure 8-3. Designs for cul-de-sac turnarounds

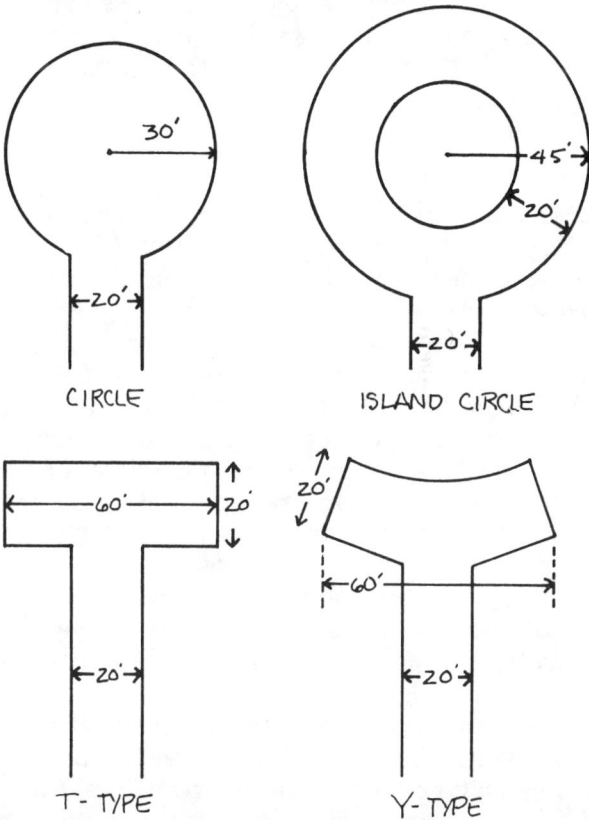

while trucks can turn by backing once. Other common road termination configurations are island circles, Ts, and Ys. Regardless of the design, a dead-end street normally should not exceed 800 to 1,200 feet in length.

The right-of-way for residential streets should only be as wide as needed for the pavement, sidewalks, and utilities. A 20-foot street with no sidewalks calls for a right-of-way of 22 feet, not the 40 or 50 feet required in many jurisdictions.

Design Speed

Design speed is one of the most influential elements in setting the geometric parameters of roadways. However, for a place or lane, use of design speed can result in overdesign of the street. The minimum design speed found in most design publications is 25 mph, yet this level of design is not necessary for a street which may only be a few hundred feet long and provide access to just a few houses. Conversely, a properly down-sized street can be the most important factor in maintaining safe speeds and reducing the expense of providing numerous traffic control devices.

Geometric Design

Design vehicles are the basis on which many localities establish their roadway design parameters. Design vehicles are selected motor vehicles with the weight, dimensions, and operating characteristics used to establish highway design controls. Examples of design vehicles are passenger car, single-unit truck, and large semitrailer.[4] For residential roadway design, the frequency of use by large vehicles does not justify using a moving van (a full trailer), for example, as the design vehicle. The geometric design of a roadway should be developed to provide adequate access for emergency vehicles. The stringency of many governmental regulations concerning land development reduces flexibility, and flexibility is necessary to provide an efficient and aesthetic subdivision.

A variety of factors other than regulations helps determine street pattern layout. In addition to the confines of the property line, street layout is contingent upon the existing road patterns, topography, soil conditions, drainage courses, and intended land use. Initial planning can be undertaken with the use of a topographical map, generally found in a scale of 1 inch to 200 feet, a survey of the site, and other information that documents the natural features of the site. Based on the features of the site, the preliminary horizontal and vertical road alignments can be designed to accommodate the anticipated lot layout and the intended subdivision design.

Horizontal Alignment

Wherever the street must change direction, a horizontal curve is used to accommodate that change. The rate of horizontal change, cross slope, and design speed all affect the motorist's comfort.

Most residential roadways are designed with a normal crown section, in which the travel lanes slope away from the centerline. Normal cross slopes can vary from 0.02 percent to 0.04 percent. Heavily used roadways, such as arterials, are designed with a super-elevation rate, which means that through a curve both travel lanes have the same cross slope. With a super-elevation rate, traffic must maintain the operating speeds for which the road was designed to diminish the pulling sensation created by the cross slope.

The sight distance across the inside of the curve determines the proper horizontal curve. Sight obstructions can vary considerably on older roadways. On new residential roadways, precautions can be taken to maintain flexible horizontal design and provide an adequate sight distance. Trees, hedges, retaining walls, guard-rails, or cut slopes within the right-of-way should be considered when evaluating the horizontal sight distance. At times, a roadway intersecting at the inside of a horizonal curve and near the point of curvature can present a sight distance problem. The roadway alignments can remain as designed if the line of sight is not obstructed within the right-of-way or within the corner lot. If the line of sight goes beyond the right-of-way line, a planting restriction should be established in order to maintain adequate sight distance—which allows the motorist to sight an object in the road and to stop before reaching it at the established design speed.

The minimum length of a horizontal curve varies considerably with each classification of roadway. For example, a minimum horizontal curve length of 100 feet can be used for a place or a lane. A subcollector with 200 to 600 ADT and certain conditions could use a 100-foot horizontal curve. A 150-foot minimum curve should be used in designing a subcollector serving 200 to 1,000 ADT.

In addition to the minimum length of curve, a minimum radius should be established to set parameters for design. Flexibility is needed in designing roadways serving residential communities because the curvature of the road determines how the road functions. The minimum radius for any place or lane should be 100 feet. For subcollectors, the minimum radius should be 200 feet, and for higher road classifications, the minimum radius depends upon the design parameters established. Compound circular curves and reverse curves are design aspects that enhance the most appropriate design for the road section. Reverse curves are generally permitted with a minimum 100-foot tangent length between the curves, but compound reverse curves are acceptable under certain design conditions and for the lower classifications of roadways.

Vertical Alignment

Vertical alignment of a roadway consists of grades and vertical curves. Design choices for grades and vertical curves must reflect expected weather conditions. The goal is to design a road that minimizes cut and fill requirements but still provides adequate sight distance along the vertical curve. Normally, the critical length of grade is not a controlling factor in the design of residential streets; however, the minimum length of vertical curve is important in providing adequate sight distance. The minimum length of vertical curve, as established for highways and applicable for residential streets, should not be less than three times the design speed. This guide can be used for both crest and sag vertical curves.

The stopping sight distance is the most critical aspect of the vertical alignment. The formulas that can be used to determine the length of vertical curve required are:

Crest Vertical Curves

$S > L \quad L = 2S - \dfrac{1398}{A}$

$S > L \quad L = \dfrac{AS^2}{1398}$

Sag Vertical Curves

$S > L \quad L = 2S - \dfrac{400 + 3.5S}{A}$

$S > L \quad L = \dfrac{AS^2}{400 + 3.5S}$

S = Sight distance, in feet
L = Length of vertical curve, in feet
A = Algebraic difference in grades, in percent

These formulas can be used when the following design parameters are used:

- Crest vertical curves—when the height of the eye is 3.75 feet and the height of the object is 6 inches.
- Sag vertical curves—vehicular headlight spread is the controlling design criterion.

Maximum and minimum gradients for residential roadway classifications have been established on tradition rather than experience. Also, different regions of the country require a different design approach to vertical alignment. Most jurisdictions permit the construction of a road with a minimum gradient of 1 percent. A 0.5 percent minimum grade is acceptable if certain precautions are taken into account, such as maintaining proper drainage in areas where the roads are virtually flat, for example, in Florida.

The maximum road gradient varies considerably from jurisdiction to jurisdiction and from designer to designer. Ideally, local conditions and experience will dictate an acceptable grade. Many localities are establishing the maximum grade at 10 percent without any flexibility. A practical gradient with a continuous grade could be as high as 12 to 14 percent, and under certain conditions, a much steeper gradient could be used. For guidance in developing residential streets, the desired maximum gradient should be 10 percent with design flexibility.

Typical Street Section

Typical street drawings show the interrelationship of the various components of a residential street (Figure 8-4). For example, a 20-foot residential street would be made up of two 10-foot travel lanes with sufficient off-street parking required in the subdivision regulations. In addition to the pavement width, the cross section shows the cross slope, or in this case, the normal crown and the necessary right-of-way. The right-of-way requirements established by the National Association of Home Builders for residential streets accommodate installation of utilities and eliminate unnecessary maintenance costs to the local jurisdiction.

Another component of street construction that is generally based on tradition or state standards is the pavement section. Rigid pavement design (concrete) and flexible pavement design (bituminous concrete) are the two methods used by design engineers to determine the required pavement thickness. Most jurisdictions do not devote time and effort to establishing pavement thicknesses for their area. The pavement designs generally duplicate state standards or adjacent jurisdiction designs which usually are based on different traffic, soil, and weather conditions.

Figure 8-4. Typical street cross section

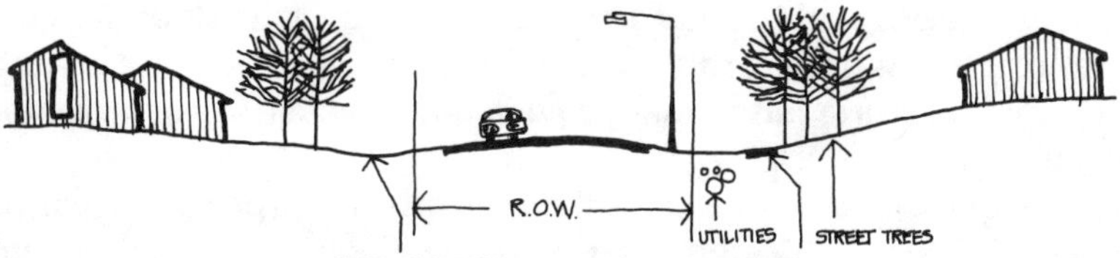

Source: National Association of Home Builders

Residential pavement depths must be based on local conditions. Excessive pavement widths are a luxury that can no longer be afforded because of escalating energy and construction costs. Consideration should be given to using a stone base in lieu of a concrete pavement section or a full-depth bituminous concrete pavement section. In addition, the stone base can be used as a road surface during construction.

Increasing emphasis is being put on developing alternative pavement designs through innovative paving technology. The paving industry is developing substitutes and additives for asphalt and portland cement to decrease the construction costs. One of the most recent and exciting changes in the paving industry is the use of sulphur as a paving material. A test run for the Federal Highway Administration showed that the stabilization capabilities of an asphaltic mix can be equalled by a 100 percent sulphur blacktop mixture. Another development that is receiving more attention is pavement recycling. Although innovation does not always receive universal support, new ideas in pavement construction should be pursued because they can lower construction costs, maintain high-quality pavements, and encourage energy savings.

Intersection Design

Proper intersection design affects safety and drainage. Considerations of efficient residential site planning can override important considerations of intersection design. NAHB recommends that four-way intersections should be avoided whenever possible. This valuable concept for designing an efficient road network should consider the classifications of the intersecting roadways. The anticipated or actual use of a road can require a traffic signal at a T-intersection rather than other traffic control devices. Intersecting residential roadways generally function more efficiently as T-intersections than as four-way stops.

To maintain adequate traffic flow on a high classification roadway may necessitate a turning lane for vehicles turning onto another classification of roadway. This procedure also improves the safety of the motorists making the turn. Lane width, transition length, travel length, and fillet radii are the design aspects of a turning lane. A left turning lane must provide ample stacking distance for the turning vehicles.

Safe sight distances at each intersection are a primary goal in proper intersection design. Many obstructions, if not taken into consideration, can reduce the intersection sight distance dramati-

cally. Again, the geometrics of the roadway will have a direct bearing on the intersection design. Common rules to follow when considering intersection sight distance include the following:
- Avoid intersections on curves.
- Strive to ensure a 90-degree intersection. A skew angle of a minimum of 80 degrees will only reduce the visibility slightly.

Another point to consider in evaluating the intersection's level of service is that future design may require installation of a signal at the intersection. If that is the case, the right-of-way alignment should make provisions to accommodate the signal facilities.

Drainage is an important factor sometimes overlooked in the design of an intersection. Open and closed drainage systems are designed differently for handling the flow of water at an intersection. The grades of each roadway at the intersection have an impact on how to handle the runoff.

Normally, the designed grade of the intersecting streets should be kept below 4 percent within 100 feet. This gradient limitation is necessary to ensure an adequate stopping area. The maximum gradient within that 100 feet should not exceed 10 percent.

At intersections, the desired design should eliminate an excessive flow of runoff at the curb line. The quantity of flow at the intersection determines the depth of flow at the curb line and the width of flow perpendicular to the curb line, the spread. Especially in residential areas where pedestrian traffic is a consideration, the drainage criteria should include the spread and depth of water to ensure a design compatible with both vehicular and pedestrian traffic.

The effect of storm drainage on the street operation can be substantial if the design does not accommodate local intricacies. For example, stormwater ponded at low points, flow adjacent to the curb, and sheet flow across the pavement can all affect the efficiency of the roadway. Sheet flow is critical because of the splash consideration and because of potential vehicle hydroplaning. However, the sheet flow is not a major component in causing hydroplaning on residential streets where the vehicle speed is low and the traffic is light.

Also to be considered is the radius of curbs at intersections. Excessively large radii cost more to build, and result in more paved area, less effective channeling of traffic, and more difficult street crossing by pedestrians, while radii too small result in vehicles driving over curbs and lawns, or swerving before making turns. While a radius of 25 to 30 feet may be necessary for heavily traveled streets, a radius of 20 feet has proven to be sufficient for most low-traffic residential streets (places and lanes).

Curbs

Curbing is used to control drainage, protect pavement edges, and protect sidewalks and lawns from encroachment by vehicles. The use of concrete curbing became popular in the United States during the early part of this century. Traditionally, concete curbing was cast in place using forms; while this method is still used, there are other methods available that involve automated curbing machines or precast curbing systems.[5] An extruded asphalt curb, constructed as a part of the pavement, can be used effectively in both rural and urban developments and is usually less expensive. This type can be less durable than concrete, which can be especially significant in areas that use snow-removal equipment.

The basic types of curb are the concrete barrier curb, the concrete mountable curb, and the asphalt rolled curb. The barrier and mountable curbs may be designed with a gutter. Figure 8-5 shows some representative curb types.

The barrier curb is the traditional system used for city streets and is appropriate for high traffic roadways with adjoining high density development and a large volume of pedestrian traffic. For suburban areas of single-family detached homes, a mountable curb is often preferred because it is less expensive to build, and in lower traffic areas, there is less of a problem with vehicles pulling off the roadway. Also, the availability of off-street parking in suburban

Figure 8-5. Curb types

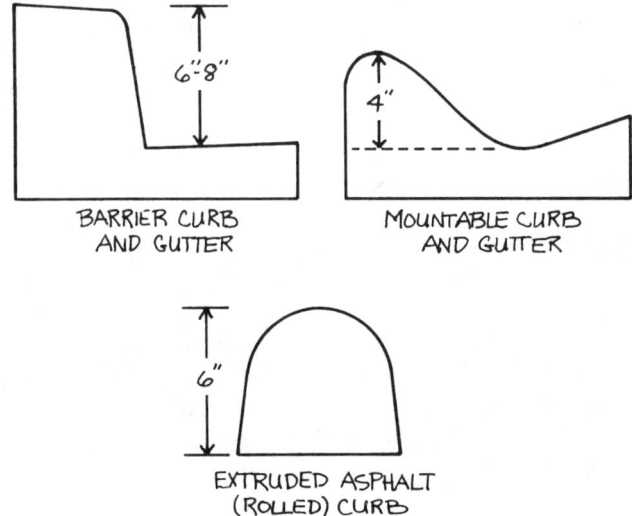

areas reduces on-street parking, obviating much of the need for a barrier curb.

The use of curbs, gutter, and stormwater drains is known as a closed system. Another option being used more frequently today is the drainage swale. This is a grass-lined open channel adjacent to the street. No curbing is used (Figure 8-6). The use of swales allows a significant percentage of the stormwater to seep into the earth immediately, while another portion may remain as standing water for hours after a rain. This reduces stormwater runoff, especially the amount of peak runoff, and helps in removing some of the pollutants, such as motor oil, from the stormwater. The environmental benefits and cost savings of open drainage systems have made the use of swales an attractive alternative to traditional curb and gutter systems.

Figure 8-6. Grass swales for drainage

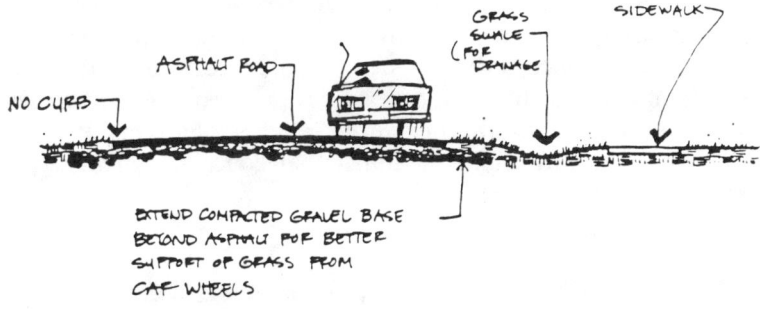

Source: HOH Associates, Inc.

Pedestrian Traffic

With increasing emphasis on comprehensive community planning, sidewalks, pathways, and bicycle paths for pedestrian circulation are being required. Obviously, pedestrian traffic needs to be separated from vehicular traffic on streets with significant vehicular volume. Again, the evaluation of a development and the need to accommodate pedestrian traffic should not be circumvented by inflexible development requirements. The location of sidewalks or pathways should be determined by the need of the subdivision and adjacent uses. The intended use and expected use of the facility should then dictate the width and material of the facility.

A pedestrian travelway can be located within a street right-of-way or can be separated completely from the street. If it is within the right-of-way, careful consideration should be given to the design requirements for an open-section roadway. Normally, the sidewalk width is 4 feet. However, in commercial centers or adjacent to schools, the width increases to accommodate anticipated heavy pedestrian traffic. A two-way bicycle path to be used only by bicycles requires a path 5 feet wide. The path or sidewalk surface is determined by the existing site conditions and can vary from a well-drained soil surface to a concrete surface. Between these two extremes are several other common surfaces, such as stone, wood mulch, and bituminous concrete. Where a path crosses any street, adequate sight distance should be available for the pedestrian. Residential street design should accommodate pedestrian and vehicular traffic while providing facilities that protect the general health, safety, and welfare of the public.

In recent years, many communities have recognized that sidewalks are expensive items that increase the cost of new housing. They have also come to appreciate that sidewalks may not be necessary on low-traffic streets. This has led many local governments to require sidewalks on both sides of major roadways only and on one side of collector streets, and to have no requirement for sidewalks on cul-de-sacs and other minor residential streets. Appendix C includes some examples of municipal codes which follow this practice.

Community Roadway Plans and Standards

Over the past several years, as local governments established their development standards, they sought methods to lessen the impact of development on existing public facilities. Their method of accomplishing this goal was to impose additional restrictions on new development, which included increased subdivision fees and provision of public facilities. Requirements to provide offsite facilities to be used by the community-at-large are being imposed, although some of these requirements have been questioned legally. Public capital improvement projects are as important to a community as a development is to the economic base. Most of the roadways built years ago are now the main roadways within a community. The new residential roadways, designed with new standards, intersect these older roads. A practical solution to this situation would be for communities to institute an improvement program that complements new development rather than to pass the improvement costs on to new residents.

Traffic analysis is another tool that jurisdictions are using to establish residential road classifications. Developers are being required to furnish a traffic report on the impact of the increased traffic on the surrounding roads to determine their classifications. Again, this requirement is shifting the responsibility and costs of these determinations to the developer.

An important aspect of any overall community plan is the development of a comprehensive roadway plan. This plan evaluates the intended land use, the existing land use, and the existing and proposed road alignments to arrive at a road classification that is suited to the anticipated traffic. A local government could meet the needs of the community by providing an adequate road network based on a comprehensive and jurisdiction-wide traffic analysis, rather than relying on a piecemeal approach. This road network plan can then be used to set the road construction project priorities for the local government.

Maintenance is an important factor in setting any government's development standards. This section on residential streets not only presents practical design concepts that can serve the needs of vehicle and pedestrian traffic; it also shows that maintenance and costs can be reduced by many means, such as reducing pavement width.

Most residents expect efficient local government maintenance service, and this service can be provided within certain fiscal constraints. When street design parameters are reduced while adequate facilities are maintained, maintenance costs to the community are kept to a minimum. Some communities, however, require a maintenance guarantee or bond. Generally, a 1-year maintenance guarantee is all that is necessary, since this will allow the local government to incorporate funds for maintenance needs in the next year's budget. It should be acknowledged that it is the inspection of the completed street, not a maintenance bond, that is the quality control mechanism. Routine maintenance of a public street is the responsibility of the local (or state) government.

Several communities require developers to post bonds in excess of 100 percent of the construction cost of the streets and storm drainage before they receive the necessary approvals. If this situation exists, a road construction bond that uses mutually accepted construction unit prices should be developed. The bond should be separated into several phases, and the amount for each phase should be released to the developer after it is completed.

NAHB's guidelines on designing and constructing practical residential streets have set principles and practices that residential communities can follow. As energy, taxes, costs, environmental concerns, aesthetic requirements, and safe but functional roadways continue to receive national attention, many communities will try new approaches to serve their future residential neighborhoods. Innovative land planning techniques will require residential street designs that complement the development design.

Chapter 9
Energy Conservation

The energy crisis of the 1970s brought a new awareness of the need to use energy wisely. Although energy availability has increased and relative costs have decreased at times since then, we are mindful that our fossil fuel supplies are finite and that long-term energy shortages will occur.

The lessons learned about energy efficiency and conservation have become permanent guidelines that need to be considered in designing and siting housing. Even in periods of less expensive energy, consumers of housing have exhibited a strong preference for energy-efficient homes.

Housing Types

The single-family detached unit is the most predominant housing type in the United States, yet it is the least energy-efficient when compared to higher density solutions.

Single-family detached units:
- Have larger floor plans than multifamily structures.
- Have greater heat loss in winter and heat gain in summer, maximizing heating and cooling requirements.
- Minimize the opportunities for shared construction such as common walls, driveways, and utilities.
- Reduce the opportunities for orientation to minimize adverse climatic conditions.
- Maximize the traveling distances.

High-density housing types such as townhouses and low- and highrise apartments offer greater energy savings than single-family units. A typical highrise apartment is 42 percent smaller and uses 34 percent less energy per square foot than a detached, one-story, single-family house.[1]

By reducing distances to services, high-density development also makes other energy-conserving options feasible such as mass transit and onsite shopping and recreational amenities.

High-density housing types are also transportation energy-efficient, according to the Argonne National Laboratory:

The highrise apartment at the upper end of the density scale requires much shorter streets than a single-family detached subdivision with the same number of units. For a 1,000-unit conventional subdivision 60,000 feet of road will be needed. A 1,000-unit high-rise complex requires only 8,950 feet, 86 percent less. The highrise complex will require somewhat wider streets for adequate traffic handling. Because most of the energy used in this country is used in the residential sector, planned and higher density development provides one of the most important means of conserving energy.[2]

The single-family detached house uses household-energy services far less efficiently than the highrise apartment. The difference is especially evident in heating-energy use. Increased density and planning could reduce energy and water use by an estimated 40 percent.

Heating and Cooling of Structures

The human body has an established climatic zone in which it is most comfortable. Through history, man has either settled in areas where the natural climate most closely fits this comfort zone, or altered the ambient conditions accordingly. Earlier civilizations built their habitats to maximize the natural heating and cooling potentials of the wind and sun. With the advancement of technology, man has relied less on natural systems and more on energy-intensive technological solutions.

The greatest amount of energy consumed by residential developments is in the heating and cooling of structures, the former being the less energy-efficient of the two. At a time of concern for energy supplies and costs, reexamining the energy-conserving potential of natural energy systems is essential. The principles of site planning and design can make significant contributions to energy conservation in the heating and cooling of structures: passive systems, siting of structures, and site modification.

The first step is to determine whether the principal problems are in heating or cooling. The "heating degree day index" (Figure 9-1) can be used to evaluate heating needs, and the "discomfort index" (Figure 9-2) can be used to determine cooling needs. Simply locate the project and compare the numerical value of the indices. Lincoln, Nebraska, for example, has 6,000 heating degree days and a value of 1,500 on the discomfort index; therefore, heating requires four times as much energy as cooling.[3]

Figure 9-1. Heating degree day index

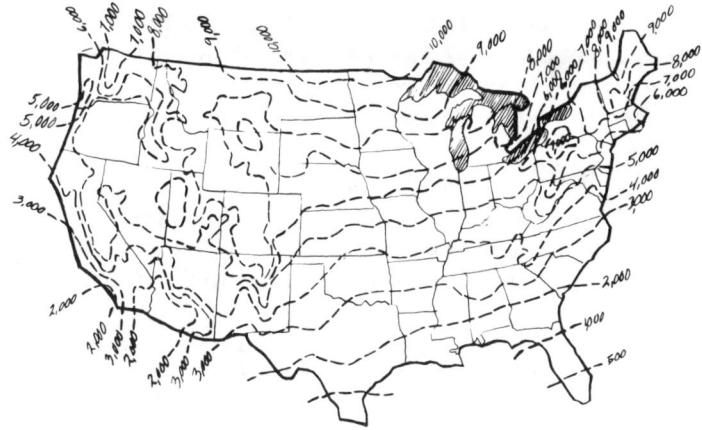

Source: Environmental Design and Research

Figure 9-2. Discomfort index

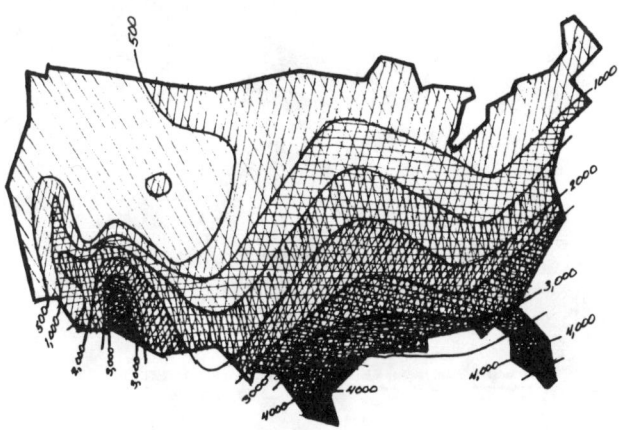

Source: Environmental Design and Research

Solar Characteristics

The builder should understand a few fundamental characteristics about the sun before designing a development that uses solar energy.

- The noon sun angle is 45 degrees higher in the sky in the summer than in winter. Therefore, the winter sun reaches farther

267

into the interior of structures and the summer sun is easiest to block (Figure 9-3).[4]

- In the temperate zone the summer sun path from sunrise to sunset is 240 degrees. Therefore, the east-to-west facing surfaces receive more sun than the south or north (Figure 9-4). A horizontal roof surface receives a greater amount of radiation than any of the sides.[5]
- During the winter months the sun's path is 120 degrees, and the south-facing surfaces receive the greatest amount of radiation.[6]
- In the winter, the sun rises in the east and sets in the west. In the summer, the sun rises in the northeast and sets in the northwest.

These fundamental characteristics of the sun, when combined with site characteristics such as topography and vegetation, deter-

Figure 9-3. Deciduous trees provide shade in summer while allowing sun to penetrate in winter

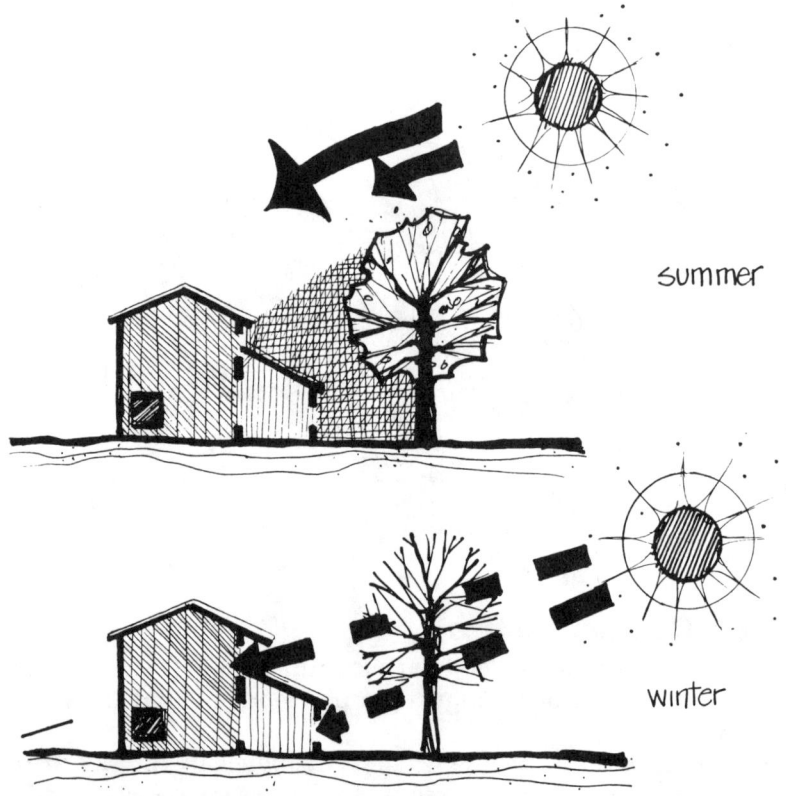

Source: Environmental Design and Research

Figure 9-4. Sun angle diagram

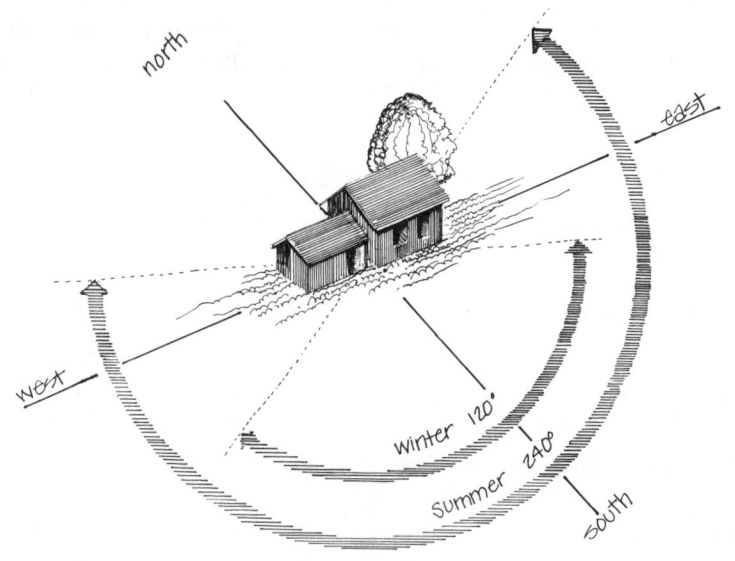

Source: Environmental Design and Research

mine design decisions based on solar radiation. The following guidelines can be applied when selecting land for development, laying out streets and lots, and locating structures to maximize beneficial and minimize adverse solar and wind effects.

Topography

The slope and orientation of the land largely determine the amount of radiation received. South-facing slopes usually receive the greatest amount of sunlight. General guidelines can be stated for positioning residential development in all regions of the continental United States:[7]

Southeast slope	Most desirable
South slope	Preferred (warm winters, early spring, late fall)
East slope	Acceptable (warm winter mornings, cool summer evenings)
West slope	Undesirable (hottest summer slope)
North slope	Least desirable (coldest in winter)

Always keep in mind that shade can be provided if the sun is a nuisance, but significant solar exposure is impossible once a dwelling is located on a shady north-facing slope.

Slope orientation can have significant effects on seasonal change. Studies in the New York-New Jersey region measured the impact of radiation on slopes of varied orientation and steepness and have shown that preferred locations can extend effects of the desired season. According to Victor Olgyay in his book *Design with Climate*:

> Slopes of 10 percent gradient with south and southeast orientation receive 20 percent or more solar radiation and will be two weeks ahead of any other slope in the arrival of spring.[8]

Street Layout

The layout of streets largely determines the orientation of the structures and lots to sun and wind patterns. East-west street layouts are usually preferable because the lots are oriented north-south.

Solar Heating

For passive solar heating, the goal is to design the structure for maximum exposure to the southeast and southwest. The fundamental principle of passive systems is very simple, but to design the dwelling that is most efficient in its relationship to site characteristics often requires sophisticated analysis and unconventional design solutions. In general, passive systems work by opening the sides of the unit that are exposed to the greatest amount of radiation and closing off all others, creating a greenhouse effect. This effect is typically accomplished by placing large double-glazed windows on the southern exposures and leaving all other exposures nearly solid walls. The same principle applies for active systems, the only difference being that the major concern is for sunlight to reach the solar collectors, usually located on the roof, rather than on the window walls. After the radiation has been trapped in the dwelling and converted to heat, a variety of methods, such as fans and rock beds, can be used to circulate and store the heat.

The future of passive and active solar heating systems is unclear. Most states require passive systems to be backed up by conventional heating systems. The cost of duplicating systems combined with the cost of large areas of double-glazed windows and extra insulation required in passive heated structures increases the house price above that of conventional homes. The extent of the construction of solar heating systems will depend upon government incentives through the tax code, state and local design standards, and the cost of heating fuel.

Tree Locations for Solar Efficiency

A major concern in the design of solar-efficient developments is the location of trees. Good tree-planting design allows solar radiation to reach windows and solar collectors during the winter months and provides shade during summer months. December 21 is the most critical day for winter heating requirements because the sun is at its lowest angle. Low sun angles cause the greatest problems by casting the most extensive shadows. Shadows can be plotted by using either a solar simulator or graphic techniques. Shadow patterns depend on site slope and orientation as well as the form of the shadow-casting object (Figure 9-5). A series of shadow patterns can be shifted about the site until no shadows conflict with the window wall or collectors.

Two major factors to consider in evaluating tree shading are the time of the year the shading occurs (species leaf-out and leaf-fall dates) and the amount of sunlight that penetrates the bare branches of deciduous trees. Both factors vary widely among species (Figure 9-6).

Avoiding shading during winter months is only one of the planning considerations for trees in energy-conserving residential developments. Beneficial effects such as shading and wind-breaking may also be important.

Morning and evening shadows determine beneficial shading of east-west windows, paved areas such as streets and parking lots,

Figure 9-5. Shadow patterns of trees vary with ground slope

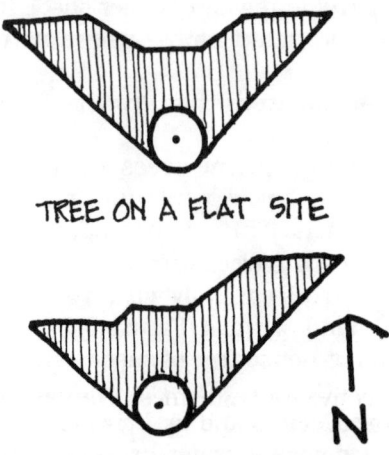

Source: Zanetto, **Landscape Architecture,** Vol. 68, No. 6 (November 1978), p. 514.

Figure 9-6. Sun penetration for various street trees

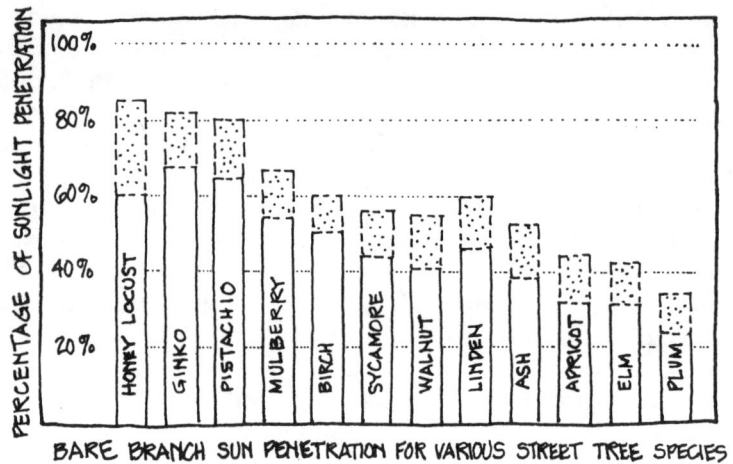

Source: Zanetto, **Landscape Architecture,** Vol. 68, No. 6 (November 1978), p. 516.

and outdoor-use areas such as patios during the summer months. The summer noon condition of June 21 is the most critical for shading such outdoor surfaces.[9]

The key rules for choosing tree species for energy conservation are:[10]

- Form—wide short trees shade better in summer and less in winter than other forms.
- Deciduous or evergreen—use mainly deciduous trees; use evergreen for wind control and where winter shade is desirable.
- Foliage and bare branch density—use relative to sunlight and wind penetration.
- Growth rates—plant trees that grow fast initially but slowly after reaching optimum form.
- Minimum pruning—prune trees up (not down) to allow breezes and winter sun below, while minimizing suckering and dense branching patterns. Thin, do not top, trees.

The key rules for locating trees are:

- Select and locate trees carefully within a 45-degree arc west of solar collectors and window walls (Figure 9-7).
- Keep south wall of house free of shadows on December 21.
- Use plan and section drawings to evaluate shadows for both conflicts with solar collectors and for beneficial summer shading.
- Remember that domestic water heating collectors, pools, and gardens need sunlight during the hot season when dwelling windows, streets, and paving need shade.

Figure 9-7. Locate trees within 45° arc

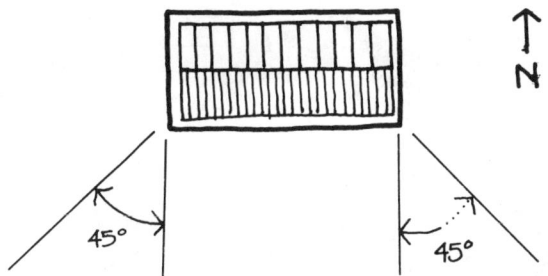

- Place evergreens to the north of structures and to the north of whole developments if north winter winds are a problem.
- Plant trees close to roadways to provide "tunnels of shade" with continuous closed canopies.
- Plant the tallest trees on the southern side of the street (Figure 9-8).

Figure 9-8. Tallest trees on south side of street

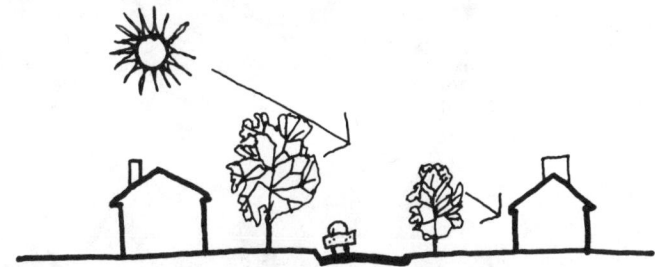

Structure relationships—Avoid obstructing winter sun by placing smaller buildings in the shadow of larger structures (Figure 9-9).

Figure 9-9. Large buildings should not block winter sun

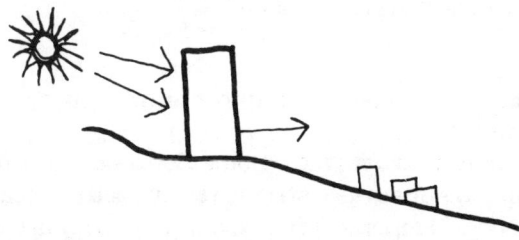

Structure orientation—Depending on the climatic region, orient the structure for optimum summer sun.

Figure 9-10. Sun pockets

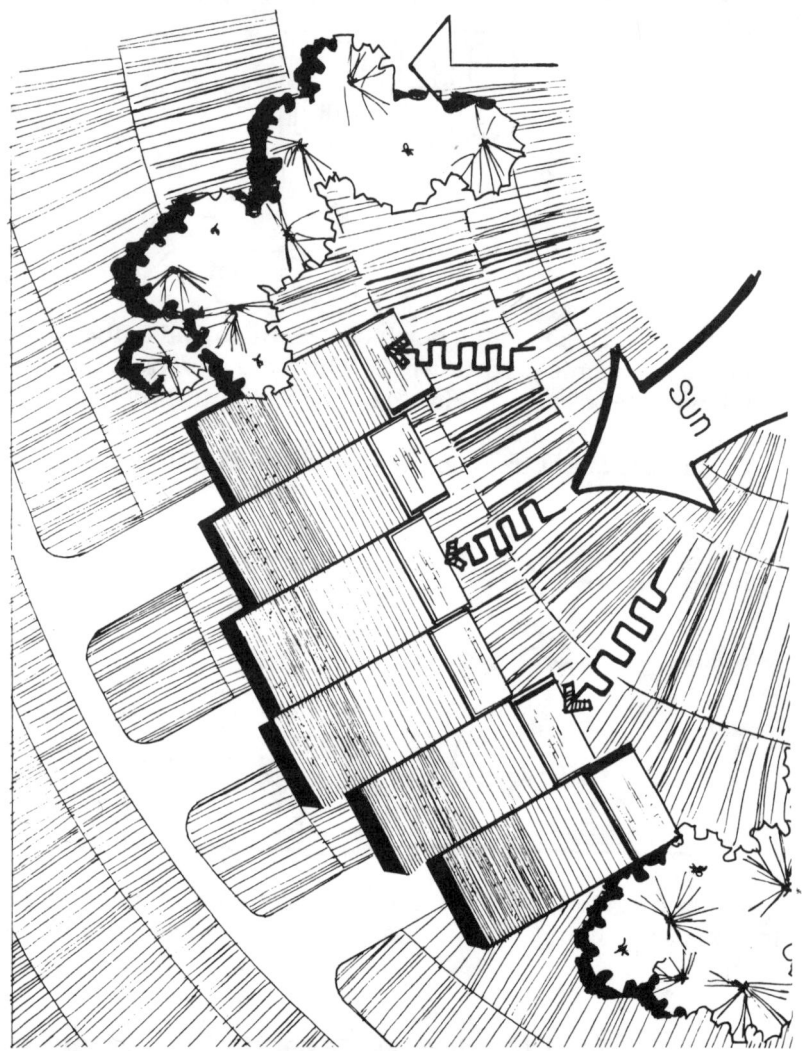

Source: Environmental Design and Research

Cluster multiple dwellings around sunny courts to create sun pockets (Figure 9-10).

Earth-protected structures—Some developers are finding subsurface or partial subsurface structures attractive because of their energy efficiency. Temperatures above the ground are consistently hotter in the summer and cooler in the winter than below the surface (Figures 9-11 and 9-12).

Figure 9-11. Comparative surface and subsurface temperatures

Source: The Center for Landscape Architectural Education and Research, **Options for Passive Energy Conservation in Site Design,** p. 19 (for National Technical Information Service).

Figure 9-12. Regional suitability of completely or partially subterranean construction

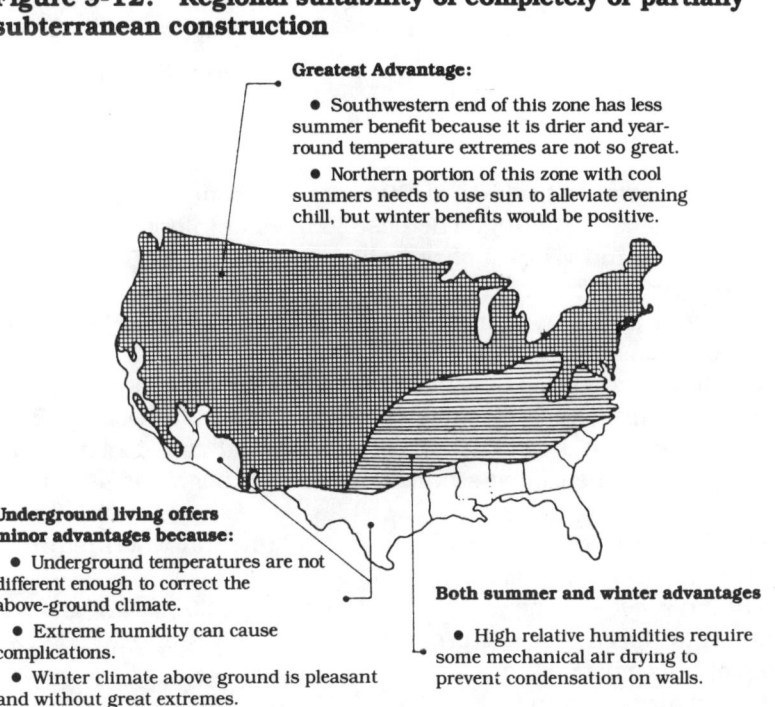

Source: The Center for Landscape Architectural Education and Research, **Options for Passive Energy Conservation in Site Design,** p. 20 (for National Technical Information Service).

Bodies of water—The temperature extremes are moderated on shoreline sites by the proximity to water. Temperatures are cooler in the summer and warmer in the winter.

Wind—Wind cools air and dwelling temperatures by increasing evaporative and convective cooling. Wind direction and velocity vary daily and seasonally, but predominant wind characteristics can be established for any given site. Studies have shown the following correlation between exterior wind velocity and the interior temperature required to offset cold air infiltration[11] (Figure 9-13).

Figure 9-13. Effect of Wind on Heating Requirements

Wind speed (mph)	Heating requirements
1/10	68.0°F
1/2	73.0°F
1	75.0°F
2	77.7°F
3	78.3°F
5	79.3°F
10	80.6°F

Records show that winds at 20 miles per hour can double the heating load of a building. The best sources of information about the direction and velocity of prevailing winds in a region are the U.S. Weather Bureau and local airports. This information should be gathered for the winter and summer seasons and represented graphically on site analysis plans.

A variety of conditions affect the specific movement of air on any site: topography, vegetation, structures, and water bodies. The builder's goal is to protect the structures from adverse winter winds and to channel beneficial summer breezes through the structure and outdoor living spaces.

The following considerations are fundamental when making gross site selection decisions:

- Wind speeds at the crest of a ridge are up to 20 percent greater than wind speeds on flat ground. Avoid the tops and windward sides of hills where wind velocities are greatest.
- Cold air settles in valley floors. Avoid them.
- Valley walls tend to be the preferable locations because they are relatively warmer than ridges and valleys.

- Shoreline developments receive cool breezes from bodies of water during the day.

Site-specific wind considerations are as follows:

- Locate garages and other rooms that are not lived in on the prevailing winter wind sides of dwellings.
- A 45-degree angle orientation to prevailing winter winds is the worst possible orientation, while a parallel orientation is the best.
- Fences, earth berms, and vegetation on the windward side of dwellings reduce air infiltration. Evergreens are year-round barriers, while deciduous vegetation provides the least protection during the worst months.
- Trying to stop the wind only makes conditions worse. Simply try to deflect the wind to avoid structures.

Vegetation can provide significant wind velocity reductions. The degree of wind reduction depends on the vegetation density, shape, and size. Vegetation can reduce wind velocity by 30 to 50 percent over a distance of 10 to 20 times the height of the windbreak (Figures 9-14 and 9-15).

Figure 9-14. Vegetation can reduce wind velocity significantly

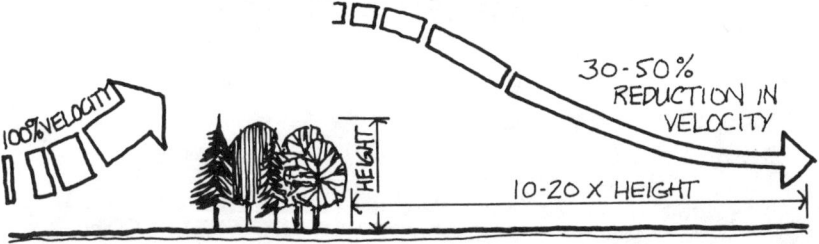

The height of the vegetation has the greatest effect on the distance of velocity reduction. As the wind is diverted upward, pockets of relatively calm air are created on both the leeward and windward sides. If the vegetation lacks enough density or branches far off the ground, little wind protection will result.

The cooling effect of summer breezes can play a beneficial role. The basic consideration is to remove all potential obstacles between the structure and the prevailing summer breezes. Sensitive designs can channel and increase available summer winds. Obviously, the ideal design minimizes the adverse effects of winter winds and maximizes the beneficial effects of summer breezes (Figure 9-16).

Figure 9-15. Using vegetation and fencing to reduce wind velocity

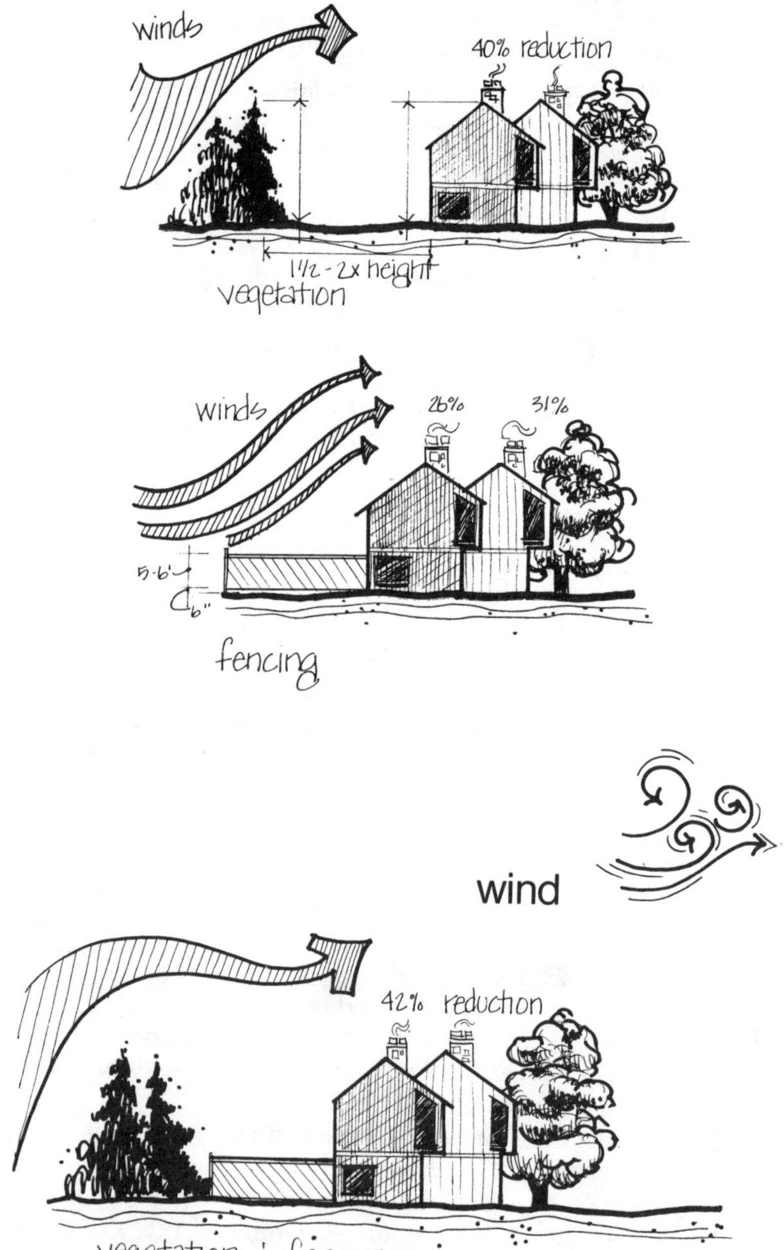

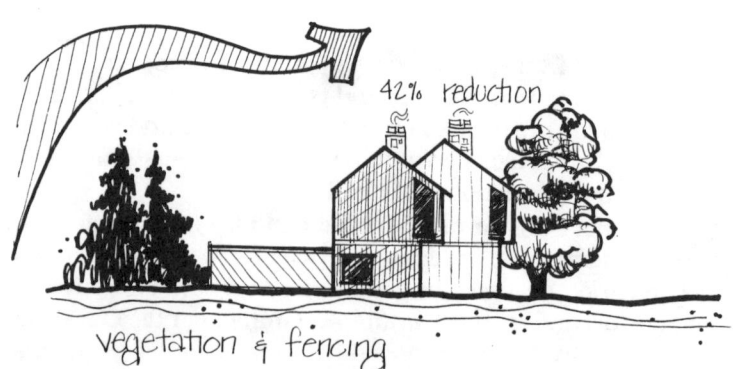

Source: Environmental Design and Research

Figure 9-16. Analysis of prevailing summer and winter winds

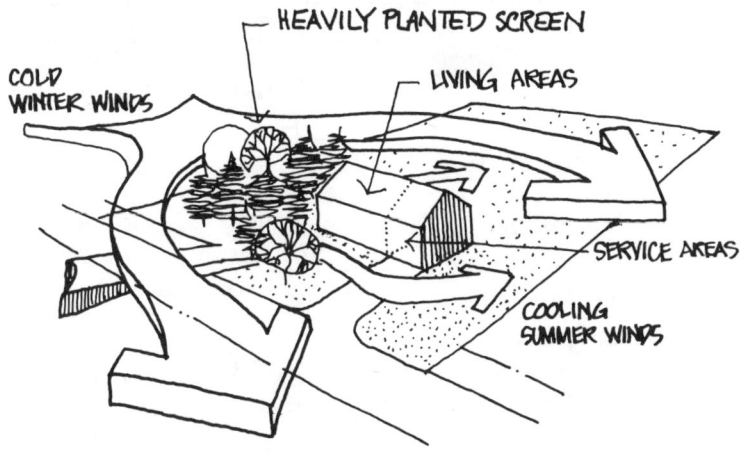

Source: The Center for Landscape Architectural Education and Research, **Options for Passive Energy Conservation in Site Design,** p. 75 (for National Technical Information Service).

Regional Site Design Guidelines

The four major climatic regions of the United States are the cool, temperate, hot-humid, and hot-arid regions (Figure 9-17), and each requires special site design considerations. Figure 9-18 provides

Figure 9-17. Climatic zones in the United States

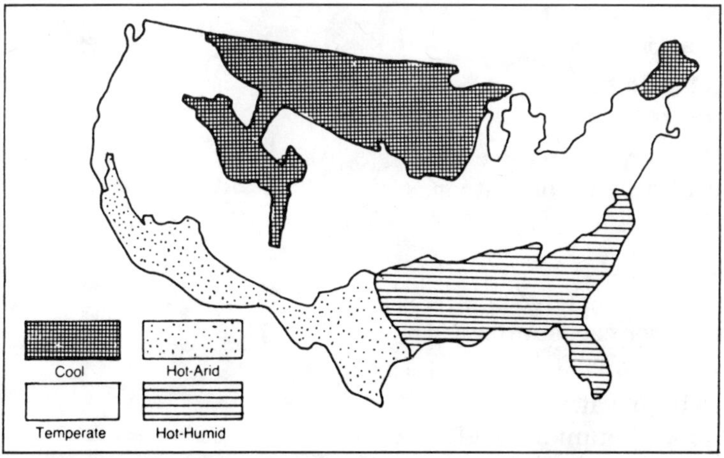

Source: Kennedy, **Integrated Community Energy Systems,** p. B.5.

279

Figure 9-18. Site selection and design guidelines

	Climatic zones			
	Cool	Temperate	Hot-humid	Hot-arid
Wind				
Locate site structures on the leeward sides of hills to protect from prevailing winter winds from the	NW	NW	E&SW	
Avoid hot desert breezes				X
Do not obstruct prevailing summer breezes from the	SW	SSW	E	EW
Solar				
Select sloping sites with south/southeast orientation for winter heating and year-round balance	X	X	X	X
Select east-west street layout	X	X	X	X
Topography				
Avoid valley floors, which are damp, cool, and potential frost pockets	X	X	X	X
Avoid ridgelines exposed to winter winds	X	X		
Select hill crests for ventilation			X	
Select sites halfway up slopes	X	X		X
Avoid slopes in excess of 20 percent because of drainage problems	X	X	X	X
Water				
Locate close to large bodies of water for cool summer breezes	X	X	X	X
Avoid high water tables because of humidity and frost	X	X	X	

Figure 9-18, continued

	Climatic zones			
	Cool	Temperate	Hot-humid	Hot-arid
Locate on mountainous or hilly coastal sites, which are open to breezes			X	
Avoid areas of coastal fog (in areas of fog seek higher elevations where fog retention is less)		X		
Avoid coastal lowland areas if dampened by the effect of dense vegetation or buildings that act as windbreaks			X	

Source: The Center for Landscape Architectural Education and Research, **Options for Passive Energy Conservation in Site Design** (for the National Technical Information Service).

site selection and design guidelines for each climatic region. These guidelines are general and require sensitive application to specific site conditions and project requirements.

Regulatory Effects on Energy Conservation

Current development regulations both encourage and discourage the design of energy-efficient residential developments. The builder is faced with trying to incorporate new bodies of knowledge and technology into standard building designs without excessive costs or unsatisfactory home appearance. The builder has insufficient standards, quantified energy savings data, and prototypes from which to draw ideas; therefore, in the interim period builders will probably be required to show good faith during the design phase. Passive solar systems are attractive because of their relatively low environmental impact, which can result in relatively easy permit review.

Future trends in land use planning will see more flexible zoning and subdivision regulations, and even energy conservation ordinances. In the past, zoning has segregated land uses, required minimum lot sizes (which has encouraged low-density residential development), and established setback requirements that necessitate detached units—none of which promote energy-efficient development. In the future, zoning ordinances will have to be amended to allow for energy-conserving solutions.

Subdivision regulations control the layout and width of streets and have an important bearing on lot configuration when each lot is required to have frontage on a public street. The introduction of performance standards and energy conservation concerns will increase rejection of traditional gridiron layouts in favor of more energy-efficient curvilinear streets with cul-de-sacs and reduced street width requirements. The reduction in street standards and flexibility in lot layout can result in significant energy savings.

Planned unit developments also offer energy conservation as they gain greater acceptance, as does clustering within traditional zoning and subdivision regulations.

The general plan adopted by the City of Davis, California, in 1973, included the following items in an energy conservation ordinance:

- Efficient land use eliminating development in a checkerboard fashion.
- Distributing city services in an efficient manner.
- Orienting houses on a north-south axis.
- Deregulating fence setbacks.
- Shading streets.
- Reducing street widths.
- Efficient transportation system, providing bicycle circulation network.[12]

After a solar-efficient development has been designed, numerous private legal devices can ensure that solar access remains intact. Restrictive covenants, easements, and homeowners association ordinances can all be used. Convenants and easements have the advantage of being available to individuals who wish to enter into an agreement. The key advantage of homeowners association ordinances is that the enforcement remains local.[13]

Until present building codes, zoning, and subdivision regulations are amended, builders may find it difficult to design energy-efficient neighborhoods. As long as codes require excessive setbacks and oversized conventional backup heating systems, builders may find the excessive construction and legal costs prohibitive. Tax breaks and incentive zoning are two major devices government will use to offset these restrictions and encourage energy conservation.

Chapter 10
Landscaping

Plant materials are used in the built environment for aesthetic and functional reasons. Developers must recognize that plants can directly affect the development's economic success. Because builders and developers seldom are experts in landscaping techniques and plant materials, they should seek professional guidance from a well qualified landscape architect.

Benefits of Landscaping to the Development

Just as builders use various building materials to create structures, they should use various plant materials to develop exterior environments. Maples, oaks, and junipers can be used in the same way the builder uses stone, brick, and wood. Collectively, plants can form walls, floors, and ceilings; frame views; articulate space; and soften or accentuate architectural forms.

Unlike manmade forms, which are usually static, plants change with their environment. Size, color, form, density, and texture are dynamic elements of plant materials that the designer can use effectively in landscaping. Functionally, plants can be used to control pollution, noise, erosion, climate, and views, either physically or psychologically. Above all, vegetation has the positive psychological effect of bringing the manmade environment in harmony with the natural environment.

The landscaping process should be planned carefully in light of the potential effects plants have on the built environment. Whether formulating personal design decisions or working with professional consultants, the developer must become educated to the potential value of the effective use of plant materials.

Existing Vegetation

If a development is going to achieve financial success, the developer must get the most out of every development dollar. To achieve this goal, the developer must give landscaping operations consideration early in the development phase—not wait until unit types, densities, distribution, and circulation are determined.

The landscaping process should begin at the earliest stage, preferably during site selection. Everything from field grasses to mature trees should be studied and assessed in terms of its potential benefit to the development. The presence of vegetation should affect both the proposed density of development and the type of development. For example, a heavily vegetated site might appear attractive because of its marketing value, but after cutting roadways and installing utilities, the developer might find that the high water table is affected, and serious dieback of the vegetation could become a detriment.

Open areas generally consume the greatest percentage of the planting budget. The savings in higher density units can offset the higher landscaping costs of the common open spaces. Lower densities in vegetated areas minimize site disturbance and the cost of clearing and replanting, and preserve the natural qualities of the site for marketing.

Following are a few basic considerations that warrant attention early in the development process:

- The natural features of the site—vegetation, topography, and open spaces—can offer opportunities to define neighborhoods and buffer use areas (Figure 10-1).

- Existing drainage courses and vegetation can reveal their po-

Figure 10-1. Natural features

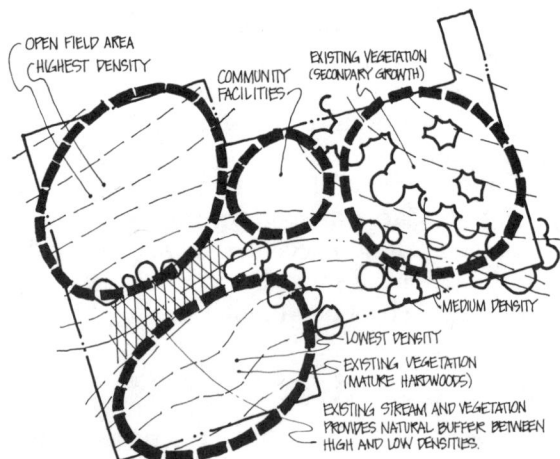

Source: Environmental Design and Research

tential for creating visual buffers between neighborhoods, providing circulation systems, and reducing storm drainage systems (Figure 10-2).

- Selection of unit types and their layout can optimize the preservation of existing vegetation (Figure 10-3).
- Dieback is apt to occur beyond clearing lines, because of sudden exposure to sun and wind, roof damage by roadway, excavation, and utility trenching. Weak, diseased trees with dead branches will do little for the development's sales effort.
- Lower densities in wooded areas help ensure that the character of the site will be preserved. Only selective plants are retained because of roadway clearing, roadway and building excavation, and utility mains and arterials. Plants adjacent to such excavation areas die back, leaving little if any effective vegetation. Lower densities in wooded areas help ensure that the character of the site will be retained after dieback.
- When possible, unit type based on site conditions should be selected to minimize clearing caused by grading operations.
- When higher densities are planned, driveways should be located to maximize preservation of vegetative masses.

Figure 10-2. Using vegetation to create buffers between neighborhoods

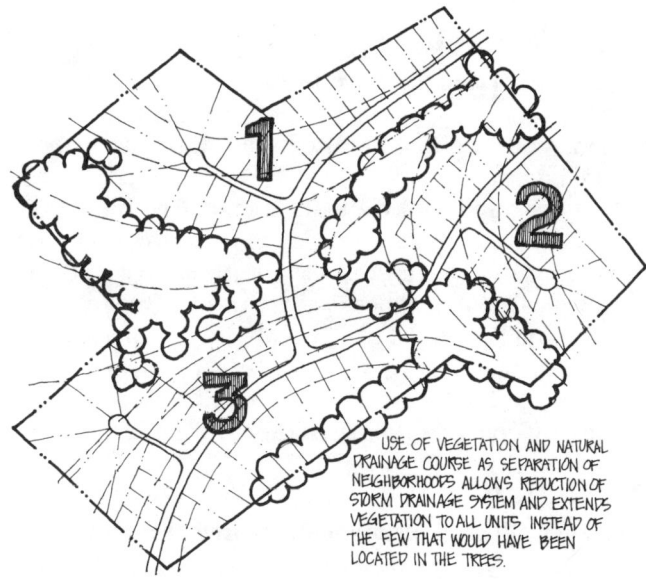

USE OF VEGETATION AND NATURAL DRAINAGE COURSE AS SEPARATION OF NEIGHBORHOODS ALLOWS REDUCTION OF STORM DRAINAGE SYSTEM AND EXTENDS VEGETATION TO ALL UNITS INSTEAD OF THE FEW THAT WOULD HAVE BEEN LOCATED IN THE TREES.

Source: Environmental Design and Research

Figure 10-3. Preservation of existing vegetation

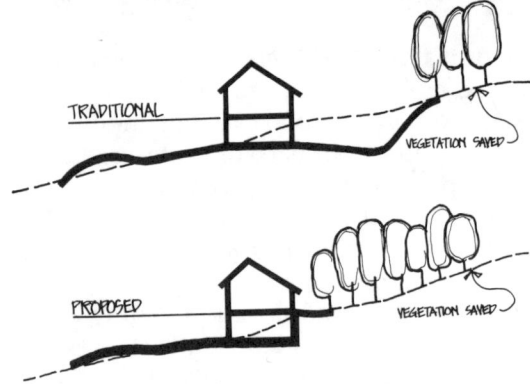

Source: Environmental Design and Research

- Driveway clearings should be used for utility corridors.
- A major portion of dieback is caused by careless construction practices and by failure to plan operations with the preservation of vegetation as an important consideration.

When analyzing site conditions and beginning the decision-making process, the developer should be familiar with specific design responses.

Preserving Valuable Vegetation

- After design documents have been completed, the site should be inspected.
- Proposed road alignments and building areas to be cleared should be staked out.
- The designer and builder should then determine if any minor adjustments should be made in order to preserve valuable vegetation. Major changes are rarely justified or necessary if accurate site surveys and logical design processes are used. Minor changes usually amount to small road and utility realignments and minor building site relocations.
- When layout is finally determined, retained trees that may be disturbed during construction should be protected adequately.

Tree Protection

- Snow fences or scrap lumber can encircle trees and make good protective barriers.
- Construction equipment should operate as far away from protected trees as is practical (Figure 10-4).

Figure 10-4. Root damage and soil compaction from weight of construction equipment

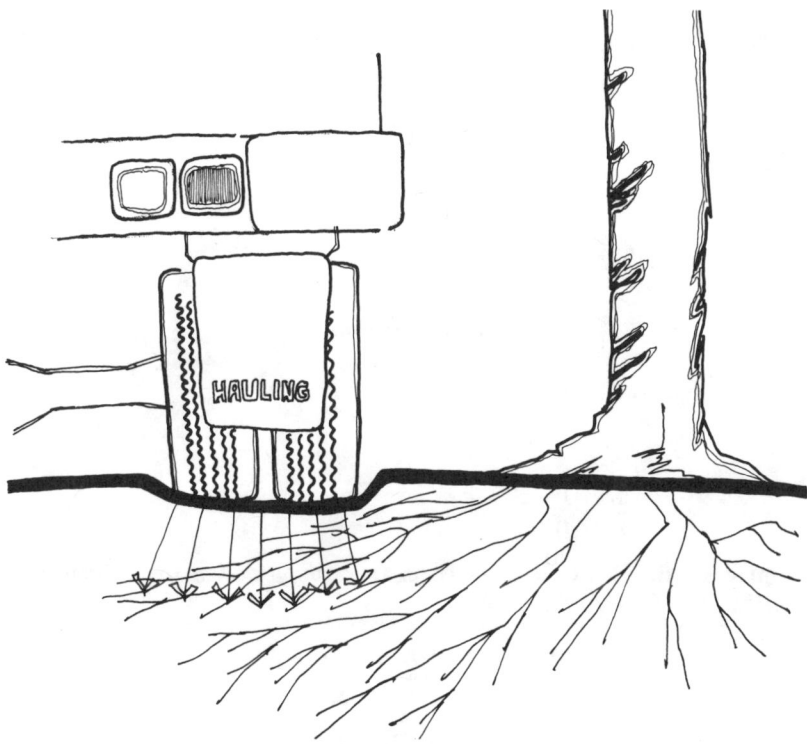

Source: Environmental Design and Research

- Topsoil, building supplies, and backfill materials should not be placed in or around the protected areas (Figure 10-5).
- Trenching should be planned to avoid damaging root systems (Figure 10-6).
- Grading that may affect surface or subsurface drainage patterns should be planned carefully to minimize the effect of too much or too little water for plants (Figure 10-7).

Pruning and Repair of Damaged Vegetation

- Regardless of how well the trees are protected, any disturbed trees should be pruned, fertilized, and watered to overcome any moisture or nutrient deficiencies that occur during construction.
- Damaged trees should be repaired as soon as possible after the damage occurs.
- Scars, broken branches, and pruned branches more than 34 inches in diameter should be coated with a tree-wound paint.

Figure 10-5. Root damage and soil compaction from storage of construction materials

Source: Environmental Deisgn and Research

Figure 10-6. Root damage from trenching operations (building footings and utility trenches)

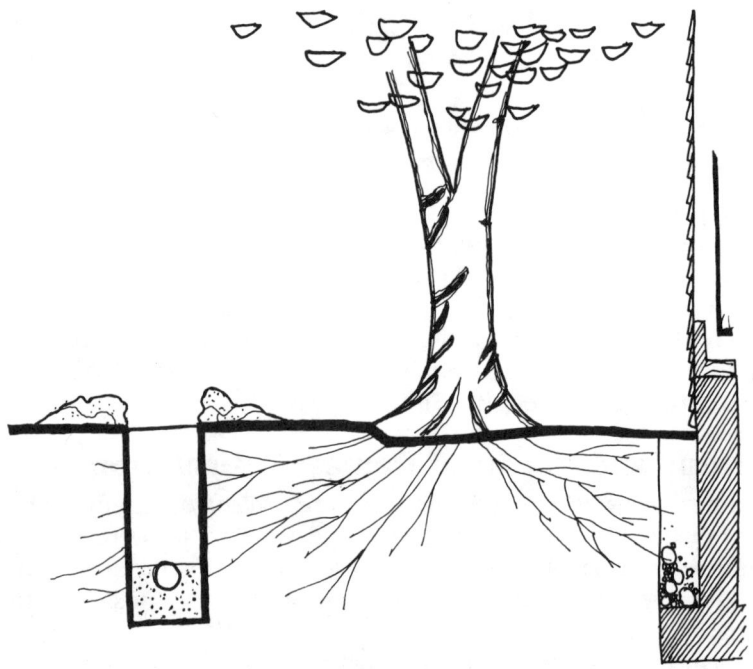

Source: Environmental Design and Research

Figure 10-7. Lowering of water table by grade changes and trenches

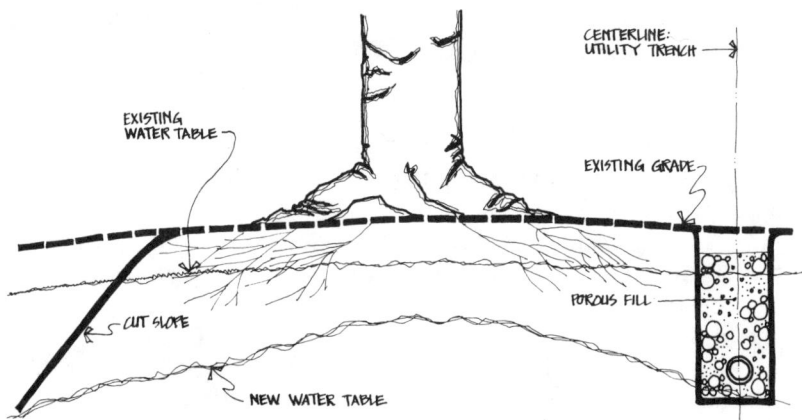

Source: Environmental Design and Research

- Professionals should be consulted for pruning, fertilizing, and repairing trees.

A little extra effort can go a long way towards saving and maintaining a tree that has years of growth behind it and that would cost money to cut.

General Guidelines

- Trees have a good chance for survival if two-thirds of the area under the branch spread remains undisturbed.
- Younger trees, sandy soils, and low water tables are favorable conditions for survival.
- Clay soils are easily compacted, which inhibits the ability of the tree to tap the soil for water and nutrients.
- Areas with high water tables often harbor shallow-rooted species that are generally difficult to protect. Minor changes to the water table can drastically affect the chances for survival.
- Trees should be thinned selectively and with great care to minimize root disturbance and wind exposure.
- Minor fill of 6 inches or less will not harm most trees; some trees have survived with 2 to 3 feet of fill around them.
- Proper aeration of the root system can be provided by gravel and coarse sand around the trees when they are filled to a depth of 2 to 3 inches.

Open Spaces

Open space with or without vegetation is set aside to enhance the development and the community. Retention of open space in the development for recreation and other uses is almost always desirable. The use and location of spaces must be considered during the design phase, before any clearing or construction can begin. As with vegetation, small pieces of open space scattered throughout the site have a limited visual impact on the overall development and little, if any, functional value.

Two basic open space considerations relate to existing vegetation:

- Existing vegetation can define an open space and at the same time provide a sight and sound buffer between activities in the open space and residential units.
- Open space facilities should be appropriate to both topography and existing vegetation. Ballfields are appropriate for large, open, flat sites; picnic areas should be shaded by vegetation and placed near natural site features.

Planting Design

As with the preservation of existing vegetation, a well conceived, efficient and effective planting plan must be developed early in the design process.

Working with and enhancing the character of the existing site is always easier and less costly than changing it drastically. Respecting the existing landscape in this way results in a better development at lower cost. Because the end result is better, sales are better, and because initial costs are lower, the development money can be spent more effectively in landscaping and other facets of the project.

How well the developer's ideas fit into the existing conditions will largely determine the aesthetic, functional, and economic success of the project.

Among the factors the developer must consider are housing type, lot type, open space, overall density, and budget. Other factors are existing vegetation, topographical conditions, climatic conditions, geological conditions, and existing land use. Careful planning is necessary to ensure a cohesive mixture of manmade and natural elements. The developer must consider these elements and determine how to use them effectively to create a successful project.

Feasibility and marketing analysis must include the appropriate planting allowances to achieve an attractive and functional development that financially rewards the developer and enhances the lives of residents. The developer should avoid creating a development that lacks interest because of the visual dominance of structures, streets, and driveways.

Previous experience, research, and professional consultation can help determine early budget figures for planting. As the planning and design process progresses, detailed costs should be developed and compared to earlier projections to permit cost control throughout the project.

To effectively develop a comprehensive planting design, other development needs—housing type, unit design, density, market unit costs—must be considered along with site characteristics. After the limitations of the site are known and their economic, aesthetic, and functional effects on the development are identified, minor adjustments in the landscape design program can be made to mitigate the constraints to the site and capitalize its assets.

The layout of structures and roadways must be considered for the most effective and efficient planting design.

A uniformity of unit design, rigid road alignment, and constant unit setback creates a sterile environment, necessitating a large planting budget to overcome the monotony.

Varied setbacks, improved circulation lines, and mixed complementary unit types diminish the developer's dependence on plants and allows the planting designer to place the material more effectively (Figure 10-8).

Figure 10-8. Variations in setback

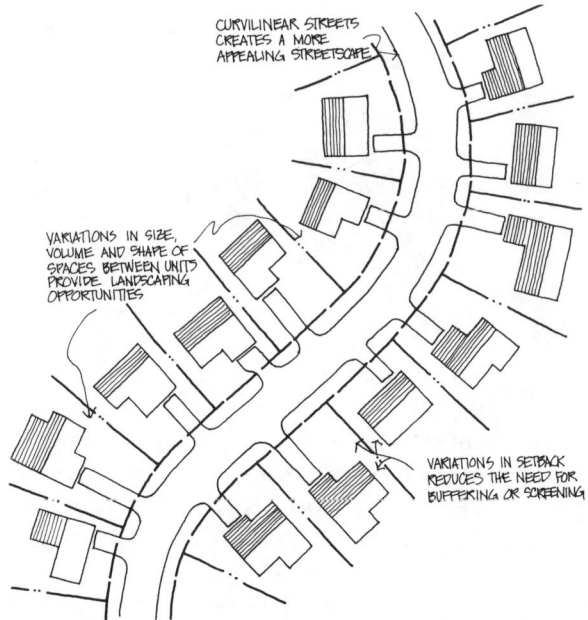

A cluster arrangement is one of many alternatives available to the developer to create usable open space and small-scale residential neighborhoods (Figure 10-9).

The placement of plants should remain a consideration throughout the design process. The designer should keep in mind the following planting objectives as the subdivision is laid out:

- Definition of the development's entrance space.

- Creation of streetscapes at a residential scale through street tree planting that provides a sequence of visual barriers and overhead planes (Figure 10-10).

- Relief from the monotony of flat, open sites by defining open spaces and providing vertical elements softening the dominant architectural elements and breaking up the repetition of units by clustering vegetation.

- Definition and reinforcement of vehicular and pedestrian circulation patterns.

- Avoidance of the monotony caused by overuse of a single specimen, while still using a dominant species or group of species as a unifying element.

Figure 10-9. Clustering enhances planting design opportunities

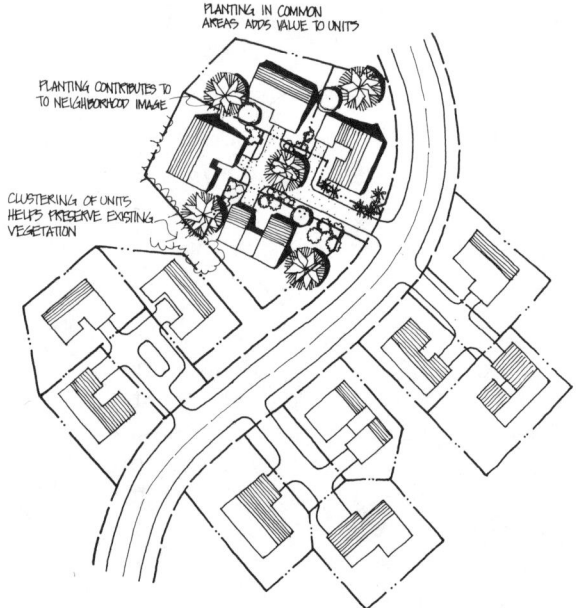

Figure 10-10. Spatial sequence created by street tree plantings

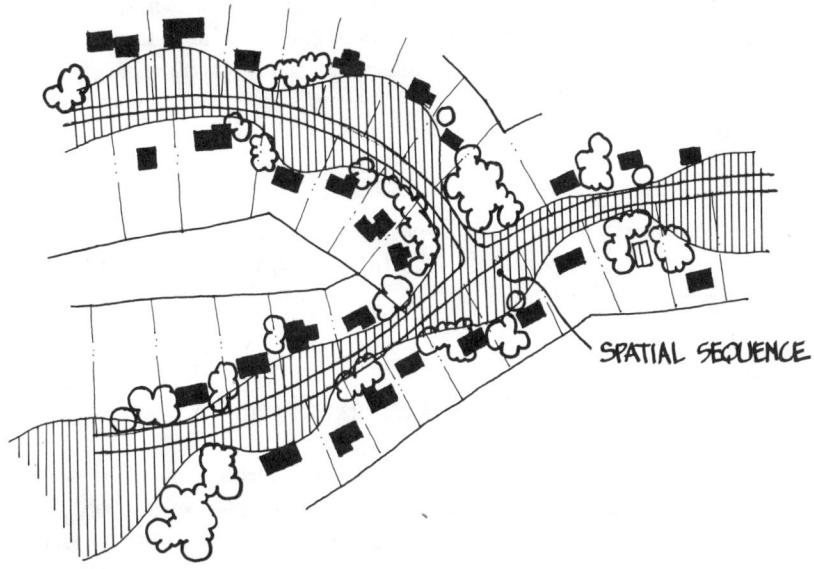

Source: Environmental Design and Research

- Avoidance of chaos by using a limited variety of species.
- Designing and locating planting in response to the development's specifically identified site needs.

Functional Uses of Plant Materials

In addition to creating a pleasant living environment, the proper use of plants can address many functional needs of the developer. Plants can control micro-climates, minimize objectional noises and views, prevent erosion, enhance wildlife, and serve other functions in the ecosystem.

Climate Modification

Plants can have a positive effect upon human comfort and energy conservation by influencing the development's micro-climates. Using plants for energy conservation is not a new idea. Long before sophisticated, mechanical heating and cooling techniques were available, people used vegetation to shelter themselves from the elements. In times of high costs, energy conservation concepts should play an important role in the building industry.

Plants can help control micro-climates for human comfort and energy conservation by directly affecting humidity, air movement, and air temperature—the elements that affect human comfort. Coniferous trees grouped closely together and oriented correctly buffer winds effectively. Deciduous trees provide shade from the sun in summer, yet allow the sun to penetrate in the winter. Shade trees act as natural humidifiers, releasing moisture into the air or absorbing it.

Erosion Control

Vegetation on steep embankments has proven to be an effective means of controlling erosion. Plants with shallow fibrous root systems are most effective.

Safety

Properly selected and placed plants can improve safety. They can—
- Act as a safety barrier between vehicular roadways and pedestrian users. Rosa Rugosa (Rugosa Rosa) has been effectively used in median planting to prevent crossover of vehicles into opposing traffic.
- Reduce headlight glare.
- Physically separate pedestrian and vehicular traffic.

Placed carelessly, plants can also create hazards. They can—
- Cause injuries if planted improperly in active recreation areas.
- Restrict sight at vehicular and pedestrian intersections.
- Block critical signs.
- Increase security concerns by visually isolating an area.
- Directly affect residents' safety if trees are easily susceptible to wind damage.

Maintenance

Maintenance costs—often passed on to the homeowners' association, community, or individual homeowner—continue to rise with inflation, and for this reason careful attention should be given to the species of plants used:
- Certain species of plants are highly subject to wind damage, temperature extremes, drought, fire, disease, and insects. The use of such species can increase maintenance costs because of increased pruning, replacement, fertilization, and spraying.
- Plants properly placed can minimize vehicular damage to lawns and still allow pedestrian access.
- Some plants leave large amounts of litter that must be cleaned up.
- Some shade trees, such as Norway Maple, in lawn areas can

hinder maintenance of a vigorous stand of grass underneath.

• Plants that grow extremely tall can block out desirable views, interfere with overhead utilities, and obscure signage, causing unnecessary costs and ultimately negating the desired visual effect of the selected plant. Mature plant heights are predictable and deserve consideration.

View and Noise Control

Plants can be used like fences to control views. A heavy conifer planting can effectively screen cars, roads, service areas, houses, and other views that can be objectionable. Deciduous trees can be used in much the same way except that their value for visual screening is reduced when their branches are bare in winter. They can, however, screen effectively even in winter if the plants are massed and the species has a high bare-branch density. Rows of shrubs or trees can provide walls of privacy in a development. Species selection, quantity, size, and spacing are factors that determine the effectiveness of a planted buffer.

Plants can also be used to direct views, as well as to create and reinforce them. For example, two groups of trees with their overhead branches touching may create a frame for a view in the distance. A row of street trees may direct the view to the end of the street or to an intersection. A large group of flowering trees or a group of different species in fall foliage can create dramatic effects and draw attention to a specific use area.

Noise can be filtered through large masses of trees. Trees are rarely planted specifically to reduce noise because both the size and number of trees required is enormous. However, the allowance of a buffer zone on a wooded site between a road and the first group of houses can reduce the noise impact of the roadway. Plants can also be used to screen noise abatement walls which greatly reduce noise levels. The plants can also reduce the ricocheting of sound from solid walls.

Plant Selection and Purchase

The planting budget should work for the developer. The developer must establish goals and then select and locate plants that will meet these goals, always designing to respond to resident, development, and site needs through a logical and comprehensive process.

The selection of specific plants is the culmination of the design process and requires a thorough understanding of plant requirements and physical characteristics. To acquire this understanding, the designer must—

- Determine the desired character of each plant mass and specimen plant: size, color, height, spread, evergreen versus deciduous.
- Determine which species in the region meets these characteristics.
- Find a convenient, reliable source for plants.
- Select the best specimens from available stock. Even if all phases of plant selection are being handled by a landscape architect or other design professional, each developer should be familiar with the methods of selection.

Finding a reliable source for plants and landscaping services is best accomplished by seeking references. Local nurseries that have established a good reputation are worth the extra cost they may demand and are likely to remain in business through the guarantee period.

Seek competitive pricing and investigate guarantees and other policies thoroughly. Remember, plants are a tremendous investment. Because laypersons cannot always determine a plant's health, opting for a budget variety is rarely beneficial.

The climate zone map (Figure 10-11) shows the standard areas that correspond to the hardiness ratings assigned to various species of plants. For example, a Norway maple is a Zone 3 species, which means it would survive in areas within Zone 3 or a higher zone. It would probably not survive in Zone 2. Site-specific conditions may create zones within a zone.

Other factors to consider include soil acidity, air quality, dry or wet conditions, proximity to seashore, soil classification, and local ordinances. All of the species selected should be compatible with these factors or the plants' chances for survival will be reduced severely.

Generally, plants selected should have the following characteristics:

- Strong fibrous root systems
- Freedom from disease
- Straight, structurally sound stems
- Full branches and good proportions
- Conformity to *The American Standard for Nursery Stock*, published by the American Association of Nurserymen.

Tree and Shrub Planting Methods

Tree locations should be staked out according to the planting plan as soon as area construction is completed and the site is ready for

Figure 10-11. Plant hardiness zones

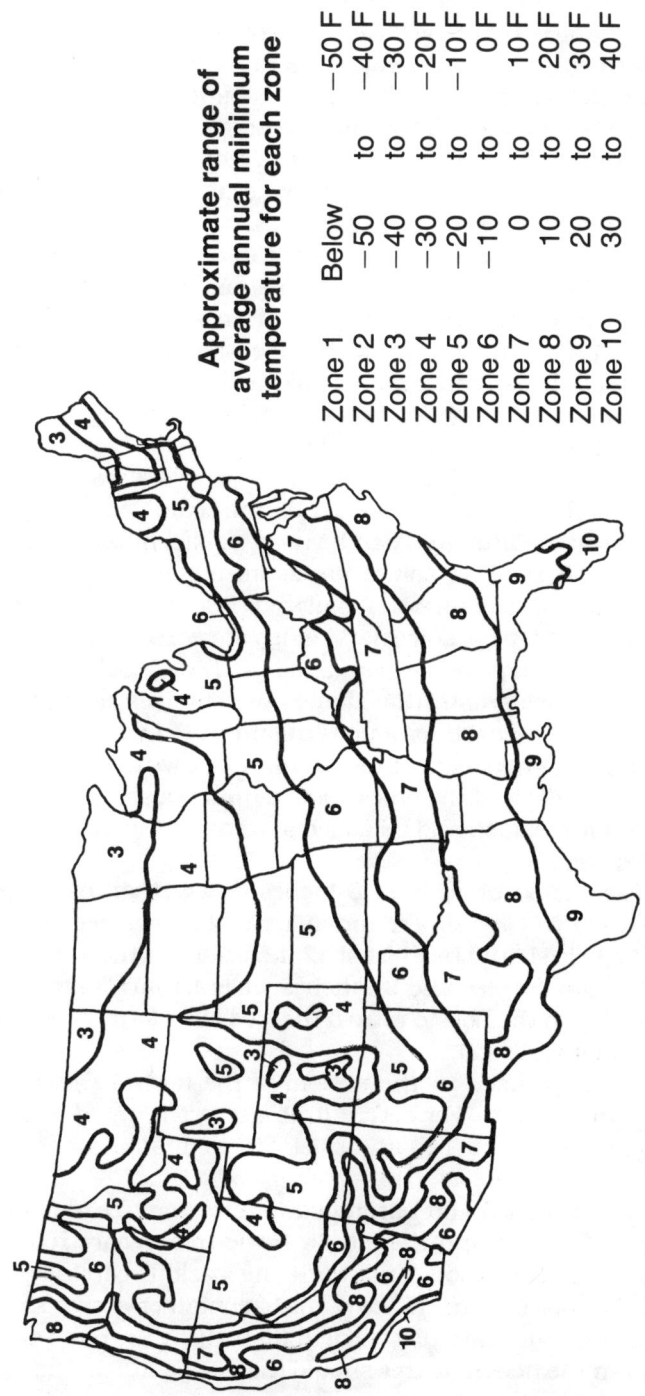

Source: U.S. Department of Agriculture

plants. At this time, tree locations must be adjusted to accommodate site changes that may have occurred during construction. Minor adjustments can usually be made for interference with utilities, rock projections, and other features. In addition, the plant composition may be modified to capitalize on opportunities that arise in the field. Although most adjustments are minor, they must fit into the overall effect of the planting scheme. Care should be taken to maintain the established planting goals.

After layout is completed, tree holes can be dug either by hand or with a backhoe. The backhoe can do a fast rough job and is economical for large planting operations. Trenching is a fast and economical method of digging for hedge plantings. Whatever the method used, backfill material should be left next to the hole. Any rocks, chunks of clay, or dead roots should be removed at this time and carried off the site.

A suitable soil condition is essential for a successful planting operation and is relatively easy to obtain. Loam generally provides a suitable soil medium and can be used as backfill without further preparation. If existing soil is not loam, organic matter must be added. If the soil has not been analyzed, field observation can help determine what type of soil exists. When squeezed in the hand, clay soil retains the shape of the grip. Sandy soil does not hold its shape, and loam soil holds its initial shape but crumbles easily. Clay and sandy soils can be used for a planting mixture by mixing one part organic matter, such as peat moss or humus, with two parts existing soil. Regardless of the type of soil, a high phosphorous fertilizer, such as bone meal, should be added at a rate of 5 pounds per cubic yard of backfill.

The hole should be at least 6 inches deeper than ball depth for small trees (1 to 1½ caliper) and at least 12 inches deeper for large trees. The hole should be at least 12 inches wider than the width of the ball for small trees and 24 inches wider for large trees. Backfill is then added to the hole to return the tree to its former relationship to grade (Figure 10-12).

Gravel can be used in the bottom of the hole to ensure proper drainage in clay soil. For severe drainage problems, a 4-inch clay drainage tile connected to an outlet can be installed beneath the gravel.

If the tree is balled and burlapped, remove the tree and fold back the burlap from around the trunk. If the tree is bare root, prune off broken or dead roots and work the backfill carefully in and around the root system. If the plant is container-grown stock, remove the container carefully without disturbing the roots and place the plant in the hole. The tree should then be positioned as desired,

Figure 10-12. Tree and shrub planting detail

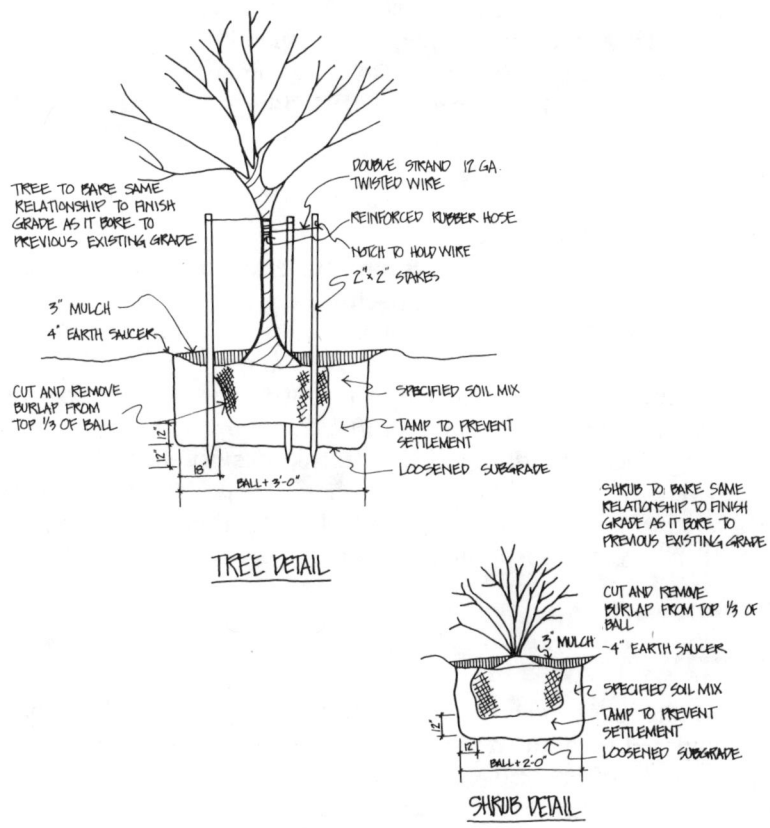

the hole filled in with backfill material, and thoroughly watered. Never handle the tree by its trunk or branches; move it by the root, ball, or container.

Different species of trees have different nutrient requirements other than phosphorous, and additional fertilizers should be watered in at this time. Also, to help the tree survive, a watering basin (about twice the diameter of root spread) formed in the backfill often helps. Fill the basin with a material such as pine bark to prevent evaporation.

Deciduous tree trunks should then be wrapped with a protective tree wrapping material from finished grade to the first branch. All trees and some large shrubs should be staked to prevent winds and other elements from moving the tree.

Pruning new trees helps them recover from shock during planting operations and may have a considerable effect on the tree's ability to survive. Any damaged branches, as well as branches that rub against or cross each other, should be removed. One-quarter to one-third of the top growth (twigs and small branches) should be removed to compensate for any loss of the root system. Lower branches should not be pruned at this time, nor should trees be pruned to alter form. Excessive pruning can do more harm than good.

Tree and Shrub Spacing

The spacing of plants is an important element in the execution of an effective planting plan. Spacing may vary considerably, depending on the developer's goals. For example, if an immediate visual impact is desired, major shade trees may be spaced 25 to 30 feet on center. If initial marketing impact is not critical, however, spacings of 40 to 50 feet may be sufficient.

Spacing also depends upon the desired design effect. If the development of a natural woodland's character is desired, then the trees need to be closer together, 20 to 40 feet on center. If the trees have been selected to be viewed individually when mature, they need to be farther apart.

Lawns

The efficient and effective establishment of lawn areas also should be considered early in the design process. The presence or lack of onsite topsoil affects budget considerations and must be taken into account in early site preparation operations. In all areas of the development where existing grades will be modified, the developer should have all topsoil stripped and stockpiled.

Good topsoil is becoming a scarce commodity in the construction industry because traditional practices have left topsoil buried under site fills or mixed with subsoils during cutting operations.

Topsoil should be left around existing vegetation that is to remain. Topsoil stockpiles should be placed in convenient locations but out of the way of construction operations. Otherwise, unnecessary expenses for hauling topsoil and relocating stockpiles will be incurred.

Topsoil Spreading

Before the topsoil is placed, the subgrade should be free of ruts and smoothly graded with a positive slope (2 percent minimum) for drainage. (Minimum slopes may vary some from region to region and should be verified.) The subgrade should also be scarified to a 2-inch depth. Once the subgrade has been prepared, topsoil should be spread to a uniformly compacted depth, recommended to be a minimum of 3 inches and 4 to 6 inches for seeded areas.

Since the mixing of additives with topsoil is a common practice and is highly technical in nature, a sample of topsoil should be taken to local testing laboratories or extension services to determine the proper amount and types of additives that should be used.

Topsoils should be worked with a disc harrow and raked to smooth-even grade, free of objectionable materials such as stone more than 2 inches in diameter, roots, lumps, clods, and sod. For areas that will be seeded with field grasses, not mowed lawn areas, raking of topsoil with a york rake is sufficient. Mowed lawn areas should be hand raked after they are york raked.

Final grading should not be undertaken when the soil is too wet or too dry. It should be damp.

Four to 7 days before seeding operations, fertilizer containing nitrogen, phosphorous, and potash should be applied. The application rate depends upon local conditions and should be determined by an expert in the area.

Seeding

Cross-sowing is often recommended to ensure a uniform distribution of grass. Cross-sowing is sowing half the seed mixture in one direction and resowing the area with the remaining mixture at a right angle to the first sowing. If the lawn is not cross-sown, care should be taken to distribute the seed evenly at 5 to 6 pounds per 1,000 square feet. When the area has been seeded, roll the seeded area lightly to set the seed firmly in topsoil. Water thoroughly after rolling to a depth of approximately 2 inches with the spray.

The timing of planting operations is critical to establishing a uniform stand of grass. Hot and dry months should be avoided; spring and fall conditions are preferable.

Sodding

Developers often sod special areas, such as those around the sales offices and model units. Preparation and fertilization of the sod bed is the same as for seeding. In the sodding operation, it is critical to maintain tight joints between sod strips and to follow a watering program for the first 3 weeks to prevent the sod from drying out before the roots are able to tap moisture in the subsoil. Normal watering after the first 3 weeks is sufficient in most areas of the country.

Landscaping for Individual Units

The concepts and techniques discussed earlier for planting of developments are applicable to planting of single units.

The homeowner can benefit from access to a model site plan that outlines a planting concept and perspective. The model plan should emphasize simplicity and provide a list of recommended shade trees, flowering trees, evergreens, and shrubs. The planting of model homes in accordance with these guidelines would be additional incentive to homeowners to blend their plantings with the overall landscape design.

Notes

Chapter 3. Local Land Use Regulations and Plan Processing

[1] Donald A. Krueckeberg, Editor, *Introduction to Planning History in the United States* (New Brunswick, NJ: Center for Urban Policy Research, 1983)

[2] Seymour I. Toll, *Zoned American* (New York: Grossman Publishers, 1969)

[3] *Standard Zoning Enabling Act* (Washington, D.C.: U.S. Department of Commerce, 1926)

[4] *Village of Euclid v. Ambler Realty Co.*, 272 U.S. 365 (1926)

[5] See for example:
Urban League of Essex County v. Mahwah Township, 207 NJ Super. 169 (Law Div., 1984)
Affordable Single Family Housing: A Review of Development Standards (Chicago: American Planning Association, 1984)
New Jersey Model Subdivision and Site Plan Ordinance (New Brunswick, NJ: Center for Urban Policy Research, 1986)

[6] Rahenkamp, Sachs, Wells, and Associates, Inc. American Society of Planning Officials, and David Stoloff, *Innovative Zoning: A Local Official's Guidebook* and *Innovative Zoning: A Digest of the Literature* (Washington, D.C.: U.S. Department of Housing and Urban Development, 1977)

[7] John Rahenkamp Consultants, Inc., *61 Corridor Study Area: A Development Standards Guidebook*, prepared for the City of Charleston, Charleston County, and Dorchester County, South Carolina, 1986

[8] Frank S. So, David R. Mosena, and Frank S. Bangs, Jr., *Planned Unit Development Ordinances* (Chicago: American Society of Planning Officials, 1973)

[9] "PUD Is Good for Everybody," *House & Home* 36(3), September 1969, pp. 72-79

[10] June R. Vollman, "Here's a New System for Figuring Project Feasibility," *House & Home* 44(4), October 1973, pp. 110-117

[11] Colleen Grogan Moore, *PUDs in Practice* (Washington, D.C.: Urban Land Institute, 1985), p. 40

[12] Nadine Huff, "Negotiating Rezoning Conditions in Fairfax County, Virginia," *Urban Land*, November 1981, p. 13

[13] Zoning Attorney Marc Bettius, quoted in Nadine Huff, "Negotiating Rezoning Conditions in Fairfax County, Virginia," *Urban Land*, November 1981, p. 13

[14] J. Michael Stimson, "If There's a Way Out of the Impasse Among Housing, the Community, and the Environmentalists, the Way Is Impact Zoning," *House & Home* 42(2), August 1972, pp. 58-67

[15] Michael J. Frank, "Performance Zoning: How It's Doing in the Place Where It Began," *Planning*, December 1982, pp. 21-23

[16] Peter J. Pizor, George H. Nieswand, and John A. Swanson, *A Transfer of Development Rights Sampler: A Collection of TDR Ordinances from Municipalities in Eight States* (New Brunswick, NJ: Department of Environmental Resources, Cook College, 1979)

[17] Peter J. Pizor, "Making TDR Work," *APA Journal*, Spring 1986, pp. 203-211

[18] John Rahenkamp Consultants, Inc.

[19] H. Milton Patton and Janet W. Patton, "Harbingers of State Growth Policies," *Management and Control of Growth: Issues, Techniques, Problems, Trends, Vol. 3*, edited by Randall W. Scott (Washington, D.C.: Urban Land Institute, 1975), pp. 318-327.

[20] *Home Builders League of South Jersey, Inc. v. Township of Berlin*, 81 NJ 127 (1979)

[21] *Oakwood at Madison, Inc. v. Township of Madison*, 72 NJ 481 (1977)

[22] *Southern Burlington County NAACP v. Township of Mount Laurel*, 92 NJ 158, 456 A.2d 390 (1983) (Mt. Laurel II). See also its predecessor, Mt. Laurel I, at *Southern Burlington County NAACP v. Township of Mount Laurel*, 67 NJ 151, 336 A.2d 713, cert. denied, 423 U.S. 808 (1975)

[23] *The Fair Housing Act of 1985*, 1985 NJ Laws, ch. 222. See also Rose, New Jersey Enacts a Fair Housing Law, 14 Real Est. L. J. 195 (1985)

[24] *Surrick v. Zoning Hearing Bd.*, 476 Pa. 182, 382 A.2d 105 (1977)

[25] *Kelly v. Zoning Hearing Bd.*, 87 Pa. Cmwlth 534, 487 A.2d 1043 (1985); *Appeal of Elocin, Inc.*, 501 Pa. 348, 461 A.2d 771 (1983)

[26] *Asian Americans for Equality v. Koch*, 492 N.Y.S. 2d 837 (Sup. Ct. 1984), Fair Housing-Fair Lending Rep. ¶ 18,039 (Aug. 6, 1985)

[27] *Soares v. Town of Atkinson*, Dkt. No. E-36-80 (N.H. Oct. 26, 1984), Master's report approved October 30, 1984

[28] *City of Boca Raton v. Boca Villas Corporation*, 371 So. 2d 154 (Fla. App. 1979)

[29] National Association of Home Builders, *Housing America—The Challenges Ahead: The Long Range Planning Report of NAHB*, 1985, p. 94

[30] Walter S. Sachs, Jr., "Everybody's Talking about the Advantages of PUD, But, Does the Green-Look Really Pay Off in Long Green?" *House & Home* 39(6), June 1971, p. 26

[31] John Rahenkamp, Kathleen McLeister, and Robert W. Ditmer, "How to Predict Your Chances of Getting Zoning Approval," *House & Home* 50 (2), August 1976, pp. 88-91

Chapter 4. Financing Land Development: An Overview

[1] Anthony Downs, "The Triple Revolution in Real Estate Finance," *Real Estate Review*

[2] The Tax Reform Act of 1986 was signed into law on October 22, 1986

[3] John Wiedemer, *Real Estate Finance*, 3rd Edition (Reston, VA: Reston Publishing Co., 1982)

[4] Alvin L. Arnold, *Real Estate Investor's Desk Book* (Boston: Warren, Gorham & Lamont, 1982)

[5] C. F. Sirmans, *Real Estate Finance* (New York: McGraw-Hill Book Company, 1985), p. 34

[6] William R. Beaton, *Real Estate Finance* (Englewood Cliffs, NJ: Prentice-Hall Inc., 1982), p. 236
[7] Sirmans, p. 237
[8] Ibid., p. 333
[9] Ibid., p. 235
[10] Arnold, p. 6-64
[11] Richard Harris, *Construction and Development Financing* (Boston: Warren, Gorham & Lamont, 1982), p. 3-9
[12] Ibid., p. 6-68
[13] Joseph Garrett, "How Home Builders Use Conventional Forward Take-Out Commitments," *Real Estate Review*, p. 73
[14] Ibid., p. 75
[15] James D. Noteware, "Ten New Trends in Financing," *The Journal of Real Estate Development* 1(2), Fall 1985

Chapter 8. Residential Streets

[1] American Society of Civil Engineers, National Association of Home Builders, Urban Land Institute, *Residential Streets* (Washington, D.C., 1974)
[2] Bucks County (PA) Planning Commission, *Performance Streets*, 1980
[3] American Association of State Highway and Transportation Officials, *A Policy on Geometric Design of Highways and Streets* (Washington, DC, 1984)
[4] Ibid.
[5] Robert J. Southerland, "Concrete Curb Systems," *Landscape Architect*, Nov./Dec. 1985

Chapter 9. Energy Conservation

[1] A. S. Kennedy, et al., *Factors That Influence the Acceptance of Integrated Community Energy Systems* (Argonne, IL: Argonne National Laboratory, January 1978), p. B.24
[2] Kennedy, p. B.26
[3] James Zanetto, "The Location and Selection of Trees for Solar Neighborhoods," *Landscape Architecture* 68(6), November 1978, p. 515
[4] Zanetto, p. 515
[5] Victor Olgyay, *Design with Climate* (Princeton, NJ: Princeton University Press, 1963), p. 87
[6] James R. Wright and Paul R. Aehenbach, "Energy Conservation in Buildings," *Scientific American Roundtable*, January 1974, p. 159
[7] The Center for Landscape Architectural Education and Research, *Options for Passive Energy Conservation in Site Design* (Reston, VA: The Center, 1979, draft), pp. 14-15
[8] Olgyay, pp. 49-50
[9] Zanetto, p. 515
[10] Zanetto, p. 516
[11] *Options for Passive Energy Conservation in Site Design*, p. 37
[12] Planning Division, Community Development Department, City of Davis (CA), *General Plan* (Davis, CA: 1973)
[13] Zanetto, p. 516.

Appendix A

Homebuying Segments

Segment/Household Size	Characteristics/Design Implications
Young Singles/1-2	Under 30; gregarious. Unmarried, active, mobile, many interests, entertain informally. Career experimentation and enhancement; loyal to career, not employer. Few possessions; spend generously on clothes and personal growth. *Design implications:* Glitz, color, excitement, variety, experimentation, interior privacy for sleep and bath. Frequent visitors; enjoy physical activity and leisure time. Emphasize living room area and master bedroom suite.
Adult Singles/1-2	Over 30, presently unmarried (single, widowed, separated, divorced). Serious social relationships, require privacy. More mature but still experimenting; early possession buildup. Appreciate quality and dependable brands. Read consumer reports and specialized magazines about their careers and leisure interests. Active with peer groups in sports and leisure. *Design implications:* Glitz, design animation in ceiling, floor, room shapes. Serious courting for serious reasons, so need interior privacy. Minimal daily maintenance, because workplace is center of peer group time and effort. Appreciate good designs in features like fireplace, bathrooms, built-ins, workspaces. Don't waste yards or hallways on them.
Young Marrieds Without Children/2	Mature discretionary/dual income. Physically active; entertain often, both formally and informally; independent, do-it-yourselfers, maybe a sports car. Planning for future: financial, career goals, family planning. Solid friendships at work. Ambitious, travel often. *Design implications:* The look of success; emphasize entry, indoor/outdoor relationships. Feature good wardrobe and storage space, combined living/dining room, master bedroom suite, den or family room, lots of usable space that is dramatic with plenty of decorating potential.
Young Marrieds With Child/3	Under 35, child under 5, both spouses working, entertain informally, amateur gardeners, focus on child, planning on more children. *Design implications:* Emphasize kitchen (good lighting, pleasant), informal dining area, master bedroom, similar secondary bedrooms, family room with fireplace, large yard. May have pet(s); need roaming space for pets and children. Provide interior mess (play) area.
Compact Family/3	Couple, age 35+, with one child. Adults outnumber children, so design house around adult activities. *Design implications:* Emphasize adult-oriented areas, informal dining with formal living, separation of master bedroom and secondary bedrooms. Large secondary bedroom preferred.
Move-Up Family/3-4	The "monthly payment" group. Nonemployed "housewife," focus on casual and informal family activities, numerous interests, mostly child-oriented. Amateur gardeners; transitional. *Design implications:* Emphasize kitchen, informal dining area, master bedroom, smaller secondary bedrooms, fireplace in family room, large yard.
Established Family/3-5+	Making monthly payments comfortably, some discretionary income, approaching their economic and social peak, some formal entertaining, older children/teenagers, many interests, 3-car family, prefer limited maintenance. *Design implications:* Separate formal living and dining areas, den or formal family room, separate master bedroom suite, large secondary bedrooms, formal yard.

Segment/Household Size	Characteristics/Design Implications
Luxury Family/2-4+	Have arrived, tremendous discretionary income, very formal house, don't entertain often but when they do, it's formal; teenagers (maybe a small child too), less physically active, one or two formal sports affiliations, dine out often, minimal maintenance, privacy mandatory. Can come in and out of market as they please; pampered, will not compromise on space, quality, or prestige of address. *Design implications:* Formal entry, separate living and dining rooms, den, master bedroom (possibly separate) plus retreat, guest or maid's room, privacy and security are important. Large walk-in wardrobes, gourmet kitchen, wine area, classic wetbar, formal entertainment room, library, paneling, fine woods in kitchen and bath cabinets and staircase. On exterior, strong window and roof treatments, wide facade impact. In condos, still luxurious rooms, but with less yard to maintain.
Move-Down Family/2-3	40-50 years old, leaving large family house, prefer limited maintenance, informal living and formal entertainment areas. Travel often, occasional visits from family or guests, focused active and passive recreation. *Design implications:* Quality not quantity, luxury. Focus on living room and master bedroom area, adequately large secondary areas, den, dining room and breakfast nook or informal eating area, small private patio. Have accumulated possessions and don't want to give them up, so storage is important. Separate his/her closets. Fireplace, bar, reading nook, skylights, nearby recreation, status neighborhood instead of space.
Divorcee/1+	Reestablishing social lifestyle, experimenting; may be looking for serious relationships. Want freedom to travel or pursue leisure interests; may be career-oriented with social life focused on workplace. *Design implications:* Home may be a "launching pad" for social experimentation; want smaller but full kitchen; master suite desirable for romance; need potential for rootedness and security from traditional room configurations. Provide closets (not necessarily large); a sense of pampering; larger tub with jacuzzi potential; use low-maintenance materials.
Single Female With Child/2+	Child-oriented. Must find a suitable place to live with child; child is focus of lifestyle; limited social life. *Design implications:* Privacy from child yet ability to monitor (no matter what age). Interior play area, important TV space. Bright, informal, easily maintained eating area with kitchen, no dining room, but perhaps an area for infrequent formal meals. Doesn't expect luxury, but appreciates appointments and materials above price range. Make-up area, separate storage and clothes closets for child and her, smaller secondary bedroom, prefers separate full bath for child.
Empty Nester-Never Nested/2	Mature, self-sufficient couple, no debts, occasional overnight guests, active in leisure activities, entertain often; want privacy, minimal maintenance and investment in house costs. Mobile in attitude but permanent in residence. *Design implications:* Formal living and dining areas, den, guest suite, large master suite and retreat, informal eating nook in kitchen, low-maintenance yard.
Young Retiree (Active)/2	Active in community, enjoy passive recreation, semiformal entertaining at home, privacy important, don't travel much. Often retired civil service or military in 40s and 50s, work part-time but enjoy some

Continued

Segment/Household Size	Characteristics/Design Implications
Young Retiree (Active)/2 Continued	sports (tennis, golf, swimming), people-oriented. *Design implications:* Quality rather than quantity, secondary bedrooms usable for hobbies too, option of separate master bedrooms (good-sized), storage space. Room configuration should be functional yet formal and traditional. Separate his/her closets, ordinary baths with limited sex appeal. One-car garage.
Passive Retiree/2	Not physically able to engage in active sports. Prefer walking, family and group activities, cardplaying, reading, travel. *Design implications:* Avoid stairs and heights. Conservative one-story and end units are preferred. Grab bars and other safety features should be subtle in design. Interior privacy is important; also, separate (and equal) bedrooms. Include a garden or patio area and a nicely lighted, full but compact kitchen (not too small). Good window treatment is appreciated. Lower appliance shelves, pantries and switches.
Widow-Widower/1	Initial period of severe readjustment followed by "life goes on;" reexamination of friendships and purpose of life. Budget-conscious and will listen to advice; privacy and comfort are important. *Design implications:* Interior privacy; no fanciness unless affluent. Wants a full kitchen and has time for maintenance. Wants a feeling of home, a fireplace; tends to use formal areas rarely, so living and dining rooms can be smaller; has possessions that are vital links to past, so needs wall space and storage. Security features appreciated; perhaps a hobby or work area; extra sleeping area for visiting children or guests. Neighborhood very important.

Special Homebuying Segments*

Second Homebuyers-National Origin/2+	Affluent empty nesters who travel, pre-retirees, active retirees, self-employed, corporate chiefs. *Design implications:* Spacious luxury, detached home, many amenities, with view of golf course or other premium features.
Second Homebuyers-Regional Origin/2+	Often same as above, but in lower income bracket. *Design implications:* Compact luxury, usually attached units, turnkey delivery as an option (with furnishings).
Investors	Local and out-of-state. Many may eventually live in community where investment home is located.
Aesthetics/1-2+	Often single, with a profession as a writer, artist, musician, architect, decorator, or similar. Borderline or actual elitist. Freedom and the avant-garde are important to them. *Design implications:* Thematic architecture or traditional with strong architectural feeling: wood, masonry, roof lines, animation, fireplace, interior garden, circular staircase, lofts, beams, clerestory, skylight, or other natural design elements. Provide a work area. Choose thematic decoration, such as Oriental. Likes to be in peer group neighborhood.

* These are important, identifiable segments in many regional marketplaces. Since they can represent a large part of a higher density project's target market, their needs should be carefully addressed.

Segment/Household Size	Characteristics/Design Implications
Glitz/1-2+	Seek that which is new and "in." Gregarious. Spend much of their income. *Design implications:* Heavy design and merchandising orientation. Sell show-off features with "sizzle:" mirrors, chrome, avant-garde, entertainment, balcony or interior decks to view guests, music room, large TV, bar, European kitchen with every gimmick, wine rack.
Boomers/1-4+	78 million post-WWII baby boomers, ages 20-39. Beware of stratifying them beyond the segments below, because they are found in many different market groups (except retirees). But in the year 2012, their median age will be 55—then watch the boom in the retirement, travel, tourism, recreation, and resort markets). 70 percent of the women are in the work force. Individual incomes are unimpressive, but when combined through marriage, 30 percent have a household income of $30,000 or more. 51 percent live in someone else's household (often a parent), only 8 percent live alone and only 18 percent head their own households. 59 percent of female boomers are married and 76 percent of these have one or more children. Approximately 6 percent of boomers are young affluent urban professionals.
Young Boomers/1-3+	Aged 20-29, focus on workplace and career development, gaining maturity but still experimenting, somewhat egocentric. 45 percent of these households have children. Median household income is $17,800; will follow tradition to become homeowners as soon as they can afford to. *Design implications:* Singles will postpone home purchase for immediate gratification of clothes, travel, recreation, spouse-searching. This is an excellent apartment market: offer touches of luxury so they can feel that their jobs pay off. Otherwise similar to other young segments.
Older Boomers/3-5+	Aged 30-39 and much more settled, assured of their careers and their personal lives. 68 percent of these households have children under 18. Median household income is $24,800 and can expand rapidly. Similar to other young married segments.
Snowbirds and Desert Rats	Fall into two groups: fun-loving escapists and self-gratifying achievers. Fun-lovers of all ages have a vacation mentality, want to live out their fantasies, travel to experience different locations and ways of life. *Design implications:* both unusual and traditional interior and exterior designs. Feature drama: partying rooms, bold masonry fireplaces (with woodbox), lofts that convert to sleeping areas, lots of natural wood. Small spaces are fine as long as they're fun. Location is all-important; try timeshare. Self-gratifiers of all ages want to live their fantasies now, transfer work ethic into wish fulfillment. Often singles and divorcees, ambitious, heavy investors in brand-name material goods for prestige and comfort. *Design implications:* Showcase entertainment areas, bar, gourmet kitchen with European styling, worksaving appliances. Feature fireplaces, wood beams and paneling, good ceiling height, lots of closet space. Want to be seen and appreciated for their accomplishments. They spend beyond their means, so will accept rental unit that satisfies their lifestyle and location needs.

The Goodkin Group

Appendix B
Resident and Nonresident Preference Questionnaires

These two questionnaires are designed to elicit information on home and community preferences, lifestyle, and household characteristics. They are geared to residents of the builder/developer's built communities and to residents of other communities. The interviewer should ask these questions to the resident personally.

Resident Preference Questionnaire
Anywhere, USA

This questionnaire is designed for the resident presently living in one of the builder/developer's built communities. It can provide helpful information for learning which marketing techniques drew the resident in, the consumer's preferences and lifestyle, and economic and household information. Additionally, the questionnaire can yield information for making improvements to the existing community, and for learning the future housing plans of the resident.

The interviewer's comments are in italic.

Hello, I represent the developers of Anywhere, U.S.A. Your responses to the following questions about the attractions of the area will be used to make the community more convenient and enjoyable for you. Your cooperation is appreciated.

Name _____ Date _____ 19____

Address _____
Residential   Development
Development _____ Code _____

City _____ Zip _____ Sex of Respondent
                                         ☐ Male   ☐ Female
Interviewer _____

1. *How did you first hear about the Anywhere, U.S.A. area?*
   ☐ Newspaper advertisements   ☐ Driving by
   ☐ Employment   ☐ Billboards
   ☐ Other residents   ☐ Friends
   ☐ Other _____

2a. Did you consider any of the other developments or residential areas here?
☐ Yes ☐ No
(If no, go to question 3.)

b. Which developments? (List nearby communities)
☐ _____ ☐ _____ ☐ _____
☐ _____ ☐ _____ ☐ _____
☐ _____ ☐ _____ ☐ Don't know

c. (For each development chosen, ask *What made you decide to reside here instead of [name of development]?* Write development name and reason given.)
_____
_____

3. Which of the following choices best describes the kind of residential community you prefer?
☐ Adults and children of all ages
☐ Restricted to adults over the age of 21
☐ Restricted to adults over the age of 45

4. As a resident, what elements of Anywhere, U.S.A. appeal to you? What are your preferences?
_____
_____
_____

5a. Are there other facilities you would like added to the present community? _____

b. If yes, *What are they?* _____
_____
_____

6. Could any aspects of Anywhere, U.S.A. pose problems for you? _____
_____

Characteristics of Present Home

Now I'd like to ask you some questions about the characteristics of your present home.

1. How long have you lived there? _____ Months _____ Years

2. Is it a:
☐ Apartment ☐ Mobile home
☐ Other _____
                        (specify)

3. What are your favorite aspects of the home or apartment?
_____
_____

4. Do you have any problems with your present home or apartment? _____
_____

5. What is your best estimate of the square footage of your home? _____
_____

6. *Regarding square footage, do you consider your present home to be adequate?* ☐ Yes ☐ No

7. (If rent, ask:) *What is your monthly rent?* $ _____

8. *In general, has living here fulfilled your expectations?*
   ☐ Definitely yes ☐ Partly yes ☐ Definitely not
   Comments _____
   _____

9. *How many days or evenings per month do you have friends over?* _____

10. *Do you have friends over for:*
    ☐ Casual visits   ☐ Parties
    ☐ Dinners   ☐ Community-oriented activities

11. *How many days per month do you go to outdoor activities with other residents?* _____

12a. *Do you have particular hobbies or interests?*
     ☐ Yes ☐ No
  b. *If yes, Could you tell us a couple?* _____
     _____

Outdoor Activities

Now I'd like to ask you some questions concerning outdoor activities at Anywhere, U.S.A.

1. *How do you feel about the development of the following outdoor recreation facilities?*

	Prefer	Acceptable	Object to
Network of attractive pedestrian paths	_____	_____	_____
Jogging courses	_____	_____	_____
Tennis courts	_____	_____	_____
Bicycle paths	_____	_____	_____
Golf courses	_____	_____	_____
Solar-heated swimming pools	_____	_____	_____
Athletic fields	_____	_____	_____
Others _____ (specify)			

2. *Do you want an outdoor exercise program made available for all the residents?* ☐ Yes ☐ No

3. *What outdoor activities do the members of your household participate in, in Anywhere, U.S.A.?* _____
   _____
   _____

4. If a community recreation center exists for the residential development, ask *How many days per month do you use it?* _____

5. *If a community recreation center and activities program were constructed for the entire Anywhere, U.S.A. community, which of the following would you prefer to have?*
   - ☐ Center for different clubs or activities
   - ☐ Tennis courts, swimming pool, exercise facilities
   - ☐ Play areas for children
   - ☐ Potential for day care center
   - ☐ Adult education courses
   - ☐ Other _____

   (specify)

6. *What would be the most dues per household per month that would be acceptable?*

   $ _____ Per month   ☐ Not acceptable

7a. *Would you prefer local recreation centers for each residential development?*
   ☐ Yes   ☐ No

   b. *If yes, What facilities would you prefer?*
   _____
   _____

8a. *Do members of your household go to other areas nearby for outdoor activities?* ☐ Yes   ☐ No
   (If no, go to question 9.)

   b. *What are some of the things you do?* _____
   _____

   c. *During an average month, how many days do you go to those areas?* ____

   d. *How long does it take to drive to the place most often used?* _____

9a. *During an average month, how many days do you go to other areas to eat at restaurants?* _____

   b. *How many days a month for entertainment?* _____
   Comments _____

   c. *What is the average driving time to these places?*
   _____

10. *How many days a month do you use each of these community outdoor areas of Anywhere, U.S.A.?*
    - _____ Campgrounds   _____ Horse trails
    - _____ Boat docks   _____ Golf course
    - _____ Equestrian center

    Comments _____
    _____

11. *Which areas would you like to see expanded?*
    - ☐ Campgrounds   ☐ Horse trails
    - ☐ Boat docks   ☐ Golf course
    - ☐ Equestrian center

    Comments _____
    _____

Previous Residence

Now I'd like to ask a few questions regarding where you resided before.

1. Where was the community? _____

2. What type of home did you live in?
   - ☐ Single-family
   - ☐ Condo/townhouse
   - ☐ Apartment
   - ☐ Mobile home
   - ☐ Duplex
   - ☐ Other _____
     (specify)

3. Did you—
   - ☐ Own   ☐ Rent   ☐ Other _____
     (specify)

4. How many bedrooms and baths did it have?
   _____ Bedrooms   _____ Baths

5. Did it have—
   - ☐ Family room   ☐ Den   ☐ Dining room

6. The approximate total square footage? _____

7. What was the reason for moving from there? _____
   _____

8. Do you currently own other property here?
   - ☐ Yes   ☐ No

Future Plans

I have some questions concerning your plans for the house you would like to purchase in the future.

1. First, how long do you plan to live at your present residence?
   _____ Years   _____ Months

2. When you move, do you plan to move within Anywhere, U.S.A. or to another community?
   - ☐ Anywhere, U.S.A.
   - ☐ Other _____
   - ☐ Don't know
     (specify)

3. If other area, reason for the choice? _____

4. If you were to move to a new house now, how many bedrooms would you prefer? _____

5. Which of the following rooms would you also want in your new home?
   - ☐ Family room
   - ☐ Den
   - ☐ Additional bathrooms (How many?) _____
   - ☐ Dining room
   - ☐ Enclosed patio

6. If you were to purchase a three-bedroom house, which of the following bedroom arrangements would you prefer?
   ☐ All three bedrooms grouped together
   ☐ Master bedroom separated from the others
   ☐ Guest room separated from the others

7. If you were purchasing a house now, what price range would you consider?
   $ _____

8a. Assuming your home has only one eating area in it, would you prefer:
   ☐ A separate dining room close to the kitchen
   ☐ A large country kitchen with a table
   ☐ A small kitchen with an eat-in nook connected

  b. Or, would you definitely prefer two separate eating areas, a dining area and an informal eating area?
   ☐ Yes   ☐ No

9. In the purchase of a home, which of the following features would you prefer to have, assuming that all of them would add to the cost of the home?

	Prefer	Don't Prefer
☐ Fireplace	☐	☐
☐ Wet bar	☐	☐
☐ Sunken conversation pit	☐	☐
☐ French doors	☐	☐
☐ Skylights	☐	☐
☐ Central forced air	☐	☐
☐ Planter areas	☐	☐

10. Which of the following kitchen features would you prefer?

   Standard
   ☐ Formica® countertop
   ☐ Single oven
   ☐ Conventional window

   Added expense
   ☐ Double ovens
   ☐ Single oven plus microwave
   ☐ Greenhouse window
   ☐ Microwave

11. What are your reasons for buying a new home: (Check all applicable)
   ☐ Tired of renting   ☐ Investment to dwell in
   ☐ Closer to work   ☐ Investment for rental
   ☐ Want larger home   ☐ Retired
   ☐ Want a better location or   ☐ Want better schools
     neighborhood   ☐ Children have grown up
   ☐ Want smaller home   ☐ Other _____
                                           (specify)

12. In addition to new home developments, would you be looking at resale (used) homes?   ☐ Yes   ☐ No

13. Considering the expense of land (at approximately $ _____ per acre), how large a house lot do you prefer?
   ☐ Less than ¼ acre   ☐ 1 to 2 acres
   ☐ ¼ to ½ acre   ☐ 2 to 5 acres
   ☐ ½ to 1 acre   ☐ Other _____
                                     (specify)

14. *Of the following, which outdoor features do you prefer?*
    - ☐ Picnic and/or barbecue facilities
    - ☐ Fenced rear yard
    - ☐ Fenced front yard
    - ☐ Swimming pool
    - ☐ Tot lot or playground

15. *Given equal square footage, which do you prefer?*
    - ☐ Rooms on two floors
    - ☐ All rooms on one floor
    - ☐ Split level

16. *Between the two, do you prefer:*
    - ☐ Clusters of 4 to 12 detached houses around a central open court or cul-de-sac
    - ☐ Rows of houses on streets

17. *If condos were constructed adjacent to a golf course, would you consider residing there?* ☐ Yes   ☐ No

18. *Would you consider residing in the following types of attached housing?*
    - ☐ Expensive condos
    - ☐ Duplex
        - ☐ Expensive
        - ☐ Less expensive
    - ☐ Quadruplex (four attached units)

19a. *In what geographic community is the male head of household employed?* _____

   b. *Is he employed—*
   - ☐ Full time
   - ☐ Part time
   - ☐ Unemployed
   - ☐ Retired
   - ☐ Military
   - ☐ Other _____ (specify)

   (If he is not employed, go to question 21a.)
   c. *What occupation?* _____
   d. *Employer or company?* _____

20. *How long a drive or commute does he have in minutes?* _____

21a. *In what geographic community is the female head of household employed?* _____

   b. *Is she employed—*
   - ☐ Full time
   - ☐ Part time
   - ☐ Unemployed
   - ☐ Retired
   - ☐ Military
   - ☐ Other _____ (specify)

   (If she is not employed, go to question 23.)
   c. *What occupation?* _____
   d. *Employer or company?* _____

22. *How long a drive or commute does she have in minutes?* _____

23. What mode of transportation do the heads of household use to get to work?

Male
- ☐ Own auto
- ☐ Carpool
- ☐ Other _____
  (specify)
- ☐ Bus
- ☐ Walk

Female
- ☐ Own auto
- ☐ Carpool
- ☐ Other _____
  (specify)
- ☐ Bus
- ☐ Walk

Education and Income

Please read over the following questions and check off your responses. (Present page to the respondent to read over and respond.)

1. What is the highest level of education completed by the head of household?
   - ☐ Less than 4 years of high school
   - ☐ High school graduate
   - ☐ Some college
   - ☐ College graduate
   - ☐ Post-graduate

2. What is your marital status?
   - ☐ Married
   - ☐ Single
   - ☐ Divorced
   - ☐ Separated
   - ☐ Widowed

3. What is the range of your household's total income before taxes?
   - ☐ Less than $7,000
   - ☐ $7,000 to 9,000
   - ☐ $9,000 to 11,000
   - ☐ $11,000 to 14,000
   - ☐ $14,000 to 19,000
   - ☐ $19,000 to 24,000
   - ☐ $24,000 to 29,000
   - ☐ $29,000 to 35,000
   - ☐ $35,000 to 45,000
   - ☐ $45,000 to 60,000
   - ☐ $60,000 to 75,000
   - ☐ More than $75,000

Thank you for your cooperation. You have been very helpful. Have a good day.

Nonresident Preference Questionnaire

This questionnaire is designed to elicit marketing information from residents of other communities.

Hello, your responses to the following questions about the attractions of your home and community are to be used for the development of more enjoyable and convenient communities. Your cooperation is appreciated.

Name _____ Date _____ 19_____

Address _____
Residential
Development _____ Development Code _____

City _____ Zip _____ Sex of Respondent
                                                    ☐ Male   ☐ Female
Interviewer _____

1. Did you consider other communities or developments?
   ☐ Yes   ☐ No   ☐ If so, which _____
   _____
   _____

2. What attracted you to each one? _____
   _____
   _____

3. What aspects of the community do you like?
   _____
   _____

4a. Do any aspects of the community pose problems for you?
    ☐ Yes   ☐ No
 b. If yes, what are they? _____
    _____
    _____

5. Which of the following choices best describes the kind of residential community you prefer?
   ☐ Adults and children of all ages
   ☐ Restricted to adults over the age of 21
   ☐ Restricted to adults over the age of 45

Present Residence

These questions are about the characteristics of your present house.

1. Is it a:
   ☐ House   ☐ Apartment
   ☐ Condominium/townhouse   ☐ Mobile home
   ☐ Other _____
                        (specify)

2. It is a—
   ☐ Two-story   ☐ One-story   ☐ Split-level

3. Do you—
   ☐ Own   ☐ Rent

4. How many bedrooms and bathrooms does it have?
   _____ Bedrooms   _____ Bathrooms

5. Do you have a—
   ☐ Den   ☐ Family room   ☐ Dining room

6. What features of the house are your favorites?
   _____
   _____
   _____

7. Describe one or two problems regarding your present house.
   _____
   _____
   _____

8. What is your best estimate of the square footage of your home? _____

9. *Regarding square footage, do you consider your present home to be adequate?* ☐ Yes   ☐ No
Comments _____
_____
_____

Future Plans

1. *For how long do you plan to reside at your present residence?*
   _____ Years   _____ Months
   (If respondent is not planning to move, go to question 8.)

2. *When you move, do you plan to move near here or to another community?*
   ☐ Near here   ☐ Other _____
   ☐ Don't know   (specify)

3. *If other area, reason?* _____
   _____

4. *If you were to move to a new house now, how many bedrooms would you prefer?* _____

5. *Would you prefer the house to be:*
   ☐ Detached   ☐ Attached
   ☐ Cluster   ☐ Doesn't matter

6. *Which of the following rooms would you also want in your new home?*
   ☐ Family room   ☐ Dining room
   ☐ Den   ☐ Patio or decks
   ☐ Bathrooms _____
                              (how many?)

7. *If you were purchasing a house now, what price range would you consider?*
   $ _____

8. *Given equal square footage, which do you prefer?*
   ☐ Rooms on two floors   ☐ Split-level
   ☐ All rooms on one floor

9. *If you were purchasing a house now, what range of square footage would you consider?*
   _____ to _____

Community

These questions pertain to the community setting.

1. *Not considering expense, which of the following do you prefer?*
   ☐ Location close to a community center
   ☐ Situated on the golf course
   ☐ An equestrian-oriented community
   ☐ A country estate lot
   ☐ A lake-front house
   ☐ Doesn't matter

2. *If condos were constructed adjacent to a golf course, would you consider residing there?*
   ☐ Yes ☐ No

3. *Would you consider residing in the following forms of attached housing?*
   ☐ Duplex
   ☐ Quadruplex
   ☐ Expensive condos
   ☐ Townhouse
   ☐ Less expensive condos

4. *The following are elements that appeal to people for a planned community. What four would cause you to consider a definite change from the present environment?*
   ☐ The country atmosphere
   ☐ Affordable houses
   ☐ The quality of the house
   ☐ Program of community activities
   ☐ Good place for children
   ☐ Uncongested roads
   ☐ Good climate
   ☐ Friendly people
   ☐ Outdoor activities
   ☐ Proximity to employment
   ☐ A good investment

Outdoor and Recreation Activities

Now I'd like to cover outdoor and recreation activities.

1. *How do you feel about the development of outdoor recreation facilities?*

	Definitely prefer	Acceptable	No difference	Object	Exist at present
Tennis courts	☐	☐	☐	☐	☐
Golf courses	☐	☐	☐	☐	☐
Athletic fields	☐	☐	☐	☐	☐
Others	☐	☐	☐	☐	☐

   Comments _____

2. *In what outdoor activities do members of your household participate?*
   _____
   _____

3. *Have you ever heard of Anywhere, U.S.A.?*
   ☐ Yes ☐ No

4. *If yes, have you ever gone there?*
   ☐ Yes ☐ No
   Comments _____

5. Looking at the residential developments in Anywhere, U.S.A. pictured before you, would you consider residing there—

	Definitely	Possibly	Would not consider
For a primary residence	☐	☐	☐
For retirement	☐	☐	☐
For a second home	☐	☐	☐

Reason _____

_____

6. What would a planned residential community in the Anywhere, U.S.A. area have to offer for you to reside there?

_____

_____

Composition of Household

Your cooperation has been very helpful. Now I have just a few questions about your household.

1. What is the total number of persons living in your household? _____

2. How many persons are in each of the following age groups:
   ____ 6 or under   ____ 13-17   ____ 25-44   ____ 65 or over
   ____ 7-12   ____ 18-24   ____ 45-64   ____ Refused to answer
   (Total number must equal response to question 1.)

3. Do you have grown children who are no longer living at home?
   ☐ Yes   ☐ No

4a. In what geographic community is the male head of household employed?
   _____

   b. Is he employed—
   ☐ Full time   ☐ Retired
   ☐ Part time   ☐ Military
   ☐ Unemployed   ☐ Other _____
                                    (specify)
   (If he is not employed, go to question 6a.)
   c. What occupation? _____
   d. Employer or company? _____

5. How long a drive or commute does he have in minutes?
   _____

6a. In what geographic community is the female head of household employed?
   _____

   b. Is she employed—
   ☐ Full time   ☐ Retired
   ☐ Part time   ☐ Military
   ☐ Unemployed   ☐ Other _____
                                    (specify)
   (If she is not employed, go to question 8.)
   c. What occupation? _____
   d. Employer or company? _____

7. *How long a drive or commute does she have in minutes?*
   _____

8. *What mode of transportation do the heads of household use to get to work?*

   Male
   ☐ Own auto
   ☐ Carpool
   ☐ Bus
   ☐ Walk
   ☐ Other _____
               (specify)

   Female
   ☐ Own auto
   ☐ Carpool
   ☐ Bus
   ☐ Walk
   ☐ Other _____
               (specify)

Thank you very much for your time.

Appendix C
Ordinances Specifying Street Width, Curbing, and Sidewalk Requirements

Raleigh, N.C. City Code
Sec. 10-3047. Paving widths.

(a) The paving widths between facing of curbs and the paving widths on streets without curbs shall be constructed as follows:
  (1) Major thoroughfare streets to be determined by the council after considering requirements of the developer, the public, the city and the state highway department but providing for minimum widths according to desired standards as set forth in the thoroughfare plan for the Raleigh urban area.
  (2) Minor thoroughfares, according to desired standards as set forth in the thoroughfare plan for the Raleigh urban area.
  (3) Commercial and commercial cul-de-sac streets, not less than forty (40) feet.
  (4) Collector and collector cul-de-sac streets, not less than forty (40) feet.
  (5) Residential and residential cul-de-sac streets, not less than thirty (30) feet.
  (6) Minor residential and minor residential cul-de-sac streets, not less than twenty-six (26) feet.
  (7) Marginal access streets, not less than eighteen (18) feet serving residential properties and not less than twenty-four (24) feet serving nonresidential properties.
  (8) Residential service and residential service cul-de-sac streets, not less than twenty-two (22) feet.

(b) Collector cul-de-sac streets which serve nonresidential properties and all commercial cul-de-sac streets shall terminate in a paved turning circle with a minimum diameter of ninety (90) feet; and all other cul-de-sac streets shall terminate in a paved turning circle with a minimum diameter of seventy (70) feet.

Sec. 10-3051. Sidewalks.

(a) Sidewalks shall be constructed on the street right-of-way in accordance with city standards. Sidewalk surfacing conforming to all the provisions of Sec. 7-2002 of this Code shall be required, as follows:
  (1) Major thoroughfares, minor thoroughfares, commercial, commercial culs-de-sac: sidewalks on both sides.
  (2) Marginal access, collector: sidewalks on one side.
  (3) Collector cul-de-sac, residential cul-de-sac, minor residential, residential: No sidewalks unless the street is within one-half mile linear traverse of a school, park, shopping area or focus area as shown on the comprehensive plan, in which case sidewalk on one side will be required. However, if the city council finds as a fact that any street which would otherwise require sidewalk, according to the above criteria, has too little pedestrian use to make sidewalks beneficial, the requirement for sidewalk may be waived.

Grandview, Mo. Subdivision Ordinance

6-4 Sidewalks.

Sidewalks shall be installed by the subdivider on at least one side of all residential local streets, except cul-de-sacs, and on both sides of all other streets. Sidewalks abutting arterial streets shall not be less than five (5) feet in width. All other sidewalks shall be not less than four (4) feet in width. All sidewalks shall be constructed of portland cement concrete. Sidewalks shall be located in the platted street right-of-way, usually one foot from the property line. Walks shall also be installed in any pedestrian easements as may be required by the Planning Commission. All sidewalks shall be handicapped accessible.

Bucks County (PA) Model Ordinance

004.3 Cartway width and curbing. Cartway width and curb requirements shall be determined on the basis of the intensity of development proposed and the manner in which parking shall be provided, as follows:

DESIGN FACTORS			STREET STANDARDS		
Intensity of Development	Parking Provisions		Cartway Width	Driveway Access Permitted	Curb Required
	On-lot[1]	Spillover			
Frontage on open space. No residential lot frontage.	None[2]	None[2]	18'	No	No[3]
Lots 5 acres or larger deed restricted against further subdivision.	On-lot	On-lot	16'	Yes	No[3]
Lot widths 100' or greater	On-lot	On-lot	18'	Yes	No[3]
Lot widths 40' - 100'	On-lot	On-street	26'[4]	Yes	Yes
Lot width less than 40'	On-lot from rear alley, or in parking lot.	On-street	26'[4]	No	Yes
Lot width less than 40'	On-lot	Off-street parking lot	20'	Yes	Yes

[1] As required by Zoning Ordinance.

[2] It is assumed that no parking will be provided on-street and that no individual residential lot will have off-street parking with direct access from this street. Access to a common off-street parking lot shall be permitted.

[3] If curbing is required for stormwater management or road stabilization, add 2 feet to the cartway width.

[4] Cartway width may be reduced to 20 feet for marginal access streets.

Source: Bucks County (PA) Planning Commission, *Performance Streets*, 1980

Additional References

The following NAHB publications provide additional information on land development. These publications are available through NAHB Bookstore (15th and M Streets, N.W., Washington, D.C. 20005; 800-368-5242; 202-822-0463):

Alternatives to Public Sewer

Community Applications of Density, Design and Cost

Community Design Guidelines: Responding to a Changing Market

Cost Effective Site Planning

Financing Land Acquisition and Development

Fire Separation Requirements for Attached Single Family Homes (Townhouses)

Higher Density Housing: Planning, Design, Marketing

How to Win at the Zoning Table

Land Buying Checklist

Planning for Housing

Residential Erosion and Sediment Control

Residential Wastewater Systems

Security and Material Controls on the Job Site

Index

Absorption, 26-27; market rate and phasing, 65-66; projections of, 24
Access, for wastewater treatment plant, 232
Acquisition and site selection, 102-106
Adirondack Park Commission, 86
Adjustable rate financing, 100. See also Financing.
Aerial photographs, and land development loan application, 106; and satellite photos, 87
Aerobic tanks, 231, 237, 239; versus septic tanks, 241
Aesthetic considerations, 59; blue-green area for stormwater management, 180; grading, 179; of natural and open drainage, 196; and plants, 283
Air rights, 84
Alexandria (VA), private water system in, 222
Ambler Realty Co. v. Euclid, 70-71
American Association of Nurserymen, 296
American Association of State Highway and Transportation Officials, 253
American Standard for Nursery Stock, 296
Anaerobic wastewater treatment, 231
Apartments, 65; and U.S. Census, 89; rentals of, 53
Appraisal reports, accuracy of, 111; and land development loan application, 106; for site selection, 103
Aquifers, recharging of major ones, 206-207
Architect's fees, and land development financing, 106
Architectural context, 56
Architectural drawings, information to joint venture partners, 116
Argonne National Laboratory, 265-266
Arid regions, and wind erosion, 162
Arterials, super-elevation rate, 255

Automobile ownership, and residential streets, 249
Average Daily Traffic (ADT), 250

Bank reports, 22
Basements, 39, 195
Basins, for sedimentation, 167
Beacon Hill Vistas, Laguna Niguel (CA), 139
Bedrock, 41-42; and onsite sewage system, 237
Benches, for erosion control, 164
Benching: See Terracing of slopes.
Berms, definition of, 164; on windward side of dwelling, 277
Bicycle, paths for, 261, 262; traffic, and grate inlets, 190
Biological tower, 232
Blackwater, definition of, 246; treatment of, 246-248. See also Septic tank disposal systems.
Boulder (CO), growth limits in, 88-89
Boundaries, legal, 39
Builder/developer, and constituency building, 91-94; in zoning has burden of proof, 90, 91
Building codes, and energy efficiency, 282; require stormwater management, 207
Building specifications, information to joint venture partners, 116
Buyer, lifestyle of, 19

California, 86, 88-89, 282; Beacon Hill Vistas, Laguna Niguel, 139, 140-141; Turtle Rock Glen, Newport Beach, 134
California Coastal Zone Conservation Act of 1972, 86
Canada, paving in, 206
Capital, cost to developers, 100
Cayuga Heights (NY), 51-68
Census, U.S., 22, 31
Census Bureau, U.S., 89

331

Channel modifications for flood plains, 194
Channels, 164; maintenance of, 175
Chemical binders, 163
Chesapeake Bay Critical Areas legislation, 86
Circulation patterns of vehicles and people, plant enhancement of, 292
City Beautiful movements, 69
City of Boca Raton v. Boca Villas Corp, 88
City planning profession, 69
Clay soil, 178
Clean Water Act of 1977, and closed drainage system, 197; Section 208, 202; Section 404, 61
Climate, 40; control with plants, 283, 293-294; environmental condition, 39; and erosion, 162; site analysis issue, 38, 50. See also Precipitation.
Climate zone, and plants, 290, 296
Closed drainage system, 197-202; and cluster zoning, 204; components of, 197; construction and maintenance costs of, 197; with curbs, gutter, and stormwater drains, 261; location of, 197-199; pipe sizes in, 199
Clubhouse, 64
Cluster developments, and detention ponds, 208, 211; and energy efficiency, 282; infrastructure cost savings, 152; and open space, 292; and performance zoning, 84; to reduce nonpoint source pollution, 203-204; trade-offs, 92
Colorado, 88-89; and metropolitan service district, 120-121; Stoney Brook, Denver, 136
Colorado State University, 190
Columbia, Maryland, 79
Commerce Department, U.S., 70
Commercial banks, commitment fund source, 114; construction loans, 100, 108; financing for commercial projects, 102; land development financing, 106-107; for residential lending, 102; source of permanent financing, 114
Commercial development, and construction financing, 109; lending for, 102; permanent financing for whole project, 114
Commercial and industrial buildings, and rooftop storage for stormwater, 212
Community center, 63

Community land use, and housing, 150
Community roadway plans, and standards, 262-264
Commute patterns, 21
Compaction methods, 176
Compatibility, in housing types, 153-154
Competition, 18-19
Competitive advantage, 22
Competitive audit, 24, 26
Concrete pipe, 200
Condominiums, 59, 64, 65; associations, 214; U.S. Census, 89; ownership of quadruplex, 136; ownership of triplex, 134; presale requirements, 113; units, 53
Conflict-of-interest laws, and zoning ordinances, 76
Conservation department, 37
Construction damage, and erosion/sedimentation control, 171-172
Construction financing, 100, 108-114; and first liens, 104; versus land development loans, 106. See also Financing.
Consumer research, 24-25
Cooling needs, 266
Cooperative housing, permanent financing for whole project, 114
Cornell University, 51, 55, 64
Corps of Engineers, U.S. Army, 86
County tax assessor's office, 31
Covenants, 40, 48; and single-family houses, 65
Cross-sowing, definition of, 301
Cul-de-sacs, 250; turning requirements for, 253
Culverts, 202
Curbs, automated curbing machine, 259; concrete, 87, 259; and cluster zoning, 204; and gutters, 76, 187-189; purpose of, 260-261; radius of, 259; types of, 260-261

Dams, as floodwater control plan, 194
Davis (CA), 282
Debt financing, difference from equity financing, 115; and syndication, 119
Deed, restrictions on and single-family houses, 65; review of, 48
Defense, U.S. Department of, 86
Delaware, state planning regulations in, 86
Demographics, 19, 87; and land development loan application, 106

Densities, 35; and planting design, 290
Deregulation, of financial markets, 99
Design, advantage, 22; standards in subdivision ordinances, 75; team, 30
Design vehicles, definition of, 254
Design With Climate, 270
Detention, definition of, 210; ponds, 211; temporary stormwater storage, methods of, 208-213
Deteriorated community areas, and tax increment financing, 121
Developer, and community working together, 80; creditworthiness of for land development loans, 106; equity of, 115; financial options of, 99-102; as joint venture partner, 115-116; and need for technical information, 93; responsiveness to community needs, 93; and sources of funds, 100; and water supply system, 217
Development, agencies for, 29; conditions of, 30; costs imposed by local governments, 262-263; and higher density, 80
Development financing, and higher rates of interest, 100
Development projects, accelerate economic performance of, 102
Development rights, transfer of, (TDR), 84-85
Development suitability, composite, 61-63
Discomfort index, 266
Disposal structures, 165
Dispute settling method, part of joint venture agreement, 117
Ditches, 164
Diversion and water interceptor dikes, 164
Domestic investment groups, joint venture capital source, 115
Downzoning, and TDR, 84
Drainage, 29, 30, 42; during cut and fill operations, 178; and erosion, 165; and overland flow, 196; of site, 55; and slopes, 43; and subdivision needs, 184-185; as utility, 215
Drainage pipe selection, factors in, 199-202
Drainage swales, 177; versus curbs, 261
Drainage systems, 185-190; advance planning for, 184-185; natural open, 195-197; as utility maintained by locality, 197-198
Driveway, clearings for utility corridors, 286; maximize vegetative masses, 285
Droughts, and erosion maintenance, 175; risk level of, 172
Dry ponds, stormwater temporary storage sites, 210. See also Detention ponds.
Dry wells, 207
Duplex, 132-134; entrances to, 132; housing choice, 159
Dutch drains, definition of, 206

Earth-protected structures, 274
Earthwork and stormwater management, 161-215
Easements, 34; on building lot for closed drainage system, 197; and rights-of-way, 35
Economic forces, and market conditions, 19
Economics, data for land use decisions, 87
Economy, of community, 53
Electricity, for wastewater treatment, 232
Elevator, in highrise, 146; and vertical barrier, 70
Emergency storage pond, for wastewater treatment plant, 232
Employment conditions, 19
Employment Service, U.S. and State, 22
Endangered species, 37
Energy conservation, 265-282; with plants, 293-294; regulatory effects on, 281-282; and weather patterns, 38
Energy efficiency, 154, 282; and consumer preference, 265
Energy utilities, and utility plan, 35
Engineers, and consultants on land development financing, 106; and design of grading plans over geological hazards, 178; survey by, 30
Entrance space, definition by plants, 292
Environmental conditions, 39, 40-47; barriers and construction lending, 110; from erosion and sediment control programs, 171; and information overlay, 59-60
Environmental impact statement, and impact zoning, 82; and land development loan application, 106
Environmental laws, 29; and water quality, 202

Environmental Protection Agency (EPA), 86, 234-235; Sec. 208, 86, 215
EPA: see Environmental Protection Agency.
Equity capital, sources of, 115-119
Equity financing, 115-119
Erosion control, with plants, 283, 293, 294; rates of, 171-172
Erratics, definition of, 42
Estimates, in construction lending, 110; of development costs and land development loan application, 106
Europe, oxidation ditch system of wastewater disposal, 235; paving in, 206
Excavation, and rock conditions, 42
Exclusionary zoning: see Zoning.
Exterior use areas, in small lot housing, 128-130
External conditions, site analysis issue, 50

"Fair share" analysis of the market, 27
Fannie Mae: see Federal National Mortgage Association (Fannie Mae)
Farmland preservation, through TDR, 84-85
Feasibility study, 29-39, 58-59; and land development loan application, 106
Federal Emergency Management Administration (FEMA), 190-191, 195; National Flood Insurance Program, 181
Federal government, and land use regulation, 86
Federal Highway Administration, 190; culvert design brochure of, 202; test of sulphur as paving material, 258
Federal Home Loan Bank Board Regulation 41c, on appraisal reports, 111
Federal Housing Administration (FHA), 177
Federal National Mortgage Association (Fannie Mae) auction rates, 113
Fences, on windward side of dwelling, 277
Fertilizing, professionals for, 289
FHA: see Federal Housing Administration.
Field auditor, 26
Fill areas, grading of, 178
Fill material, disposition of, 178

Filtration, 167-169
Financial commitment, 111, 113
Financial markets, deregulation of, 99; partial deregulation of, 100-102
Financial statements, information to joint venture partners, 116
Financial subsidiaries of major manufacturers, and funds for developers, 100
Financing, adjustable rate, 100; balloon payments, 104; borrower's financial statement and land development loan, 106; capital cost to developers, 100; declining credit option, 105; equity financing, 115-119; interest rate, 102, 113; and land acquisition, 103-106; of land development, 99-123; and market research, 28; options available to lenders, 99-102; permanent, 114-115; phased disbursement of land development loans, 108; purchase money mortgages, 104; uncertainty of, 100. See also Commercial banks; Savings and loans; Insurance companies; Wall Street firms.
Financing advantage, 22
Fire, and demand for water, 218-219
Fire hose, lengths of, 221
Fire hydrant, spacing of, 221
Fire and police protection, 55; and metropolitan service districts, 120; and subdivision zoning, 96; water storage for, 219
Fixed option, 105
Flexible downdrains, definition of, 165
Floating zone concept, 79-80
Flood, during construction, 171
Flood control ordinances, 207; during construction, 171; hazard areas and state and local regulations, 191
Flood plains, 190-195; building codes for, 191; determining limits of, 192; management objectives, 191-192, 194; and residential construction, 195; and site design, 192-194; zone, 44
Flood waters, velocity of in residential areas, 192
Flood-prone areas, and National Flood Insurance Program, 191
Florida, 86, 126-127; growth cap ordinance struck down in, 88; Key Colony, Key Biscayne, 147; roads in, 257
Flumes, definition of, 165
Focus group interviews, 25

Foreign investment groups, joint venture capital source, 115
Forest, and water erosion, 174
Fragipan, 37, 62-63
Front yard, zoning definition of, 72
Frontage requirements, 35
Full credit option, 105
Fund commitments, for future, 100
Furniture stores, 22
Future trends in land use planning, 282

Garages, and wind, 277
Garden apartments, 143-144, 160
General obligation bonds, for metropolitan service districts, 120
Geological conditions, in grading, 178; information on, 36; and planting design, 290
Geological survey, onsite factors, 56
Geological Survey, U.S., 36, 56
Geology, 29, 41-42, and environmental conditions, 39; and site analysis issue, 50
Georgia, The Valley on Roswell Road, Atlanta, 144-145
Germany, Zone Plan in, 70
Glaciated areas, 41
Government-developer cooperative effort on stormwater management, 181, 208
Grading, 174-179; costs of, 178-179; needs, 29; and plant's water needs, 287
Grading Schedule for Municipal Fire Protection, 219
Grading Schedule for Municipal Protection, 221
Grass swales, versus concrete curbs and gutters, 87
Grasses, 37; and erosion control, 163
Grate inlet, definition of, 190
Gravel, for planting, 298
Greenbelts, 139
Greywater, definition of, 246
Ground cover, and erosion and sedimentation control, 162-163
Groundwater, and onsite sewage system, 237; recharge potential of, 180
Growth management, 88-89
Guide for Determination of Required Fire Flow, 219
Gully erosion, 164
Gutters, and cluster zoning, 204; flow velocity in, 190

Hawaii, state planning regulations in, 86
Hazardous waste, 48
Hazen-Williams formula, for pipe capacity, 220
Heather Glen, San Diego (CA), 139, 142
Heating, degree day index, 266; of structures, 266-281
Hedge planting, trenching for, 298
Height restrictions, 35
Highrise apartments, 146, 160; energy efficiency in, 265, 266
Highway, engineering in 1950s, 249; standards for, 249; and transit funding decisions, 86
Historic buildings, and TDR, 84
Home Builders League of South Jersey, Inc. v. Township of Berlin, 87
Homeowners associations, 127; and solar access, 282; and stormwater management, 214
Hospitals, and metropolitan service districts, 120
Households, age of, 21, 31; size of, 21
Housing types, choice based on compatibility, 153-154; considerations for choosing, 150, 159; cost of, 76; and energy efficiency, 265-266; planning for, 150-152; planting design, 290; selection of, 125-160; and site specifics, 158-160; and sun access, 154-157
Humidity, and plants, 293
Hydraulic analysis, 192, 194
Hydrology, 44, 181-190; environmental condition of, 50

Illinois, Wood Creek Courts, Chicago, 128-130
Impact zoning, 82-83
Income per capita, 31
Infiltration/velocity reduction, for stormwater management, 206-208
Inflation, and investment return, 99, 100; and lender expectations, 99, 100-102; loans during, 112
Infrastructure, considerations of, 96; and cost savings from cluster plans, 152; definition of, 83
Infrastructure financing, and land development financing, 106; and metropolitan service districts, 120-121; and tax-exempt bond market, 119; and tax increment financing, 121-122

335

Infrastructure payments, and tax-exempt bond market, 119
Inlets, definition of, 197
Institutional lenders, and land development loans, 106-107
Insurance companies, source of permanent financing, 114
Insurance Services Office (ISO), 218, 219, 221
Interest rates, for construction funding of residential properties, 113; variable for developers, 102
Intersection design, 258-259
Interstate highways, 250
Island circle, cul-de-sac turnaround, 254
Ithaca (NY), 51, 52, 53, 57

Johns Hopkins University, The, 190, 217
Johnson, Robert L., 208, 210
Johnstown (PA), 190
Joint ventures, 97, 105-106, 115-117; agreement with development entities, 100; financing land acquisition, 103, 105-106; funding sources for, 115-117; partnership agreement, 116-117; for surrounding land, 33

Kansas, 126
Key Colony, Key Biscayne (FL), 147
Kutter formula, for pipe capacity, 220

Labor, U.S. Department of, 22
Labor and materials bond, for first-time developers, 111
Lakatos, David, 196
Land acquisition, financing, 103-106
Land area, for wastewater treatment plant, 232
Land development, and area demographics, 106; financing of, 99-123; loan application process, 106-107; loan offer, 107; and minimizing lender risk, 107-108; and property lien, 106
Land management, ordinances, 75; tools of, 87
Land planner, 29
Land planning, 29-30
Land swap, 33
Land use, 39; changes for erosion and sedimentation control, 162; and Clean Water Act Sec. 208, 202; growing sophistication of control over, 89-94; incompatibility of, 32; management approaches to, 77; mixed, 79; and planting design, 290; and PUD, 79; regulations, 86-88: see also Local land use regulations; Site analysis issue, 50
Landing, The, Fort Worth (TX), 131-132
Landowners selling to developers, and joint capital source, 115
Landscape architect, 283
Landscaping, 283-302: see also Plants.
Lane, design speed of, 254; minimum radius on, 255; versus street, 251
Large-scale projects, 32
Lawns, 300
League of Women Voters, 92
Least-cost housing, 76
Legal conditions, zoning, 40
Legal fees, expenses for site selection, 103
Legal newspapers, 22
Legal restrictions, 39, 48; site analysis issue, 50
Legume, and erosion control, 163
Lender equity participation, and shorter terms, 102
Lenders, and market research, 27-28
Lending market, and legislative reforms, 100
Level spreaders, definition of, 165
Life insurance companies, and construction loans, 108; financing for commercial projects, 102
Lincoln (NE), 266
Litigation, costly in time, 93
Loam, for planting, 298
Loan analysis, and creditworthiness, 110-111; by lender for construction loan, 110-111
Loan commitment and closing, for construction loan, 110, 111-112
Loans, length of, 100
Local Government Comprehensive Planning and Land Development Act (FL), 86
Local land use regulations, and plan processing, 69-98
Location, advantage of, 22; for housing choice, 158
Long Island (NY), 207
Long-term lease, 33, 103, 105
Long-term lending, sources for, 100-102

Looping, definition of, 221
Lot size, and onsite sewage system, 237
Lot type, and planting design, 290
Lowrise apartment, energy efficiency in, 265

Mail interviews, 25
Mailing lists of prospects, 25
Maine, state planning regulations in, 86
Maintenance, erosion and sedimentation control, 161-162; equipment for erosion control, 175; of infiltration system, 207; plant costs passed to homeowners association, 294-295; in underground storage, 212
Manholes, 225-226, 229
Manmade environmental conditions, 47-48, 61; noise, 47-48; odors, 47-48; views, 47-48
Manning equation, 190, 196, 220
Manual for the Construction of Residential Basements in Non-Coastal Flood Environs, 195
Manual of Water Distribution Systems and Development Standards, 220
Maps, 39, 50, 110
Market absorption rate. See Absorption rate.
Market analysis, consumer research budget, 25; expenses for site selection, 103
Market capture, 26-27
Market data, sources of, 22
Market indicators, 53
Market research, 17-28; cost of, 27; data, 29-30; definition of, 17; on housing type, 150; how to use, 18-22; information, 18; by outside consultant, 17; selecting a consultant, 17-18; team approach to, 18
Market segments, 21
Market study, 30-31
Marketing approach, part of land development loan application, 107
Maryland, 79, 86; and flood plain improvements, 194; and TDR, 84
Maryland State Department of Natural Resources, and flood plains, 194
Mass transit, 33, 265
Master plans, changes in, 48

Material shortages, and construction lending, 110
Metropolitan service districts, 120-121
Microclimate, 40-41; definition of, 40
Midrise, 146, 160
Mineral rights, 84
Minimum, floor area requirements, 87; lot sizes, 35
Minor drainage systems, 185-190
Mobile homes, 21
Monetary policy, and real estate, 102
Montgomery County (MD), and TDR, 84
Mortgages, for single-family homes, 114
Mortgage bankers, commitment fund source, 114; and construction loans, 100, 108
Mortgage companies, source of long-term lending, 100
Mortgage pools, for residential lending, 102; source of long-term loans, 100
Mount Laurel Township (NJ), 77
Move-in analysis of buyers at competitive projects, 25
Moving companies, 22
Mulch materials, 163, 174
Multifamily housing, 18, 21, 143-149; compatibility with community, 154; syndication financing for, 117
Multifamily rental, permanent financing for whole project, 114
Multilevel house, 126
Multiplan configurations, and view, 158
Municipal, provision of sewage treatment, 217; provision of potable water, 217; ratings on fire fighting resources, 219; utilities, 53, 55; zoning ordinance, 71-73

NAHB: see National Association of Home Builders.
National Association of Home Builders, *Practical Stormwater Management: Planning and Design Perspectives*, 196; on intersection design, 258; residential street guidelines of, 263-264; right-of-way requirements for residential streets, 257; streets with roadside swales, 187
National Bureau of Standards, formulas for pipe capacity, 220
National Flood Insurance Program, 181, 190-191

337

Natural drainage systems, 195-197; environmental conditions, 60; environmental preservation, 128-130; environment with plants, 283; site features, 284; site resources, 161
Nebraska, 266
Negotiation, and conditional zoning, 81-82
Neighborhood characteristics, 29; zoning protection for, 70
Nettings, 163
New Hampshire, and Mount Laurel approach, 88
New Jersey, 77, 85, 86; slope orientation and seasonal changes, 270; Supreme Court of, 87
New York, 86, 88-89, 207; Savage Farm, Cayuga Heights, 51-68; slope orientation and seasonal changes, 270
New York City, Fifth Avenue, 70; TDR for historic structures, 84
New York State, Electric and Gas right-of-way, 63; Freshwater Wetlands Act, 61
New town, 32
Newspaper, real estate section, 22
Nitrogen removal, with oxidation ditch, 235
Noise, 30, 32, 39; barriers with plants, 45, 283, 293
Nonvegetative covers, for erosion control, 174
Nonvegetative soil stabilization, 163-164
Norway Maple, 294-295

Oak Cliff, Wichita (KS), 126
Oakwood at Madison v. Township of Madison, 88
Odor, 39
Offering memorandum, part of syndication document, 118
Office of Coastal Zone Management, 86
Office structures, and highrise and midrise housing, 154
Offsite factors, 32-34, 53
Olgyay, Victor, 270
One-stop building permit program, 97
Onsite factors, 36-39, 56-59; shopping, 265
Open space, 290; and development, 177; facilities appropriate to site, 290; and flood plain areas, 192;
and planting design, 290; and PUDs, 80
Option, for land for development, 97-98; versus ownership, 96
Optional Method of Wastewater Flow Estimating, 223
Oregon, state planning regulations in, 86
Outfall sewers, 224

Parking, 63-64, 78-79; and precast lattice blocks, 206; and stacked flats, 144
Parking lot storage, for stormwater, 210-212
Parks, 55; and metropolitan service districts, 120
Partnership agreement, part of syndication document, 118
Passive solar systems, low environmental impact of, 281
Pathways, 261
Patio house: see Zero lot line.
Patios, and tree shading, 272
Pavement, deterioration and stormwater runoff, 189; grading requirements for, 177-178; and infiltration, 206; of sulphur, 258
Peaking, definition of, 223
Pedestrian traffic, 261-262
Pedestrian travelway, 262
Pennsylvania, 190; fair share doctrine in, 88; mound system in, 243
Pension funds, for joint ventures, 115; source of long-term loans, 100; source of permanent financing, 114
Percolation rates for septic fields, 30; tests for, 36
Performance bond, for first-time developers, 111; for phased disbursement financing for land development, 108
Performance zoning, 83-84
Permanent loan to builder, same as construction loan, 112
Personal assets pledged, for construction loans, 111
Personal guarantees, for land development financing, 108
Petaluma (CA), growth limitations in, 88-89
Phasing, 65-68
Photography, aerial and satellite, 87
Physical site factors, flood zone, 38
Physical surveys of land, and land development loan application, 106
Pinelands (NJ), 85

338

Pinelands Commission, The, 85-86
Pipes, capacity of, 220; costs of, 226; for drainage, 199-202; galvanized steel, 200; maintenance and manholes, 226; materials, 199-200, 226; pressure, 220
Place, design speed of, 254; minimum radius of, 225; versus street, 251
Planned unit development (PUD), 79-80; and presale requirements, 113; and TDR, 85
Planning, coordination of, 32; engineering studies for site selection, 103; and erosion control, 163
Plants, and air movement, 294; and air quality, 296; and architectural form, 283; to articulate spaces, 283; budget for, 290; budget variety of, 296; change with environment, 283; in development process—considerations, 284-286; design with, 290-292; for energy conservation, 293; for floors, 283; for exterior structures, 283, 292; functional uses of, 293-295; for noise control, 295; for privacy, 295; uses of, 283; for view, 295
Plat approval, includes permits, 97
Police protection, and subdivision zoning, 96
Pollution, control with plants, 283; reduction of point and nonpoint source, 202-204, 215
Pond, 64-65
Population centers, 31, 33
Population profile, and education of planning boards, 89
Positive cash flow, for investor/lender, 102
Practical Stormwater Management: Planning and Design Perspectives, 196-197
Precipitation, 38, 40-41, 181
Preservation of existing vegetation, 285
Preventive maintenance, for erosion control, 175
Price advantage, 22
Project analysis, for loan commitment, 111
Project cost statement, and property analysis, 110
Projections, in construction lending, 110
Property analysis by lender, for construction loan, 110

Property appraisal, for construction loan, 111
Property tax equalization plans, 77
Proposed development, 32; fiscal effects of, 89
Pruning, professionals for, 289
Public facilities, inventory of, 53; stormwater control, 214-215
Public financing agencies, source of permanent financing, 115
Public meetings, and building support, 92-93
PUD: see Planned unit development (PUD).
Pumps, 220
Purchase money mortgage, financing land acquisition, 103-105
Putt, Robert A., 210

Quadruplex, 136-139; 158-159

Rail systems, and intensity of land use, 70
Rainfall, 171-172, 174; See also Precipitation.
Ramapo (NY), growth limitations in, 88-89
Ranch house, 126
Raw land purchases, financing of, 103, 104
Real estate financing, and Tax Reform Act of 1986, 102, 117, 119, 122
Real estate investors, and high investment returns, 99, 102
Recreation areas, 33; development of, 60; in high-density development, 265; and metropolitan service districts, 120; buyer preferences, 19; and PUDs, 80
Regional commissions, proliferation of, 86
Regional site design guidelines, 279-281
Regulations and restrictions on site, 48
Regulatory barriers, and construction lending, 110
Regulatory reform, and least-cost housing, 76
Release provisions for sold lots, 107
Resale market, 18, 22
Residential and nonresidential tenants, 147
Residential areas, sewage design parameters, 223-237
Residential basements, floodproofing of, 195

339

Residential construction, and erosion control, 162, 169-170; financing and full payment at construction's end, 108; and flood plains, 195; funding for land acquisition, 103-106; location of, 32; and take-out commitments, 112-114
Residential financing, commitment costs, 113; permanent, 114-115; lending sources for, 100-102
Residential properties, and construction funding for, 112-114; and metropolitan service districts, 120-121
Residential Stormwater Management, 179, 190
Residential take-out funds, sources of, 113
Restrictions, 40
Retention, definition of, 210
Retention facilities, aesthetic benefit from, 213; costs of, 213; design parameters of, 213; sites of, 212-213
Right-of-way requirements, 34, 56; for residential streets, 257
Roads, see Streets, Lane, Place.
Rock and gravel, for permanent stabilization of erosion, 163
Rolling option, 105
Rooftop, stormwater temporary storage site, 210, 212
Rosa Rugosa, as median planting, 294
Runoff, estimations of, 183-185
Rural density transfer zone, 84-85

Safety improvement, with plants, 294
Salts for de-icing, alternatives to, 202
San Francisco Bay Commission, The, 86
Sanitation service, and metropolitan service districts, 120
Savage Farm, Cayuga Heights (NY), 51-68
Savings and loan associations, and commitment fund source, 114; and construction loans, 100, 108; financing for commercial projects, 102; and funds for developers, 100; joint venture capital source, 116; and land development financing, 106-107; and legislative reforms, 100; for residential lending, 102
Schools, capacities and subdivision zoning, 96; proximity of, 32
Section downdrains, definition of, 165
Sediment control, 166-169;

considerations, 161; and control ponds, 55; deposition of, 162; overcontrol of, 171; planning of, 169-175; and pollution guideline, 202; and stormwater management, 172-173; trapping, 167
Seeding, 301
Seepage basins, recharge aquifer, 207
Seepage pits, reduce local flooding, 207
Semiarid regions, and wind erosion, 162
Septage, definition of, 239
Septic fields, 36
Septic tank disposal systems, 237, 239-246
Setbacks, 35, 72, 78-79; variations, 291
Sewage, 223-237; amount produced, 223-224; design for residential areas, 223-237; in-house connection built by builder, 224; public facilities for, 233-237; system, 55; treatment is municipal function, 217
Sewerage, 224-225; pressure and vacuum, 227-229
Sewers, 34, 35; curves in, 225-226; gravity in, 227; interceptor, 224; public, 39, 237
Shade, provision for, 224, 269, 272, 294
Shopper surveys, 25
Shopping centers, 32, 52
Shoreline developments, and climate, 276
Shrubs, 37; and erosion control, 163; planting methods for, 296-300
Sidewalks, 261; need for, 262; widths of, 262
Single-family homes, 18, 21, 30, 65, 126-141; attached structures, 154; detached, 53, 125-127, 158, 265-266; detached on large lot, 126, 159; detached on small lot, 128-130, 159; site analysis for, 39
Site accessibility, 39, 48, 53, 55
Site analysis, 39-50; details of, 59-63; for housing type, 150; manmade conditions, 39-40; natural environmental conditions, 39; summary of factors in, 50; versus feasibility study, 39
Site constraints, 29-30
Site construction, 30
Site development costs, summary of, 153
Site feasibility study, 39